Bible Difficulties Solved

Bible
Difficulties
Solved

Answers to More than
500 Baffling Questions
from Genesis to Revelation

Larry Richards

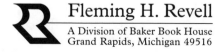

Fleming H. Revell
A Division of Baker Book House
Grand Rapids, Michigan 49516

Copyright © 1993 by Larry Richards

Published by Fleming H. Revell
a division of Baker Book House Company
P.O. Box 6287, Grand Rapids, MI 49516-6287

Printed in the United States of America

Library of Congress Cataloging-in-Publication Data

Richards, Larry, 1931–
    Bible difficulties solved / Larry Richards.
       p.   cm.
    ISBN 0-8007-1681-7
    1. Bible—Criticism, interpretation, etc.   2. Bible—Evidences, authority, etc.
I. Title.
BS511.2.R49   1993
220.1—dc20   92-598

Contents

New Testament

Preface

The Bible is the most important book in the world. Christians are convinced that it is a thoroughly trustworthy, completely reliable message communicated by God through the human writers of Scripture. Most people in our culture respect the Bible. Yet now and then criticism of the Scriptures captures the popular mind.

For instance, many people believe that the Bible is not entirely accurate about historical matters. Others say that the God of the Old Testament is cruel and vindictive and not at all like Jesus Christ. A surprising number of people who respect the Bible dismiss its creation story as a myth and uncritically accept the so-called scientific theory that all life spontaneously generated from nonliving matter. They uncritically accept the notion that a process of evolution brought forth the myriad of complex life forms that fill the earth's biosphere.

Others have been confused by some supposed error in Scripture and become convinced by critics that if the Bible contains a single mistake, the foundational Judeo-Christian concept of God is not only shaken but shattered. "Where did Cain get his wife?" and "The Bible says the sun 'rises,' while *we* know the earth rotates," represent the most popular—and superficial—attacks on the veracity of God's Word.

Yet significant questions are raised in a variety of Bible passages. Can we accept the description of the long lives enjoyed by those who lived before the Genesis Flood? How do we explain God's command to the exodus generation to totally exterminate the population of Canaan? Did Jesus really mean it when he said one must hate parents, spouse, and children to follow him?

In writing this book I begin with this simple assumption: The Bible is reliable as well as relevant. It is a book whose message was inspired by God and which conveys trustworthy information. Confident that Scripture is authentic revelation, I intend to look at many of the objections, concerns, and attacks on Scripture's reliability. At the same time, I will look at a variety of passages that are difficult simply because what they teach is not easily understood.

My hope is that this book will serve as a resource for believers who do trust their Bible and are convinced that there *are* answers to difficult questions even though they have not known where to look for them. I cannot guarantee that every solution I offer to these difficulties is the correct one. But I can assure you that there *is* a solution and one which preserves the integrity of Scripture as the fully trustworthy revelation of our loving God.

Larry Richards

Introduction

Let's begin with an admission. There *are* errors in the Hebrew and Greek texts of the Bible. Every person who has studied the Bible in its original languages is aware of these errors and what caused them. In his *Encyclopedia of Bible Difficulties*, Gleason Archer lists the following types of errors. All of these occurred in the *copying* of the text and do not affect the inerrancy of the original manuscripts. These copying errors include:

Haplography	Writing *once* a letter or word which should have been written twice.
Dittography	Writing *twice* a letter or word which should have been written once.
Metathesis	Transposing the *proper* order of words or letters.
Fusion	Combining the last letter of a word with the word *that follows* it.
Fission	The improper *separation* of one word into two.
Homophony	Confusing words that sound alike, such as *beat* and *beet*.

A variety of other similar errors can creep in when any document is being copied. But scholars called *lower critics*, who work with and compare the various manuscripts we possess, have been very successful in developing modern texts which approximate the original. For instance, the Dead Sea Scrolls contained a copy of the Book of Isaiah that was over a thousand years older than any other manuscript of that book. Yet the copyists had worked so carefully that the Dead Sea texts and the earlier Hebrew texts of Isaiah were substantially the same. The great number of New Testament texts available to scholars has made it possible to identify and correct nearly all copying errors. The New Testament words still in question fill hardly one-half of one page of a Greek New Testament. Not one of these uncertain words brings into question a single New Testament doctrine or historical statement.

What all this means is very simple. While there are copying errors in our texts of the Old and New Testaments, none of these errors is *substantial*. That is, none brings into question any significant historical or doctrinal affirmation of the Bible.

Many of the Bible difficulties fall into the category I call unsubstantial. For instance, the numbers given for census counts, or for the size of a group of people in a battle or at a particular center often vary between the accounts in 1 and 2 Samuel, 1 and 2 Kings, and 1 and 2 Chronicles. Most often these discrepancies rest on copying errors. Such errors easily affect numbers in the Old Testament, because numerical values were indicated by letters of the alphabet supplemented with dots written over them. As one or more dots was left out or added, as one letter was mistaken for another by the copyist, discrepancies did arise. Yet it is clear that such disagreements raise no substantial issue. They are easily explained. And whether an army contained 330,000 or 33,000 men, the text is primarily and rightly concerned with who won the battle.

While we can readily admit that there are copying errors, charges of *substantial* error are different. These hold that the original text contains flagrant errors or presents teachings that cannot be reconciled with later teachings.

Charges of *scientific error* range from dismissal of the Bible's creation account in favor of the current theory of evolution, to the assumption that the stories of long lives before the Flood cannot be true, to the isolation of verses which seem to teach that the earth has four corners (and thus is flat) or that the sun rises (and thus the sun travels around the earth rather than that the planet earth rotates). These difficulties can be solved. Some are solved by the acknowledgment of real conflicts but argument that the Bible's world view is correct; others by the use of scientific knowledge to explain the phenomena; and still others by the demonstration of how poetic or phenomenological language is used nonscientifically.

Charges of *historical error* range from the long-disproved argument that a primitive Moses could not have written the first books of the Old Testament because writing was unknown in his day, to charges that archaeological discoveries show the Jews were a nomadic people who drifted into Palestine rather than the conquerors described in the Book of Joshua, to supposed evidence that the Book of Daniel was written in the second century B.C. rather than in the fifth century B.C., as the book itself implies. Such difficulties must be dealt with by reference to archaeological finds, and while some charges cannot be disproved because data is not yet available, we can point out that, over and over again, when new finds bearing on a question have been made, the Bible account has consistently been authenticated.

Charges of *moral flaws* typically draw attention to the sins of men and women of faith, or accuse God himself of vindictiveness or of holding primitive values. Why should God have rejected Cain's well-meant offering? How could God impose the death penalty, and how could he display such insensitivity as to condemn homosexuals whose only crime is to prefer an alternate lifestyle? How does the Old Testament's eye-for-an-eye rule of *lex talionis* ever find a place in the same book with Jesus' instruction to love your enemies? How could a truly trustworthy God send a lying spirit to deceive Ahab and draw him to his death in battle?

Such questions cannot be answered by saying, for example, that God *did not* reject Cain, although in a real sense he didn't. The teaching of the text, however, can be explained and the ultimate answer presented: God, not modern man, is the measure of morality. He is loyal, just, loving, and good in all he does, and he displays values that we ourselves are to adopt.

The Bible is frequently charged with *conflict* or *inconsistency*. Critics may ask, How does it happen that Matthew speaks of two demoniacs healed in Gadara, and the other Gospels mention only one? Why is there a difference in the line of Jesus' ancestors as traced by Matthew and as traced by Luke? Did David kill Goliath, or is the chronicler right when he ascribes the killing to El-Nathan, and how in the world could such an obvious discrepancy have crept unnoticed into the Old Testament? Or, how can the New Testament speak of faith alone being required for salvation, and in other passages introduce conditions such as "confess with your mouth" or "repent"? Such charges of conflict need to be examined one by one, for there are a variety of reasons for the apparent or real differences between the supposedly contradictory passages.

Then there are charges *based on misunderstanding*. Many sayings in the Old Testament and New Testament may be hard to understand without a knowledge of Hebrew or Greek idiom. Did God really make Pharaoh reject Moses' demands by hardening his heart? Did God hate Esau and condemn him before he was born? What did Jesus mean when he said we should lose our lives for his sake? What is Ezekiel speaking about when he says, "The soul who sins is the one who will die" (18:4)?

Does God really visit the sins of the fathers on the children to the fourth generation?

These passages, like others that are difficult to understand, must be looked at individually. When they are understood the difficulty is resolved, and wonderful truths often emerge.

This is perhaps the most exciting thing about studying the Bible, and even about examining the difficulties that people raise. We need not fear an honest look at difficult passages or difficult questions. For the Bible *is* a trustworthy, reliable revelation from God. The Bible can withstand examination. As we seek to solve Bible difficulties, our faith is strengthened, not destroyed.

Genesis

Genesis

Who wrote Genesis, and what themes and issues does it deal with?

Genesis follows the pattern of other ancient writings and does not identify its author directly. (For instance, of thousands of Akkadian and Sumerian extant compositions dating from around 2,000 B.C., only three are known that make specific references to their authors.) But both tradition and internal references credit Moses with the substantial authorship of Genesis, as well as of Exodus, Leviticus, Numbers, and Deuteronomy, the five books known as the Pentateuch.

Mosaic authorship was vigorously attacked by German scholar J. Wellhausen in 1885. He argued that these first books of the Old Testament were created during or after the Babylonian exile of 598–539 B.C. While the arguments Wellhausen advanced have long been disproved, his anti-Mosaic bias still dominates in scholarly schools. These schools of thought also reject the portrait of Israel's history found in the Pentateuch. That history is vital because it lays the foundation for a biblical understanding of God, of humankind, and of the material universe.

In a carefully woven, always consistent account, Genesis introduces a God who creates the material universe and all that is in it. Genesis introduces humanity as a special creation of God, describes the sin that instilled corruption into our race and into history, and in the account of the Genesis flood affirms that God will surely judge sin. Yet Genesis looks forward as well as back. In the story of Abraham, Genesis introduces the theme of redemption. The promises God gave to Abraham reassure us that the universe not only has its origin in God's creative act but that history flows purposefully toward God's intended end—the ultimate blessing of humankind in and through Abraham's seed, Jesus Christ (Gal. 3:6–9, 16).

Genesis records foundational teachings on creation, on the origin of humankind, on sin, and on the fall, judgment, covenant, and redemption to come. Therefore it *is absolutely critical to the Bible's central teachings.* Genesis is either an authentic document or a fraud; either an honest portrait of historic events through which God revealed himself to humanity or a hoax as untrustworthy in its account of the past as are its authors.

So the question is important. Is Genesis, with the other books of the Pentateuch, the patchwork creation of a committee of deceptive religious zealots, intent on inventing a history that might possibly hold a shaken Jewish community together? Or are these books substantially the work of Moses, who is portrayed in them as the agent not only of Israel's deliverance from slavery in Egypt but also as the prototype prophet through whom God revealed himself and his will to his chosen people?

Conservatives point to various lines of evidence in support of substantial Mosaic authorship. The word *substantial* is important, for it does not rule out some editorial work in later times, such as the introduction of clarifying statements about place names and events (Gen. 12:6; 14:14 with Josh. 19:47; 36:31). Nor does it rule out the use of written or oral traditions by Moses in describing patriarchal times. *Substantial* Mosaic authorship means that Moses wrote or supervised the writing of the bulk of the Pentateuch and that these books are rightly viewed as both a divine revelation and an accurate, eyewitness account of events described as happening in Moses' lifetime. What lines of evidence support this view? They are both external and internal.

External evidence

Centuries before Moses, individual authors are known to have produced works which include such diverse materials as are found in the Pentateuch.

Archaeologists agree that the contents of the Pentateuch are historically accurate in detail after detail, and that literary forms (such as the suzerainty-covenant structure of Deuteronomy) date from the era implied in Scripture, not from later times. Whatever work later editors may have done, many archaeological finds support the substantially Mosaic character of Genesis and the tradition of Mosaic authorship.

Jewish tradition as far back as it can possibly be traced affirms the Mosaic authorship of the Pentateuch and says that Hebrew scribe Ezra (c. 450 B.C.) assembled the Old Testament books in their final form.

Internal evidence

Although the books are anonymous, Moses is described as being ordered by God to write historical facts (Exod. 17:14; Num. 33:2) and laws (Exod. 24:4; 34:27).

As early as Joshua 23:6 the Pentateuch is identified as the Book of the Law of Moses and is so identified in a number of Old Testament books (1 Kings 2:3; 2 Kings 14:6; 1 Chron. 15:13; 2 Chron. 8:13; 25:4; Ezra 3:2; Neh. 8:1; Dan. 9:11; Mal. 4:4).

Most significant, Christ himself authenticated Moses as the author of these early books, referring specifically to Deuteronomy 24:1–4 as Moses' command (Matt. 19:7; Mark 10:3) and to Moses as the lawgiver (John 7:19) who wrote truth which is to be believed (John 5:45).

For those who view Scripture as the reliable, inspired and trustworthy Word of God, the Bible's own testimony to Moses' substantial authorship of Genesis and the other books of the Pentateuch is decisive.

Genesis 1

What does the Bible teach about creation? And what makes this teaching so important?

The Bible's view of creation, so familiar to us, was and is unique. Ancient Mesopotamian societies viewed the material universe as the vast corpse of a fallen deity. The Greeks viewed matter as something that always existed. Modern scientists propose an unexplainable "big bang" by which matter came into existence, gradually coalescing into galaxies, suns, and planets, on which life is supposed to have been generated spontaneously from nonliving matter. Only the Bible describes the material universe as the product of a creative act performed by a personal being. In this, Scripture is in direct conflict with both the ancient myths and the modern myth—promoted as scientific—the theory of evolution.

This difficulty is more apparent than real. There is *no* conflict in the Bible's presentation of creation. Scripture is totally consistent with itself. The conflict is between the Bible's view of origins and the view held by others in modern society. Some well-meaning Christians attempt to harmonize the secular and biblical views. They propose a theistic evolution, or argue that the sequence of creation events as described in Genesis is essentially the same as the sequence of developments proposed by evolutionary theorists. But despite their efforts, an absolute conflict of views *does* exist. Evolution conjures up a universe which is impersonal and without meaning: The universe began as an anomaly; life's appearance was a matter of mere chance; human beings are merely one branch of animal life; each individual's identity is destined to be snuffed out after a tragically limited life span.

In contrast, the Bible portrays a universe intentionally created by a loving God. He shaped earth to be the home of humankind and filled it with complex life forms. God created human beings in his own image and likeness, and despite man's present fallen state each individual is precious to him. One day this material universe will have served its purpose, and God will create a new heaven and earth to be the home of those once-fallen creatures who have turned in faith to him and have been cleansed and changed through the sacrifice of his Son. It is their destiny—our destiny—to live forever in fellowship with God and with a vast family of the redeemed.

One thing is abundantly clear. These two visions are diametrically opposed. They cannot both be correct. Either Scripture's portrait of a universe filled with purpose and of a future bright with hope is true, or evolution's dismal description of a chill, impersonal cosmos void of purpose and empty of any personal hope of life beyond the grave is correct.

Which is correct, and how can we know? We can appeal to three primary lines of evidence: the scientific, the philosophical, and the supernatural.

Scientific evidence is assembled from data evaluated for its fit with either the creationistic or evolutionistic view. A number of books are available which provide overviews and in-depth studies of the data. My book, *It Couldn't Just Happen* (Word, 1988), for example, is an exploration of the weaknesses of evolutionary theory and a survey of the lines of evidence which support creationism.

Philosophical evidence involves reasoning not so much from scientifically assembled data as from general knowledge of the material universe.

For instance, evolutionary theory cannot explain the origins of man's unique moral sensibility. Yet comparative anthropology shows that every human society defines human actions morally, labeling some acts wrong and others right. While the *specific* wrongs and rights may differ, the *issues* which man's sensibilities identify as moral issue are the same across cultures. For instance, while sexual practices may differ, every society describes some sexual practices as wrong and others as right. It is on this basis that Paul can say in Romans that those with no knowledge of the law who "do by nature things required by the law . . . are a law for themselves" (Rom. 2:14). Paul's point is that God is more than willing to judge pagans, but not on the basis of Mosaic law. He will judge on the basis of their own standards of right and wrong. This is possible because every person has fallen short of his own standards, however low those standards may be. While the theory of evolution in no way can explain the existence of a moral sense in human beings, the Bible does. God created human beings in his image, and thus human beings even in their present fallen state are necessarily moral beings.

Another example of philosophical evidence is the so-called argument from design. No one picking up a watch and observing its regularity in keeping time would ever imagine that the watch just happened. They would instantly know that it had been made. In the same way, the regularity, the harmony, the intricate and yet balanced relationships that we observe in the material universe testify that the world was created by a person. Paul affirms this argument. In Romans 1:19, 20 he writes: "What may be known about God is plain to them, because God has made it plain to them. For since the creation of the world God's invisible qualities—his eternal power and divine nature—have been clearly seen, being understood from what has been made, so that [those who suppress the truth] are without excuse" (see also Ps. 19:1–4).

Supernatural evidence involves proof that the Bible is no mere human document but is inspired by God. Isaiah points often to the great contrast between the Lord and idols. They are deaf and dumb, while God acts, hears, and speaks. Thus God says, "I make known the end from the beginning, from ancient times, what is still to come" (Isa. 46:10). In context, Isaiah here not only predicts the fall of Assyria but names Cyrus as the one who will set God's captive people free some 150 years later. This is only one of dozens upon dozens of spectacular prophecies whose fulfillment demonstrates the fact that a God who knows the future speaks in Scripture through human beings who *could not* by themselves see beyond the present moment.

These lines of evidence, the scientific, the philosophical, and the supernatural, are strong and remind us of a vital truth: When a true conflict exists between the perception of reality accepted in human society and the view of reality revealed in Scripture, we must choose between the two. We cannot compartmentalize and accept as true an evolutionary view of the world that is in essential conflict with the view of reality found in the Word of God. What we will do, what we must do, is choose and then stand confidently by our choice.

Genesis 1

What were the "days" of Genesis 1? And must a Christian accept the twenty-four-hour day theory?

Christians with a high view of Scripture generally agree that the story of creation is no mere myth or story without historical foundation intended only to express the Hebrew view of God and his relationship to the material universe. But Bible-believing Christians are divided as to whether or not the days of creation were seven consecutive twenty-four-hour days. Various ways that conservative Christians have looked at the seven days, listed alphabetically, include:

Day-age theory	God's creative activity took place in a twenty-four-hour period, but then God permitted a geologic age to pass during which time the things that he had made (vegetation, sea creatures, etc.) were permitted to develop gradually.
Gap theory	God's original creation was ruined by Satan's fall (Isa. 14:13–15). The seven days of Genesis describe the repair of that catastrophe. Dinosaurs belonged to the original creation.
Indefinite-age theory	Each day is not a twenty-four-hour period but rather an indefinite geological age. Thus there is no real conflict between the Bible and evolutionistic theory, as evolution was the process God used in creating.
Seven-day theory	God created in six consecutive twenty-four-hour days, an unknowable period of time ago.
Revelatory-day theory	The days in Genesis are not days during which creation took place but days during which God showed Moses what he had done.
Revelatory-device theory	The author of Genesis simply uses days to organize his material.

The validity of these views is often hotly debated. Day-age theorists point out that the Hebrew *yom* (day) can mean any period of time during which certain events take place, as in the phrase "the day of God's wrath" (Job 20:28), or "the day of salvation" (2 Cor. 6:2). If the days of creation are understood in this way, it in no way diminishes the basic teaching of the Bible that all which exists is God's creation, was called into being by him, and depends on him for its survival. On the other hand, twenty-four-hour-day theorists argue that the language of the text, which ascribes a morning and an evening to these days (Gen. 1:5, 8, 13, 19, 23, 31), requires acceptance of their position. Also, Exodus 20:8–11 appears to treat the days literally. Yet, the seventh day has no evening. According to Jewish rabbis this means God's sabbath is still being celebrated. How then could six of the days be literal twenty-four-hour days and the seventh not?

Speculation and argument are always of interest. But this is one question that will not, and need not, be resolved. For the issue is not how God went about creation but that God *did* create. It is not necessary that we know how he did this. It is necessary that we affirm the fact that he did it. Everything in the material and spiritual world exists because God called it into being. This is the unmistakable message of Genesis 1. This is the unshakable bedrock of Scripture's vision of reality.

Genesis 1:21, 24, 25

What does Genesis 1 mean by "according to their kinds"? How does this relate to the various classifications of modern biology and zoology?

The Hebrew word *min* (kind) is a general term that occurs just thirty-one times in the Old Testament. Barton Payne has noted that *min* cannot be identified with modern biology's order, family, genus, or species. In fact, *min* is used to distinguish between plants or animals within each of these categories. What does *kind* then mean in Genesis 1? It simply identifies a basic form of life which reproduces after its kind (basic form). Clearly, within the genotype of each *min* is great flexibility, so that microevolution—small-scale hereditary changes that result in the formation of slightly differing new varieties—is provided for by the original creative act. The differentiation of a prototype dog into various modern breeds, like the differentiation of Adam's descendants into the various races of humankind, is all implicit in God's original command: "Let the land produce living creatures according to their kinds" (Gen. 1:24).

Genesis 1:26, 27

What is the image and likeness of God, in which the Lord created humanity?

Two related Hebrew words, *selem* (image) and *demut* (likeness), form this phrase, which occurs only three times in the Old Testament (Gen. 5:1–3; 9:6). Linked they make a unique theological statement: God cannot be understood by comparing him to any creature (Isa. 40:18), while human beings can only be understood in relationship to the Lord. It is futile to view humans as nothing more than highly evolved beasts, for while their physical elements were formed from the dust of the earth, human beings also have a spiritual and psychological dimension, granted when God breathed into the first human the breath of life and he became a living being (Gen. 2:7).

Some have assumed the image and likeness was an original holiness enjoyed by Adam and Eve before the fall. Yet clearly the image and likeness persist *after* the fall (Gen. 9:6). It is better to take this phrase as a summary statement. All that makes God a person—emotion, will, intellect, imagination, love of beauty, moral sensitivity—he shared with humankind. Although these capacities were corrupted in Adam's fall, they continue to set human beings apart from the animals. They also continue to witness to the existence of our creator and remind us that anyone who seeks to understand human nature must begin by confirming our likeness to God.

Genesis 1:28

Are overpopulation and the depletion of earth's limited resources sanctioned by the command to "fill the earth and subdue it"?

In 1967, a famous article in *Science* (vol. 155, March 10, pp. 1203–7) charged that Christian doctrine lay at the root of the earth's ecological crisis and pointed to this verse as the Western world's claimed license to misuse natural resources. In fact, the dominion or rule God gave humanity over his creation (v. 26) carries with it an obligation to guard and care for nature. The Hebrew word *radah*, which is used here, always indicates dominion exercised by human beings rather than by God. But the world remains God's possession (Pss. 24:1; 50:10–12), so that humankind is responsible to God to work and take care of the land (Gen. 2:15). While *subdue* indicates that the natural world resists taming, it does not convey a license to exploit. Rather, it reminds us that in placing humankind in charge of our planet God gave us a challenge and a truly significant work. The truth is that the foundation for true sensitivity to ecological issues is rooted in a deep awareness that the earth is the Lord's and that God has given us the privilege of managing it for the benefit of all living things, to his greater glory.

Genesis 1, 2

Do these two chapters give contradictory pictures of creation? Does the use in Genesis 1 of Elohim *as the name of God, and in Genesis 2 of* Yahweh *as the name of God, prove the two accounts were derived from different sources?*

The two chapters do not contain two different creation accounts at all. Genesis 1:1 through 2:3 is an overview, something like an "establishing shot" in TV or the movies, that shows a person at a distance, standing in a field surrounded by plants and animals and gazing upward at the heavens. Genesis 2:4–15 is a closeup, focusing in tightly on the person's face, capturing his wonder and delight as he wanders through God's garden. Genesis 1 is the creation story. Genesis 2 provides more detail about the most significant creation of all, that of human beings.

Why, then, the use of two different names for God? Some argue that this difference indicates two different authors, one who knew God only as *Elohim* and another who knew him as *Yahweh* (Jehovah). The assumption that the use of different names for God indicates different authors or source documents has led to the development of the "documentary hypothesis." This hypothesis supposes that the works of authors *E* and *J* were patched together with material from priestly and Deuteronomistic traditions in the fifth century B.C. to produce the early parts of our Old Testament.

The argument that Genesis 1 and 2 are different accounts of creation drawn from different sources, although accepted by many modern critical schools, fails on at least three counts.

1. The relationship of Genesis 1 and Genesis 2 should be seen as an overview (Gen. 1) that is followed by a closer examination of creation's most significant feature (Gen. 2), rather than as two different creation accounts. In fact, no known creation story from the ancient Middle East has a structure similar to Genesis 2, indicating that it is not intended as a creation account.

2. The study of comparative literature shows that it was common practice in the ancient Middle East to refer to a people's high gods by more than one name. The Egyptians' god Osiris was also called Wennefer,

Khent-amentiu, and Neb-abdu. Bel, of Babylon, was also known as Enlil and Nunamnir, while Sin was also called Nanna. In Canaan the king-god was known as El and Latpan, while Baal was often called Larpan. In view of the fact that alternate names for gods were consistently used in the same documents in other ancient cultures, it is hard to accept the argument that the use of different names for God in the Pentateuch proves the *E* and *J* material in Genesis 1 and 2 must have been written by different authors.

3. *Biblical names* have theological significance. *Elohim* was the culture's general name for God. On the other hand, *Yahweh* is God's personal name and is associated with his redemptive, loving involvement with humankind. (See the section on Exodus 6 for further discussion of the name *Yahweh*.) It is thus completely appropriate for Moses to use *Elohim* in his record of God's work as the creator of the material universe in Genesis 1 and to use *Yahweh* in his account of God's unique, intimate, hands-on involvement in the creation of Adam and Eve in Genesis 2.

Genesis 2:10–14

Where was Eden?

The Bible does indicate the general region in which Eden was located. The word was apparently an early name for a wide area including Mesopotamia and perhaps most of the fertile crescent. The garden God planted for Adam and Eve was in the eastern part of this region (Gen. 2:8) and known for its association with four rivers, two of which, the Tigris and Euphrates, are well-known today. The two locations most scholars identify as possibilities lie in the mountains of Armenia and at the head of the Persian Gulf. The exact location, however remains uncertain.

Genesis 2:16

Was it fair for God to test Adam, knowing he would fail? Why did God tempt Adam instead of let him enjoy his innocence?

God had made Adam in his own likeness and image. To be truly like God, who is a moral being, Adam had to have the opportunity to exercise moral choice. The tree God planted in Eden, whose fruit he told Adam not to eat, was not an intended trap for Adam. It was a positive gift, a way to enable Adam to exercise his moral capacity and imitate God by choosing what was good. Without the tree, Adam would have been a mere puppet. Without the opportunity to exercise moral responsibility Adam would have been without a quality essential to the image and likeness that God graciously shared with humankind.

Most of us tend to look at spiritual tests and temptations negatively. But they are not traps intended to cause us to sin. They are opportunities to demonstrate our commitment to God and, by obeying him, to strengthen our character and display his redemptive work in our lives.

Genesis 2:20, 21

Why would God make Eve from Adam's rib rather than shape her as he had Adam? Is this just another proof of the Bible's chauvinistic attitude toward women?

It is, in fact, just the opposite. If God had made Eve from clay *after* he created Adam, it might be argued that women are different from and, as a later creation, inferior to men. In forming Eve from Adam's rib God confirmed woman's *identity with* man. Eve was thus a full partner with Adam in God's gift of the divine image and likeness. This total identity of male and female as equal participants in God's image and likeness was immediately sensed by Adam, who said, "This is now bone of my bones, and flesh of my flesh" (2:23).

The same thing is taught in the much-misunderstood phrase that identifies Eve as a "suitable helper" for Adam (2:20). The Hebrew *'ezer* here means a "strength" or "power," as in Deuteronomy 33:36, 39, and *kenegdo* means "corresponding to him" or, according to some, "equal to him." The point, however, is the same. Adam searched the animal kingdom and could find no one corresponding to himself, no one who like him was shaped in the image and likeness of God, no one with whom he could have a true, deep, significant, person-to-person relationship. The search made Adam aware of his deep need for an equal. When that need was finally felt as an ache and emptiness, God acted. He made woman, not to be an inferior, not to be chattel, not to be a plaything, but to be a power, a being, equal to man.

Genesis 2:17

God warned Adam that the day he ate fruit from the forbidden tree he would "surely die." But when Adam did eat, neither he nor Eve dropped dead. Clearly God was wrong or lied to frighten Adam. So either the Christian's belief that God knows the future or notion that God is trustworthy must be in error.

The words *die* and *death* have a variety of complex meanings. By death the Bible means (1) the end of biological life, as in Hebrews 2:14–15; (2) sin's active corruption of man's nature, as in Ephesians 2:1–6 and Romans 8:5–8; (3) the state of alienation from and antagonism to God that sin causes, again as in Ephesians 2:1–6; and (4) that final, eternal separation from God in the lake of fire that Revelation 20:14 identifies as the second death.

So the question is not why Adam did not drop dead biologically when he sinned but *in what sense did he die?*

The answer to this is fourfold. When Adam sinned, the process that leads inexorably to biological death began to operate. When Adam sinned, the image of God within him was misshapen and distorted, and Adam became "dead in transgressions and sins" (Eph. 2:1–6). When Adam sinned, his act alienated him from God, and he fearfully fled the Creator's presence (Gen. 3:10). When Adam sinned, he passed from life to death and, without a subsequent act of faith, would have been destined to suffer the second death (Rev. 20:14) of everlasting separation from God.

When we understand the range of meanings of death in both Old Testament and New Testament, it becomes clear that, in the most significant sense of all, Adam *did* die the day he ate the forbidden fruit, just as God had said he would. Later, Adam and Eve produced children who were according to Adam's likeness. This likeness included their being spiritually dead and alienated from God (Gen. 5:1–3; Rom. 5:12–13). Yet this dread testimony of Scripture is in a sense good news. It explains the origin of the evil and wickedness that mar society, and it reminds us to turn from our own flawed efforts to please God and instead to find in Christ his gift of forgiveness and new life.

Genesis 3:5

What is the meaning of Satan's promise, "You will be like God, knowing good and evil"?

There are five Old Testament passages in which knowing good and evil are mentioned: Deuteronomy 1:39; 2 Samuel 14:17; 19:35; 1 Kings 3:9; and Isaiah 7:15. These, with Genesis 3:5, agree that knowing good and evil is the prerogative of God. That is, God alone has in himself the capacity to distinguish between that which is good and that which is evil. He alone is truly an autonomous (free, sovereign, and independent) person.

Satan's statement contained both truth and falsehood. In disobeying God, Adam and Eve declared their independence from him. They did come to know (experience) evil and its consequences. But the freedom they declared trapped them, forcing them to rely on their own faulty judgment and forcing God to condemn them for their sins. Satan's promises seem appealing on the surface. But any truth his words contain conceals a deadly trap.

Genesis 3:16

What is the meaning of the curse on Eve, who represented all women, that "I will greatly increase your pains in child- bearing"?

Some have taken this to indicate that the act of giving birth itself is to be painful. Others have noted that some women have a pain-filled monthly cycle.

It's more likely, however, that the verse speaks of the entire process of bringing children into the world and rearing them to adulthood. Adam and Eve introduced sin into the world and into the race. A woman's real distress is seeing how sin can and often does spoil the lives of the offspring she loves.

Genesis 3:16

What is the meaning of the second part of the curse on woman: "Your desire will be for your husband, and he will rule over you"?

The word *desire* means not sexual desire but orientation. It means that, rather than look to God for security and direction, women will tend to look for these things in their husbands. As a result men will gain a power over women that was not contemplated in the original creation. Rather than live together in partnership, history has shown, fallen humanity has tended to develop societies in which women have fewer rights than men and are subordinated to them. God did not ordain male superiority. That male claim is a direct result of the fall and an expression of injustice in any marriage or any social order.

Genesis 3:21

Why did God clothe Adam and Eve in animal skins following their sin?

Bible students see in this act history's first sacrifice. It was God's first instruction in the terrible truth that sin merits death. But it was also God's first proclamation of the gospel, the good news that God in grace will accept the death of a substitute in place of the death of the sinner. Of course, no animal's death could serve as an adequate substitute for any human being. But throughout the Old Testament animal sacrifice provided an object lesson. The repeated sacrifices were repeated promises that one day, through a sacrifice's substitutionary death, God would redeem mankind.

Genesis 4:5

Why was Cain's offering of fruit and vegetables not acceptable to God? Was God unnecessarily harsh with Adam's first son?

In a recent book entertainer Steve Allen complained that God was unfair in rejecting Cain's offering. Hadn't Cain worked hard? Didn't he bring his best to the Lord? So Allen rather angrily concluded that in rejecting Cain, Yahweh was acting like a petty tyrant. Jewish sages have also expressed puzzlement, and one line of teaching in the Mishnah (an ancient rabbinical commentary on the Old Testament) suggests that Cain brought rotten fruits and vegetables and thus showed open contempt for the Lord. Yet the text itself contains clues that help us solve this difficulty. The Genesis text has God asking Cain, "If you do what is right, will you not be accepted" (4:7)? This clearly implies that Cain *knew* what was right. He knew the appropriate offering to bring to God and chose not to bring it. This verse also shows God's grace, for Cain was still invited to bring the correct offering.

What, then, was right, and how would Cain know it? Throughout the Old Testament, only animals are brought to God as sin offerings. This principle had been taught to Adam and Eve when, after they sinned, God killed animals to provide a covering for them. They passed this knowledge on to their sons Cain and Abel. But Cain refused to approach God with the blood of a sacrifice and offered works of his own hands—the vegetables he had grown. Much later Paul wrote: "He saved us, not because of righteous things we had done, but because of his mercy" (Titus 3:5). Cain was rejected because he insisted that God accept his works. Cain did this by refusing to approach God in the appropriate way to seek mercy.

Genesis 4:17

Where did Cain and the other sons of Adam find wives?

Genesis 5:4 tells us that during Adam's long life he "had other sons and daughters." Clearly the children of the first pair married brothers or sisters. While in later eras law and custom forbade the marriage of brothers and sisters (Lev. 20:17), at the beginning no other possibility existed.

Genesis 5

How could people before the flood live such long lives? Does the existence of similar tales in Middle Eastern literature reveal these tales (and early Genesis as well) as unbelievable ancient myth?

Other cultures in Mesopotamia did have similar traditions. For instance, the *Sumerian King List*, which dates to between 2000 and 2250 B.C., names eight kings said to have lived prior to a great flood who enjoyed lengthy reigns. The shortest reign was supposed to have been 18,600 years, the longest 43,200 years. In comparison, the longest lived person listed in Genesis 5, Methuselah, is said to have lived 969 years. The Genesis account thus appears quite restrained.

Actually, what the *Sumerian King List* shows is that ancient peoples retained knowledge of a great flood and of long lives before it, suggesting that a historical reality lies at the root of these common traditions.

But is the Bible's report of such lengthy lives unscientific? Actually, not at all. Medical researchers now know that many if not most human diseases are genetic, caused when malfunctions occur in the duplication of the human genetic code. This code is unbelievably complex, so complex that if we assigned a letter, such as *a* or *b*, to each molecule in the chromosomes that carry genetic material, the letters in a human-beings code would fill a thirty-two volume *Encyclopedia Britannica* thirteen and one-half times. The wonder is not that people lived so long just after God created humankind, before multiple errors in duplication weakened our race; the wonder is that God designed humanity so well that most of us remain healthy despite the billions upon billions of duplications of the genetic code that have taken place since creation. Truly we are "fearfully and wonderfully made" (Ps. 139:14).

Genesis 5

Do the genealogies in this chapter prove that the Bible inaccurately assumes that earth was created only a few thousand years ago? After all, when a nineteenth-century bishop named Ussher added up the ages provided in Hebrew genealogies, he concluded that creation took place in 4004 B.C.

The math may not be wrong, but Ussher's assumptions were. Hebrew genealogies were used to trace roots and lineage and typically included only key persons, not everyone in the family line. The phrase *was the son of* or the word *begat* are used in a general sense meaning "descended from" or "was the ancestor of." This approach to genealogical records is common to many non-Western cultures as well as to Hebrew culture. For this reason Old Testament and New Testament genealogies are *incomplete*. Adding up ages given in Genesis 5 gives no clue at all to the date of creation.

Genesis 6:2

Who were the sons of God referred to in this passage?

The sons of God who "saw that daughters of men were beautiful" and "married any of them they chose" have puzzled Jewish and Christian commentators alike. It is clear that the text regards this as unnatural and a terrible sin. In the rest of the Old Testament the phrase *sons of God* is used for either angels (Job 1:6, 2:1; Ps. 29:1, 89:6) or human beings who enjoy a covenant relationship with the Lord (Deut. 14:1, 32:5; Ps. 73:15; Hos. 1:10). This has led some to argue that the *sons of God* here are fallen angels. They are sons only in the sense of having been created by God. This is supported by the reference to Nephilim who were the supposed offspring of the union of the sons of God and daughters of men. This reference is similar to the myths persistent in many ancient religions about children fathered by a pagan deity who appeared in human form. Others dismiss this theory as pure paganism and argue that angels, who, the Bible teaches, are spirits (Heb. 1:14), could not possibly father children. It is far more likely that the text refers to intermarriage between the godly line of Seth and the line of Cain. The consequence was a loss of spiritual sensitivity and responsiveness. This led to such corruption of society that the flood became a moral necessity.

Genesis 7

Was the Genesis flood universal or local in extent? And if it was universal, why is there little geological evidence of such a great cataclysm?

Some biblical scholars and most Christian geologists tend to argue for a limited, local flood. They note that God's intent was to "destroy all life under the heavens, every creature that has the breath of life in it" (Gen. 6:17). They further argue that, in this early age, human and animal life probably had not spread beyond the Mesopotamian basin. Thus the fulfillment of Genesis 6:17 would only require a local flood to wipe out the earth's limited human and animal population. Reference to water covering "all the high mountains under the entire heavens" (7:19) is phenomenological; that is, only the heights the people of that time could *see* were covered. Otherwise there is not enough water on the planet and in the atmosphere to cover mountains such as Everest. The reason there is no geological evidence of a flood is that, while the flood was great enough to accomplish God's purpose, it was not worldwide.

This, however, does not seem to do justice to the Genesis text, which portrays a cataclysm of awesome proportions (7:11), with waters that rose "greatly on the earth" (7:19) and caused the deaths of "every living thing that moved on the earth" (7:21). And the ark came to rest "on the mountains of Ararat" (8:4).

Proponents of a universal flood deny that there is no geological evidence and argue that the Genesis flood has actually shaped the major features of earth's surface. They say it took no more water than is now found in our seas to cover a relatively flat preflood earth, and it was the pressure of those waters that forced the sea beds down and the mountains upward. Mountain ranges, the tops of which often contain sedimentary rock that prove they once lay under water, were formed as the tremendous pressure of the waters that covered the whole earth pressed the sea beds down and caused the faulting and cracks that thrust the mountains up. Thus the high mountains of Genesis 7 that were covered by the waters are *not* the Mount Everests and Mount Hoods of today. For this reason the argument based on there not being enough water to cover earth is irrelevant.

Certainly, debate on the extent of the Genesis flood will continue, and the two sides will never agree. But the purpose of Genesis 7 is not to pose a theological/scientific puzzler. It is to show that God is the moral ruler of his universe, and that God *has* intervened to severely judge human sin. The Genesis flood stands as a warning to all those who suppose that God does not care what human beings do, or that if he cares, he is unable to act in space and time.

Genesis 7, 8

How long did the Genesis flood last?

The text provides a time frame. In modern terms:

The Ark built	6:14	120 years
Animals enter	7:10	10 May
Flood begins	7:11	17 May
Waters increase	7:12	26 June
Waters inundate earth	7:24	
Ark touches ground	8:4	13 October
Waters recede, mountaintops visible	8:4	1 January
Windows opened, birds sent out	8:6	10 February
Dove sent	8:10	17 February
Dove sent again	8:13	24 February
Ark door opened	8:13	1 April
Land fully dry: the family exits	8:14	23 May

Thus from beginning to end the Genesis flood extended two weeks beyond a full year.

Genesis 7:2

This verse says Noah took seven pairs of animals into the Ark, but Genesis 6:19 says he took "two of all living creatures, male and female." Here is an obvious discrepancy that shows an error in the Bible and probably indicates that two different stories were patched together by the editors of Genesis.

This is an old argument and, like many complaints, a weak one. Certainly, if this is such an obvious discrepancy, the supposed editors of Genesis would no more have made this blunder than Moses would have. In fact, it's not a blunder, but an expansion of the instructions given Noah. The first reference is to a pair of every kind of animal; the second is a special instruction to take extra pairs of ritually clean animals (see Lev. 11). Why the extra animals? First, for sacrifice (8:20), and second, after the flood was over, predatory animals would have needed to eat some of the nonpredatory clean animals to survive. Only if Noah were *not* told to take extra pairs of the clean animals would there have been a problem.

Genesis 9:6

How can Genesis 9 imply that a person who kills another should be killed in turn? The Ten Commandments say, "You shall not murder" (Exod. 20:13).

Two different Hebrew words help us resolve this supposed inconsistency. *Harag* is the usual word for the violent killing of people by others. It is used for a range of both unjustified killings, as Cain's murder of Abel (Gen. 4:25), and the justified execution at Elijah's command of some four hundred prophets of Baal (1 Kings 19:1). This word thus looks at killing as an event, without making moral distinctions. Another word, however, *rasah*, is unique to Hebrew, without cognate words in other Semitic languages. *Rasah* is best understood to indicate a personal killing, whether accidental homicide or premeditated murder. This word is never used to denote either judicial executions, ordered by competent legal authority, or killing in war.

The use of these words in Scripture makes it clear that the commandment of Exodus 20:13, which says "You shall not murder" (*rasah*), is *not* a blanket condemnation of all killing. In fact, Genesis 9:6 holds the community *responsible to kill* the person who murders another.

Old Testament law codes call for restitution in the case of most crimes. But Genesis 9:6 reminds us that God made human beings in his own image. Thus nothing is as precious as a human life, and there is no price great enough to balance the scale when a murder has been committed. By calling for the death penalty, Old Testament law confirms the significance of human life, reminding everyone that nothing can make up for the taking of another life. Society *must* call for the death penalty for murder, not as a means of prevention but as a powerful statement about the sanctity of human life.

It is important to note that Old Testament law carefully distinguishes between intentional and accidental homicide. Several extended passages speak of cities of refuge to which a person who accidentally killed another could flee and find safety (Num. 35). But there is no provision of such grace for the murderer. As Numbers 35:31 says, "Do not accept a ransom for the life of a murderer, who deserves to die. He must surely be put to death."

Genesis 9:25

What was the curse Noah placed on his youngest son, and why did he say Canaan would be a slave?

The word translated "curse" here is *'arar* and serves as an announcement of a punishment that God imposes. This is the first time in the Old Testament that a man utters a curse, here obviously with divine authority. The cause of this curse was Ham's act of deriding his father when he found him lying naked in a drunken stupor. The curse predicted the political subjection of the Canaanites as a people to descendants from Noah's other sons. Note that the curse involved only one branch of Ham's family. Note, too, that the curse did not *cause* Canaan's later subjugation but did preannounce a divine judicial sentence on the Canaanites for later moral choices that reflected the flaw observed here in their ancestor, Ham.

Genesis 10

What is the significance of the "table of nations" in this chapter?

This chapter contains the oldest known ethnographic document in existence. It identifies, using location, language, or descent, the tribal groups that became the peoples of the world known in ancient times. Modern research has shown this table of nations to be a strikingly accurate record of nations and peoples that existed many centuries before the writing of the Old Testament. The map on page 33 shows the location and modern designation of many of the peoples named in Genesis 10.

Genesis 11:28

Where was the city of Ur that Abraham originally came from, and what was it like?

Some scholars have suggested that Abraham's family came from a location referred to as "Uru" in documents found in excavations at Ebla. This would place the family near Padan Aram, where the brother of Abraham, Haran, lived (Gen. 12:4).

This text, however, specifically identifies this city as Ur of the Chaldeans, located near the shore of what is now the Persian Gulf.

Table of Nations
Genesis 10

GOMER

TIRAS?

JAVAN

JAVAN

MESHECH

Lud?

TUBAL

Asshur

▲ Mt. Ararat

MADAI

Arphaxad

Aram

Tigris R.

Euphrates R.

Elam

CANAAN

PUT?

MIZRAIM

Nile R.

CUSH

| Miles | 0 | 200 | 400 | 600 |
| Kms | 0 | 300 | 600 | 900 |

Excavations at Ur conducted between 1922 and 1934 reveal that in Abraham's time Ur was a vigorous, wealthy city. The *Revell Bible Dictionary* says,

> Ur was dominated by a giant three-stage ziggurat, reaching some 70 feet above the flat plain below. On it were shrines to Nannar, the city's god. The city was enclosed by oval walls some 30 feet high, which protected not only the city but two harbors. Streets were carefully laid out. House walls faced the streets, and homes featured an inner courtyard onto which their rooms faced. Among the more spectacular finds from Ur's early period are beautifully worked gold jewelry and objects, gold-inlaid musical instruments, and colorful mosaics illustrating civil and military life. In addition, a number of clay tablets were recovered, including a Sumerian dictionary and a mathematical text recording cube roots. There were also business records, which show the people of Ur were actively involved in international trade.

Our current knowledge of the civilization Abraham left reminds us both of the paganism that he abandoned in response to a revelation from the true God and of his commitment stimulated by his faith in God. Abraham, wealthy and successful, abandoned worldly comforts to spend his life wandering a land that God promised would one day belong to a mighty people descended from him.

Genesis 12:1–3, 7

Have the promises God made to Abraham been kept? And if so, how?

The striking feature of these verses is God's repeated use of the phrase *I will*. These are unconditional promises. They are a clear commitment by God to act, with no reference at all to anything that Abraham might be required to do. When we ask if God has kept his promises, we need to remember that most prophetic images of the future speak of a time future to our own. Because some promises made by God have not yet been kept does not mean God lied or was mistaken or that he has changed his mind. It simply means that history is not over yet.

Still, most of the commitments God made to Abraham *have* been kept—and wonderfully so. How? Note:

"I will make you into a great nation" (v. 2).	Childless Abraham became the ancestor of both the Arab peoples

	through Ishmael and the Jewish nation through Isaac.
"I will bless you" (v. 2).	God guarded Abraham throughout his lifetime, and did bless him greatly.
"I will make your name great" (v. 2).	Three great world religions, Islam, Judaism, and Christianity, all venerate Abraham as the founder of their faith.
"I will bless those who bless you, and whoever curses you I will curse" (v. 3).	Throughout history, nations that have welcomed the Jewish people have experienced times of blessings, while those who have persecuted them have suffered severe decline.
"To your offspring I will give this land" (v. 7).	This promise is yet to be fulfilled, even though a Jewish state once again exists in Canaan.

Genesis 12:10–20

How could God bless Abraham when he told such terrible lies and betrayed his own wife, Sarah?

Abraham was not blessed because he was sinless, which he was not. He was blessed because he had faith in God, and God was committed to him. Romans 4:3 says: "What does the Scripture say? 'Abraham believed God, and it was credited to him as righteousness [which he did not have].'" This is a great blessing for us, for just as Abraham had flaws, so do you and I. If God only blessed folks who were perfect, not one of us could expect anything good from God.

Another thing to remember is that when faith in God launches us on our new life in Christ, we have a long way to go. It's not surprising if we stumble and fall as we start out on faith's journey. True, Abraham fell. And it was not the only time. But Abraham grew, too, and despite his flaws increasingly became a man we can admire and emulate.

Genesis 14:1–4

Isn't the story of a coalition of kings raiding the cities of the plain rather unbelievable?

Not really. The Mari tablets, which describe conditions near the patriarchal period, speak of coalitions of kings from the east raiding city-states in Syria-Palestine. Archaeologists have found a string of Middle Bronze Age settlements along the route Genesis says the kings took, and both the names of people and places fit what we know of Abraham's time. We even know the reason for such raids. Copper, asphalt, and manganese were valuable natural resources of the region. Rather than being unbelievable, many details of the story fit the times exactly. What *is* unbelievable is the notion that a story so accurately set some 2000 years B.C. could have been made up by editors writing at a much later date.

Genesis 14:18

Was Melchizedek a historical figure or a mythical figure? Was he, as some say, the preincarnate Christ?

The pre-Christian Jewish rabbis were fascinated by this figure, and some suggested that he was an angel or other supernatural being. The writer of Hebrews argues that the fact that neither Melchizedek's parents nor his death are mentioned indicates that Christ's priesthood is patterned on Melchizedek's priesthood rather than on Aaron's. But this argument presumes that Melchizedek is a *type* of Christ—a real person who in some respects resembles, and thus foreshadows, the work or person of our Lord. However, there is no indication that the preincarnate Christ ever served as a type of the incarnate Jesus.

In fact, the Old Testament text treats Melchizedek as a person who was well established in his own milieu. He was king of Salem (later, Jerusalem) and "priest of God Most High." This title was never applied in Scripture to anyone other than Yahweh. The fact that his parents and his death are not mentioned, while relevant to the author of Hebrews, is irrelevant to the role he played in the story of Abraham; his parents and death should not be expected to be mentioned, any more than Abimelech's ancestry or demise are recorded in the Genesis text (Gen. 20). It's best, then, to take Melchizedek as a historical person, a worshiper of the true God who praised the Lord for Abraham's victory over the invading kings and blessed the patriarch, just as Genesis describes him.

Genesis 15

What is a covenant, and how was God's covenant with Abraham different from most?

The Hebrew term for covenant is *berit*, one of the most significant words in the Old Testament. It indicates a binding agreement, with its specific nature depending on the relationship it governs. In business a covenant was a contract. Internationally it was a treaty. Within a state it served as a constitution, spelling out the mutual obligations and privileges of the governed and the governor. Between individuals it might simply be called a legally binding agreement.

Typically a covenant defined the obligations of all parties covered by the agreement they promised to fulfill. And, typically, the covenant spelled out penalties for nonperformance. Thus the covenant was an *if-then* kind of document, with *if not-then* clauses.

There were also different kinds of covenants: a covenant of salt, a covenant of blood, etc. The most binding of ancient covenants was the covenant of blood, in which the parties both passed between the divided halves of sacrificial animals, a symbol that they pledged their very lives to live up to the terms of the agreement between them.

This background helps us understand the uniqueness of the covenant that God made with Abraham in Genesis 15. First, it was a covenant of blood, the most binding of all ancient legal formulations. The sacrificial animals were carefully divided and laid on the ground. But then God caused Abraham to fall into a deep sleep, and *God alone passed between the pieces of the sacrificial animals.* God committed himself unconditionally to keep the promises originally recorded in Genesis 12 and reaffirmed here in Genesis 15. Abraham did not pass between the sacrifices. He made no commitments to God, so nothing that he did or failed to do could relieve God of the commitment he made to keep his promises. Thus Hebrews 6:17 calls this covenant an oath, and says, "Because God wanted to make the unchanging nature of his purpose very clear to the heirs of what was promised, he confirmed it with an oath."

What, then, is the Abrahamic covenant? It is a legally binding oath, formally taken by God, to confirm for all time his firm intention to keep his promises to Abraham—*whatever Abraham or his descendants might do or fail to do.* God did this because he wants us to rest assured. When we put our trust in God, he commits himself to us, fully and completely. As Hebrews 6:19 says, "We have this hope as an anchor for the soul, firm and secure." How good it is to know that we can count completely on our God!

Genesis 15:17

The Bible often talks of the sun setting and rising. Does this show that the writers of the Old Testament thought that the sun revolved around the earth? How can we trust a book filled with such prescientific errors?

This kind of objection is one of the most foolish of those raised to challenge the trustworthiness of the Bible. The person who considers this an error ignores the fact that every modern newspaper reports the time of the daily sunrise and sunset. Certainly newspaper editors do not believe the sun really sets or rises. Why use these terms? Because every language is filled with *phenomenological terms and phrases*. That is, people speak in terms that tell how things *appear to them*, rather than in terms that provide scientific descriptions. The sun appears to rise, so we naturally call it sunrise. And the sun appears to set, so we, like the Hebrews, call it sunset. In describing things in terms of how they appear to us, neither we moderns nor the ancient Hebrews intend to describe the solar system scientifically. Thus the charge of scientific error is utterly meaningless and false.

Genesis 16

Was Abraham's taking Hagar to bed an immoral act? Why did Abraham do it?

In Abraham's day, custom permitted a childless wife to give her maid to her husband as a surrogate mother. Any child conceived was considered to be the child of the wife, not the servant. So even though the act fell short of God's created ideal for marriage, measured by the standards of the day Abraham's act was not immoral.

Abraham, however, did not inquire whether this union was God's will. Instead, he reluctantly gave in to the urging of Sarah. The results were not what Sarah expected. When Hagar's pregnancy demonstrated that Abraham was capable of fathering children, Hagar felt and showed contempt for her mistress. Later, when Abraham and Sarah had Isaac, the hostility between the two women was so great that Sarah insisted both Hagar and Ishmael be sent away. Hostility still dominates in the Middle East between Jews (Abraham's descendants) and Arabs (Ishmael's descendants).

How much wiser we all would be to seek guidance from God in all our choices, rather than to measure our acts simply by their acceptability in our society.

Genesis 17:5

What is the significance of the change of Abram's name to Abraham?

The name Abram means "father"; Abraham means "high father," that is, "father of a multitude." We can almost hear the snickers as childless Abram announced to his many herdsmen and their families that from now on he was to be called Abraham. That simple announcement was a tremendous act of faith and helps us appreciate Abraham's strengths despite Scripture's honest report of his flaws.

Genesis 18:13 with 17:17

These verses record that both Abraham and Sarah laughed when they heard the promise that Sarah would have a child. Yet only Sarah was rebuked. Why?

This is one of those difficulties which cannot really be solved, except on the basis of an assumption. The Hebrew word for "laugh" (*sahaq*) can mean either "laughter in joy" or "incredulity." In the latter sense, the meaning can shade into mockery or derision. Since the same word is used to describe both Abraham's and Sarah's first reaction to the preannouncement of Isaac's birth, we can only assume from the rebuke given Sarah that Abraham's incredulity shaded toward faith and Sarah's toward ridicule. Despite the rebuke, God blessed Sarah, and the incredulity turned to joy when the promise was fulfilled.

Genesis 19

Where was Sodom, and how was it destroyed?

Sodom, Gomorrah, and the other cities mentioned here lay in the broad valley near what is now known as the Dead Sea. Some believe that their remains lie under the south end of that sea, although this is far from certain. How they were destroyed is, however, not a mystery. The area held rich deposits of bitumen, a semisolid residue of petroleum or asphalt. It is likely that God used an earthquake and storm to ignite this highly flammable substance. The resultant fiery explosions would perfectly fit the Bible's description of dense smoke and a rain of burning sulfur (19:24, 28).

Genesis 19:5

The Old Testament describes Sodom as very wicked and focuses on a virulent homosexuality that found expression in the men's attempt to rape the visiting angels. Is the Bible's attitude toward homosexuality always this negative?

The modern demand that homosexuality be accepted as a morally valid alternate lifestyle finds absolutely no support in the Bible. Literally every mention of this practice in Scripture condemns it in the harshest of terms. Old Testament law says, "Do not lie with a man as one lies with a woman; that is detestable" (Lev. 18:22). In Romans 1 Paul describes both male homosexual and lesbian practice as unnatural (v. 26) indecent acts (v. 27) that are motivated by shameful lusts (v. 26). He calls such practices perversions (v. 27). First Timothy 1:9, 10 lists perverts among the "ungodly and sinful, the unholy and irreligious." First Corinthians 6:9 categorizes them with the wicked who "will not inherit the kingdom of God."

It is popular in contemporary society to call for tolerance for almost any way of life, and gay activists have been successful in enlisting media and popular support for their position. Yet it is clear from Scripture that whatever our society may decide, homosexuality is something that God does *not* intend to tolerate, but will surely judge.

Genesis 21:32; 26:1

Both these texts refer to Gerar as the land of the Philistines. But archaeological evidence shows that the Philistines did not settle along Canaan's coast until centuries later. Obviously, the Bible is in error. Also reference to Philistines in Canaan proves Moses could not have written this book.

While there is general agreement that massive settlement of the coast of Canaan by sea peoples from Crete took place around 1200 B.C., there is no reason to suppose Philistine settlements did not exist long before this time. In Abram's time as in the time of Moses a variety of peoples had settled in Canaan, including Hittites from the far north. Certainly the seagoing peoples who traded the Mediterranean had established colonies along the shores of the entire basin for centuries prior to Abraham's time. There is no reason to suppose that Philistines, whose forefathers came from Crete, were not among them.

Genesis 21:8–20

Why did Abraham send Ishmael away? Was this a moral or legal act?

Abraham rejected Sarah's urging to send Ishmael away until he was specifically directed to do so by God. He was undoubtedly motivated by love for his son, as well as by established custom of the era. Archaeological finds have shown that custom guaranteed the son of a handmaiden a significant inheritance in case the husband's primary wife later had a child. In this case God not only commanded Abraham to send Ishmael away but personally guaranteed Ishmael's survival and subsequent blessing (21:13). Why did God command this apparently cruel separation? Because it was essential that there be no confusion over who was to inherit the covenant promises given Abraham and thus which family line would be the agent of authentic revelation and the ultimate salvation of humankind.

Genesis 22

How could God tell Abraham to sacrifice his son Isaac? Does this story indicate that God once accepted human sacrifice?

Not at all. The Bible consistently condemns human sacrifice (Lev. 20). God did tell Abraham to give him Isaac as a *'olah*, (whole burnt offering). And Abraham certainly understood the command in this way. Yet Abraham was also aware that God could not and *would not* permit Isaac's life to end. Abraham said to his servants as he and Isaac headed up the mountain to sacrifice, "We will come back to you" (22:5), and to Isaac, "God himself will provide the lamb for the burnt offering" (22:8). The book of Hebrews adds to our understanding by noting that Abraham was so sure God would give him descendants through Isaac that he "reasoned that God could raise the dead" and would, if need be (Heb. 11:19).

We realize, then, that this incident was exactly what the Old Testament says it was, a test that enabled Abraham to exhibit the extent of his now-mature faith (Gen. 22:12). God never intended that Isaac be sacrificed. In fact, the only human sacrifice God has ever called for is that which he himself willingly made in Jesus, when he gave his own Son for the redemption of humankind.

Genesis 24

Did Isaac's marriage to Rebekah involve incest?

The laws governing this issue recorded in Leviticus 18 do not forbid sexual relationships in marriage between first cousins. In later times, however, such marriages were frowned upon, as they are in our own time.

Genesis 25:31

What was the birthright that Esau traded for a bowl of red stew?

Esau's birthright was the customary claim of the firstborn to the intangible rights of his father, as well as to double the material wealth granted to any other brothers. We are familiar with the tradition. For instance, the firstborn son of a king is first in line to succeed his father to the throne. In Abraham's case, the intangible asset was God's covenant promise. The fact that Esau was willing to trade the covenant away for a bowl of stew shows his complete disinterest in spiritual things. Esau was a total materialist. In contrast Jacob, despite his tendency toward deceit, placed a high value on the spiritual, and eagerly desired to be in the covenant line.

Genesis 26

How could Isaac duplicate Abraham's failure and lie to Abimelech? That ruler must have died decades before.

In Semitic languages *Abimelech* means "my father is king." *Abimelech* was most likely a royal title, not a personal name. So it is not necessary to assume the text indicates Abraham and Isaac dealt with the same individual.

Genesis 27

Why was Isaac's blessing so vital to his two sons?

The Nuzi tablets, documents dating from the fifteenth century B.C. and reflecting customs established for centuries, report a lawsuit between three brothers. One brother won the right to marry a woman named Zululishtar by showing that the marriage was authorized in his father's deathbed blessing. Thus the oral blessing served as a will with legal validity recognized in any ancient court. In addition, the blessing had special spiritual significance. While other peoples felt that blessings, like curses, had magical powers to affect the future, the Hebrews believed that God worked through the blessing of prophet and patriarch and empowered those blessed for the future. Both these features of the oral blessing made Isaac's blessing important to the brothers.

Genesis 27

How could God bless a liar like Jacob, who used deceit and fraud to cheat his brother of his rightful inheritance?

First, we need to remember that God did not bless Jacob *because* he lied and used deceit but in spite of it. Since "all have sinned and fall short of the glory of God," (Rom. 3:23), the only people God *can* bless are sinners. You and I can take our place alongside Jacob and be humbly grateful that God loves and blesses us despite our faults.

But don't suppose that Jacob got away with his fraud without paying a price. His action so provoked his brother that he had to flee for his life to his mother's relatives. There he himself was cheated by his uncle, learning how it felt to be the defrauded one rather than the defrauder. And his mother, who plotted with him, was deprived of her favorite son's company for the rest of his life.

And it was all unnecessary. God had told Rebekah that he intended Jacob to inherit the covenant promises (Gen. 25:23). If she and Jacob had only waited, God would have worked it all out for them, and their lives might have been very different.

Genesis 28:10–22

What did Jacob see in his dream at Bethel?

The famous ladder that Jacob saw, rendered stairway in the New International Version, is the translation of the Hebrew word *sullam*. This word occurs only in this verse. Assuming that the root of this word is *sll*, it seems most likely that the word indicates a point of contact, a place where communication between heaven and earth can occur. What is most important in the description is that what Jacob saw was a pathway oriented toward the earth with its top set in heaven. This stands in sharp contrast to Genesis 11:4, which reports people's efforts to build a tower, with its foundation set on the earth, which would reach into the heavens. What the text tells us is that God is the one who initiates communication with man. The shining pathway Jacob saw stretching up the hill of Bethel and on into the heavens is another reminder that any link between earth and heaven can exist only by the grace of God.

Genesis 29:27

Did Jacob wait seven years after he married Leah to wed her sister, his true love, Rachel?

This verse indicates Rachel was given to Jacob just seven or eight days after he married Leah. He committed himself to serve Laban seven more years as a bridal price, but he did not have to fulfill this contract before the wedding took place.

Genesis 29, 30

The fact that Jacob (Israel) had four wives is taken by the Muslims to condone polygamy. How can we say that the Bible teaches monogamy and yet honor Jacob as one of the founding patriarchs of our faith?

We do not build doctrine on reports of how God's people behaved but rather on the direct teaching of Scripture. It is true that Jacob's multiple marriages fall short of God's ideal as revealed in the creation account. But archaeology has shown that his relationships were fully moral according to the standard of the times. What Jacob did, therefore, was moral and right *as far as he knew.*

In fact, however, even a quick reading of these chapters makes it clear that polygamy led to significant pain and strife. Leah knew and was crushed by the fact that Jacob loved Rachel more than he loved her. She then used her ability to produce sons for her husband to hurt her sister, creating a tragic sense of rivalry and antagonism. Jacob himself was constantly plagued by his wives, who even insisted he take their maids as secondary wives to extend their competition over who could produce the most sons. Certainly the story told in these chapters helps us see at least one reason why polygamy is not God's will for his human children. The jealousy and competition stimulated by such relationships distorts the good God intends to bring into our lives through marriage.

Genesis 30, 31

Clearly, Laban cheated Jacob. But didn't Jacob cheat Laban right back and so gain large flocks at Laban's expense? Are we to conclude that it's all right to cheat others if they cheat us first?

Jacob did not cheat Laban, even though his uncle had changed his wages ten times (31:7). Archaeological finds show that work contracts generally were renewed at shearing time. The fact that Jacob fled at that time (31:19) indicates that he had fully and completely fulfilled his contract with Laban before leaving. As far as gaining large flocks at Laban's expense, Laban had freely agreed to give Jacob the speckled and streaked animals, because these were *uncommon* in that day. Thus Laban's agreement was motivated by greed and was unfair to Jacob. God's intervention caused the multiplication of the speckled and streaked animals and was a divine judgment on the deceitful Laban. So in no way can we accuse Jacob of cheating his uncle.

Genesis 31:34

Why did Rachel steal her father's household gods? Did this act indicate that she was committed to paganism?

Certainly Rachel was brought up as a pagan, unaware of her own great-uncle Abraham's faith in the one true God. But an article in *Biblical Archaeologist* (Summer 1983) reports: "The family gods, perceived as responsible for good fortune and passed down from one generation to the next, were at the heart of the family, and the individual who possessed them also held the paternal authority of the head of the house." Rachel may have been brought up as a pagan, but it's most likely that she took the family's household gods either to attack the father who had rejected her and her children, or to establish the future right of her own sons as heir to her father's estate.

Genesis 32:27–28

What is the significance of changing Jacob's name to Israel?

Names had great significance in the biblical world and were intended to communicate something of the essence of the person or thing named. Thus the change of Jacob's name to Israel clearly had great significance not only for him but for the people who took his name as their own. What does the name Israel mean? From among several possible meanings the best seems to be "God perseveres" or "he perseveres with God." Despite personal and national flaws and failures, God never gave up on his Old Testament people, and despite serious lapses of faith, Israel as a covenant people struggled to maintain its relationship with him.

The name *Israel* is used in seven distinct ways in the Old Testament. It is important to understand these ways to correctly interpret passages where the name is found:

1. As the personal name of Jacob-Israel.
2. As the name of the Old Testament covenant community made up of descendants of Abraham, Isaac, and Jacob.
3. As the name of the nation—either the territory or the people— formed by the covenant people after the Exodus.
4. As the name of the northernmost of the two Jewish kingdoms that were established after the division of the unified kingdom that had been ruled by David and Solomon.
5. As the religious and political entity reestablished in Judea after the Babylonian captivity.
6. As true believers within the larger community, who are distinct from the physical descendants (Rom. 9:6–8).
7. As a prophetic entity established at history's end.

Genesis 32:30

Jacob said he "saw God face to face." But later God told Moses, "You cannot see my face, for no one may see me and live" (Exod. 33:20). Is this a contradiction?

Not really. In Hebrew, "seeing one's face" often is used idiomatically to mean to be in a person's presence. Jacob concluded that the being with whom he had wrestled was God, and he was awed to realize that he had been in the presence of the Lord and survived. In the passage in Exodus Moses asked to see God's glory. Moses meant that he wanted to see God as he really is, unmasked, in his essential nature. God replied that no one could be in his unmasked presence (again using the phrase *see my face* idiomatically) and live. Jacob survived a contact with God who was masked as an angel or human being. Moses could not survive a contact with God if God had been unmasked, burning bright in his essential glory. There is no conflict here at all.

Genesis 39

When did Joseph enter Egypt?

The dating of biblical events prior to the time of Solomon has been the subject of serious debate. Conservatives generally accept a dating system ably defended by Gleason Archer. This system relies on dating provided in the Bible, and is supported by the consistency of the patriarchal narratives with what is known of life in Palestine in the second and third millennia B.C. Briefly, Archer dates Old Testament events up to the time of the Exodus as follows:

Abram's birth	2166 B.C.
Abram enters Canaan	2091 B.C.
Ishmael is born	2080 B.C.
Isaac is born	2066 B.C.
Sarah dies	2029 B.C.
Isaac marries Rebekah	2026 B.C.
Jacob is born	2006 B.C.
Jacob goes to Haran	1929 B.C.
Joseph is born	1915 B.C.
Joseph taken to Egypt	1898 B.C.

Genesis 39

A foreigner like Joseph could never have obtained high position in Egypt. This whole story is highly unlikely.

On the contrary, an Egyptian document dating from the mideighteenth century B.C. gives the names of some eighty members of a Theban household. More than forty are identified as Asiatic. The point is that it was quite common in Joseph's time for Asiatics to fill a number of posts, in private households and certainly in Pharaoh's administration as well. Joseph's interpretation of Pharaoh's dream so impressed Pharaoh that he elevated Joseph to one of the most important posts in his bureaucracy, if not the most important.

While Joseph's name has not been found on any written list of viziers of ancient Egypt, no complete list has ever been found, and many gaps currently exist. Significantly, the symbols of office and the honors Joseph received are authenticated by inscriptions and carved images of the royal court. The Genesis reports of details about the inner workings of the Egyptian court are so accurate that they clearly could not be mere fiction.

Genesis 44:5

This text has Joseph telling his servant to identify the silver cup placed in Benjamin's sack as one which "my master drinks from and also uses for divination." In view of the Bible's hostility toward occult practices, how could Joseph associate himself with divining?

Joseph's earlier interaction with Pharaoh's servants (40:8) and with Pharaoh himself (41:16) shows that he gave God full credit for his ability to interpret dreams. He did not claim any occult powers. Why does Genesis 44 speak of divining? Most likely Joseph's instruction to his servant was intended to mask his identity from his brothers by misdirecting them (44:15), lest the intimate knowledge he had shown of the family (43:33, 34) betray him.

Genesis 48:17–22

With Joseph's two sons taking his place as the founder of one of Israel's tribes, the number of tribes must be thirteen. Why does the Bible keep speaking of the twelve tribes of Israel rather than the thirteen?

The number twelve symbolizes the completeness and unity of God's Old Testament people. After the exodus the tribe of Levi was set aside to serve God and the community as priests and Levites. This tribe inherited no land in Canaan but was given cities in the territories of the others. In honoring Joseph by making him, through his sons, the father of two of Israel's tribes, God guaranteed that twelve territories would be occupied in the promised land.

Genesis 49:10

Does this verse predict a scepter for Judah as a messianic prophecy about Christ?

The verse has been understood by Jews in the pre-Christian era and by most Christian commentators as a prediction concerning Christ. David, Israel's great king from the tribe of Judah, prefigures his even greater descendant. In this sense the verse may indicate the throne of Israel is reserved for a member of the tribe of Judah—David first, and then Jesus.

Exodus

Exodus 1

Why would God permit the Hebrew people to spend such a long time in slavery if he really cared for them? Is the biblical story in conflict with the Christian's notion of a good and loving God?

During the centuries that the Hebrew people resided in Egypt, Canaan, the land God promised to Abraham's descendants, was a frequent battlefield. Great powers of the north and Egypt in the south struggled to dominate the smaller city-states that developed in Canaan. If the Hebrews had remained in Canaan, they surely would have been decimated by the warring locals or by the great powers. But, safe in Egypt, the people multiplied greatly (1:7). As slaves the Hebrew people were kept from assimilating with the Egyptians and were also moved to cry out to God, looking to him for a future deliverance. When God's time came, and Moses appeared to deliver Israel, the people were numerous enough to be able to marshal the army necessary to take the Promised Land by force.

Often the things that appear most painful in our lives are God's blessings in disguise, recognized as such only when the passage of time unveils the purpose God has had in mind.

Exodus 1:20, 21

How could God be "kind to the midwives" who lied to Pharaoh? Certainly they should have let the Hebrew boys live. And we can see how lying might seem necessary when they were confronted by Pharaoh. But to be blessed for lying? And, if there were so many Hebrews, how could just two midwives have served them?

49

50

Old Testament

Egyptian practice involved setting up bureaucracies for nearly every function. These two women, both of whom bear Hebrew names, most likely supervised a larger group of midwives drawn from the slave population. Nothing in the text supports the assumption that the midwives lied to Pharaoh. Perhaps the midwives purposely arrived late for most Hebrew births.

Exodus 3:21, 22

Is there any possible moral basis for the Israelites plundering the Egyptians?

This apparent conflict was heightened in older translations of the Bible, which portrayed the Hebrews as borrowing jewels from the Egyptians which they never intended to return. Actually, the Hebrew word *sa'al* simply means to "ask" or "request." The request was for gifts, not for a loan.

Why should the Egyptians have given their valuables so freely? By the time the request was actually made Egypt had experienced ten devastating plagues. The Egyptians were desperate for the Hebrews to leave and were glad to do anything that would hasten their departure (Exod. 12:33).

As for the moral basis, it was only right that the Hebrews who had served the Egyptians as slaves for so many decades be paid at last for their work. God simply saw to it that they were paid in full.

Exodus 3:14, 15

What is the significance of the name LORD?

Certainly God's words to Moses, "This is my name forever, the name by which I am to be remembered from generation to generation," make it clear that the name LORD is extremely significant.

Scholars agree that this name *Yahweh* was constructed from the Hebrew verb for "to be"; thus the I AM of Exodus 3:14. It seems best to take its essential meaning as "the one who is always present." God wants us, as he wanted his Old Testament people, to know him not just as a God who acted in the past or who will act in the distant future but as one who is with us now, ready and able to act in our present. Whenever we find LORD in our English translations, with its small capital letters, we know that the Hebrew contains this wonderful name of our God.

And we are reminded that we worship a God who is with us now and forevermore.

Exodus 3:18

Why did God tell Moses to ask permission from Pharaoh only for a three-day journey, when all along God intended to free his people completely?

The answer may well be that God in grace asked a small favor from Pharaoh, which he could have granted without cost, rather than immediately demand the greater sacrifice. God often asks us to do little things before he calls for complete commitment, to help us develop the habit of obedience. In Pharaoh's case, even this easy request met an angry refusal. Pharaoh's blunt rejection of this reasonable request shows us that his heart was arrogant and hard long before God exerted greater pressure on that king.

Exodus 4:21

How could God blame and punish Pharaoh for refusing to let Israel go, when the Bible says God is the one who hardened Pharaoh's heart?

Heart is a broad term in the Hebrew and indicates the inner person and his or her capabilities. Here clearly the will is involved; it is Pharaoh's intent to reject God's command. This intent is mentioned often in Exodus 4–14, and the seventeen different references to it alternate between statements that God hardened Pharaoh's heart (as here and in 7:3), descriptions that simply affirm that "Pharaoh's heart became hard" (7:13; 8:19), and statements that "Pharaoh . . . hardened his [own] heart" (8:15, 32).

The critical issues are (1) whether Pharaoh operated as a free and responsible person in refusing Moses' requests, or whether (2) he was caused to act against his own will by the action of God? It is clear from the text and from the phrase that gives us trouble itself that Pharaoh *was* acting as a free and responsible person. To say that God *hardened* Pharaoh's heart (intent, will) indicates that God simply strengthened the intent to refuse Moses' request which Pharaoh already had. Clearly God did not cause Pharaoh to act against his own will. Thus Pharaoh was responsible for his intent, even though God hardened him in it.

For those who still feel this is unfair, there is another observation to make on this text. If we ask *what God specifically did* that hardened Pharaoh, what we see in Exodus is simply that God *progressively revealed more of himself and his power through the series of miracles that Moses performed.* It was God's revelation of himself to Pharaoh that hardened that ruler in his determination to resist the Lord. It is the same today. Just as the heat of the sun that softens wax also hardens clay, so God's self-revelation softens the hearts of those who believe and hardens the hearts of those who refuse to believe. There is no difficulty here. This is a reminder that you and I must always keep ourselves open to the Lord, that the more he reveals himself to us the more tender our hearts will be.

Exodus 4:22

In what way was Israel God's firstborn?

The literal firstborn was the eldest son, who held a special position in the family with special rights, privileges, and responsibilities of inheritance. When used figuratively, as here, firstborn indicates the special place Israel has within the whole family of God, the special privileges this chosen people enjoyed, and its special responsibilities.

Exodus 4:24

Why was the Lord about to kill Moses?

Moses had neglected to have his son circumcised, apparently due to the opposition of his wife (vv. 25,26). Circumcision symbolized inclusion in the covenant line of Abraham. Certainly one who was to lead the covenant people had to serve as an example of obedience to God and his precepts despite the opposition of his wife. Zipporah understood the cause of Moses' critical illness and so circumcised their child against her will.

Exodus 5:7

How was straw used in making bricks?

The bits of straws that the Egyptians typically mixed with the clay strengthened the bricks and made them harder.

Exodus 6

Who was the Pharaoh at the time of the exodus?

The Bible does not give the name of the Pharaoh Moses confronted. Egyptian records, like the records of other ancient monarchs, boast of the rulers' victories and fail to mention their defeats. So there is no direct evidence as to the identity of the Pharaoh of the exodus.

Scholars who argue for a late date of the exodus (around 1200 B.C.) assume that the Pharaoh in question was Rameses II. Conservative scholars, however, believe that the traditional early date of about 1445 B.C. fits not only specific biblical evidence (1 Kings 6:1) but also the majority of the archaeological evidence as well.

If the exodus did take place in the 1440s B.C., the Pharaoh who oppressed Israel and from whom Moses fled when he went to Midian, would be Thutmose III, who died in 1447 B.C. The Pharaoh Moses later confronted would have been his son, Amenhotep II, who ruled until 1421 B.C.

Interestingly, there is apparent corroboration for this conclusion in what is called the dream stele of Thutmose IV. This pharaoh promised the god Harmakhis, who promised in a dream that he would ascend Egypt's throne, to clear the Sphinx of sand so the chapel between the statue's paws could be opened for worship. This implies that Thutmose IV did not *expect* to become Pharaoh, because his older brother would normally have succeeded Thutmose III. But this brother would have been killed in the tenth plague, when the death angel struck down the firstborn of every Egyptian household.

Exodus 6:16–20

Exodus 12:40 says that the Israelites were in Egypt 430 years. But here the text lists only three generations between Levi and Moses. This couldn't be.

Hebrew genealogies do not list *every* person in a family line but emphasize the key people. Actually, 1 Chronicles 7 identifies ten persons between Ephraim and Joshua, so we know that there were at least ten generations between the patriarchs and the exodus. Ten generations of forty-three years each allows plenty of time for the seventy-three persons who entered Egypt to multiply to the two million who left it 430 years later.

Exodus 7:11, 22; 8:7

This text says that the Egyptian magicians duplicated two of the authenticating miracles performed by Moses. It's one thing to believe that God can perform miracles. It's a different thing entirely to believe in magic.

There are two possible solutions here. One is simply that the magicians of Egypt, like modern magicians, used deception. The other is that the supernatural actually was involved. To believe that Satan can cause what 2 Thessalonians 2:9 calls "counterfeit miracles, signs and wonders" is very different from believing in magic. Jesus himself warned of a coming time when false Christs and prophets will perform great signs and miracles. It would be foolish not to assume that at least some of the supposed miracles associated with pagan religions were not real or were caused by Satan rather than God.

Exodus 7–11

Why did God bring all those terrible plagues on Egypt? Why didn't he just move the Egyptians to let his people go, without making them suffer so?

God never causes suffering gratuitously. The Book of Exodus gives three purposes that God intended to accomplish through the devastating scourges that struck Egypt. First, these mighty acts that God performed would serve forever as a reminder that God is the one who brought his people out of bondage (Exod. 6:7). Second, the plagues were a "judgment on all the gods of Egypt" (Exod. 12:12). That is, they demonstrated the powerlessness of Egypt's gods to help the people of that land. And third, the plagues served as an unmistakable witness to the pagan Egyptians that they might know that "I am the LORD" (Exod. 7:5). These last two purposes are clear evidence that grace was actually being expressed in and through these national tragedies. In exposing the barren nature of Egypt's hope in her gods, and in revealing himself as the one true God, the Lord was inviting the people of this benighted land to turn to him.

Exodus 12

Does the evidence show that the exodus really took place around 1290 B.C. rather than around 1445 B.C., the date the numbers given in the Bible suggest?

Twenty years ago only the most conservative of scholars would have held out for a 1445 B.C. exodus. Today more and more questions are being raised about the 1290 B.C. theory.

Gleason Archer sums up several arguments advanced for the later date and gives the reasons why they are not conclusive.

Argument	Response
Exodus 1:11 says the Israelites slaved in the city of Rameses. So the exodus must have been *after* this king's rule.	This is an example of inserting the name after the event. Rameses' reign began in 1300 B.C., and the work project was undertaken prior to Moses. Moses could hardly have been eighty years old just ten years after he would have been born.
Josephus says the Semitic Hyksos were in power in Egypt when Jacob migrated there. They did not seize power before 1750 B.C. Four hundred thirty years afterward would give a date for the exodus much closer to the time of Rameses II than Amenhotep II.	The text makes it clear the Hyksos did not rule at the time of the migration (Gen. 43:32; 46:34). It is more likely that the "new king, who did not know about Joseph" (Exod. 1:8) was a Hyksos, and that the concern over the multiplication of the Hebrews was linked to the Hebrew loyalty to the old regime. Later, after Amose expelled the Hyksos, the Asiatic Hebrews would have understandably remained under suspicion. Thus the biblical account simply does not fit with Hyksos rule in Joseph's time.
Archeological evidence points to a destruction of key cities in Canaan in the thirteenth rather than the early fourteenth century B.C. Hazor, for instance, was said in the Book of Joshua to have been destroyed in the Hebrew invasion. It must have taken place at the	The archaeological evidence of destruction does not indicate who caused it. The Book of Judges describes an unsettled land marked by continual warfare. And we know from passages like Judges 5, 6 that many cities destroyed by Joshua were later rebuilt. While Katherine Kenyon's analysis of Jericho has long been assumed to prove the late date, recent work by Bryant G. Wood, based on

later rather than the earlier date.

firmly established methods, has
shown conclusively that this key city
did fall about 1400 B.C., thus fully
supporting the traditional date.

Exodus 12:29–30

The account of the death of Egypt's firstborn raises a serious moral difficulty. Was it fair for God to take the sons of all the people when it was clearly Pharaoh's sins that deserved judgment? After all, the common people had no control over Pharaoh, who was an absolute ruler.

There is no indication that the Egyptian people ever opposed Pharaoh's policy or spoke out against the enslavement of the Jews. If Pharaoh's actions were so out of harmony with the will of his administration and people he would have been unable to impose his policies. For this reason a later Pharaoh who sought to wean Egypt from the worship of many gods to the worship of the sun failed completely to do so. Even in our own day we apply this same principle of national responsibility for the acts of a ruler. Hitler's policy of exterminating the mentally and physically infirm and the Jews was tolerated by the German people, who today acknowledge their share of the guilt. Saddam Hussein's cowardly terrorist attacks on Israel during the more recent Gulf War were cheered by his people, as was Iraq's occupation of Kuwait. The people of Egypt, like the German and Iraqi peoples, were guilty of their leaders' acts. The death of all firstborns was a just penalty imposed by a righteous and moral God for centuries of persecution of Israel.

Exodus 12

What is the significance of the annual Passover festival?

The Old Testament identifies Passover as a *zikkaron*, a "memorial" or "commemoration" (12:14). This technical theological term indicates a recurring event or a place intended to remind God's people of some historic act of his in their behalf. Through the *zikkaron* the believer was enabled to sense his own personal identity with that past act and thus to see it as an act God performed for him personally. The Passover, then, became an occasion on which succeeding generations of Jews might identify with the exodus generation and realize afresh that God is each Jew's personal redeemer. This is why the father was to say to the youngest child each time the Passover meal was eaten, "It is the Passover sacrifice to the LORD, who . . . spared *our* homes when he struck down the Egyptians" (12:27).

The communion service, called a *remembrance* in 1 Corinthians 10, serves this same purpose for Christians. As we partake of the cup and the bread, we are taken back in time and realize that each of us individually stands at the foot of the cross. It was for *me* that Jesus died, and because he died I will live.

Exodus 13–14

What was the Red Sea that opened to let the Israelites pass and then closed again on the pursuing Egyptian army?

The Hebrew *yom suph* means "sea of reeds," that is, a body of water whose shallows supported great fields of papyrus reeds. Scholars agree that this body was not the Red Sea but one of the large, shallower bodies of water that lie between Goshen, where the Israelite slaves had lived, and the Sinai Peninsula. The exact location of the crossing is unknown.

Exodus 16:31

What was manna?

Some have struggled to give a natural rather than a supernatural explanation for the food that supported the Israelites in the wilderness. One candidate is a tiny, sweet substance produced by certain insects. The fact that these insects could not have produced enough food to sustain the large numbers of Israelites specified in the Bible has then been used to argue that Old Testament numbers are exaggerated, and that only a few thousand Israelites actually fled Egypt.

The Bible, however, makes it clear that manna was provided for God's people supernaturally. As Jesus said, manna was "the bread from heaven" (John 6:32).

Exodus 20

How are Christians to understand and apply the Ten Commandments?

The Bible speaks of the Mosaic law as a whole as a covenant God made with Israel (Jer. 31:31, 32). And the New Testament insists that the Christian is "not under law, but under grace" (Rom. 6:14). None of this means, however, that the Ten Commandments have no application to Christians. They are clear statements of general moral principles. The principles they embody reveal much about the moral character of the God who gave them. They also reveal moral standards which make clear what God expects not only of his Jewish people but of all people who live in a personal relationship with him.

While stated in the negative as "thou shalt not," each commandment has clear, positive implications that give us practical guidance for maintaining a right relationship with God and with other people.

The Commandment	Its Positive Implications
1. *You shall have no other gods before me (20:3).*	God merits our complete loyalty. We give our allegiance totally to him.
2. *You shall not make for yourself an idol (20:4–6).*	Nothing in the material universe can represent God or may be allowed to take his place in our hearts.
3. *You shall not misuse the name of the LORD your God (20:7).*	Never assume that *God* is an empty or meaningless word. God is real, and we are to be constantly aware of this fact and to trust him to act in our lives.
4. *Remember the Sabbath day by keeping it holy (20:8).*	Set aside time to worship, honor, and remember the Lord—and to rest.
5. *Honor your father and your mother (20:12).*	Show respect for your parents when they are young and old.
6. *You shall not murder (20:13).*	Consider every person an individual of worth and value, and actively protect and guard one another's lives.
7. *You shall not commit adultery (20:14).*	Be loyal to your spouse and the covenant you made to commit yourself to him or her alone.
8. *You shall not steal (20:15).*	Show concern for others by protecting their right to their possessions. Do not use others for your own material gain.
9. *You shall not give false testimony against your neighbor (20:16).*	Guard the reputation of others as well as their lives and property.

10. *You shall not covet (20:17).*   Value people, not things. Let
                                      other people be more important
                                      to you than what they have or
                                      than what you do not have.

Exodus 20:8

*Do Christians violate the commandment to "remember the Sab-
bath day" (Jewish Saturday) by worshiping on Sunday?*

While the principles embodied in each of the other nine commandments are repeated explicitly in the New Testament, the New Testament never even implies that Christians are to worship on the Sabbath. Instead it is clear that Sunday replaced the Sabbath as the
Christians' day of worship. Although the first Jewish converts to Christianity continued to worship on the Sabbath, it is clear that soon the
first day of the week, Sunday, was kept as the Christians' holy day (Acts
20:7; 1 Cor. 16:2). What explains this shift? While the Sabbath is associated in the Old Testament with God's act of creation (Exod. 20:11),
Sunday is associated with the resurrection of Jesus (Matt. 28:1; Mark
16:2; Luke 24:1; John 20:1). This event, which is the focus of Christian
faith, took priority in the church's thought, and thus the day of worship
was changed to reflect the new reality. A third-century document titled
The Teaching of the Apostles says that "the Apostles further appointed"
the first day of the week as a day of worship "because on the first day of
the week our Lord rose from the dead, and on the first day of the week
he ascended up into heaven, and on the first day of the week he will
appear at last with the angels of heaven."

Exodus 20:13

*How can some Christians justify war and capital punishment
when the sixth commandment says, "You shall not murder"?*

The Hebrew language makes a clear distinction between personal killings, such as murder and manslaughter, and judicial executions and killing in war. This commandment uses the word for personal
killings, and thus the New International Version rightly reads, "You shall
not murder," rather than the older, "Thou shalt not kill." For more, see
the discussion of Genesis 9:6, page 31.

Exodus 20:14

Did Old Testament multiple marriages, like that of Jacob, who had four wives, violate the commandment against adultery? How could God bless, and God's people honor, a person who lived in adultery all his life?

The relationship that Jacob had with Rachel, Leah, Bilhah and Zilpah were legal marriages according to the laws and customs of the patriarchal age. The law against adultery is against illicit sexual relationships outside of marriage, and thus did not apply to Jacob.

In fact, the Old Testament does not specifically forbid multiple marriages. Jesus' argument from creation in Matthew 19 certainly implies a monogamous union, and the quick appearance in Cain's line of multiple marriages (Gen. 4:19–23) is clear evidence that these are not God's will for humankind. But it would be unfair to apply a standard that is understood millenniums later to a person who lived a righteous life according to the standards of his time.

Exodus 21:1

How can you justify the practice that Moses' law governs the selling of oneself or one's children into slavery. Yes, the NIV says servant, but older versions are more honest. No God who institutes slavery can be considered moral.

This difficulty needs to be answered in several ways. First, Old Testament laws did not *institute* slavery. They *regulated* an already existing institution. Comparison with the practices of other cultures of that time shows that the slave in Israel had many more rights and much greater protection under law. For instance, the granting of freedom should a master injure the slave and the ruling that a slave must be released after seven years are unique to Old Testament law. Second, selling one's children into slavery was frequently an economic necessity. Parents did not sell children to make a profit but because they could not support them. In a sense, slavery in Israel was often a lifesaving institution. Third, slavery was one of the social mechanisms by which Old Testament law sought to reduce poverty in Israel. A person who found himself in debt could sell himself to a successful individual. He would use the money to pay off his debt and then work for his master for seven years. During this time he might gain skills that would enable him to make it on his own. After the seven years were up, the slave was not only freed but was supplied by his master with the capital he needed to make a fresh start (see Exod. 21:2–11; Lev. 25:39–55; Deut. 15:1–18). While individual slaves might be misused by wicked masters, slavery in Israel was hardly the awful institution that it was in other cultures or in the United States thousands of years later.

Exodus 21:23–25

The biblical principle of an eye for an eye sounds terribly primitive and brutal. How can anyone imagine that the God of the Old Testament, who introduced this principle, is anything like the God of the New Testament, who through Jesus taught us all to love our enemies?

This so-called *lex talona*, or "law of the jungle," is a very advanced principle that was essential to maintain social harmony in Israel.

Israel had no police force, jails, or national courts. Disputes were brought to local elders for settlement. Crimes were considered to be committed against an individual, not against the state. Penalties were paid to the individual harmed, with the intent being to restore what had been taken from him or her. In the case of theft, not only was what had been taken restored, but often it would be repaid two or more times over. But what then about injury cases?

In many societies a crime is considered to be a matter between the victim and the perpetrator. For this reason terrible feuds have developed. One person hurts another; in anger that person strikes back; the terrible cycle of injury piled upon injury continues. The eye-for-an-eye principle of Old Testament law stopped this cycle before it could begin. If someone harmed another by blinding one eye, the most the injured could do to the other was to take his eye. In practice, this meant that an injured person set a price on the harm done to him and that the elders of the city became involved in negotiations until the case was settled by a payment mutually acceptable to both parties. The eye-for-an-eye principle meant simply that the harmed party had no right to demand more in retribution than he had in fact had done to him.

Understood this way, the *lex talona* is not a law of the jungle at all. It is a principle of law that is intended to maintain social harmony in a community where people are held responsible for acts that harm others, but where justice, rather than revenge, rules. There is no conflict at all with the principles of relationship Jesus introduced. Old Testament law calls for forgiveness and the restoration of harmony after the victim has been indemnified for the harm done to him.

Exodus 31:18

Does God really have fingers? Are verses that use such anthropo-morphic language evidence that the Old Testament's view of God is primitive and completely out of harmony with Jesus' view that "God is Spirit" (John 4:24)?

The use of anthropomorphic language does *not* suggest a primitive view of God. Hebrew is a very graphic language and frequently uses concrete images in figurative or symbolic ways. To say that the stone tablets of the law were inscribed by the finger of God was clearly understood by the people of Moses' time to mean nothing more than that God had personally conveyed these laws to Moses.

There are so many similar uses of language in the Old Testament it is hard to imagine that anyone could raise such a foolish objection. For instance, for God to put something under his heel is to subdue it. To say his eyes are on something or someone is to affirm his watchful presence. To meet God face to face means to meet with him personally. To ascribe an act to God's mighty arm simply means it was accomplished by his great power.

None of these or similar uses of language suggest for one moment that the Hebrews thought of God as anything other than a transcendent Spirit whose nature could never be captured by any image shaped by man (Exod. 20:4).

Exodus 33:11, 20

These two verses obviously conflict with each other. How can God say, "You cannot see my face," while the same passage indicates that God spoke with Moses "face to face"?

The answer lies in the different ways that *face* is used in the Old Testament. See the discussion of this question under Gen. 32:30, page 46.

Exodus 34:7

This verse actually says God "punishes the children . . . for the sin of the fathers to the third and fourth generation." How can any-one consider this a moral thing to do? Besides, Ezekiel chapter 18 repudiates this principle. So even the Old Testament does not try to justify this morally indefensible position.

This verse does not paint God as the vindictive pursuer of the children of the guilty but emphasizes a significant truth. The choices that a person makes affect not only his or her own life but influence that person's offspring as well. The effects of our choices echo in our offspring for generations. Those who, in this context, reject and violate the principles expressed in God's Ten Commandments distort the moral character of their offspring and make them terribly vulnerable to divine punishment for their own acts.

Ezekiel 18 deals with another issue entirely. In Ezekiel's day the people of Judah were indifferent to God, arguing that repentance would make no difference, for God had determined to punish Judah because of the sins of their forefathers. Ezekiel makes it clear that, even in times of national disaster, each individual's moral commitment *does* make a difference. God treats individuals on the basis of their own moral choices and does *not* punish them for what their fathers or grandfathers did.

Leviticus

Leviticus

Who wrote this book, and what issues and themes does it deal with?

This third book of the Old Testament was written by Moses (see Genesis, page 13). The name means "concerning the Levites." This book focuses on worship, giving detailed instructions as to how the priests and Levites were to perform their duties, as well as instructions to the people on how to maintain the ritual and moral holiness essential for fellowship with God.

Leviticus 1–7

Animal sacrifices were clearly vital in Old Testament worship, just as they were in most pagan religions. But even the New Testament points out that "it is impossible for the blood of bulls and goats to take away sins" (Heb. 10:4). How then can Leviticus say that God gave the Israelites animal blood to "make atonement for the man's sin" (Lev. 4:26)?

The Hebrew word used to describe the effect of Old Testament sacrifices, translated as "atonement," is *kapar* (verb) or *kippur* (noun). Most believe the root means "to cover" and see in it the imagery of sins covered by the blood of the sacrifice. Certainly atonement, and the blood sacrifices that accomplish it, is the avenue through which God's Old Testament people appropriated the forgiveness God offered to believers. How then can the New Testament say that the blood of animals offered in the Old Testament could never take away sins? The answer is found in making a critical distinction. The *basis* on which God forgives human beings of any era, Old Testament or New Testament, is and has always been the sacrifice of Christ. It is his blood that is efficacious and truly takes away, rather than simply covers, human sin.

It would be wrong to assume that Old Testament believers saw in the animal sacrifices a foreshadowing of the cross and that they believed in Jesus and relied on his sacrifice for them centuries before he was born. But it would be right to say that the sacrifices offered in Old Testament times were a way through which the Old Testament believer could express faith in God's promise to forgive, and that *faith in God's promise* has always been the key that unlocks the door of salvation. Thus the basis on which God saves is the blood of Christ, not of animals. But the faith that appropriates salvation was, in Old Testament times, expressed by the offering of the animal sacrifices that God ordained.

There is one more important contribution that animal sacrifices made. They did foreshadow the sacrifice of Christ. The blood on Old Testament altars was a constant reminder that the sinner deserves death but that God will accept the life of a substitute in place of the life of the sinner. This repeated object lesson undoubtedly prepared true believers in Israel to understand the meaning of Jesus' death. And it enables us to understand the crucifixion as a substitutionary offering of Christ for us. He truly did die for us that through his death we might have eternal life.

Leviticus 10

Why were Nabad and Abihu killed by fire from God? Surely this incident is evidence that the Old Testament view of God is primitive, for his action here is clearly vengeful and cruel.

In verse 10 of this chapter, God explained to Aaron, the father of the two who were killed, that priests were charged to "distinguish between the holy and the common, between the unclean and the clean" and to "teach the Israelites" (10:10, 11). In offering "unauthorized fire," the two sons of Aaron showed their disregard for God's commands, which were to be taken seriously and observed in every detail. The punishment of the two sons of Aaron was severe but was required by the high position they held. It clearly underlined for all time the need for the priests to treat God's commands with utmost respect.

Leviticus 11

Was "unclean" food unhealthy? What was wrong with eating the animals forbidden in Old Testament law?

Some have tried to explain the Mosaic list of animals that were not to be eaten by seeking some health reason. This crops up even in our own day. There is a strange rumor that pork is dirty meat because the pig does not fully assimilate its food and so stores waste material in its flesh. In fact, there is nothing intrinsically dirty about the animals Israel was forbidden to eat (Acts 10:9–23).

In fact, many of the Mosaic rules concerning the clean and unclean have absolutely no relationship to sanitary or health issues. Instead they were intended to serve as a constant reminder to the Israelites that they were different from all other peoples of the world. God had chosen them, and God was concerned about every detail of their lives from birth to death: whom they married, what they ate, how they planted and harvested their crops, etc.

Today you and I can see in these strange Old Testament rules concerning cleanliness a vivid reminder that God does care completely for us. In all we do we are to recognize his presence, be thankful for his good gifts, and honor him in the doing.

Leviticus 17:11

All this emphasis on blood in the Old Testament and New Testament is primitive, a carryover from ancient superstitions. How can anyone respect the Bible when it is filled with such primitive notions?

Leviticus 17:11 makes it very clear that *blood* stands for life. Whenever sacrificial blood is mentioned, we are to understand it as symbolic of the life of a substitute offered in expiation for a sinner who deserves to die. In fact, the revelation that God gave his Son as a substitutionary sacrifice to pay for our sins, a reality pictured in the Old Testament blood sacrifices, is a stunning and totally unique teaching of the Bible. Thus biblical blood sacrifice is very different in its essential nature from the blood sacrifice practiced in ancient and modern pagan religions.

In pagan religions blood sacrifices are typically bribes people offer to the gods in hopes of avoiding punishment or gaining some favor. What is fascinating, however, is the fact that the practice of sacrifice is almost universally observed in primitive religions. This fact suggests that there is a common *basis in the history of our race* for the belief that sacrifice is an essential element in religion. Rather than prove that the biblical faith grew out of paganism, the almost universal practice of sacrifice in pagan religions suggests that human awareness of the necessity of sacrifice grows out of a common racial memory of the fall and the remedy to which Scripture testifies.

Leviticus 18:5

Christians say that salvation is by faith. Is this contradicted by this verse, which says, "Keep my decrees and laws, for the man who obeys them will live by them"?

Not every verse in the Bible that speaks of life and death refers to eternal life or eternal punishment. In fact, the Old Testament's references to life and death typically are to the biological rather than the spiritual or eternal. This is particularly so when Old Testament law is referred to. Deuteronomy 27 in particular spells out the blessings in this life that an obedient Israelite could expect, and also the punishments that could be expected for persistent disobedience. Any generation of Israelites that took the Old Testament law seriously was very much aware that, in this life, "the man who obeys them [God's laws] will live by them."

Leviticus 20

Why do so many crimes listed here and elsewhere in the Old Testament call for the death penalty? It may be possible to argue that murderers deserve to die, but do adulterers and homosexuals and mediums and fortune tellers? That's pretty severe.

Actually, there are far fewer crimes for which the death penalty is prescribed in Old Testament law than in other law codes of the ancient world. For instance, unlike other Middle Eastern law codes, Mosaic law does not call for death in the case of any crime against property.

The question then is, What is the rationale for those crimes that did deserve the death penalty? What did they have in common? Two things. Crimes that called for the death penalty threatened the whole community either by undermining the family or faith in God. Sexual deviation threatens the family and distorts that covenant relationship which is to govern a husband's or wife's commitment to his or her spouse. The worship of pagan deities, and the practice of the occult that was an integral part of it, denied the commitment God's people were to maintain to him. By permitting either unfaithfulness to one's spouse or to God to develop

68

Old Testament

in Israel would so affect the community's faith that the very existence of the nation as a people of God would be threatened.

While this may seem an extreme view, even a brief look ahead at the Israelites' journey to Canaan and at events that took place during the period of the Judges shows that loose sexual practices and involvement in pagan practices led to national disaster. Only by the most severe penalties, intended to maintain the purity of the community of faith, could that purity be preserved and the nation as a whole experience the blessings of God.

Leviticus 24:10–22

Why was the blaspheming son stoned to death? Here is another indication that the God of the Old Testament is cruel and capricious and very different from the God the New Testament describes.

More than swearing, or "cussing," is involved here. The text says that this son of an Israelite mother and an Egyptian father "blasphemed the Name *with a curse."* This means that the individual invoked the name of God as part of an occult curse directed against someone he was hostile to. This was a clear violation of the command not to use God's name in vain, and also a violation of commands forbidding God's people to engage in occult practices. Thus the death penalty was not only called for, it was required.

Why was the entire assembly told to stone the offender? This mode of execution was used to symbolize important aspects of Old Testament law. Each member of the faith community was to accept responsibility for maintaining the holiness of the community. If anyone was aware of a crime committed by a fellow Israelite, he was to bear witness of it before the elders of the community. If a person was guilty of a capital crime against the community (see Lev. 20, above), it was the responsibility of the entire community to put him to death. Thus there is a great difference between the lynch mobs or vigilantes of our Old West who acted outside of established law, and the citizens of Israel who acted as agents of the law when stoning offenders.

Leviticus 27:30–33

Is tithing binding on Christians as well as on God's Old Testament people?

Old Testament passages that define tithing include, in addition to this passage, Numbers 18:21–32; Deuteronomy 12:5–14; 14:22–29; and 26:12–15. Another frequently quoted verse is Malachi 3:10, which urges the Jews of that prophet's day to "test me in this, . . . and see if I will not throw open the floodgates of heaven and pour out so much blessing that you will not have room enough for it." Strikingly, no New Testament passage calls on Christians to bring ten percent of their income as an offering. Instead 2 Corinthians 8–9 simply invites generous giving in response to the needs of others and as expression of love for God.

Some persons note that Abraham gave a tithe to Melchizedek before the Mosaic law was given (Gen. 14:20); they assume that this established a precedent which both Moses and Christians must follow. But this act had special symbolic implications related to establishing Christ's priesthood (Heb. 7:6–10). When we do look at the law, we note several critical things. First, the tithe was paid *only on what the land produced,* that is, its crops and animals. The basis of the tithe was that the land belonged to God, and thus the tithe was rent, owed to God, on the land he permitted Israel to live on. Second, the tithe was intended for the support of those who gave their lives to lead Israel in worship, the Levites and the priests. Third, one tithe every three years, or perhaps a second tithe every third year, was collected and retained locally for the care of widows, orphans, and homeless strangers.

In Old Testament times tithes, which should be seen as rent paid God for the use of his land, were supplemented by freewill offerings. These were voluntary contributions, given spontaneously and freely as gifts, not from a sense of obligation nor with an intent to merit God's blessing. God, who has given wonderfully to us (Ps. 68:9), is deserving of all that we might be moved to give him. While some Christians may choose to take the tithe as a minimum standard by which to measure their giving, they should not suppose that the tithe is required by Scripture. As Paul says in 2 Corinthians 9:7, "Each man should give what he has decided in his heart to give, not reluctantly or under compulsion, for God loves a cheerful giver."

Numbers

Numbers

Who wrote this book, and what themes and issues does it deal with?

This is the fourth of the five books of Moses which launch the Old Testament (see Genesis, page 13). The book picks up the story of the exodus generation; it proves essential genealogical information and reports on the travels of God's people from Sinai to the borders of Canaan and back into the wilderness for forty years of wandering. The theme of Numbers is the disastrous results of the failure of the exodus generation to trust God. Because of this the conquest of Canaan had to wait until a new generation could grow up, a generation that, unlike the former, *did* trust God completely.

Numbers 1

This book and the rest of the Old Testament books frequently report statistics on the size of armies and tribal groups. These numbers often do not agree with each other. This certainly proves the Bible cannot be trusted. How trustworthy are these statistics?

Two different issues are involved in this question. First, why are there discrepancies between the statistics given in the Books of Samuel and Kings and the Chronicles? And second, aren't the large numbers given in Scripture for tribal groups and armies simply unbelievable?

To deal with the first difficulty we need to note that in the hundreds of statistics, a great majority *do* agree. And some of the supposed disagreements, on closer examination, are because the authors made their counts at different times or included or left out groups not considered by the other. Even so, some eighteen cases of real discrepancy do occur, as for example between 2 Samuel 23:8 and 1 Chronicles 11:11, or 1 Kings 4:26 and 2 Chronicles 9:25. The question here is whether these discrepancies reflect error in the original text or later transmission error. If the error crept in as the manuscripts were copied again and again over the centuries, we can hardly use them to argue that the *Bible* is in error. It would be the *copyist* who made the error, not the original author.

In fact every likelihood is that the errors *are* errors in transmission. In Old Testament Hebrew, letters represented numbers. Thus *a* stood for *one*. To multiply the number, dots were placed over the letter. Thus *a* with two dots represented 100. It is easy to see how a manuscript could become worn or cracked, the faded or smudged dots become more and more difficult to read and finally very difficult to copy accurately.

Such copying errors can also lead to seemingly serious historical problems. For instance, 2 Kings 18:13 says, "In the fourteenth year of King Hezekiah's reign, Sennacherib king of Assyria attacked all the fortified cities of Judah and captured them." Since we know the date of that invasion was 701 B.C., and was the year Hezekiah took the throne (2 Kings 18:1, 9, 10), it is clear that the original text of 18:13 must have read the *twenty-fourth* rather than the *fourteenth* year of Hezekiah. This modest change easily corrects a copyist's error.

But another objection raised to the numbers given in Scripture has nothing to do with discrepancies. It has to do rather with the assumption that the large tribal numbers and the armies reported in the Old Testament simply could not be accurate. To support this, one theory suggests that the word for "thousand" (*'elep)* is related to the noun *'allup*, meaning "chief" or "commander of a thousand." Based on this assumption some have revised the numbers so that a figure like 45,000 would be read as 46 chiefs and 500 men.

This creative theory does not, however, explain passages such as Exodus 38:25, where *'elep* is clearly used as a "thousand" in recording the half-shekel tax collected for each adult Israelite male. Here the number of half shekels collected *exactly equals the 603,550 males that Numbers 2:32 reports were counted in the census taken after the Israelites left Egypt.* Clearly in this case *'elep* is used in its normal sense, and there is no reason to assume that it should be read as "chiefs" or "clans" when it is found in other statistical references.

Why then not accept the numbers as accurate? Some say the Desert of Sinai could never have supported so large a number. It surely could not have without the supernatural supply of manna provided by God. But reducing the numbers does not eliminate the supernatural element, for the desert could not have supported the 30,000 the critics suggest as a more reasonable number, either.

Other objections have focused on the supposedly impossible size of the armies raised in the time of David, or the troops led by Asa against the Ethiopians (2 Chron. 14:8–12). However, it is important to remember that the armies of Israel were essentially *militia*. These fighting men were not a professional army drawn from the general population but represented all men in the population available for fighting. Other ancient Middle Eastern sources also report extremely large armies. Shalmaneser III's records give specific numbers for the coalition forces ranged against him at Karkar, and although the Assyrian was thrown back, he reports some 14,000 of the coalition forces killed in the battle. Sennacherib, in records of his invasion of Philistia and Judah in 701 B.C., reports taking 200,150 prisoners. And Herodotus claims that Xerxes, in the fifth century B.C., assembled an army of 1,700,000 for his invasion of Greece. If we add to this the information from records at Ebla, which suggest a population of some 260,000 in the area, and from Nineveh, which suggest perhaps a million in Nineveh and its surrounding territories, the large numbers given in the Bible do not seem as unrealistic as the critics suggest.

What we have to conclude is that the statistics in the Bible must be considered accurate in nearly every case. Where discrepancies do occur, they can be explained either as copyists' errors, or by reference to differing, and sometimes unknown, factors taken into account by the writers.

Numbers 4:3

The explanation just given for differences in statistics found in the Old Testament surely cannot explain the discrepancies between this verse, Numbers 8:24, and Ezra 3:8 concerning the age Levites were to begin to serve God. This has to be viewed as an error in the Bible.

Not at all. The Levites came to "serve in the work" at the tabernacle from age thirty to fifty. Numbers 8:24 says they came "to take part" in the work at age twenty-five, apparently undergoing a five-year apprenticeship before being allowed to serve in the work. Ezra 3:8 depicts an unusual situation, in which the small number of Levites available (Ezra 2:40; Neh. 7:43) required letting men of age twenty enter into their apprenticeship. Also, at this particular time the tabernacle no longer existed, and a temple had not yet been built. Therefore, the particular sacred duties for which the men aged thirty to fifty alone were qualified were not involved.

Numbers 11:31–34

Why did God punish the Israelites with a plague after giving them the quail they had demanded? He did not punish them earlier when he granted the same demand (Exod. 16).

In each case the demand reflected an attitude of disbelief and ingratitude, which was tantamount to an overt rejection of God by the people he had rescued. So we cannot explain the different reaction on the basis of any deterioration of attitude between the incidents in Exodus and Numbers. What *had* changed was very basic and simple. God had introduced his law, and the people of Israel had bound themselves to obey it. Before the giving of the law there was no objective basis for divine discipline, so God withheld the punishment that Israel's earlier rebelliousness surely merited. But now the relationship between Israel and God as Israel's monarch had been firmly established, so rebelliousness could be disciplined. In this way the cause-and-effect relationship between disobedience and punishment can be understood. God graciously withheld punishment earlier because that cause-and-effect relationship had not yet been established by the definition of clearly understandable standards.

There is another important point to consider. Without discipline, God's people had shown a consistent *decline* of both faith and obedience. From murmuring and complaining the people drifted to open rebellion until they nearly stoned Moses (Exod. 15:22–17:16). In the same way, a child who is constantly indulged becomes less and less manageable and more and more unhappy. So the introduction of law, and even the seemingly harsh punishments that befell the Israelites after Sinai, were motivated by love. Only an obedient people, who had learned that God could be trusted and that he must be obeyed, could possibly take Canaan, the Promised Land, and enter into the blessings God intended Abraham's descendants to enjoy.

This is a reminder for us as well. Hebrews 12:6 says that "the Lord disciplines those he loves, and he punishes everyone he accepts as a son" (see also Prov. 3:11, 12). God disciplined Israel, and he disciplines us, because he loves us and yearns to help us develop the character and faith that will enable us to experience his very best.

Numbers 12:3

If Moses really wrote this book, he would not have spoken of himself in this way.

Actually, such comments by ancient authors are not uncommon. In this case, the comment may be offered in explanation of the fact that Moses did not defend himself when he was attacked by Miriam and Aaron, and so is clearly appropriate. Most scholars, however, take this verse as a gloss or comment added by a later scribe. The translators of the New International Version indicate this possibility by putting the verse in parentheses.

Numbers 12:14

Did fathers really spit in the faces of their daughters? What a terrible thing for a father to do!

It's hard to see this as a moral difficulty, for this passage does not command, or even suggest, that any father actually do so. In the East spitting is a rebuke and sign of contempt. A parent who spits in a child's face condemns his or her actions and shames the child until he or she is forgiven. The meaning of the verse is thus clear. If a human father condemned an action of his daughter, she would be "in disgrace for seven days." God himself condemned Miriam's action, so at the very least she should be expelled from the camp, unable to approach or worship God for seven days.

Numbers 22:12–23

Why does this passage describe God as being, "very angry" (22:22) with Balaam when he responded to King Balak's summons? Didn't Balaam piously tell Balak he could only speak what God commanded him?

God had clearly informed Balaam *not* to go and not to try to put a curse on Israel (22:12). Balaam thus knew what God's will was. God granted Balaam permission to go following Balaam's second request, but this was *permission*, not *direction*. Later writers who comment on the incident are critical of Balaam's motives (greed) and his actions, for when he found it impossible to curse Israel, he advised Balak to try to corrupt Israel morally and religiously and so manipulate God into cursing them against his will (Num. 31:16; 25).

Even aside from the way in which future events demonstrated Balaam's character, this passage reminds us of an important truth. God may permit us to choose something that is less than his best. But if we know what God's will is, pleading for permission to do what we know is contrary to it is foolishness indeed.

Numbers 30:3–5

Does the law of vows show that the Old Testament discriminates against women? Why shouldn't a woman be allowed to make a vow on her own, without giving a father or husband veto power?

The Hebrew word for vow here is *neder*, which indicates a vow to do something positive, such as offer a sacrifice, rather than *'issar*, which indicates a pledge to abstain from something. It is likely, then, that the vow in view here would have been costly to the family. Since the father or the husband was legally responsible for the security of the family, he must be allowed final say in a vow that might seriously affect the family's finances.

It is important to note that a widow or divorced woman, who was responsible for herself, had no such restriction imposed on her. This rule concerning vows thus was in no way a slight on women. It instead simply reflected economic realities of the time and God's caring involvement in every detail of his people's lives.

Numbers 31

How can the genocide of the Midianites and God's brutal command to totally wipe out the peoples of Canaan be justified morally?

It is important to understand the cultural background when we consider the conquest of Canaan and the destruction of the Midianites. The national character of the Midianites is displayed in the Midianite strategy, developed by Balaam, of attempting to corrupt Israel morally and spiritually (Num. 25). The fertility religions of the area emphasized both sex and violence. Ritual prostitution and sexual orgies were part of religious celebrations that attempted to stimulate the gods and goddesses to their own sexual acts, which were thought to guarantee the fertility of the land and domesticated animals. On the one hand, the utterly debased morals and religion of the peoples of the region merited divine judgment; on the other hand, it threatened the continued purity of God's people once they settled in the land. The commands to totally wipe out the inhabitants of the land have to be understood as a judicial sentence, imposed by God to be executed by his people.

What is perhaps most stunning in this regard is a statement made to Abraham and reported in Genesis 15. There God informed Abraham that his descendants would spend some four hundred years in Egypt, in part to delay that judgment that must in time be imposed. Why? Because "the sin of the Amorites (representatives of all the peoples of Canaan) has not yet reached its full measure" (Gen. 15:16). The wonder is not that God ordered the ancient Israelites to wipe out the corrupt peoples of Canaan, but that God waited so patiently until the sins of those peoples reached full measure and literally demanded punishment.

Numbers 35:30

Does this verse mean that a person cannot be convicted and condemned for murder on circumstantial evidence alone? In that case, anyone could kill, as long as no one was there to witness the act.

Old Testament law is careful to protect the innocent from false accusations by people who hate them or who hope to benefit from their misfortune. For this reason two witnesses are consistently required in Old Testament law (Deut. 19:15). However, a witness (Hebrew, *'ed*) need not necessarily observe an act, but could be a person who *had knowledge relevant to the case* (Lev. 5:1). For instance, a killing might take place in the fields where no one saw the act. But if the killer had threatened to harm the victim, or if the killer had been observed previously hiding the tool used as a weapon near where the killing took place, this evidence would be relevant to the determination of guilt or innocence. In fact, the law requiring witnesses does *not* rule out circumstantial evidence at all. It simply rules out accepting as evidence the word of a single individual who might vindictively and falsely accuse someone to whom he or she is hostile.

Deuteronomy

Deuteronomy

Who wrote this book, and what themes and issues are found in it?

Tradition and the contents of the book (Deut. 1:1; 31:9, 24, 26) suggest that the author of Deuteronomy was Moses, around 1400 B.C. (see Genesis, page 13). While many modern scholars argue that the book was written much later—in the time of Josiah—the traditional view is certainly correct. In Deuteronomy seventy references to events of the exodus are in the past tense, while references to entry into Canaan are in the future. The nations mentioned in Deuteronomy are those of Moses' time. Most important, the structure of Deuteronomy is modeled on a structure for ancient political treaties that were only in use in the age of Moses (1500–1200 B.C.). Writers or editors working in the time of Josiah, some eight hundred years after Moses, would hardly have reflected ancient times so accurately.

The name *Deuteronomy* means second law; it serves as Moses' restatement to a new generation of Israelites of the divine law given forty years earlier on Mount Sinai. Key words in Deuteronomy are *love* (thirty-one times), *obey* (thirty-one times), and *this law* or *this book of the law* (twenty-four times). These key themes remind us that a relationship with God is not an impersonal kind of thing and that our obedience must grow out of and reflect a love that we have for the God who first loved us.

Deuteronomy 5

The Ten Commandments are supposed to be words God himself spoke to Moses. But the words quoted here are not the same as

those quoted in Exodus 20. Surely this proves that the Bible's
words cannot be inspired. If they were, the words in both places
would have to be the same.

Throughout, Deuteronomy is a summary and paraphrase of laws given on Sinai and recorded in Exodus, Leviticus, and Numbers. In many ways Deuteronomy is a sermon, an exhortation to the new generation of Israelites, intended to prepare them for their entry into the Promised Land. It is not necessary when paraphrasing previously revealed information to use the exact words to communicate the same meaning. Even a cursory comparison of this statement of the Ten Commandments with their form in Exodus 20 shows that there is no real difference.

Deuteronomy 6:4

Here the Old Testament clearly states, "The LORD our God, the
LORD is one." How then can Christians hold that God exists as a
Trinity?

In context this verse affirms both the unity and the uniqueness of Israel's God. He is not one among the many gods and goddesses worshiped in the ancient world; he *alone* is God, and the others are but myths and fiction.

Thus, as far as the intent of the verse is concerned, there is no conflict with the New Testament's fuller revelation that the unique God of the Old Testament exists in three persons. In fact, even the Hebrew word used here, *'ehad*, may be interpreted to express a compound unity, as it clearly does in Genesis 2:24 where it is used to say that a man and his wife are one flesh. If in Hebrew two can be one, there is no conflict with the doctrine of one God who exists as a Trinity. Actually, plural language is frequently used in speaking of God in the Old Testament (as in Gen. 1:26: "Let *us* make man in *our* image"). The New Testament doctrine is suggested in its multiple references to God's Spirit. However, it is in the New Testament, where Jesus is clearly presented as God and one with God from eternity (John 1:1–3), that the Trinity doctrine is made totally clear. Jesus claimed that "I and the Father are one" (John 10:30), and identified the Holy Spirit as one like, yet distinct from, himself (John 14:15–17). The deity of Jesus is explicitly claimed by Christ in the Gospels and taught in the epistles (Rom. 1:4; Phil. 2:5–11; Col. 1:15–20). In Ephesians 1 we see the distinct roles of Father, Son, and Holy Spirit in our salvation.

It is very difficult for us to conceive of one God who exists in three persons. Also, every analogy, from the single egg which has shell, white, and yoke, to Augustine's analogy of the Trinity as a tree with roots, trunk, and branches, falls short. But these are not reasons to reject a concept taught so clearly in the New Testament and supported by the careful use of the language in the Old Testament.

Deuteronomy 7:2

How could a good God possibly order Israel to destroy totally the people living in Canaan?

This question comes up whenever such a command is found in the Old Testament (see the discussion of Num. 31, page 75). On one hand, the call to exterminate the Canaanites was a judicial sentence pronounced by God, in view of the debased moral and religious practices of those peoples. The degraded nature of these practices has been confirmed in many archaeological finds.

This chapter of Deuteronomy adds another reason for the command to destroy the Canaanites. God, through Moses, warned, "They will turn your sons away from following me to serve other gods, and the LORD's anger will burn against you" (7:4). Only by totally isolating Israel from corruption *within the Promised Land* could the purity of Israel's faith and worship be maintained. In fact, Israel did not obey God's command to drive out or destroy the Canaanites, and Israel was corrupted by the peoples that, in disobedience to God's command, they permitted to live in the land.

Deuteronomy 10:12

How can the call to fear the Lord and the call to love the Lord be found in the same verse? Aren't fear and love incompatible emotions?

Fear is a complex concept in our language, with meanings that range from utter terror to a mild anxiety about the future. The Hebrew word *yare'*, used commonly for "fear," also means "religious awe." In this sense to fear means to recognize God as creator and Lord: the one who is, and who is always with us, always active for us. Thus the Old Testament call to fear God is a reminder to acknowledge him as the most significant reality in our lives, so that we would not only love him but also show our respect for him in all that we do. Fear and love for God are entirely harmonious concepts in the Old Testament. Each calls us to make God the center of our thoughts and of our lives.

Deuteronomy 13:6–11

How could a good God call on his people to turn over a loved one to be executed? This surely is incompatible with the revelation of God seen in Jesus and must reveal the Old Testament as a primitive document.

There is no sense of glee underlying the command to show even a loved one no pity. And this is no general command to turn a loved one over to the executioner for minor offenses. Instead, the command concerns a loved one who has chosen to worship other gods and "secretly entices you" to join that worship. In such a case God's people must be more committed to God than to even the nearest loved one and so "purge the evil from among you" (13:5).

The command recognizes a terrible reality. If the people of Israel failed to maintain their commitment to God, more than one individual would die. By surrendering a corrupt loved one an Israelite would prevent many from slipping off into idolatry (13:11) and might well save the nation from the apostasy that in later centuries did lead to destruction and exile.

Deuteronomy 15:4, 11

How can God say that "there should be no poor among you" and in the very same passage predict that "there will always be poor people in the land"? This is contradictory.

The contradiction is emphasized in older translations, which rendered verse 4 as a promise: "There *shall be* no poor among you." But even then there was no real contradiction, for the passage goes on to say, "if only you fully obey the Lord" (15:5). In context, this passage concerns one of the several social mechanisms provided in Old Testament law to protect the poor and to alleviate poverty. What are these provisions?

1. Interest-free, forgivable loans made to those in need (Lev. 25:35–37; Deut. 15:1–3; 23:19, 20).

2. Yearly access for the poor to unharvested produce in the fields of others (Lev. 19:10; 23:22) and to all crops which grew of themselves every seventh year, when the land was not to be planted or worked by its owners (Exod. 23:10–11).

3. Preservation of family capital by the return of ancestral lands to the original family every fifty years (Lev. 25:13–14).

4. Impartial justice, which favored neither the wealthy nor the poor in disputes (Exod. 23:3, 6).

5. Voluntary servitude, allowing a poor person to sell himself to a successful fellow countryman for seven years (Deut. 15:12–18; Lev. 25:39–54). At the end of this time, hopefully trained and equipped for better care for himself, the slave was to be freed and given money and goods that allowed him to make a fresh start for himself and his family.

6. Organized collections, taken every third year as tithes and stored up locally for distribution to not only the Levites but also "the aliens, the fatherless, and the widows" (Deut. 14:28, 29).

Taken together, these social mechanisms would eradicate poverty as a social evil. Thus we might understand Deuteronomy 15:11 to mean that there would always in every generation be a *need for these mechanisms to be at work*. However, most readers understand 15:11 more pessimistically as a prediction. There would be no poor only if the law's provisions for their relief were put into practice. Unfortunately, there is no record of any Old Testament generation actually putting these mechanisms into practice, although individuals like Boaz (Ruth 2) did show generosity toward the needy.

Old Testament laws concerning the poor and oppressed remind us that God calls us to care for the needy. They also remind us that laws are meaningless in themselves. It is only when people are willing to put into practice the way of life that the Bible calls for that Scripture will make a positive difference in any individual's life.

Deuteronomy 18:9–13

Why are occult practices so strongly condemned in the Old Testament? Does this mean Christians are prohibited from going to astrologers or palm readers or fortune tellers? What about looking at a newspaper horoscope?

In Old Testament times, occult practices were critical elements of pagan religions, through which their practitioners attempted to gain supernatural guidance or helpful information about the future. In these same religions magic and occult incantations were used to manipulate deities, either to force or to win them to a course of action desired by the practitioner. It is clearly because of the integral association of the occult with paganism that all such practices were forbidden to the people of Israel.

Today many occult practices, such as astrology and palmistry, are not directly associated with pagan beliefs. Does this mean that they are acceptable for Christians? Not at all. Certainly Israel, like Christians today, did need supernatural guidance in many situations not covered by Old Testament law. But Deuteronomy 18 goes on to promise that God will provide Israel with prophets who will speak in his name and give God's people the guidance they need. The point is that *the only source of supernatural guidance to which God's people were to appeal was God himself.* It is the same for us today. God has given Christians his Holy Spirit to serve as our guide and teacher. To look for guidance to any occult source, whether it be to the daily horoscope or the local spiritualist, is to look *away* from God. Today, as in the past we are to depend wholly upon the Lord and trust him to lead us step by step into the future he has planned for us.

Deuteronomy 20

Is there such a thing as a just war? How could a good God give rules for such a terrible thing as war?

War is always horrible. But the Old Testament recognizes that at times war is a necessary evil. Some wars of Israel were punitive in nature. God's people or other nations were instruments God used to punish evil in society (Hab. 1:5–11). Other wars were defensive or required for national security. Some of the wars reported in the Bible were commanded by God, while others clearly were expressions of a ruler's sinful desire for self-aggrandizement.

Whether or not Christians today take a pacifistic stand or hold that defensive or certain other types of war are justified, it is clear that the *rules of warfare* found in the Old Testament were unique in ancient times. In Deuteronomy 20 certain categories of men were excused from service on religious or humanitarian grounds. While any city lying within the boundaries of the land set aside for Israel was to be destroyed completely, cites outside the land were to be offered terms of peace and well treated. Particularly interesting is the prohibition, unique to Israel, against destroying fruit trees when besieging an enemy city. In comparison with the practices of other peoples, women prisoners of war were treated humanely (Deut. 21:10–14), and hygienic practices to be followed by armies on the march were carefully spelled out (23:9–14).

The Old Testament does look forward longingly to a coming era of peace on earth. This time of peace, however, is connected with the dominating presence of the Messiah, who alone is able to impose peace on earth, and then only after the Lord's army wins a terrible final battle against the marshaled forces of this world (Isa. 13:4; 24:21–23; 29:5–8; Zech. 14:5).

Deuteronomy 21:18–21

How could a God of love ever require parents to condemn their own little boy to death just because he was "stubborn and rebellious"?

First, *son* does *not* imply a little boy or even a youth. It is clear from the context that an adult son is meant. How? The *Expository Dictionary of Bible Words* (Zondervan) notes that "the two Hebrew roots for 'stubborn' are *sarar* and *qaseh*. The first means 'stubbornly rebellious' and the second indicates a hard, obstinate attitude. Both are translated 'stubborn' and portray unbelief's antagonistic attitude toward God as a response to his self-revelation." This, plus the formula, "You must purge the evil from among you. All Israel will hear of it and be afraid" (21:21), puts this injunction in the same category as the earlier penalty imposed for inciting worship of a pagan deity (Deut. 13:11). So there clearly was much more involved in having a "stubborn and rebellious son" than a child's rejection of parental guidance or refusal to show respect. This was an essentially religious sin. The rebellion was against God and the lifestyle the Lord commanded his people to live. The death penalty was imposed only because such people threatened the integrity and purity of the nation as a people of God.

Deuteronomy 22:5

Does this prohibition against men and women wearing each other's clothing mean that girls today should not wear slacks?

The prohibition is intended to remind Israel to maintain a distinction between men and women. This is not because one sex is better than or inferior to the other. Instead, the ruling implies that God's people are to acknowledge his wisdom in creating two sexes and to affirm the worth and value of each sex by gladly affirming one's own.

In biblical times the clothing worn by men and women was quite similar, but the cut of the outer robe made the sex of the wearer clear. As long as the clothing worn by men and women today is essentially masculine or feminine, it certainly fulfills the intent of this Old Testament ruling. There is nothing wrong with slacks in themselves. It is only when clothing is intended to conceal or confuse the sex of the wearer that the principle expressed in this Old Testament ruling would apply.

Deuteronomy 24:1–3

Is it incompatible for Moses to give rules on how to get a divorce, and then for Jesus to say, "What God has joined together, let man not separate" (Matt. 19:6)?

Divorce is a complicated and very sensitive topic. Many people honestly hold strongly divergent viewpoints. This topic is best examined in the context of Matthew 19:6 (see page 252). However, it is important to note one thing. Jesus explained that Moses permitted divorce "because your hearts were hard" (Matt. 19:8). Divorce never represented God's ideal, but was *permitted* because in his grace the Lord knew that at times the hardened hearts of sinful human beings would distort this positive relationship into something negative and damaging. The question for Christians is not whether divorce is *encouraged* in the Old Testament; it is not. The question is whether God continues in the age of grace to deal graciously with those who try in marriage but fall short. Certainly grace was exhibited in the age of law, and the divorced were not only permitted but, in most cases, expected to remarry (Lev. 21:7, 14; Ezek. 44:22).

Deuteronomy 26:12–15

Does this passage suggest that believers who are obedient to God have a right to demand that God bless them? If so, it certainly conflicts with the New Testament teaching that we have been given a gracious gift by God not because of our merits.

The law covenant under which Israel lived was an *if-then* covenant. That is, it explained to Israel what they could expect from God, conditioned on their behavior. If the nation was obedient and faithfully observed God's laws, then the Lord would bless them. If, on the other hand, the nation was disobedient and refused to observe God's laws, he would discipline them to bring them back into a right relationship with him. In essence God had, in the law, expressed his intent to bless the obedient and to punish the disobedient. Based on this feature of the Mosaic law, God's Old Testament people did have a right to expect the Lord to graciously keep his promises. But they had no right to *demand* that he bless them, or do so immediately.

It is very difficult to transfer this principle of Old Testament law, which related specifically to the nation as a whole and only indirectly to individual Israelites, to Christian life today. What can we can say, however, is that disobedience leads us out of that circle within which God showers his blessings, while obedience puts us in the place where God can freely pour them out upon us. What blessings he chooses to bestow, whether spiritual or material, are matters for him alone to determine. And they are always expressions of grace. For even in our obedience we fall short of perfection, and our best falls far short of meriting a divine reward.

Deuteronomy 29:29

What are "the secret things" that belong to God?

Some have interpreted this verse as a reference to the future, which God alone can know. Others see it primarily as a reference to the limitations of human wisdom generally. Either understanding underlines the text's major point. What Israel has is God's law. Whatever God's people may *not know,* they do know this much of his will. And so it is appropriate to concentrate on doing what one does know, rather than to speculate about what one does not.

Deuteronomy 34

How could Moses have written a book that contains a report not only of his death but also of subsequent events?

It is not necessary that Moses have written every word found in the books of Genesis, Exodus, Leviticus, Numbers, and Deuteronomy to identify him as the author of the Bible's first five books. It would be foolish indeed to suggest that including a report of the main figure's death in a historical work implied the main figure could not be the author of the main text. There is no reason to doubt that Deuteronomy 1–33 was Moses' work just because chapter 34 provides an obituary.

Joshua

Joshua

Who wrote this book, and what major themes and issues does it deal with?

No author is identified either by the book or by tradition, but its references to Jerusalem as a Jebusite stronghold (15:8; 18:26) and other features suggest it was written during the time of the judges, prior to 1200 B.C. The book tells the story of Joshua's conquest of Canaan and subsequent distribution of the land to Israel's twelve tribes. The events recorded in it probably span some twenty to twenty-five years, with initial events taking place around 1390 B.C. The book serves as a reminder that when God's people are obedient, they are able to claim and to enjoy his promises.

Joshua

Have archaeological findings made it impossible to accept the biblical and traditional date for the conquest of Canaan? And what about the modern theories that there never was a conquest and that the Book of Joshua is a totally fabricated religious history?

Conservative, liberal, and secular scholars have long disagreed over the date of the conquest of Canaan. The conservatives tend to hold to a 1390 B.C. date and appeal to archaeologist John Garstang's dating of the fall of Jericho. The liberals argue a 1200 B.C. date and point to conclusions supporting this late date for Jericho's fall reached later by archaeologist Kathleen Kenyon. More recently several Israeli scholars have argued that there was no conquest at all. They say that either nomadic tribes drifted into Palestine, settled for a time in hilly areas, and later took over the lowlands as well; or the outlying villagers rebelled against their masters in ancient cities and took them over. These theories treat Joshua, and the whole Pentateuch, as a religious invention intended to create a unified identity for a dozen diverse tribal groups and bond them together as one people.

These secular theories can be dismissed as totally speculative. The biblical description of Hebrew hill-country settlements found in Judges fits the archaeological data at least as well as it fits the modern theories. The critical question is the date of the conquest. Here the pivotal argument is over the dating of Jericho's fall. John Drane, in a 1987 work published by Harper and Row, *Introducing the Old Testament,* notes that "twenty years ago it would have been difficult to find any reputable scholar who would not have dated the exodus and Israel's entry into Canaan somewhere between about 1280 and 1240 B.C. But today an increasing number are inclined to give more weight to an older view that dated these events about 1440 B.C." (p. 57). In particular, recent work by Bryant G. Wood, using well-established methods of pottery analysis supported by carbon 14 dating, have shown that every line of archeological evidence actually supports a violent overthrow of Jericho about 1400 B.C. It is largely the compelling nature of his findings, scrupulously documented, that has led many to reevaluate other less important arguments for the later dating of the conquest of Canaan. With this linchpin date established, the weight of the evidence supports the traditional date of 1390 B.C. for the conquest. This is in harmony with dates and spans of years mentioned in the Bible itself. (See also Exodus 12, page 54.)

Joshua 1:14

Why were there only 40,000 men from the trans-Jordan tribes in the invading army, when Numbers 26 says the males numbered 110,000? Isn't this a discrepancy?

The text of Joshua says "all your fighting men" (warriors). The Numbers census included all those "able to serve in the army" (26:2). We can only assume that the fighting men in Joshua were the military core of the trans-Jordan tribes, and that the rest of the 110,000 total male population stayed behind to care for flocks and herds and to guard the women and children.

Joshua 2:4, 5

How could God approve of Rahab's lie and bless her for it? Leviticus 19:11 and Proverbs 12:22 forbid and condemn lying.

It is tempting to note that in Rahab's case, as in the case of the midwives who similarly deceived Pharaoh in Moses' time (Exod. 1), there were extenuating circumstances. After all, if the Israelite spies had been discovered, Rahab and her family as well as the two men she hid would surely have been executed. Even if we accept this argument, there is no way to argue that a lie told in a life-threatening situation justifies the little white lies that many wish to tell.

But the question here is one of moral consistency within the Scriptures. How can a God who forbids lying bless a person like Rahab who tells lies? The answer, of course, is that God must always bless sinners, because all human beings share Rahab's flaw. Rahab was blessed not *because* she lied but because she had faith in Israel's God and expressed it by risking her own life to save the two Hebrew spies. Her faith was expressed not in the lie but in committing herself and her family to God's care.

Joshua 3:14–17

Was the crossing of the Jordan a miracle or just a natural event, as these verses seem to suggest?

The *Revell Bible Dictionary* defines a miracle as "an event that so overrides what observers understand of natural law that it creates wonder and serves as evidence of God's active intervention in this universe" (p. 699). Several things mark Israel's passage over the Jordan as a miracle. First, the text says they crossed "on dry ground" (v. 17), despite the flood waters that had soaked the river bed and the surrounding fields. Second, while a landslide upstream is credited with blocking the waters, the *timing* of the event, so that the waters were "cut off" (v. 16) as soon as the priests' "feet touched the water's edge," (v. 15) is clearly supernatural. While the means God used to stop the waters may have been natural causes, the timing and details of the event were clearly miraculous.

Joshua 6

Why were the Israelites given such strange instructions for the attack on Jericho?

Some have explained the fall of Jericho's walls by an earthquake set off by the stamping of feet and shouting of the Israelite hordes following the seventh day's march around that city. The explanation, intended to make sense of the strange story of Jericho's fall, misses the point. A major theme of Joshua is that obedience brings blessing, while disobedience brings defeat. God's instructions were intended to demonstrate this principle. Israel need not understand God's commands, only obey them.

Joshua 7

Why was Achan killed? Furthermore, why did his family have to die with him? That is morally indefensible.

Achan's disobedience had led to the death in battle of thirty-six Israelite soldiers in the defeat at Ai (Josh. 7:5). Achan's disobedience—theft of property God had commanded be destroyed—directly resulted in the Lord withdrawing his protection from his people. So Achan was not only condemned because of his disobedience but because his act had led to the deaths of so many fellow soldiers.

But what about his family? Some have noted that a theme of corporate responsibility runs through the Old Testament and is reflected in other ancient cultures. That is, the individual is in some sense responsible for the behavior of the group, and the group is similarly responsible for the individual. But the best solution to this problem is suggested by Joshua 7:22, which says that Achan's loot was "hidden in his tent." As the entire family shared the tent, it is unlikely that any of them would have been unaware of Achan's acts and thus would have been participants with him in his crime.

Joshua 8

Archaeology has shown that Ai was unoccupied at the time of the conquest, both the early and late date. This proves that Joshua is inaccurate.

Most archaeologists have assumed that Ai was situated at a site named Et Tell, even though the topography of the area does not fit the biblical account. Excavations show that a large city was destroyed about 2200 B.C. and no other major city ever constructed there. To explain the conflict between the Bible and archaeology, some have argued that the Ai of Joshua's time was an outpost settlement of Bethel. Recently archaeologists have found evidence that suggests Et Tell was not the site of Ai at all, and have suggested a place known today as Khirbet Nisya, a little southwest of Et Tell. While more archaeological work needs to be done, it seems most likely that Ai never was situated at Et Tell, which makes the fall of that city in 2200 B.C. irrelevant to dating the conquest of Canaan.

Joshua 10:12–14

How can the long day reported in this chapter be explained? If the sun really did "stand still," there should be some record of this unusual phenomenon in the records of other ancient peoples.

The language of 10:12–14 has been interpreted in several ways. Some have taken the Hebrew word *dom*, translated "stand still," in verse 12 in its basic meaning of "cease," or "be silent" and suggested that Joshua asked that the sun stop pouring out its heat, which was weakening the Israelite warriors. However, the phrase *the sun stood still* (v. 13) does not seem to support this interpretation. Others suggest an "optical prolongation"; that is, that God caused visible sunlight to shine on the area, perhaps by refracting the rays in some way. Some, however, insist that the Bible's report that "the sun stopped in the middle of the sky and delayed going down about a full day" (v. 13), must be taken literally. Interestingly, authors of several books have included reports that some astronomers have checked Egyptian, Chinese, and other ancient astronomical records and concluded that a day is missing from their calculations. Unfortunately, this support for the conviction that Joshua 10 reports a real miracle cannot presently be documented. But there is little doubt that the biblical text itself does describe a miracle which, unless Joshua's description is purely phenomenological and thus limited to Canaan, would have had worldwide impact.

Judges

Judges

Who wrote this book, and what themes and issues does it deal with?

No author is identified in the book itself. Tradition suggests that Samuel, the last of the judges, may have collected and reported the stories in this book. The Book of Judges covers several hundred years, from the death of Joshua and his fellow leaders of the conquest to the time of Samuel. During this period the Israelites were drawn again and again into apostasy and subsequently subjected to domination by foreign peoples. When suffering caused an oppressed generation to turn back to the Lord, he provided a military and/or political leader called a judge, who restored his oppressed followers to freedom and then led them during the rest of his or her life. Just as the Book of Joshua illustrates the principle that obedience brings victory and rest, so Judges demonstrates the fact that disobedience brings disaster and defeat.

Judges 1:7

Is it realistic to suppose that a tiny land like Canaan could have produced seventy kingdoms? This is an obvious mistake. Why were these kings' thumbs and big toes cut off?

The Hebrew *melek* means "king," but can just as well be translated as "governor," "prince," "chief," or in modern terms perhaps "mayor." The word does not indicate a specific office or form of government but simply indicates a person with civil authority. Thus the sev-

91

enty kings of this passage were undoubtedly rulers of the many independent city-states that we know dotted Canaan in this period. It is also likely that the seventy represented successive rulers of the same city-states, captured in a series of campaigns over a period of many years. The captives' thumbs were cut off so that they could never again hold weapons. Their big toes were cut off so that they would be unable to maintain their balance and run.

Judges 2

How do archaeological findings fit the picture of early Jewish settlement given here and in the book as a whole?

Careful surveys of settlement patterns in Canaan reveal a great number of small villages set in the hill country, and the persistence of earlier, more advanced Canaanite city civilizations in the valleys. These villages were located in areas of little rainfall. Their existence was made possible by the development of plastered cisterns to hold water for family needs. This picture of two cultures in Canaan, the poorer groups isolated in less-fertile hill areas, and the wealthier in control of the fertile valleys and plains, exactly fits the picture given in the Book of Judges.

While we seldom have archaeological corroboration of specific events reported in Scripture, there is often clear corroboration of the historical and cultural settings in which the events are placed. For instance, the structure of Deuteronomy reflects a suzerainty treaty format current only from about 1500–1200 B.C., the era in which the book claims to have been written. Archaeological surveys of Israel show settlement patterns between 1300 and 1000 B.C. that fit the portrait provided in Judges.

Judges 3:11

The Book of Judges carefully records the number of years each judge is said to have ruled. Added together, they total 410 years. But at most this period could only have stretched from about 1390 to 1050 B.C. How can this be explained?

A look at a map along with a careful reading of Judges provides a simple answer. Note on the map the seat of each judge named in this Old Testament book, and the location of the enemies who oppressed the Israelites. The answer to the time problem is simply that no judge ruled *all* of Israel, but in only one or a few of the tribal areas.

Likewise, the foreign oppressors, who were also frequently localized, launched incursions into areas lying next to their territories. This means that several of the judges undoubtedly ruled concurrently, and some of the oppressors harassed different Israelite tribal areas at the same time.

Judges 4:1

How could Hazor be an oppressor if the city was destroyed by Joshua, as reported in Joshua 11:10, 11?

The event reported in Joshua probably took place about one hundred years before the story told here in Judges. So there was plenty of time for the city to be rebuilt. Still, the occurrence of the name *Jabin* in both stories has led some to suppose there was one destruction of Hazor. However, this name is most likely a hereditary title, recurring from generation to generation. There is certainly no compelling reason to question the resurgence of Hazor, which was located in a strategic position controlling the principal trade route between Egypt and the Asian empires. Archaeologists have discovered that Hazor was a dominating city in Canaanite times, extending over 200 acres and with a population estimated at 40,000 people.

Judges 5:24–27

This account of Sisera's death differs from that in Judges 4:18–21. Not only is this a factual discrepancy, but there is a cultural problem, too. For Jael to murder Sisera would be to violate one of the most binding of all cultural obligations: the obligation of hospitality shown to guests.

Judges 4:18–21 and 5:24–27 together provide a complete, certainly *not* contradictory, account of this event. After welcoming Sisera, giving him refreshments and a place to sleep, Jael drove a tent peg into his skull. The fact that one story gives more details than the other hardly makes them contradictory.

On the other hand, Jael's killing did violate one of the ancient Middle East's most important customs, which committed a host to offer protection to a guest. At the same time, Jael as a Kenite was linked by ancient bonds to Israel. How could she support a brutal oppressor of God's people? In addition, Jael was alone, or else her husband would have greeted the guest. As a woman, how could she have resisted Sisera's demand of a place to rest and to hide?

It may be significant that there is no record of a divine commenda-
tion granted Jael for her act. At the same time, Deborah celebrated the
killing as if it were a commendable act of valor in war.

Judges 6:17

*Gideon repeatedly asked for a sign to confirm the fact that God
was really speaking to him. Was this an act of unbelief? Later
Gideon set out a fleece and asked God to provide proof the Lord
would do what he promised (6:36, 39). Is putting God to the test
forbidden in Deuteronomy 6:16? Is this a good pattern for us to
follow in seeking God's will?*

God frequently provided a sign or miracle as confirmation
that he was the one speaking (Exod. 4:1–9; Isa. 7:11–12). Gideon's first
request was completely in harmony with the Old Testament's teaching
that one who spoke God's word would be authenticated as a divine
messenger by some miraculous sign or by the fulfillment of a specific
prophecy.

In classifying Gideon's later requests for further confirming signs it
is important to note the context of the Deuteronomy 6:16 prohibition.
In the wilderness God's people rebelled and demanded a sign to prove
that God was among them (Exod. 17:17). The demand in this context
grew out of, and was an indication of, unbelief. In contrast, when Gideon
realized that it was God who spoke to him, he immediately obeyed and
at personal risk did tear down his town's pagan altars. Thus the context of Gideon's request was not one of unbelief or rebelliousness but
one of faith and commitment. Rather than demand that God prove himself, Gideon simply asked for reassurance that he had truly understood
what God intended him to do. Setting out the fleece for Gideon was an
expression of his own weaknesses, not an arrogant demand that God
prove himself.

It may well be that God will graciously confirm the leading he has
given us by some sign. But let's not use Gideon as an excuse. If we
intend to use Gideon's case as a precedent, let's remember that both a
true knowledge of God's will and initial obedience to it *preceded* the
sign.

Judges 11:29–40

*Did Jephthah actually offer his daughter as a burnt offering?
How could a person who practiced human sacrifice become a*

judge in Israel and be commended in the New Testament's list of Old Testament heroes of the faith (Heb. 11:32)?

The Old Testament displays an absolute revulsion toward human sacrifice (Lev. 18:21; 20:2–5; Deut. 12:31; 18:10). While some argue that Jephthah must have fulfilled his vow by killing and burning his daughter, this is not required by the text or by Hebrew practices. Old Testament law introduces a principle in Exodus 38:8 and illustrates it in 1 Samuel 1:28 and Luke 2:36, 37. This principle is that a person or thing dedicated to God might fulfill the vow by a lifetime of service as well as by the surrender of a life.

Indicators that this is what happened in the case of Jephthah's daughter are: (1) the knowledge Jephthah had previously displayed of Old Testament history and law, as in his letter to the Ammonites (10:15–27); (2) every sacrifice to the Lord required that a priest officiate and that no Hebrew priest would offer a human sacrifice; (3) the reaction of Jepthath's daughter who went out with her friends to lament not over her imminent death but "because I will never marry" (11:37). All this leads us to the conclusion that Jephthah *did* fulfill his vow by dedicating his daughter's life to the service of the Lord.

Judges 14:4

How could God motivate Samson to do wrong? Surely this does not fit with the Bible's insistence that God is good and does not "tempt anyone" with evil (James 1:13).

It is always important to distinguish between cause and effect. The text does not say that God caused Samson's passion for the Philistine girl. It does say, however, what the Bible everywhere teaches: God is able to use even man's failings to produce something good. Samson's motives were his own, and his carnal passion expressed a flaw in his own character, not in God's nature. But this flaw was from the Lord in that Samson's passion was channeled in a direction which would lead to a confrontation with the Philistines, who dominated the Israelites. Samson was responsible for his passions. God was responsible for pointing him in a direction that would ultimately fulfill God's purposes.

The great tragedy here is that Samson was so insensitive and unresponsive to God that he could only be moved to confront Israel's enemies by manipulation of his own base motives. Unlike the other judges, who faced Israel's enemies for the sake of God and their oppressed countrymen, Samson was only moved by his own self-centered anger against a personal affront.

This is a reminder for us. God can and will use us, even if his purposes are accomplished against our will. How much better to gladly seek his guidance and avoid the sins and suffering that plagued Samson all his life.

Judges 15:4

How could Samson catch three hundred foxes? Foxes are elusive, solitary animals. Even the most skilled trappers could hardly have caught so many in such a brief time.

This objection surely has force, unless we want to retreat to the miraculous and suppose that God led the three hundred to trot right up to Samson and surrender. But there is more than one option to this. For instance, as Israel's judge Samson might well have ordered others to hunt the foxes. In accordance with the custom of the time, Samson as leader would be credited with having accomplished the task himself. Another and perhaps more likely suggestion is rooted in the meaning of the Hebrew word in the text. This word, *su'al*, is not only used of foxes but also of jackals, which hunt in packs and are more easily trapped.

Many supposed discrepancies in the Bible are much like the objection of critics to Samson's foxes. The objection seems reasonable on its face. But with even the slightest effort, reasonable alternatives can be found. People who persist in seeing such discrepancies don't *want* to find answers that support a high view of Scripture. If they honestly did try to solve the problems they pose, they would soon find alternatives at least as reasonable as their objection that preserve the Christian's view that Scripture is the revealed and trustworthy Word of God.

Judges 19:18–24

How could a man offer his daughter to be raped so he might protect a guest? And how could the Levite, who seems to be the hero of this story, turn over his concubine to the rape gang?

First, let's be clear that neither of these acts is represented in the text as God's will. The Bible simply tells the story of what happened, accurately and honestly. Second, recorded events must be understood in the context of the author's intent. Here at the end of the Book of Judges the author has included three related but separate stories intended to show the spiritual and moral depravity that corrupted Israel during this era. The story of Micah's idols (Judg. 17, 18) shows the corruption of the Israelites' faith by religious concepts they adopted from pagan neighbors; the story of the Levite's concubine (Judg. 19) shows the moral corruption that always accompanies corruption of faith; and the story of the civil war that followed (Judg. 20, 21) shows the breakdown of social order that takes place in times of moral and spiritual decline. Understood in this context, the story of the Levite and his host actually *condemns* both of them for their actions.

Ruth

Ruth

Who wrote this book, and what themes and issues does it deal with?

The bright little Book of Ruth serves as a counterweight to the tragic pictures in the Book of Judges.

The events in each book take place during the same historical period. While Judges shows Israel's national decline, Ruth reminds us that there were individuals in this age who remained faithful to God and his law. The book also serves an important historical purpose since Ruth and Boaz, the heroine and hero of this book, became the great-grandparents of David, the king who formed God's people into a powerful kingdom and led the nation back to heartfelt worship of the Lord.

Ruth 3:9

If Ruth is such an example of godliness, why did she sneak out to the fields at night to seduce Boaz and get him to marry her?

Ruth 3:9 tells us that when Boaz woke up at night, he found Ruth sleeping at his feet, and that she asked him to "spread the corner of your garment over me." The notion that this was an immoral proposition results from a failure to understand the customs of those ancient times. It is very clear from the reaction of Boaz, who immediately took steps to win the right to marry Ruth, that to throw the mantle over a woman meant, at that time, to claim her as a wife. Thus, rather than proposition Boaz for any immoral act, Ruth instead took this very private moment to express her desire to marry the man who had been so kind to her.

98

Ruth 3, 4

What customs are seen in the story of the marriage of Ruth?

The customs in this story are those of levirate marriage and redemption by a near kinsman. Levirate marriage provided that when a man died childless, his nearest male relative might marry his widow (Deut. 25:5, 6). The concept of redemption by a kinsman was a basic provision in Old Testament law. It also permitted (or obligated) a kinsman to save the property of a poor relative when it was in danger of being sold and thus passing out of the family. This was a costly procedure, with no guarantee of repayment. In the case of Ruth, both customs applied. Here a near kinsman who became Ruth's husband would have to redeem (buy back) the lands of Ruth's first husband and then turn them over to any son that Ruth might have. In many cases this might mean impoverishing his present family to supply an inheritance to a child yet to be born.

In Ruth's story a nearer kinsmen than Boaz to her dead husband lived in the area. But he was unable or unwilling to take on the expense both of buying back her family land and taking on another(?) wife and thus risking his own children's inheritance. He declined, and Boaz quickly exercised his options as near kinsman to claim Ruth and repurchase the lost family land.

1 Samuel

1 Samuel

Who wrote this book, and what themes and issues does it deal with?

The Book of 1 Samuel, which in the Torah (Hebrew Old Testament) is bound with 2 Samuel as a single book, does not name its author. While some speculation has focused on Nathan the prophet as a likely candidate, there is no way to learn who penned these two historical books.

The books are, however, very significant. Together they tell the story of the last judge, Samuel, of the institution of the monarchy under flawed King Saul, and the rise of Israel to prominence under godly King David. This period in Israel's history is critical historically and prophetically. David was not only the ideal ruler of Israel's past golden age but was also a prototype of the Messiah, who came from his line and who was destined to rule over the whole world.

1 Samuel 1:11

Was Hannah bargaining with God in her promise to give God back a son if only he would give her one? How does this fit with Jesus' prayer in Gethsemane, "May your will be done" (Matt. 26:42)?

Yes, it *was* bargaining with God. And a bargaining attitude is not encouraged in Scripture. However, we must get away from the notion that prayer is a mechanical kind of thing, or that we must approach God with exactly correct form and content or he will not listen. Hannah's vow was torn out of her by pain and longing. God did not answer Hannah's prayer *because* she offered him her son, and he did not reject her prayer because she was willing to offer her heart's desire in return for his blessing. Let's remember that prayer is an expression of our relationship with a God who loves us dearly. Honesty and trust are more important than "doing it right."

1 Samuel 2:25

Did God keep Eli's sons from repenting? What else could "for it was the Lord's will to put them to death" mean?

Although priests, Eli's sons openly ignored ritual regulations concerning sacrifice (2:12–17) and had illicit sex with women who served at the tabernacle (2:22). The phrase in verse 25 expresses God's judicial sentence, and the word *for* is to be understood as "therefore."

1 Samuel 4:3

The movie Raiders of the Lost Ark *made the ark seem magical, a terrible weapon to be used by Israel against its enemies. Does this story in 1 Samuel make the ark seem magical, too? Why else would the Israelites cheer and the Philistines fear when the ark was brought into the army camp?*

In Israel's religion the ark of the covenant represented the presence of God among his people. Both the Israelites and the Philistines *assumed* that if God was present he would be able to defeat Israel's enemies. This *was* a magical view of the ark, but it was also a mistaken one. The ark was one of God's *symbols*, it was not God. The Israelite and Philistine views were essentially pagan, not biblical. The God of Scripture fills the universe: he is present everywhere, ever able to aid his people in whatever their circumstance. Rather than rely on God himself, the Israelites wrongly relied on the *material symbol* of God's presence and so turned the ark of the covenant into an idol. The defeat that followed served as divine rejection of the magical view of the meaning of the ark. This was a lesson that the makers of the movie either did not understand or chose to ignore.

1 Samuel 6:19

Why did God strike seventy persons dead for curiously peering into the ark after it had miraculously returned from its capture by the Philistines?

In Israel's religion the ark *was* the material symbol of God's presence; Moses' law underlined its holiness. That is, the ark was an object associated with and consecrated to God. Old Testament religion placed great emphasis on maintaining a distinction between the sacred and secular (Lev. 10:10, 11), and many Old Testament laws dealt with the treatment to be accorded to holy things, such as sacrifices and holy days like the sabbath. The ark was so holy that, according to Numbers 4:20, even the Levites who served in the Tabernacle "must not go in to look at the holy things, even for a moment, or they will die" (see also Num. 4:5, 6, 15–20).

Earlier the ark had been treated as a deity by the Israelites; but the army that relied on its magical powers had been crushed (1 Sam. 4). Events proved the Israelites' view of the ark to be wrong. The Philistines tried to treat the ark as the symbol of a defeated pagan deity but were subjected to terrible plagues. So events proved their view wrong, too, and after seven months they hurriedly sent the ark back to Israel (1 Sam. 5, 6). At Beth Shemesh the people treated the ark as a mere curiosity, crowding around and pawing at it to see inside. When seventy died, events proved *this* view to be wrong, too, and at last the Israelites got the message. "Who can stand in the presence of the LORD, this holy God" (1 Sam. 6:20)? This third tragedy was necessary to remind Israel of a reality that Eli's evil sons and the whole nation had forgotten: God is to be treated with respect and awe. His word and his religion are to be honored in everything.

The death of the seventy was tragic. But only when God's people lived in awe of God, loving and obeying him, could far greater disasters be avoided, such as the defeat at Aphek where *34,000* died.

1 Samuel 8

Moses predicted that Israel would have a king, and even laid down rules for the monarch to follow (Deut. 17:14–20). Why then was God displeased when Israel demanded a king?

A number of Old Testament passages speak of Israel as having a king (Gen. 49:10; Num. 24:17). The issue here is one of *motive*.

Israel wanted a king so they could be like the other nations and would have a human leader to rely on in times of war (1 Sam. 8:10–18, 20). This was an overt rejection of God, who not only was Israel's king but who had committed himself to fight for his people when they were obedient (8:7). Right and wrong are as much a matter of motive as of the act itself. It was not necessarily wrong to ask for a king. What was wrong was Israel's motives.

1 Samuel 9:12, 19

This passage and others in Joshua and Judges describe worship at high places. But doesn't the Bible condemn this practice? Surely this shows the Bible is inconsistent.

The Canaanites, who preceded Israel worshiped their pagan deities at altars built in hilltops and in sacred groves of trees. Israel was forbidden to worship Yahweh at these pagan sites (Num. 33:52; Deut. 7:5; 12:3). However, before the temple was erected at Jerusalem (1 Kings 3:2), certain special sites *were* set aside by God for the Israelites to worship (Exod. 20:24; Deut. 12:5, 8–9, 13–14). It is clear that prior to the building of the temple acceptable worship *was* offered by accredited priests like Samuel at various sites. This is especially understandable at this time, when the tabernacle site at Shiloh had been destroyed and the ark had no sanctuary (1 Sam. 4–6).

1 Samuel 9:17

Why did God choose Saul to be king? God must have known his flaws and the disaster that would follow.

Sometimes God is limited by what his people will accept. Saul's impressive height helped make him acceptable to the people (1 Sam. 10:24). Saul also demonstrated a number of positive traits as he began his rule, which shows he was initially a good ruler (1 Sam. 11:12–15). God also granted Saul special powers (1 Sam. 10:6). Taken together we see that the Lord gave Israel the best man available who would be acceptable to the people. So certainly God cannot be blamed for the flaws the future revealed in Saul. The whole history of Saul underlined the danger in the people's determination to rely on other humans rather than on God.

1 Samuel 10:6

Why would the coming of the Spirit on Saul and his change into "a different person" not protect him from his later failures? Are we vulnerable to this today?

God does not treat anyone as a puppet. The gift of the Spirit to Saul and the even greater gift of the Spirit to us today means that we can overcome sin and live for the Lord. But that gift does not mean that we must do this. Like Saul, you and I have the freedom and the responsibility to choose. We can live in harmony with the Spirit, respond to God's guidance, and overcome sin. Or, like Saul, we can refuse to hear God's word, go our own way, and fail. Vulnerable? Certainly.

But empowered? Yes, as long as we choose to follow our Lord.

1 Samuel 11:10

Was the promise of the people of Jabesh Gilead to surrender to the Ammonites nothing but a trick to give Saul time to raise his troops? Must we conclude, from example if not by precept, that at times lying is not only the best but perhaps the only course?

The original Hebrew text here says, "Tomorrow we will *come out* to you." The term *come out* was taken by the Ammonites as a promise to surrender. But that word is also used when an army comes out to attack an enemy force. In this case the New International Version's word is unfortunate, for by this play on words the people of Jabesh Gilead both deceived their enemy and told the strict truth. They did intend to come out to the Ammonites—and fight them.

By the way, the Ammonite demand to put out the right eyes of the Israelites may seem strange. Soldiers in battle peered around their shields with only one eye, usually the right, exposed. By putting out the right eyes, the Ammonites eliminated the men of this city as a future military threat against them.

1 Samuel 13:5

Which is right, the NIV, which says the Philistines had 3,000 chariots in their force at Micmash, or older versions, which say 30,000?

The Hebrew text says 30,000. But the text also mentions only 6,000 horsemen. From what we know of the makeup of military forces in the ancient world, this proportion of horsemen to chariots is most unlikely. The best solution is that the original listed 3,000 chariots. How this kind of numerical mistake might be made is resolved in the explanation of Numbers chapter 1, page 70.

1 Samuel 13:13

Why would one foolish act disqualify Saul as the founder of a dynasty? Isn't that rather harsh? After all, anyone can act foolishly.

Each of the three Hebrew words translated *"fool"* focuses attention on a *moral* deficiency. In contrast, English *fool* focuses attention on mere carelessness or lack of sense. Saul's foolish act was to rebel against "the command the LORD your God gave you." Since Israel's king was, like her people, subject to the written law and to the prophets (Deut. 17:14–20), Saul's readiness to disregard God and choose his own way disqualified him as the founder of a dynasty and eventually led to his death.

1 Samuel 14:37–45

Why was Jonathan identified by God as a guilty party in this incident? Why was his father ready to execute him?

Even though unwittingly, Jonathan had violated the oath-command of Saul, the king. It was a foolish command but, once pronounced the curse was binding. When God identified Jonathan as the person who came under the curse, the army interposed and vowed in God's name that he should *not* be killed. Saul gave in, perhaps after the army rescued Jonathan by providing a ransom or substitute animal sacrifice to satisfy the legalities. This story is particularly ironic because Saul, who had consciously and deliberately disobeyed God, was ready and willing to kill his son for unwittingly disobeying *him*. What an exalted view he had of his own human majesty and what a low view of God's majesty! No wonder Saul was rejected by God.

1 Samuel 15:11

The text says God was grieved to have made Saul king. Does this mean God had not known what would happen? If so, this does not fit with the Christian doctrine of an all-knowing, all-powerful God.

The Hebrew word translated "grieved" is *niham,* a word which indicates strong emotion and concern. The implication of regret reflected here does not mean that God did not know ahead of time, or was helpless to affect what happened. It is true that *niham* can convey the idea of a change of mind, and in fact does so in verse 29 of this chapter. But here the idea that God was grieved simply expresses the fact that God is a person who permits human beings to stray (for man does have free will) but who cares deeply when that straying brings personal or national disaster.

1 Samuel 15:22

This saying is often taken to indicate that sacrifice is a primitive idea the ancient Hebrews shared with their pagan neighbors, a practice God simply permitted but did not require. Is that what is intended?

Not at all. The concept of sacrifice is basic to both the Old Testament and New Testament. The saying "To obey is better than sacrifice" (15:22) simply points out a basic feature of Old Testament law. Sacrifices were offered *after a person had sinned.* If the person had obeyed in the first place, sacrifice would not be required. While a person in right relationship with God could bring free-will offerings as an evidence of devotion, God was and is more delighted by a devotion that is expressed in glad obedience to his commands.

1 Samuel 16:10

If the Bible is really accurate, how can this verse indicate Jesse had eight sons, while 1 Chronicles 2:13–15 names only seven?

The most likely reason for this is that one of the eight sons died while young and still unmarried. Typically Hebrew genealogies include only those who have some significance for future generations, or who made some unusual mark on their own times. There is no conflict here that cannot be easily explained by established Hebrew custom.

1 Samuel 16:1–3

1 Samuel contains many instances of lying or deceit on the part of Samuel and David. But here it is God himself who tells Samuel

*what to say and do. Does God really condone these things as a
means to a good end?*

Gleason Archer in his *Encyclopedia of Bible Difficulties* (Zondervan, pp. 175–176) suggests three things to remember when reading biblical accounts of real or apparent falsehoods.

1. Even though Scripture records human dishonesty of men, this does not necessarily mean that it approves or condones such a sin. The same is true of other types of sin committed by religious leaders.
2. The duty to tell the truth does not necessarily carry with it an obligation to tell the whole truth about the matter, especially if lives would be endangered or lost as a result of this information, or if divulging all the details would violate a trust of secrecy or amount to a betrayal of another's confidence.
3. The mere recording of an episode involving subterfuge or deception does not imply that the person resorting to it was acting responsibly on the highest level of faith or furnishing a valid example of conduct that believers might justifiably follow today.

1 Samuel 16:14

*This verse says that the Holy Spirit "had departed from Saul." How
can this be, since the New Testament promises God will never
leave the believer?*

In the Old Testament the Holy Spirit is frequently described as "coming upon" someone (10:5–6,10; Judg. 15:14). This phrase describes God's act of giving an individual divine power or special ability for the completion of a unique task. The New Testament passages that say God will never leave the believer, and verses that indicate each believer has a special relationship with the Holy Spirit (Rom. 8:9; 1 Cor. 12:13), do not speak of the same thing as the "coming upon" references to the Spirit's work in the Old Testament. Therefore, the description of the Spirit departing from Saul simply means that the divine power or ability he had previously enjoyed was withdrawn.

It is striking that the Holy Spirit's influence was replaced by "an evil spirit from the LORD." This statement does not mean that God did evil *to* Saul. It implies two things. First, evil spirits can operate only in areas where God withdraws his active presence. And second, disobedience like Saul's opens an individual to evil influences. Here, and in 18:10 we see not a vindictive act performed by God but the consequences of Saul's rejection of God. How much better to remain committed to the Lord and be assured of his guarding presence in our lives.

1 Samuel 17

We all know the famous story of how David killed Goliath. Did he really do this, or is 2 Samuel 21:19 right in saying Goliath was killed by a warrior named Elhanan?

Folks who raise this question like to imply that David sort of took over another person's reputation after he was king, or that the writers of these historical books did this for him. After all, glorifying the ruler was common practice in the great ancient empires of the Middle East. The solution comes from a parallel passage in 1 Chronicles 20:5, which says that Elhanan "killed Lahmi the brother of Goliath." What we have in 2 Samuel 21 is simply a copying error, with the phrase *the brother of* mistakenly dropped from the original.

1 Samuel 17:56

According to chapter 16 David was at Saul's court before the fight with Goliath. But this verse says Saul didn't know David. This is an obvious discrepancy.

Actually, this shows how carelessly some people read the Bible. The text says that Saul asked, "Whose son is that young man?" (17:55) and then ordered his commander to "find out whose son this young man is." The Hebrews typically identified persons not only as individuals but also by their families; thus the importance of genealogies. It was one thing to recognize David as a favorite harpist, but another thing entirely to see him bravely face Goliath. The significance of his role as a warrior representing Israel's entire army made the king rightly concerned about his lineage. So it's not that Saul didn't know David. It's simply that now Saul needed to know *who* David was.

1 Samuel 18:10

How can a good God send an evil spirit like the one that tormented Saul?

See 16:14 above.

1 Samuel 19:11–24

How could David have permitted an idol in his house? For that matter, how could Saul, who rooted out those who practiced occult arts, have let his daughter, David's wife, worship an idol?

The Hebrew word translated here is *teraphim*, which is mentioned only fifteen times in the Old Testament and is not the ordinary word for idol. At the same time it is clear that they were cultic objects (Gen. 31:19, 34–35; Judg. 17:5). In this case the object was in the home of Michal, where David lived with this daughter of King Saul. Some who assume that this object was an idol and used in worship blame Michal and not David for its presence. However, no one knows just what this *teraphim* was or what its function was. All we really know is that, throughout the Old Testament the term is used negatively and is associated with pagan worship.

1 Samuel 21:4

Only the priests were allowed to eat the consecrated bread that Ahimelech gave to David (Lev. 24:9). How can this act be justified?

Ahimelech did question whether or not David and his men were ceremonially clean before giving them the consecrated bread. This priest and David seem to have understood the principle that Jesus drew from the incident centuries later. Ceremonial law was not to be given greater priority than human need (Matt. 12:3, 4; Luke 6:9). Providing food for David's exhausted and weakened men was well within the spirit of Old Testament law.

1 Samuel 23:1–6

How did David "inquire of the LORD" (v. 1) and how did God answer him? Are we to assume he heard God's voice?

The answer to this is in verse 6, which explains that Abiathar son of Ahimelech "had brought the ephod" when he fled to David.

The ephod was a sort of vest worn by Israel's high priest. Most believe it contained a pocket in which were kept the Urim and Thummim, which were used to discern God's will. Most believe these were stones or gems on which *yes*, *no*, and *maybe* were inscribed. When David or another person addressed a question to the priest, he reached into the pocket of the ephod and drew out that stone which contained God's answer.

Because God guided the high priest's hand, the answer was considered
to be God's own.

1 Samuel 24:5

Why should David be conscience-stricken for cutting off part of
Saul's robe? After all, he had just spared Saul's life, even though
his men had urged him to kill the king.

One possible answer is that the act had symbolic implications. Royal robes were distinctive; their borders and decorations served
as a sign of the wearer's position. This robe was identified with Saul himself as ruler of Israel. David may have felt either that cutting off part of
Saul's robe was an implicit attack on the person of the king or that it
symbolized wresting the kingdom from Saul. Note that earlier (18:4)
Jonathan took off his robe and handed it to David, an act that symbolized Jonathan's recognition of David as the one God had anointed to follow his father, Saul, as ruler.

The pang of conscience was apparently brief, however, since shortly
afterward David displayed the piece of robe as proof that he could have
killed Saul if he had chosen to (24:11). In this case David realized that
his act symbolized his true intent and that it should not be interpreted
to mean something he had not intended.

1 Samuel 28

Did the witch of Endor (a spiritualist or medium) really have
supernatural powers? Can such people really contact the dead?

The Bible does not dismiss all practitioners of the occult as
frauds. It *does*, however, forbid all such practices, on the basis that any
spiritual powers contacted are demonic in character and intent. It follows that any supernatural contacts made by mediums, spiritualists, or
channelers are not with dead loved ones, but with other, malignant spirit
beings.

Still, is this passage evidence that the medium of Endor at least *did*
contact a real person—and a man of God at that? The text hardly supports this interpretation. Verse 12 makes it totally clear that the witch
was terrified when Samuel's spirit actually appeared. *She had not expected*
a real apparition herself. And after Samuel appeared, he addressed Saul
directly, not through the stunned and silent medium.

What happened here is that God intervened and used the occasion to deliver his final word of judgment to Saul. The story demonstrates that personal existence does persist after biological death. It also shows that the pretensions of practitioners of the occult collapse in screams of fright when such persons are confronted with spiritual realities.

1 Samuel 31

This report of Saul's death does not square with the account in 2 Samuel 1. This surely shows that there are errors in Scripture.

Any discrepancy is only apparent and can easily be resolved. Saul was wounded severely, and when his armorbearer refused to dispatch him, he fell on his sword. The story told to David by the Amalekite (2 Sam. 1) either was true, and Saul's attempt at suicide had failed, or it was false, and the Amalekite lied in hopes of being rewarded by David for killing David's enemy. It is most likely that the Amalekite came across Saul's dead body and made up his story in hopes of gain. That was a big mistake. Rather than reward the Amalekite, David accepted his story and had him executed for the crime of killing God's elect.

This, by the way, was not only right but was also very wise. The history of the ancient Middle East is filled with reports of the assassinations of rulers. David wanted to establish unmistakably that the person of any ruler of Israel anointed in God's name must be inviolate.

2 Samuel

---

2 Samuel

Who wrote this book, and what themes and issues does it deal with?

See 1 Samuel, page 100.

2 Samuel 2:8

Why is Saul's son called Ish-Bosheth here, and Esh-Baal in 1 Chronicles 8:33?

The word *baal* has the general meaning of "master" or "owner." It also had a religious meaning, being on the one hand a general name standing for "god" and on the other a title given to Canaanite deities, who were the supposed owners of the territory in which they were worshiped. In Scripture, because of this pagan association, proper names that originally contained *baal* are often changed to *bosheth*, which means "shame," to avoid idolatrous connotations.

It is important to note here that Saul's naming his youngest son *Esh-Baal*, "Baal lives," need not imply that Saul had abandoned Yahweh to worship Canaanite baals. It may simply reflect the early use of *baal* as a generic word for "god."

2 Samuel 3:39

Why didn't David punish Joab for the murder of Abner? Wasn't this at best a sin of omission?

David's motives here are never explained. It may be that at this critical juncture the loyalty of the northerners was controlled by their commander, Joab. It is very likely that David simply could not bring Joab to trial without causing a rebellion. However, it must be remembered that in Hebrew culture a curse uttered against an inferior was considered a binding act, with the ability to effect actual punishment. In cursing Joab, David not only condemned his faithful military commander but also actually did punish him. In the end David also called on Solomon to execute final judgment on Joab, and put him to death (1 Kings 2:5–6, 29–35).

2 Samuel 5:5

How could David reign over Judah for seven and one-half years, if Ish-Bosheth ruled only two years over the northern tribes (Israel) before he was assassinated?

After the defeat at the hands of the Philistines, when Saul was killed, the northern territories were controlled by these invaders. It may well have taken Abner five years to throw back the Philistines and consolidate his gains. Only then did Abner call representatives of the ten tribes to Mahanaim to officially crown Ish-Bosheth king. While this is not explained within the text, it seems the most reasonable explanation of the five-year gap and certainly fits practices of the times.

2 Samuel 6:20

Was David's dance when the ark was brought to Jerusalem lewd, as Michal seems to suggest? What does this mean, that David "distinguished himself today disrobing in the sight of the slave girls"?

Verse 14 says David wore a linen ephod, the simple garment worn by priests and Levites when they ministered at the tabernacle. There is no implication in Michal's criticism that in his ecstatic dancing David threw this off. The story simply portrays a proud princess, critical of David's failure to maintain his royal dignity. David reminded Michal that God had chosen him to be king in place of Saul. One reason for this was that David, unlike Saul, had a heart for God.

2 Samuel 7

What was the real nature of God's promise to David?

Psalm 89 identifies this as a covenant promise, a firm commitment made by God to David and the people of Israel. Specifically, the promise guarantees: (1) that David will have a son and successor (Solomon); (2) that David's son will build the temple David yearned to construct; (3) that the throne (the royal line) of this kingdom will be established forever; (4) that, despite the sins of members of this line, the right to the throne will never be taken from the family; and (5) that David's house, throne, and kingdom will endure forever.

Some might point to this passage and argue that these promises were *not* fulfilled. The Babylonians stripped the Jews of their independence in 586 B.C., and the Romans destroyed the last Jewish attempt to reestablish a kingdom when they smashed Jerusalem in A.D. 70. Today there may be a Jewish state, but there is no Jewish *kingdom*, and no one from David's line rules in Jerusalem. Certainly the promises recorded in this passage have not been kept. Thus, either God is unable to guarantee the future and is not the person Jews and Christians claim him to be, or the Bible is in error in reporting these promises as a guarantee given David by God.

The solution, of course, is to carefully review the terms of the promises. Solomon did succeed David and was firmly established in his kingdom. Solomon did build the temple. And, despite the ups and the terrible downs experienced by the nation during the kingdom age, a lineal descendant of David did rule on the throne of Jerusalem throughout this time. More important, David's line persisted during the era of subjection to the Gentiles. As the genealogies in Luke and Matthew demonstrate, Jesus himself is from David's family. And because Jesus lives today as our resurrected Lord, *there has always been a member of the royal line qualified to take the throne of Israel.* And *this* is what God promised David: a house forever.

But what about the permanent establishment of the kingdom? Christians see this prophetic promise fulfilled in two possible ways. Some believers see the promise fulfilled in Christ's present spiritual reign as Lord and head of the church. Other believers fully expect that when Christ returns, he will establish a kingdom here on earth and rule the world from Jerusalem as David's greater son. After the Old Testament promises concerning this earthly kingdom have been fulfilled, and after a great final rebellion also described by many of the prophets, this world will end, and Christ will rule his saints forever in eternity.

Whatever position one may take on eschatology, it is clear that, as far as the Bible is concerned, the promises to David *have been* or *will be* fulfilled. There is no basis here for arguing that the Bible is inconsistent, or in error.

2 Samuel 12:14

This story implies that the baby of David and Bathsheba died as a punishment to the sinning pair. How could a loving God do such a terrible thing, especially when God says children should not be put to death for their parents' sins?

Many scholars suggest two explanations. One is that in biblical times a "unitary" view of sin persisted, so that all family members were viewed as responsible for a member's sinful acts. Another is that the child's death was seen as an "atonement" for David. David was forgiven, but even forgiven sin must be punished, and so the child had to die.

It is always an error to read modern moral assumptions into biblical accounts, or to revise biblical moral standards to make them fit contemporary mores. Even so, the scholarly explanations compound rather than reduce the moral questions raised by the death of David and Bathsheba's son. In trying to resolve the moral problem, we want to notice first that David's punishment is announced in 2 Samuel 12:10–13. The divine judgment on David has been fully expressed *before* the child is mentioned. Thus the statement concerning the death of the child is *carefully distanced by the author from the issue of David's punishment.* It is also distanced from the issue of forgiveness. In Hebrew ritual forgiveness *follows* the offering of an atoning sacrifice (Lev. 1–7). Here forgiveness is announced *before* the child is mentioned. Thus the statement concerning the death of the child is *also carefully distanced by the author from the issue of David's forgiveness.* Whatever the reason for the child's death, it has nothing to do with either David's punishment or David's forgiveness.

The author links this death to the contempt David's unfaithfulness to God arouses in the enemies of the Lord. The child cannot live to continue to be a symbol stimulating contempt for God in the Lord's enemies. In this, God exercises grace and displays it to the nation, to David and Bathsheba, and to the child as well. This is grace toward the nation, for living the child would serve as a reminder of *successful* sin and might well stimulate others to act irresponsibly as David had. This is grace toward David and Bathsheba, because however much they might try to love the boy, he would be a constant reminder of their sin and shame. And this is grace toward the boy, for while innocent of any wrongdoing, he would sense the shame felt by his parents and the amused contempt of the general population, and suffer greatly for it. In taking the boy as an infant, God protected the nation, removed the parents' shame, and saved the child himself from a lifetime of ridicule and undeserved contempt. The death of the child was an act of grace, not of judgment; of compassion, not of revenge.

And let's remember David's words as we keep not only the infant's death but death itself in perspective. When the child died, David said, "I will go to him, but he will not return to me" (12:23). David's child died biologically but lives eternally. Life is a gift, and death is to be avoided. But death is a defeated enemy for the believer, and the blessings of eternity outweigh those of time as much as earth outweighs a grain of sand.

2 Samuel 14:27

How can 2 Samuel 18:18 say Absalom had no sons, when this verse claims that Absalom has three?

Absalom says in 18:18, "I have no son to carry on the memory of my name." It's apparent that Absalom's three sons all died before he did, and before they were old enough to wed and have children. There is no discrepancy here at all.

2 Samuel 21:1–15

How could David let the Gibeonites execute seven innocent descendants of Saul as revenge against the dead king? This surely is a moral discrepancy.

During his reign Saul broke the commitment made by Joshua at the time of the conquest (Josh. 9) and tried to exterminate the Gibeonites, a Canaanite people who lived as a subject people in Israelite territory. God struck the land with a three-year famine as punishment, and so David asked the Gibeonites how he could make amends. When they asked to execute seven of Saul's descendants, David agreed. And after the executions, God again answered prayer. So both David and God seem to have approved this vengeance, and we are left with the moral problem: How could they do this?

Perhaps the solution is found in examining the assumption that these descendants of Saul were innocent. 2 Samuel 21:1 reports that the Lord revealed that the famine came "on account of Saul *and his blood-stained house.*" This suggests that the family of Saul was actively involved in the attempt to exterminate the Gibeonites, and that rather than ask for the right to execute the *innocent,* the Gibeonites actually asked David for the right to execute the *guilty.* In this case there is no moral conflict. The perpetrators of this early holocaust directed against the Gibeonites were rightly and judicially condemned, and the land was purged of its guilt.

2 Samuel 24

Why was it wrong for David to count his fighting men? And why did God punish the people for David's sin?

The passage is filled with puzzles. For one thing, while this passage and 1 Chronicles 21 suggest that God and Satan both incited David to number the people—each, of course, for his own reasons. We know nothing of David's personal motives. Note, by the way, that it is basic to Old Testament thought: that even though either God or Satan is said to stimulate a person to an action, the person is still fully responsible for the choices he or she makes. Neither God nor Satan forces a person to act against his or her will. Since we are not told David's reasons for conducting this military census, we remain puzzled as to why he insisted on taking it. And we also remain puzzled as to just why the action was wrong. However, even the spiritually insensitive Joab realized that it *was* wrong (1 Chron. 21), and so we are sure the sin was willful.

It is not surprising that David's sin had an impact on the people of his nation. No national leader can make choices that do *not* affect the people he or she governs. Still, the fact that 24:1 tells us "the anger of the Lord burned against Israel" at this time makes it clear that, while David's sin was the *occasion* for divine judgment, the *cause* of the judgment was not David's act but the people's sin. So, clearly the people did *not* suffer because of David's sin but because of some unnamed sin of their own.

2 Samuel 24:9

Here, again, numbers in this passage and in 1 Chronicles 21 differ. How can an inspired book have so many numerical errors?

Actually, there are not that many numerical errors, given the frequency with which statistics are given in the Old Testament. Most discrepancies are relatively easily explained (see comments on Numbers 1, p. 70). Here two sets of numbers are involved.

2 Samuel 24:9 gives 800,000 as the adult male population of Israel, but 1 Chronicles 21:5 says the population was 1,100,000. 2 Samuel 24 lists 500,000 for Judah, while 1 Chronicles 21 makes it 470,000. One passage must be wrong. Well, perhaps.

It may be, however, that an answer is suggested by the use in 2 Samuel of *fighting men* (warriors) and its absence from 1 Chronicles 21. The smaller number may reflect the fact that while there were 1,100,000 men of military age available to David, only 800,000 were experienced troops.

The discrepancy between the 500,000 and 470,000 troops may also be explained in the details of these texts. Chronicles tells us that Joab did not complete the census and, in fact, left out the tribe of Benjamin (21:6). The larger figure in 2 Samuel may include an estimated 30,000 troops from Benjamin to make up a realistic total. Thus these discrepancies may be more apparent than real, if the text is read carefully.

The second so-called discrepancy is in the amount paid by David to Araunah. 2 Samuel 24:24 says David paid fifty shekels of silver for the threshing floor and the oxen. 1 Chronicles 21:25 says David paid six hundred shekels of gold, nearly two hundred times as much. How can we explain this? A threshing floor is a small, hilltop area, usually only a few hundred square feet in size. The much greater price recorded in 1 Chronicles suggests that while David paid only fifty silver shekels for the oxen and threshing floor, he also purchased the entire site—the larger area where the threshing floor was situated. As the temple was later built on this site and covered many acres, we have good reason to suppose that the 600 gold shekels were paid for the fields and hill surrounding the threshing floor, and not for that tiny location at all.

1 Kings

1 Kings

Who wrote this book, and what themes and issues does it deal with?

1 and 2 Kings are books of history that cover Israel's kingdom age, from the rule of Solomon (971–921 B.C.) to the fall of Jerusalem to the Babylonians in 586 B.C. In the Hebrew Bible the two books are treated as a single work. The unknown author is primarily concerned with showing how the rulers' faithfulness to or abandonment of God affected the state of the nation, and so focuses our attention on the goodness or wickedness of rulers. During this era the united kingdom of David and Solomon was divided into two competing nations: Israel in the north, and Judah in the south.

1 Kings 2:23

Was it unjust of Solomon to execute Adonijah for asking to marry Abishag?

Adonijah had attempted to gain the throne and thwart his half-brother Solomon's rightful claim. Solomon spared his life. But when Adonijah asked to marry a girl who had been David's concubine during his last days, Solomon recognized this as a political act. Marriage to even a secondary wife of David was a step toward legitimizing his claim to be David's successor. Solomon ordered Adonijah's execution because the request made it clear that Israel might be plunged into civil war by this brother who refused to give up his ambition to take Solomon's throne.

1 Kings 6:1

This passage gives very specific chronological information. But don't most scholars insist that Rameses was the pharaoh of the exodus? If he was, the fourth year of Solomon's reign could not be 480 years after the exodus.

The reign of Solomon is the first truly fixed date that scholars can agree on. That is, there is enough independent information from archaeological records to enable scholars to link the events of Solomon's reign with events in other nations and thus fix a common date for each. No events prior to Solomon can be dated with similar confidence. This is why we do not have independent corroboration of exactly when David became king, or just when the patriarchs entered Egypt, when Abraham left Ur, etc. For this reason dating depends on the Bible's own chronological notes, and general evidence gathered by archaeologists that provides a context within which the events described in the Bible fit. So when we come to a verse that provides a specific chronological note, we can either accept the notation as accurate, or we must discount it. In this case, those who assume Rameses the Great was the pharaoh of the exodus discount this verse and say it cannot be accurate. But it is just as reasonable, and much wiser, to accept the verse and discount the theory that Rameses the Great was the pharaoh of the exodus. Unless there is some clear evidence of scribal error, it is wiser to evaluate the theories of scholars by the Bible rather than evaluate the Bible by the theories of scholars.

For a discussion of the date of the exodus and who was pharaoh at the time of the exodus, see Exodus 12 (p. 56) and Joshua (p. 86).

1 Kings 7

Much wealth was lavished on the Jerusalem Temple. Could those riches have really existed? If so, what eventually happened to all that gold?

The twenty-five tons of gold for Solomon's annual income (1 Kings 10:14: 666 talents), and the even greater tonnage required to overlay the temple and create cultic objects as described in this chapter, plus additional tons used in making the shields and goblets for Solomon's household portrayed in 1 Kings 10, have led some to dismiss these records as the product of an exuberant imagination. Yet a search of ancient records shows that kings of the ancient world did gather vast amounts of the yellow treasure and use it in ostentatious ways. For instance, these ancient records say that Esarhaddon of Assyria "coated the walls" of the shrine of the god Ashur "with gold as if it were plaster." And one Egyptian monarch overlaid a 220-foot-long barge, used to carry images of his gods, with gold to the waterline. But even so, if Solomon had so much gold, we have to ask, Where did it all go? How could so much wealth disappear from history if it were real?

The fact is that Solomon's gold did *not* disappear from history. Both the Bible (1 Kings 14:25, 26; 2 Chron. 12:2–4) and Egyptian records report the capture of Jerusalem by Pharaoh Shishak about 925 B.C., shortly after Solomon's death. Shishak died about a year later. He was succeeded by his son Osorkon I. And Egyptian records report that in 921 B.C. this king donated, *as part of his gift to the gods*, a total of 383 tons of gold and silver.

Where did this pharaoh gain such immense wealth only three years or so after coming to power? The best answer is that he got it from Solomon's temple and palace, looted five years before by his father, Shishak. Does the Bible record a product of someone's exuberant imagination? Not at all. Once again we see that even in the most unusual details God's Word is accurate.

1 Kings 7:23

Here is a clear mathematical error. The value of pi is 3.13159. But calculations based on the dimensions given in this verse would give 3.0 as the value of pi. In this the Bible is clearly and unmistakably in error.

This argument is based on the established mathematical relationship between the circumference and radius of a circle, that is, if one knows the radius, the circumference is found by multiplying it by 3.13159. The verse says the giant bronze vessel Solomon cast to hold water for the priest's ritual washing was ten cubits in radius and thirty cubits in circumference. This is a 1 to 3 ratio, not a 1 to 3.13159 ratio, and thus in error. This objection is ridiculous on several counts. For instance, the object was not a circle, but a giant vessel of significant thickness. It might have been measured not around the outside but across from inner rim to inner rim. Gleason Archer has pointed out that if a rod five cubits long were used to measure the inside circumference of the vessel described, "it would take exactly six of those five-cubit measures" to complete the circumference, and the value of *pi* would be preserved. Archer's point is that a straight measuring stick such as was used in ancient times *would not measure the curvature* of the vessel, and that if we take curvature into account, the result is that Solomon's giant laver *does* in fact maintain the exact value of *pi*!

1 Kings 11:1

Why did Solomon take so many wives? Was this a violation of Old Testament law?

Moses' law said, "The king . . . must not acquire great numbers of horses for himself. . . . He must not take many wives. . . . He must not accumulate large amounts of silver and gold" (Deut. 17:16–17). Solomon violated each of these commands by building a large chariot army, collecting great wealth, and contracting multiple marriages. The many wives did not so much reflect Solomon's sexual passions as his approach to international relationships. In biblical times treaties between nations were commonly cemented by marriage. Solomon's initial tolerance of his many wives' pagan deities led in time to his own defection from Yahweh (11:4–6).

1 Kings 12

Why did Jeroboam set up worship centers at Bethel and Dan, and what were the consequences of his act?

When Solomon's kingdom divided after his death, Jeroboam, who became ruler of the northern ten tribes, feared that if his people maintained their traditional religious allegiance to the Temple at Jerusalem, they would also in time return to political allegiance to the South. Bethel and Dan were chosen as competing religious centers because of the long history of each site as a holy place. Jeroboam also restructured the religious calendar, ordained a non-Aaronic priesthood, and in general counterfeited critical elements of the Scriptural faith. This nonscriptural religion was supported by a series of evil kings throughout the short history of the northern kingdom.

1 Kings 13

Why should God have killed the young prophet who so bravely carried his message of judgment to Jeroboam? It doesn't seem fair.

Many of the moral discrepancies of Scripture that critics point out exist only because human beings persist in assuming that their own moral sensibilities are more acute than those reflected in actions attributed to God in the Old Testament or New Testament. In fact, the young prophet had carried a message of judgment to Jeroboam based on the principle that conscious disobedience to God *for whatever reason* is wrong and merits punishment. This prophet had been told by the Lord not to eat or drink while in the north. But when the old prophet of Israel told him that eating at his home would be all right with God, the young prophet accepted his word that God had changed his mind. In essence, the man of God from Judah did just what the people of the north were doing: accepting a religious innovation on the word of a mere man. The death of the prophet from Judah was not only a just judgment on him but was also a powerful object lesson for the people of the north on the dangers of substituting human judgment for the clear Word of God.

1 Kings 15:3

How can the Bible describe David as a person whose heart was fully devoted to the Lord? David was an adulterer and conspired to murder his paramour's husband. He also disobeyed God on other occasions. That's devotion?

David certainly did fail, terribly. Yet the overall orientation of David's life was godward. He did not fall into the terrible sins of arrogance that marked so many rulers of his time and so many of those who followed him on the throne of Judah. What is more, when David sinned he quickly and openly confessed his failures and sought forgiveness. This reaction is far different from that of Saul, who when caught in sin begged Samuel to honor him in the sight of the people (1 Sam. 15:30).

The fact is that every person sins and falls short. But the person who normally is devoted to the Lord is obedient to him, and when he or she does sin quickly turns back to God, and seeks forgiveness through confession.

1 Kings 18:40

How could Elijah order the death of the four hundred prophets of Baal? His point was proved in God's answer of fire.

Ahab and Jezebel were committed to replacing the worship of Yahweh with the particularly virulent form of Baal worship practiced in Tyre. We can sense something of the character of this religion by the action of Baal's prophets reported in 18:28. They slashed themselves with knives when calling on their deity, because Baal was supposed to delight in violence, and they expected the smell of fresh blood to arouse him. Later this Phoenician religion was exported to the colony established at Carthage. Today one can go just outside that city to a topheth, or sacrificial park, and see the graves where children from infancy to about four years of age were burned alive as sacrifices to the same deities worshiped by the prophets Elijah ordered slain. Archaeology has demonstrated powerfully that this group of religious leaders deserved merciless execution, not tolerance.

1 Kings 21

Was Naboth being unreasonable in rejecting Ahab's generous offer to trade fields? We cannot justify the acts of Ahab or Jezebel, but doesn't Naboth bear some of the blame?

Not at all. All family land claims in Israel and Judah were to be traced back to their original grant by Joshua at the time of the conquest of Canaan. At that time land was distributed to and within the tribal groups by lot, so that each family was to see its property as the personal gift of God. What is more, that land was not to pass out of the hands of the family. The Year of Jubilee was established so that if land was sold, every fiftieth year it would be returned to the original owner (Lev. 25:8–17). Naboth, a godly individual, was horrified that the king would want him to surrender "the inheritance of my fathers" (1 Kings 21:3). Naboth had too much respect for God to surrender his land, even to the king. So Naboth was not simply being stubborn, he was being obedient.

1 Kings 22:22

How could God use a lying spirit to trick Ahab into undertaking a war in which he would be killed? Doesn't this imply that God himself lied to Ahab?

God did permit the spirit (angel) to lie through Ahab's pagan prophets. But does this mean that God tricked Ahab into going to war? Or that God lied to Ahab? Again, it's important to read the passage carefully. Ahab was already intent on the war and had arranged an alliance with Jehoshaphat of Judah before either sought divine guidance. So Ahab could hardly be said to have been tricked into a war he had already planned.

But what about the charge that God deceived Ahab? Again, look at the passage. When a true prophet of the Lord was called, he not only revealed that Ahab would die in the coming battle but even revealed that the source of Ahab's prophet's predictions of victory was a lying spirit. God clearly revealed the *whole truth to Ahab* through his prophet Micaiah.

The fact is that Ahab was not tricked into the battle but that he chose not to believe God's prophet's clear prediction that he would die in the coming war. There is no way that God can be charged with deceit in this situation.

As for God's use of the lying spirit, the story illustrates a basic teaching of Scripture. Satan and his minions can commit themselves to do harm. But God is great enough to turn even the evil men and fallen angels to his good ends.

2 Kings

2 Kings

Who wrote this book, and what themes and issues does it deal with?

See the introduction to 1 Kings, page 119.

2 Kings 1

Was it right of God to answer Elijah's prayer and destroy soldiers who were only following orders? Did Jesus imply that Elijah was wrong when he refused to call down fire on the Samaritans?

Elijah ministered at a critical juncture in Israel's religious history. Jezebel and her son Ahaziah were still committed to stamping out the worship of Yahweh and replacing Israel's biblical faith with the religion of the Tyran Baal.

In the context of the times, Elijah's prayer and its answer were vivid demonstrations to the new king (Ahab had just died) of Yahweh's power. The fire that destroyed two companies of soldiers not only authenticated the prophet but underlined Yahweh's claim of sovereignty over Israel. This divine sovereignty placed loyalty to God higher than loyalty to the king.

When this point was made, and the commander of the third company showed respect for God (1:13, 14), no more demonstrations were required.

As for Jesus' rebuke of his disciples (Luke 9:54, 55), no censure of Elijah was implied. Instead the censure was directed against his disciples, who mistakenly assumed that the ignorant unbelief of the Samaritans was in the same category as the willfully rebellious unbelief that Elijah had confronted.

2 Kings 2:24

How could Elisha curse these youths just for ridiculing his baldness? And why would God fulfill the curse by sending bears to attack and maul forty-two of them?

The jeering phrase, "Go on up, you baldhead" (2:23), did not ridicule Elisha's lack of hair but rather the notion that Elijah had actually been taken directly up into heaven (2:1–18). It was a direct challenge to Elisha not as a man but as God's prophet. We must remember that at this time an intense struggle between Yahwehism and Baalism was taking place in Israel and that the pagan religion had the direct support of the crown. Elijah, God's champion, was no longer present, and so this gang of pagan youths took it on themselves to ridicule the man who claimed to be his successor. Elisha recognized the jeering for what it was, a challenge to God himself. The immediate fulfillment of the curse and the judgment visited on the gang helped not only to establish Elisha as a true prophet but also to inspire an essential respect for Yahweh as a real and present God.

2 Kings 3:27

Why did Israel's army withdraw after the king of Moab killed his son as a sacrifice to his gods? Was "the fury against Israel" due to the supposed intervention of the Moabite deity Chemosh, as some have argued?

Archaeology has recovered literary evidence of the pagan practice of offering a royal son as a sacrifice when the nation was in extreme danger. What puzzles commentators and has been one of the most perplexing items in Scripture is the observation that as a result there was "fury against Israel" and that the Israelite forces withdrew.

The theory that Chemosh is supposed to have acted directly against Israel's forces contradicts the Scripture's consistent portrayal of pagan deities as helpless and useless. Some have suggested that God turned against Israel for pushing the Moabites so hard that their king was forced to this extremity. A traditional Jewish interpretation is most interesting: According to 2 Kings 3:6–9, Judah and Israel warred against Moab together, accompanied by the king of Edom, who was a vassal of Judah. According to this theory the royal heir who was sacrificed was not that of Moab but was the captive son of the king of Edom. The "fury against Israel" was that of the Edomites, whose hostility at the death of their crown prince created such a threat that the coalition forces were forced to withdraw.

2 Kings 8:26

Was Ahaziah twenty-two or forty-two years old when he began his reign. This passage and 2 Chronicles 22:2 disagree.

This is another of those differences easily explained by a copyist's error, as discussed in reference to Numbers 1, page 70. The multiplier was a small mark placed above the Hebrew letter to indicate its numerical value. The fading or wrinkling of a manuscript easily made that mark indistinguishable. There are a number of instances where just this kind of scribal error seems to have taken place. This also explains the difference in the age of Jehoiachin reported in 2 Kings 24:8 and 2 Chronicles 36:9, 10.

Such errors in copying may create a discrepancy in our present text, but they hardly imply an error in the original.

2 Kings 9:1

Who were the "sons of the prophets" (KJV)?

The word *son* is extremely flexible in Hebrew and occurs some five thousand times in the Old Testament, with a variety of meanings. Here *son of* denotes membership in a group. Scholars debate whether "the sons of the prophets" were those who where in training to become prophets or those who served as a sort of guild whose members were prophets.

2 Kings 9:6–10

God condemns Jehu in Hosea 1:4. But God gave him the task of wiping out the family of wicked King Ahab. How could God condemn Jehu for doing what God himself intended him to do?

Jehu not only wiped out the family of Ahab but also killed all those in Israel who were committed to the worship of Baal (2 Kings 9:14–10:28). At this time God commended Jehu and promised him a reward (10:30). However, the same passage reminds us that Jehu did this not out of piety, but self-interest, for he never intended to follow the ways of the Lord (10:29, 31). Perhaps the best way to understand Hosea 1:4, which predicts punishment for Jehu's line, is to note that motives do count. While the havoc Jehu wrought was divine judgment from the Lord's perspective, from Jehu's perspective it was an opportunity to wipe out the royal line and establish himself as king. He was guilty, because rather than seeing himself as God's executioner he was carrying out God's commands for his own selfish purposes.

2 Kings 17:23

How can the prophets speak of the twelve tribes of Israel when ten were taken into pagan lands and never returned?

The fiction of the ten "lost tribes" has popped up in many guises. A movement known as British Israelitism proposes the engaging theory that these tribes are the real forefathers of the British people. American Indians have also been proposed as descendants of the supposed lost tribes who disappeared from history after their deportation from Israel by Assyria in 722 B.C.

In fact, no tribe was truly lost and its members fully assimilated into other peoples. When the land was divided into two kingdoms, the southern kingdom continued to worship Yahweh according to the law in the temple at Jerusalem. The northern kingdom set up a counterfeit religious system with worship centers at Bethel and Dan (1 Kings 12). At that time many from the ten northern tribes migrated to Judah to worship the Lord freely (1 Kings 12:27; 2 Chron. 11:13–17). Because of this, representatives of all twelve families of Israel were included in the southern tribes of Judah and Benjamin. None of God's people have been lost.

2 Kings 19

We know from the Taylor Prism that Sennacherib invaded Judah in 701 B.C. 2 Kings 18 calls this Hezekiah's fourteenth year, but 2 Kings 18:1 says he became king the third year of Hoshea of Israel, which was 729 or 728. Is this a historical inaccuracy?

Certainly the dating of the reigns of Hebrew kings is a complex and difficult subject. Sometimes years are calculated from the time a person became co-regent with his father, and sometimes from the beginning of his sole reign. At times, depending on the nation and custom, the number of years is calculated from the first *anniversary* of his ascension. It's no wonder that more than one book has been written on the subject. The best known is *The Strange Numbers of the Hebrew Kings*. However, we probably do not need to resort to complex calculations to resolve this particular numbers problem. It seems most likely that the word written *fourteen* was originally noted in the early system in which letters were given numerical value and place value (4, 40, 400, etc.) indicated by signs written over them. If we assume the kind of transmission error in the marking over the decade indicator as seen in other Old Testament numbers, the *fourteen* was originally a *twenty-four*, and no real problem exists.

2 Kings 20:12–15

We know that by 701 B.C. Merodach-Baladan had been expelled from Babylon by the Assyrians. So there is a clear historical error in this text, which reports an envoy coming from him after this date.

The confusion here is created by taking the phrase *in those days* (20:1) to parallel the story of Hezekiah's illness with Sennacherib's invasion reported in 2 Kings 19. In fact, the phrase simply introduces a shift of subject. This was another incident that took place during the reign of Hezekiah. We can be quite sure of this, for the same phrase is used in the same way—without any direct linkage to previous material—in Judges 17:6; 18:1; 19:1; Esther 1:2; and even in the New Testament in Matthew 3:1.

When did the incident of Hezekiah's illness and recovery take place? We know that Hezekiah died sometime between 698 and 696 B.C. Counting back the fifteen years God added to his lifespan, his illness must have taken place around 711 B.C. when Merodach-Baladan *was* in control of Babylon. This also provides an interesting insight into the reason Merodach-Baladan sent messengers to Judah. He may have been eager for the states of Syria and Palestine to open a second front against the Assyrians, with whom he was constantly at war.

2 Kings 22

What was the Book of the Law found in the temple? Is it likely that this book was an invention of priests who created the books of Moses at that time to stimulate a religious revival?

This rather interesting theory has gained much support from some scholars. There is no historical, traditional, or compelling textual support for this view. The reason for this theory is simply that this is a good place to hang the idea that the Old Testament documents simply could not be as old as they claim to be or be the authentic Word of God. It stretches credulity to the breaking point. It assumes that an entire racial history could have been created in the seventh century B.C., and that it would be accepted by a people as their history without conflicting with already existing traditions and racial memory. However, common sense is not always a critic's strong point.

As to the question of what this lost Book of the Law *was*, we do not know. Some say it was the Book of Deuteronomy. Some suggest that it was the entire Pentateuch. As to *how* the Book of the Law might have been lost, this we *do* know. Hezekiah's son Manasseh was violently opposed to the worship of Yahweh through the first phase of his reign. He not only imported foreign deities but also closed the temple and attempted to stamp out worship of the Lord. Surely one of his major efforts would be directed at destroying the sacred books that provided the foundation of Israel's faith.

Some have suggested that the sacred books were found during repairs because of a common practice in ancient times. When a cornerstone was laid, various documents were often sealed into the building. It is possible that in repairing the temple a copy of the Scriptures, the true foundation of Israel's faith, was found within its walls.

1 Chronicles

1 Chronicles

Who wrote this book, and what themes and issues does it deal with?

No author of 1 and 2 Chronicles, which appear as a single book in the Hebrew Old Testament, is identified. The book covers the history of Israel. The first chapters use genealogies to review history from Adam to the death of King Saul. The remainder of the two books reviews the history of David and of the Jewish people through the Babylonian captivity.

Although these books cover the same material as is found in 1 and 2 Samuel and 1 and 2 Kings, the material is organized with a special purpose in mind. Writing for the little group of Jews who had returned to Judea after the captivity ended, the writer was concerned with the fact that God is faithful to his covenant promises. Israel's history demonstrates that God brings disaster on the nation when its people sin, and that he blesses the nation when its people obey him. What an encouragement to the struggling community in Judea this commentary on history must have been, and what a reminder it is to us of the importance of living close to the Lord!

1 Chronicles 1–9

Why such a long, boring list of names? The Bible is supposed to be relevant to our lives. Instead we get genealogies.

Genealogies were important documents in Israel, not only as ways of guaranteeing the Israelites' descent from Abraham and thus membership among God's covenant people, but also ways of preserving the history of the people. The organization of genealogies, which typically skip generations and emphasize certain ancestors or family lines, permits the historian to accentuate various claims. Here, for instance, the central portion of the genealogy (2:18–3:24) is structured to highlight David's ancestry and descendants.

While the seemingly interminable list of names we find in this extended genealogy may seem meaningless and boring to us, the writer carefully designed the list to make important theological and historical points that his first readers surely understood, even if we do not.

1 Chronicles 11:15–19

Why did David throw away the water his men risked their lives to get for him?

When David "poured it out before the LORD" (11:18), he praised rather than rejected the men's brave act. In essence David was saying that the lives they risked to obtain the water were sacred, and therefore the water could not be used for any ordinary purpose, such as for drinking. This honest concern for the lives of his men was one of David's many attractive features and helped him win the loyalty of his soldiers.

1 Chronicles 13:7

Why did God slay Uzzah when all he wanted to do was to steady the ark and keep it from falling?

The ark of the covenant was the most holy object in Israel's religion. According to Mosaic law, it was to be carried with poles slipped through rings on its sides, not by oxcart (Exod. 25:12–15), and it was not to be touched by any person (Num. 4:15). Uzzah, whatever his intent, did touch the ark in violation of the law governing this holy object. David's subsequent anger has been reflected in the reaction of others to this story. But the incident served as a vital reminder that God is holy and powerful. He must be honored, and his word must be kept. This forceful lesson undoubtedly deepened the conviction in Israel that God was real and able to deal with their enemies in David's subsequent drive to defend and expand the united kingdom.

1 Chronicles 15:29

Why does the chronicler leave out incidents that tend to show David in an unflattering light? Here, for instance, there is no mention of Michal's angry outburst. And there is no mention later of David's sin with Bathsheba.

This certainly is not the result of a desire to hide David's flaws. When the Book of Chronicles was composed, 1 and 2 Samuel and 1 and 2 Kings had already been written, and David's great psalm of confession (Ps. 51) was part of Israel's hymnody. These negative events were on the record. The author of the Chronicles, like all authors, reported those incidents which developed his theme. That theme is God's faithfulness to David and his descendants as a basis of confidence for the exiles returned from Babylon, despite their difficult present and uncertain future.

1 Chronicles 21:5

Why is there a difference between the census totals recorded in this verse and those of the same census given in 2 Samuel 24:9?

See explanation of 2 Samuel 24:9, page 117.

2 Chronicles

2 Chronicles

Who wrote 2 Chronicles, and what themes and issues does it deal with?

See the introduction to 1 Chronicles, page 132.

2 Chronicles 2:17–18

How can anyone justify the use of slave labor to build God's Temple? Certainly this constitutes a major moral difficulty in the Old Testament.

These aliens were survivors of Canaanite tribes. They were permitted to live after Israel first invaded the land, on condition that they serve the Israelites as a labor force (Josh. 9:27; Judg. 1:28). This does not mean that the alien peoples did not have their own homes and farm their own land, but that they paid taxes to Israel in the form of labor. 1 Kings 9:21 makes it clear that the so-called forced labor was drawn from this population, and that Solomon simply assigned the men to work on the temple project in place of performing other required tasks. It would not be accurate to describe this labor force as slave labor. Rather, it is significant that aliens were *allowed* to participate in building God's Temple. Isaiah predicts that this privilege will be granted to foreigners in God's future kingdom when Jerusalem is reestablished as the site of God's rule on earth (Isa. 60:10–12).

135

2 Chronicles 7:1

*What was the "glory of the L*ORD*" that filled the Temple? And what was the significance of fire falling from heaven to burn up the sacrifice offered at the temple's dedication?*

The glory of the Lord is used frequently as a technical theological term in the Old Testament that indicates a visible invasion of the material universe by the Lord—a revelation of God's presence. God displayed his glory in the plagues that struck Egypt (Exod. 14:4), and he displays it always in the starry universe he created (Ps. 19:1). At times the glory of the Lord was displayed visibly, as here, in a boiling, fiery cloud (Exod. 29:43; Ezek. 43:4; Hag. 2:3).

The fire from heaven that burned up the sacrifice symbolized God's acceptance of Solomon's dedicatory prayer and promise to grant Solomon's requests.

2 Chronicles 9

Who was the Queen of Sheba and why did she visit Solomon?

In Solomon's time Sheba was a wealthy kingdom at the southwestern end of the Arabian Peninsula and extending across the Red Sea into Ethiopia. Israel, situated on the land bridge between Egypt and the great kingdoms of the north, controlled vital trade routes. Solomon's trading ventures (8:18) were undoubtedly of great concern to the ruler of Sheba, which had previously dominated the area's trade in gold and spices. Undoubtedly the Queen of Sheba came, not simply out of curiosity but also to work out commercial and trade agreements.

2 Chronicles 11:2–4

Does the division of the kingdom at Solomon's death violate the promises the Lord had made to David and to his people?

No. God's promise to Solomon was that he should "never fail to have a man [qualified] to rule over Israel" (2 Chron. 7:18). It is clear from God's warning to Solomon that sin, in his own life or in the lives of his descendants, would result in judgment (2 Chron. 7:17–22). Throughout the kingdom era, Judah was always ruled by a descendant of David, and during the centuries of domination by Gentiles the royal line was maintained until it culminated in Jesus Christ (Matt. 1; Luke 3).

2 Chronicles 11:20

How could Maacah be the daughter of Absalom, when his only daughter's name was Tamar (2 Sam. 14:27)?

Here is another example of an error that is actually a non-error. The word *bet*, "daughter," like the word *ben*, "son," is flexible and is often used in the sense of "descendant." Maacah was most likely the granddaughter of Absalom (1 Kings 15:2).

2 Chronicles 13

The account in 1 Kings of Abijah's rule is clearly negative. But here he seems to be treated positively. This is a contradiction.

This chapter gives about three times as much space to Abijah as does 1 Kings. The summary in 1 Kings 15:3 is negative. While there is no similar summary in this chapter, the chronicler reports at least one occasion on which he and Judah "relied on the Lord" (2 Chron. 13:18) and won a decisive victory. But this is no contradiction. The author, intent on displaying God's faithfulness to Israel when Israel relied on him, selects one atypical incident to illustrate that even when the tendency of a ruler's life was toward evil, God came to his aid when he chose to rely on the Lord.

2 Chronicles 16:12

Does this criticism of Asa for using physicians imply that believers should not go to doctors? What is the position of Scripture on the healing arts?

Asa was criticized for relying *only* on the physicians and for failing to "seek help from the Lord." This is not a condemnation of medical aid as such. It is certainly true that in Israel the medical profession did not have the great medical knowledge displayed in Egypt or Mesopotamia. But physicians are mentioned in both Testaments, and several references in the Gospels imply they were common in A.D. first-century Palestine (Matt. 9:12; Luke 4:23). Isaiah 1:6 and Luke 10:34 mention healing balms used to treat wounds, and Isaiah prescribed a poultice of figs for treatment of King Hezekiah's boil (Isa. 38:21). Gall and myrrh were mixed with wine as an anesthetic (Mark 15:23), and Paul told Timothy to use medicinal wine (1 Tim. 5:23). Christians certainly are to rely on God when they are ill. But there is no reason not to expect him to work through medical means. Our healing need not be an obvious miracle to be credited to our loving God.

2 Chronicles 18

How could God use an evil spirit to accomplish his purposes? This has to raise moral difficulties.

This story also appears in 1 Kings 22 and is discussed on page 124.

2 Chronicles 33:13–16

Is this repentance of Manasseh an invention of the chronicler? 2 Kings never mentions such a personal reformation.

The difference between the two accounts is linked to the different purposes of the two authors. The author of 2 Kings is intent on showing the impact of the king's obedience or disobedience to God's law on the history of the nation. Thus he emphasizes the evil acts of Manasseh's reign, which set the nation on its final plunge toward destruction. The author of Chronicles is concerned with displaying God's faithfulness. This is displayed beautifully in Manasseh, who was restored by God after his repentance, despite the unbelievably wicked acts he had performed. No one summarizing any public figure's life in just a few paragraphs could begin to report everything he or she did. Careful selection of what to report is necessary, and such selection will always be guided by the theme the writer seeks to develop.

2 Chronicles 35:21, 22

The text says that God spoke to Josiah through Pharaoh Neco. How could God speak through a pagan, and why would Josiah be expected to recognize God's voice, given the spokesman?

God is not limited in the way he communicates with believers. Angels, prophets, visions, dreams, and yes, even a donkey (Num. 22:30) have spoken for him. We should not be surprised if God speaks to our hearts in peculiar ways, or even through unbelievers. Our task is not so much one of choosing which sources to ignore *a priori*, but instead to remain open to the Lord and ready to do as he directs. Christ's promise reminds us that God's sheep *do* recognize his voice, whatever its source (John 10:14, 16).

Ezra

Ezra

Who wrote this book, and what themes and issues does it deal with?

Ezra was a Bible student and teacher who chronicled the history of the Jews' return to the Promised Land after the Babylonian captivity. His book of history was written about 440 B.C. and includes copies of seven official Persian documents relating to the Jews and the district of Judea.

Ezra 1:2

Did Cyrus the Persian really believe in the Jews' God, as this document seems to imply? Is it more likely Ezra made this up to magnify God's supposed influence in the pagan world?

The decree is undoubtedly authentic. But it does *not* imply that Cyrus had a personal faith in the God of the Jews. When Cyrus the Persian took over the fallen Babylonian empire he reversed their policy of deporting peoples from their homelands. He not only permitted Jews to return but also encouraged other ethnic groups to go back to their homelands. From purely political motives Cyrus credited each deity with making him ruler of the empire and encouraged each group of people to offer sacrifices to its god on his behalf.

Ezra 2

There are two lists of the family groups that returned to Judea, one here (2:3–35) and one in Nehemiah 7:8–63. The lists agree

139

that there were thirty-three families. But there are fourteen dif-
ferences in the lists. Are there?

Several explanations have been suggested for the differences in the listings. Ezra, with access to data in Babylon, may have used an early list of those who signed up to return. Nehemiah expressly identifies those who arrived in Judea in 537 B.C. The differences may be accounted for by deaths and by a change of mind on the part of some of the early volunteers found on Ezra's list.

When numerical values differ (as between Ezra 2:64 and Nehemiah 7:66), we must remember that the transmission of numbers is very difficult. These differences may be due to transcription errors (see Numbers 1, page 70). However, the fact that we do not know the reason for some of the differences in the two lists does not mean that no valid reasons for the discrepancies exists. We must be cautious and not shout error on the basis of differences like these.

Ezra 3:8–13

The chronology of the rebuilding of the temple seems confusing when we compare these verses with 4:24; 5:13–17; and Haggai 1:15. What is the explanation for the different dates given for starting the rebuilding of the temple?

The reason for the difference is that these passages speak of different *phases* of the rebuilding project. Ezra 3:10–11 deals only with laying the temple foundation, approximately 537 or 536 B.C. Local opposition caused the project to be abandoned at that time (4:24). Work was then resumed about 520 or 519 B.C. under the influence of Haggai. The temple was finally completed in 516 B.C. There is no discrepancy in the rebuilding reports at all.

Ezra 4:2

The people living in Palestine when the Jews returned claimed to have been worshiping Yahweh since the time of the Assyrians. Why did the Jews refuse to let them take part in rebuilding the temple?

Ancient peoples tended to see gods and goddesses as owners of particular regions. Thus, when the Assyrians deported the Israelites in 722 B.C. and resettled a number of pagan peoples in Palestine, these peoples simply added the worship of Yahweh while they continued to worship their own gods (2 Kings 17:24–41). There was no exclusive commitment to Yahweh, or recognition of him as the sole deity and creator of the universe. This, combined with the fact that Yahweh's covenant was made only with the descendants of Abraham, Isaac, and Jacob, made interreligious cooperation unthinkable.

Ezra 4:1–23

The material in this chapter is confusing. Where do these documents fit in the history of the return to Jerusalem?

Ezra's organization here is thematic rather than chronological. He stops his story to summarize efforts to hamper the Jews' attempts at rebuilding the temple and the city. Verses 1–5 tell of the days of Cyrus (559–530 B.C.), verse 6 of the reign of Xerxes (480–465 B.C.), verses 7–23 of the reign of Artaxerxes I (465–424 B.C.), and verse 24 of the reign of Darius I (533–486 B.C.).

Ezra 6:1

Why would the Persians search archives in Babylon for records of Cyrus' decree? Archaeology has shown that the Persian capital was Susa.

Actually archaeology has shown that there were four capitals used by Persian rulers: Babylon, Persopolis, Susa, and Ecbatana. Apparently Cyrus was resident in this latter city, which is near the present city of Hamadan in Iran, when his original decree was promulgated. Interestingly, the report in 6:2 that the decree was found "in the citadel of Ecbatana" is the only reference in the Old Testament to this site.

Ezra 6:8

Is it reasonable to suppose that a pagan monarch would actually pay for building a temple for a subject people? Didn't ancient rulers take away rather than give?

Actually, history is replete with illustrations of monarchs endowing temples in various regions of their domains. It was the policy of Persian kings to do this. Secular sources report that Cyrus repaired temples at Uruk and Ur, among others. So once again the argument that something in the Bible is not reasonable by contemporary standards is shown to be totally meaningless by archaeological discoveries.

Ezra 9:6

Why did Ezra refer to "our sins" in his prayer when he personally was totally innocent?

Ezra spoke in the first person to express his identity with the community of faith. Even though he was not personally involved in the sin, Ezra did feel a sense of responsibility for the behavior of his co-religionists. This element is common in similar Old Testament prayers (Neh. 1:6; 9:33; Dan. 9:5–19) and underlines an important principle: God's people are corporately as well as individually responsible for the purity of the faith community. We cannot excuse ourselves by saying, "*I* didn't do it." We must, like Ezra, express our concern to God and accept responsibility to try to correct the evil.

Ezra 10

How could Ezra demand that the guilty Israelites not only divorce their foreign wives but also send away the children born of them? Doesn't the Bible say God hates divorce (Mal. 3:5)? Certainly he cannot think much of abandoning children.

Old Testament law clearly forbids intermarriage between the Jews and pagan peoples (Exod. 34:11–16; Deut. 7:1–5). In this case, unlike that of Ruth, there was no conversion to Yahweh before the marriage (9:1–3). In essence, the original marriages were invalid, and divorce was not simply permitted but also required by the "commands of our God" (Ezra 10:3).

But what about sending away the wives and children? According to custom, when the divorce took place the husbands were required to return any dowry the women brought with them and return them to their parents' house. The divorced wives again became daughters and their children members of the mothers' original families. Let's not suppose these wives and families were simply turned out into the cold. They were not.

Esther

Esther

Who wrote this book, and what issues and themes does it deal with?

No author is identified in this fascinating book. It tells the story of a threat to the Jewish people that was averted by the bravery of a young Jewish woman who had become the queen of the ruler of the Persian Empire. This unusual book does not mention the name of God even once. Yet again and again it shows God at work behind the scenes of history caring for his people.

Esther 2

The Bible calls Xerxes' first wife Vashti and names Esther as his second. But we know her from secular history as Amestris. Is this an error?

Amestris is linked with the first part of Xerxes' reign. As queen mother she influenced her son Artaxerxes during his reign. It seems most likely that Amestris was the Greek name of Vashti. While Esther is not mentioned by the Greek historians who write of Xerxes, not much is said of his later reign, either. The most likely scenario is that after the death of Esther, or after her possible fall from favor, Amestris/Vashti regained her influence.

Esther 2

How could Mordecai enroll Esther in what was essentially a sexual contest to become Xerxes' queen? Does this clash with the high standards of morality in Scripture?

The Bible maintains high standards. It does not guarantee that everyone mentioned in Scripture lives up to them. We might well question not only the morality of the affair but also Mordecai's willingness to see his niece married to a pagan. The point of this story is not to create heroes, however, but rather to demonstrate that God works through and for his people to accomplish his good ends, whether or not his people merit his grace.

Esther 3:9

According to Herodotus the entire annual income of Persia was 15,000 talents. If he is right, Haman offered the king two-thirds of this amount. How could a public official ever afford that much?

On the one hand, the critics are much too willing to accept the precision of secular historians while discounting the accuracy of Scripture. However, even if Herodotus were right, the solution to this money puzzle is relatively easy. Haman intended to get the money by appropriating the property of the Jews he intended to murder. As recently as the 1930s we saw Nazi Germany loot the Jewish people whom they attempted to exterminate.

Esther 6:8

How could wearing royal robes be an appropriate reward for saving the life of Xerxes?

In Old Testament times a king's clothing was symbolic of his power and honor. Appearing in public in royal clothing would indicate the wearer was a person of the highest status.

Esther 9:1–10

How can one justify the brutal killing of the Jews' enemies? Just because someone wants to harm us, do we have a right to harm them?

Old Testament law established the principle that persons who falsely accused another in an attempt to harm him or her must suffer the fate that they intended for their victim. The refusal of the Jews to loot their enemies was intended to make it clear that their revenge was judicial in nature. In this sense the so-called revenge killings were, in fact, completely moral.

Job

Job

Who wrote this book, and what themes and issues does it deal with?

The author of Job is not identified in the text. It is, however, clear from Job's archaic language and its setting that this story took place very early in biblical times. Many believe Job to be the oldest book in the Old Testament. The book explores the familiar and painful question of why God permits the good to suffer, and whether or not personal tragedy is always the consequence of personal sin.

Job

Was Job a historical person, or a fictional character used to explore a basic philosophical issue?

In one sense, it makes little difference to argue whether Job was a real person or a fictional character. However, Job 1:1 uses a phrase commonly used to indicate historical individuals (1 Sam. 1:1; Luke 1:5). Also, Ezekiel 14:14 mentions Job along with Daniel and Noah, who are undoubtedly viewed by Scripture as historical figures. James 5:11 also treats Job as a historical person. On the other hand, there is no compelling reason to view Job as fictional. Even his name, *'Iyyub*, occurs in documents dating from the eighteen hundreds B.C., the era which the setting of the book seems to match best.

Job 2:1–2

Does Satan have access to God in heaven? And who are the sons of God who appeared regularly before the Lord?

145

Other passages in Scripture portray Satan in God's presence as an accuser of believers (Zech. 3:1). What is more significant is that all the sons of God (angels) appeared before the Lord. It is not so significant that Satan had access but that Satan was *required* to report to the Lord.

Whatever powers Satan possesses, he remains subject to God and stands today as an enemy defeated at the cross.

Job 3

How can the divergent views expressed by Job and his three friends all be inspired? They certainly differ on important points.

Inspiration guarantees that the words of Scripture convey what God intended. It does not guarantee that every person quoted is telling the truth. For instance, Satan is reported to have directly contradicted God and said, "You shall not surely die" (Gen. 3:4). This was a lie, even though it is in the Bible. We must use common sense in interpreting Scripture and be aware of context and the function of common literary forms.

Job 19:26

Does this verse really show that Job expected a bodily resurrection?

Just what Job expected is not totally clear. However, it is clear that Job expected to see God personally. This is the meaning of his idiomatic use of "with my own eyes" (19:27). The doctrine of resurrection is taught with total clarity in the New Testament and is hinted at in the Old Testament. The impression that Old Testament saints had of the future is unclear, but it is clear that Job and others were convinced that they would continue to exist as conscious, aware individuals after biological death.

Job 25:4–6

Genesis says that human beings were made in the image and likeness of God. How can this verse say man is "but a maggot—a son of man, who is only a worm"?

First, this verse reports what Bildad said. It is not a divine evaluation of human beings. Second, Bildad is using poetic hyperbole, a recognized literary device, to contrast the vast difference between God above and man below. Poetry, even Bible poetry, must be read *as* poetry and not as history or doctrine.

Job 38–42

Why doesn't God explain the reason he permitted Job's suffering?

In the end Job obtained a glimpse of God and realized that he could only worship and trust God, not question him. This is the lesson this book holds for us. Life must be lived by faith in virtue of who God is. We do not question God. We attest to his wisdom and goodness, and go on in simple faith.

Job 40:15; 41:1

The behemoth and leviathan are known to be mythic monsters feared by pagans. Reference to them here clearly shows that this part of the Bible is rooted in earlier, pagan beliefs.

The *behemoth* and *leviathan* are used metaphorically in this passage. While the pagans did believe such monsters existed, the writer of Job no more believes in their real existence than British romantic poets did in the Greek gods whose names figure prominently in their poetry. Most Bible students take the beasts described in these metaphors to be patterned after the giant hippopotamus and giant crocodile.

Job 42:7

How can God say that Job has "spoken of me what is right," when it was Job who pointed to evidence that God does not always punish the wicked or bless the righteous?

Job's dilemma was that he knew himself to be innocent of any behavior that would merit the terrible disasters he experienced, yet he believed completely in the justice of God. Job's friends shared this commitment and were driven to the conclusion that Job *must* have sinned terribly to merit such calamities. They had no *evidence* of Job's sin but chose to condemn their friend because they could not reconcile what happened to him with their beliefs about God. Job, knowing his innocence, looked with simple honesty at evidence that God does not always behave as his friends assumed he must. They each knew wicked men who prospered. They each knew apparently good persons whose lives were marked by trials and difficulties. Job was driven to *question his assumptions about God without abandoning his faith in God.* It was this that God commended. Ultimately Job realized that God is not someone believers can fit into a pigeonhole but is someone whose motives and purposes are often shrouded in mystery. We should not try to explain God's actions but simply trust God as far greater, wiser, and benign than we can imagine.

Job 42:12–17

Why weren't all of Job's blessings doubled? His flocks and herds were, but he only had twelve more children to replace the twelve he lost.

Every blessing *was* doubled. His first twelve children had died, true. But biblical faith understands that personal existence is not extinguished when the body dies. The twelve children who had died still lived with the Lord, and so the twelve more children Job fathered made his family total twenty-four.

Psalms

Psalms

Who wrote this book, and what themes and issues does it deal with?

The Book of Psalms is a collection of poems used in corporate and private worship. They were written by a number of poets over a span of several hundred years. There are five books of psalms. Each was a fresh collection added to the others from the time of King Solomon to the time of King Josiah.

The Book of Psalms powerfully expresses a full range of human emotions and explores every aspect of the believer's relationship with the Lord. As such these poems serve as a model for the individual believer's prayers and praise, as well as for praise offered by the worshiping community.

Poetry of Psalms

What rules of Hebrew poetry help us interpret the psalms?

Hebrew poetry relies on repetition of ideas rather than on rhyme. Thus the same basic thought is typically stated in an initial phrase and immediately followed by some parallel form of the same thought. While some parallelism is very complex, there are three basic forms of parallelism. Synonymous parallelism repeats the same thought in different words. Antithetical parallelism emphasizes the initial thought by expressing an opposite or contrasting idea. Synthetic parallelism develops the initial thought by adding a series of ideas that build on and expand it.

149

150

Psalm 5:5

How can a God of love "hate all who do wrong?" This is a moral difficulty and stands in direct contrast with Jesus' call to love our enemies (Matt. 5:44).

God's love for sinners is established beyond any doubt in Jesus' death on the cross. At the same time, the cross firmly establishes God's commitment to punish sin. In this psalm and in other similar expressions found in the Old Testament and the New Testament (Mal. 1:2, 3; Rom. 9:13) such statements are to be understood in a judicial sense. Those who believe in God and turn to that which is right stand safe within the circle of God's love. Those who reject God and do evil stand outside that circle in the realm of judgment. God loves (accepts, forgives) the believing sinner; God hates (decisively rejects, is committed to punish) the sinner who *will not* believe or turn to the Lord.

Psalm 10

A number of psalms have an angry, hostile tone. How can believers justify this attitude toward others, even if others have done them wrong?

These psalms are usually called imprecatory psalms because they call on God to pay back the psalmist's enemies for injuries they have done. While this has bothered some Christians, it should not. The psalmist appeals to God as judge to punish those who have done wrong. These are not curses expressing ill wishes against some harmless fellow who insulted the psalmist. These are appeals for justice, addressed to the supreme court of the universe.

The imprecatory psalms, such as 5, 7, 28, 35, 54, 55, 83, and 109, are expressions of faith and restraint. Rather than take personal revenge, the psalmists leave vengeance in the hands of God and ask only that he do justice.

Psalm 14

Who is the fool in this and other psalms, and why is his belief that "there is no God" so terrible? Are all agnostics to be viewed so negatively?

The reason that the fool is so roundly condemned in the Old Testament is that each of the four major Hebrew words translated "fool" focuses attention on *moral* rather than *intellectual* flaws. Fools are rebelliously unwilling to submit to God or to God's law and thus "are corrupt, their deeds are vile; there is no one who does good" (14:1).

Some persons are quite honestly uncertain about the existence of God. It would be wrong to lump them with those who scornfully deny God's existence and who, convinced there is no God to call them to account for their actions, plunge into unrestrained sin.

Psalm 19

What is natural revelation, and what can it tell us about God?
Can a person be saved by believing in God as he reveals himself
in nature?

Theologians make a distinction between natural and special revelation. Natural revelation is God's self-revelation through his creation and includes all that can be deduced about him through what he has made. Special revelation is God's direct self-revelation through dream, word, or action, and involves content that cannot be deduced but must be directly revealed.

Psalm 19 tells us that the created universe declares the glory of God, and that every human being hears the voice of the heavens even though no speech or language is involved. Paul develops this further in Romans 1:20. There he says that God's "eternal power and divine nature have been clearly seen, being understood from what has been made." Thus God *has and does reveal himself to all human beings.*

But Paul goes on. Rather than respond to this revelation and thereby worship God, human beings reject the evidence of creation and, in fact, "suppress the truth by their wickedness" (Rom. 1:18). Rather than being a means of salvation, natural revelation has served to demonstrate humanity's lost condition. If human beings were in right relationship with God, they would recognize and worship him through natural revelation. Because human beings are warped and twisted by sin, they reject the evidence of creation. The ancients invented wild tales of slain goddesses whose corpses became the material universe. Moderns invent wild tales of an evolutionary process by which clouds of matter and energy became stars and planets, and by which tiny single living cells generated from nonliving matter developed into the complex life forms that fill our world today. Ancient or modern, humankind proves unwilling to know God.

Can a person be saved by belief in the God revealed in creation? Yes. If a person responds with faith to *any* self-revelation of God, as Abraham responded to God's promise that he would have a son, the benefits of Christ's death will be applied (Gen. 15:6). But the great truth that drives us to witness to neighbors and send missionaries throughout the world is that it is the message of God's love expressed in Christ that has the power to turn men's hearts to the Lord and move them to accept the forgiveness Jesus bought for us at terrible cost.

Psalm 40:6

Does this verse, and other verses such as Psalm 50:14, show a gradual abandonment of the primitive notion of animal sacrifice?

Sacrifice is not a primitive notion, even though it is a feature of all ancient religions as well as of Old Testament and New Testament faiths. References such as these simply point out that obedience is more important than sacrifice. The reason is simple. Sacrifices were required after disobedience had interrupted the Old Testament believer's fellowship with God. If one obeyed and maintained right relationship with God, guilt offerings and sin offerings were not required.

The reference in this verse to the piercing of the ears is significant. An Israelite who sold himself as a slave to a fellow Israelite was bound for only seven years. But if at the end of that time he wished to remain in *voluntary, lifelong service* to his master, he could elect to do so. To symbolize this commitment, the master used an awl to pierce the servant's earlobe (Exod. 21:6). Here David, and prophetically Christ, commits himself to voluntary, lifelong obedience to God the Father, realizing that *this* is what God desires from every human being.

Psalm 51:5

How can David say he was sinful at birth and "sinful from the time my mother conceived me?" David at birth hadn't yet done anything either sinful or good.

David is simply acknowledging the fact that despite his love for God he is aware of a fundamental flaw in his nature that expresses itself in acts of sin. This flaw has always been present in him, as it is in all other human beings. Thus David, like you and me, *must* rely on God for forgiveness when he fails and for a cleansing that will enable him to do what is right.

While David's confession of his own sinfulness is poetic in nature, it is significant that he traces his flaw back to conception and speaks of himself as a person even while he was in the womb (see also 139:13). Biblically the fetus is a person from conception.

Psalm 73:20

How can God awaken when he never sleeps (Ps. 121:3, 4)?

Here we have a common metaphorical use of language. The call to awaken is a poetic appeal for God to act in the psalmist's behalf. The affirmation that God neither slumbers nor sleeps is a poetic expression of a basic reality: God is everywhere present, constantly aware, and always available to the believer.

It is important to keep two things in mind when reading the Old Testament. First, Hebrew is a language that relies heavily on imagery and metaphor. Second, we must always keep the literary form in mind when interpreting any portion of Scripture. It is foolishness to attempt to apply rules for interpreting didactic (teaching) material to the interpretation of poetry. This would never be done in secular literature and should never be done in the Bible's poetic portions. If we take these and other images found in the Old Testament as the poetic metaphors they are, many of the superficial discrepancies pointed out by some critics disappear.

Psalm 104

Does the Bible support the animal rights movement? What does the Bible have to say about animals?

Psalm 104 makes it clear that God provides, through nature, for animal as well as human life. Man's original grant of dominion over creation (Gen. 1:26) is not a license to exploit the earth or its living inhabitants, but rather implies an obligation to serve as God's agents in caring for all his handiwork. At the same time, the creation story makes a clear distinction between animal and human life, granting to humans alone participation in the image and likeness of God. Thus the insistence of some extreme animal rights activists that animals be granted the same rights as human beings and that eating meat is essentially cannibalism has no support in Scripture at all.

What *is* the basic difference between human beings and animals? The key is expressed in Psalm 73:22 and 2 Peter 2:12, which characterize beasts as creatures of instinct. What sets human beings apart is the capacity to evaluate our instincts on the basis of moral and spiritual awareness, and to choose whether or not to follow our instincts. Animals can be trained, but a moral and spiritual awareness which gives us the capacity to evaluate our actions belongs to humankind alone.

Psalm 120–134
What are the psalms of ascent and how were they used?

This remains a subject of debate. Some believe these psalms were sung by worshipers on their way up mountain roads to the summit where the temple stood in Jerusalem. Others believe they were sung by Levites standing during the festival times and that the ascent refers to the steps up to the temple compound on which the singers stood.

Psalm 137:8, 9
How can anyone possibly think a book that celebrates dashing infants against rocks is a "good book" or the Word of God?

It is certainly true that such words would be inappropriate on the lips of any Christian. At the same time, it is important to understand the context in which this cry for judgment was uttered. Psalm 137, found in the fifth book (collection) of the psalms, dates from the time of the Babylonian captivity. This psalm expresses the anguish of a person who has seen the Babylonian armies rape, murder, and pillage the people of Jerusalem and Judah. The utter brutality of the Babylonians as they callously dashed the life from Jewish infants is imprinted on the memory of the horrified author of this psalm. So the psalmist cries out to God to do justice, to visit on the Babylonians the atrocities they perpetrated on others. As they treated others, the psalmist says, they deserve to be treated themselves.

Today, in our age of grace, we realize that God often withholds judgment to give sinners the opportunity to repent and find forgiveness (Rom. 2:4). But let us never forget that ultimately justice does demand punishment for sin. When Christ returns, "[God] will pay back trouble to those who trouble you . . . [Christ] will punish those who do not know God" as they deserve (2 Thess. 1:6–9).

Proverbs

Proverbs

Who wrote this book, and what themes and issues does it deal with?

The proverbs found in this book were contributed by a number of authors, but the majority are attributed to Solomon. Proverbs is characterized as wisdom literature. Like other ancient wisdom literature, Proverbs is concerned with living a good and prudent life in this world. Its pithy sayings distill the insights of godly people into such diverse matters as wealth, poverty, child rearing, friendship, adultery, laziness, pride, wicked people, women, work, etc. The book is not organized by these topics, but these are recurring themes. Brief thoughts on these and other matters are scattered throughout the book.

Proverbs

What principles should guide our interpretation of Proverbs? Are these God's words to us, or simply man's notions about what is wise and good?

The proverbs generally are in poetic form, relying on the parallelism that is typical of Hebrew poetry to make their points. Therefore, before trying to interpret these proverbs a person should know something about this characteristic of Hebrew verse (see comments on Psalms, page 149).

Another important characteristic of Proverbs is that the sayings found here are both *universal* and *general* in character. They are universal in that the truths expressed here apply to all human beings and societies,

155

not simply to those who belong to the community of Old Testament or New Testament faith. They are general in that the truths the proverbs express are *usually*, but not always, true. For instance, Proverbs 16:7 says, "When a man's ways are pleasing to the LORD, he makes even his enemies live at peace with him." This is *not* a promise for believers to claim but it *is* a general principle that is *usually* true.

As long as we remember these characteristics of Proverbs, we can profit greatly from the insights they provide, and we will avoid misunderstanding and misapplying their words of wisdom.

Proverbs 1:7

How can "fear of the Lord" be the "beginning of knowledge"? Doesn't the New Testament teach that "perfect love drives out fear" (1 John 4:18)?

Fear in the Old Testament is frequently used with the sense of reverential awe rather than terror. Certainly God's love and our love for him free us from anxiety in our relationship with the Lord. A reverential awe of God that takes his existence and his presence seriously frees us from the temptation to sin.

Proverbs 17:5

Is there a basic conflict in Proverbs' teachings on poverty and the poor? Some verses seem to blame the poor for laziness (10:4; 20:13; 21:17), while others seem to indicate poverty is caused by social injustice, as does this verse and Proverbs 13:23.

It is clear that poverty is a complex rather than a simple phenomenon. While some slide into poverty because of laziness or a profligate lifestyle, others are oppressed by social structures that favor the wealthy at the expense of the poor. The Old Testament's position is that a society is responsible to establish a mechanism that makes it possible for anyone willing to work to escape poverty. For an extended discussion, see "Poor and Oppressed" in The *Expository Dictionary of Bible Words* [Zondervan].

Proverbs 22:6

Is it always a parent's fault if a child does not do well? Is that what this verse suggests?

We need to remember that the Book of Proverbs is both universal and general in its stance. It makes statements that are generally true but not always so. This verse points out that a parent who guides a child appropriately at each stage of his or her development sets him on a course he or she will likely follow for life. This is *not* a guarantee that if parents do their job correctly a child will always turn out right. The Bible makes it clear, by example and in teaching, that each human being is a *responsible* individual. That is, no person's life is *predetermined* by heredity or environment; each person's choices of good or evil are freely and responsibly made. Parents and others in the community can influence someone's choices, but nothing they do can program that person or rob him or her of free will.

For example, Ezekiel looks back in history and models his teaching in chapter 18 on three kings of Judah: Hezekiah—a good king and godly man—and Hezekiah's wicked father and even more wicked son. Why didn't the father tilt the direction of Hezekiah's life toward evil? Because Hezekiah was free to choose good and did so. Why didn't Hezekiah tilt the direction of his son Manasseh's life toward good? Because Manasseh was free to choose evil and did so.

Don't misunderstand the implications of Proverbs 22:6. Godly parents do all they can to influence their children for good and recognize that by God's grace generally their influence will be strong. But godly parents also realize that their children have both the freedom and responsibility to make their own moral choices. So while they rejoice in the good choices children make, they do not take credit. And if the children should make wrong choices, the parents hurt for them but realize that the guilt is theirs.

Proverbs 31:10–31

Isn't it true that the Bible is a male-dominated, chauvinist book? This passage certainly seems to teach that a woman's place is in the home.

It's true that the Bible emerged in a society that was patriarchal in structure and that many laws and customs reflect that society. But it is *not* true that the Bible is a chauvinistic document, that it says wives are to be dominated by husbands, or that a woman's place is so limited to the home that she has no right to participate in the professions of the male-dominated workplace.

This passage, sometimes used to support the "women-at-home" position, actually implies just the opposite. We must remember that Old Testament society was agrarian, with wealth measured in land and its products. The job of men was tilling the soil, using its commodities to make products to buy and sell, supervising workers, etc. What is significant about the noble wife of this passage is that *she is engaged in exactly the same kinds of endeavors as her husband.* The *Expository Dictionary of Bible Words* says:

> She supervised a staff of workers (v. 27). She served as buyer for her enterprises (v. 13). She sold what her staff produced (vv. 18, 24), and she invested her profits (v. 16). She had the freedom to give help to the needy (v. 20). She was respected for her wisdom and her responsibility (vv. 14–15; 26–31). This picture is striking, for it shows the woman of Old Testament times engaged in the functions of what today we call the business world. The Old Testament woman's activities were linked closely with her home and family, but she was not at all cast in what some think of when they suggest that women should "keep house and take care of the children." Women were viewed with greater respect in biblical times than that.

The Bible makes it clear that women are viewed as persons with a full complement of those capacities that all human beings share as persons made in the image of God.

Ecclesiastes

Ecclesiastes

Who wrote this book, and what themes and issues does it deal with?

Tradition and Ecclesiastes 1:1 suggest that the author of this book was Solomon, "son of David, king in Jerusalem."

Ecclesiastes dates from the end of Solomon's life, after his foreign wives turned his heart away from God toward their pagan deities. Having lost his spiritual moorings, Solomon suddenly felt that life had no meaning. He set out to search for its meaning. In this search he limited himself to human reason (1:12) and gathered his evidence only from the material universe (1:13, "under heaven").

The first part of this book serves as a report of this wise Old Testament ruler's exploration of those things in which most people seek meaning. His conclusion: "Everything is meaningless" (1:2). The second half of Ecclesiastes probes a second question: Since everything is meaningless, which of the choices that we have in this life are better? While Solomon concludes that some choices are to be preferred, he remains convinced that satisfying conclusions about the meaning of life simply are not available to human beings.

Ecclesiastes

Ecclesiastes is such a pessimistic book! And Solomon's dreary conclusions seem so out of harmony with many upbeat passages in the Bible. Are we forced to conclude that this so-called inspired book conflicts directly with other books that believers claim also are inspired?

159

It is important to remember that *inspired* does not mean that everything recorded is true. It is certainly not true, for instance, that life is meaningless. The inspiration of Scripture guarantees the accuracy of its account. Ecclesiastes is an accurate record of the thoughts of history's wisest person as he examined the possibility that life in this world might have meaning in and of itself. Solomon's conclusions, recorded here, remind us that unless God exists, and unless we truly are destined for eternity, life on earth *is* meaningless. The optimistic and positive outlook of the rest of Scripture is rooted in the meaning that believers find in the existence and the love of God.

Given the fact that he chose to use reason only in his search, and that he limited himself to a man's brief experience in this material universe, Solomon was right. Inspiration guarantees the accuracy of Solomon's report of his process and conclusions, not that his conclusions reflect the reality we know through Scripture's fuller revelation of God and his good purposes for humankind.

Ecclesiastes 3:19

How can the Bible say that man's fate is like the animals'? Doesn't the Bible teach that human beings exist as self-conscious individuals after biological death?

This and other sayings such as, "Eat and drink, and find satisfaction" (3:13) must be understood in the context of the book's clearly stated methodology and presuppositions. Solomon limited himself to the evidence of his senses. From all that a person can see there is no difference between a dead person and a dead cow. Biologically both have suffered the same fate. It is only when we accept the evidence of revelation that we can say with confidence that there *is* a difference between the fate of man and the fate of animals.

There are a number of other similar conclusions which, despite their inclusion in Solomon's report, are *not* true. They are Solomon's conclusions, accurately reported. But they are not a divine revelation of reality given through Solomon.

Song of Songs

Song of Songs

Who wrote this book, and what themes and issues does it deal with?

Seven references to Solomon and frequent references to the "king" have led to the traditional view that Solomon wrote this book. While both Jewish and Christian commentators have viewed this poem as a metaphor of the relationship between God and his people, the Song of Songs is best understood as a celebration of the love experienced by a man and woman—the lover and the beloved. Some people have expressed shock that a "mere love song" should be included in Scripture. But the Song of Songs is actually a beautiful confirmation of the gift God has given to human beings. This gift is the capacity to love and be loved in marriage.

The Song's Poetry

How does the Song of Songs compare with other ancient love poetry?

Many examples of the love poetry of the ancient Middle East have been recovered by archaeologists. This poetry is filled with gross and explicit sexual references, very different from the delicate, passionate images conveyed in the Song of Songs. Throughout the Bible sex is dealt with honestly and openly, yet with a unique modesty. Other cultures, like our own society today, cheapen sex by stripping the act of its mystery, and treat it in literature and other media as no more than an animal urge.

Isaiah

Isaiah

Who wrote this book, and what themes and issues does it deal with?

This magnificent book of prophecy was written by Isaiah the son of Imlah. Isaiah lived in Judah, the southern Hebrew kingdom, during the critical decades of the Assyrian invasion. The prophet saw the northern Hebrew kingdom, Israel, crushed and its people taken into captivity in 722 B.C. He lived through a period of the denuding of much of his land when the Assyrians returned in 701 B.C. At that time God turned the enemy army back to its own land before Jerusalem could be captured. Tradition tells us that Isaiah died a martyr under Manasseh, the wicked son of godly King Hezekiah.

Isaiah's writings reflect both the early and late decades of his ministry. The first thirty-five chapters of this prophecy are filled with warnings and calls to repent. A historical interlude provides a narrative account of how God turned away the Assyrians in response to Hezekiah's prayers. Chapters 40–66 then look ahead and offer comfort to a people who have escaped the Assyrians but will not escape deportation by the Babylonians a hundred years later. These later chapters reflect conditions after the Assyrian captivity and even refer by name to the Persian ruler, Cyrus, who would order the return of the Jews to their homeland in 537 B.C. (44:28; 45:1). Seeing this, and noting a shift in vocabulary between the first and last sections of the book, many scholars have argued that there must have been two or even three authors of the Book of Isaiah.

If we accept a fact asserted frequently in Isaiah, that God knows and reveals the future (46:8–10), the naming of Cyrus is hardly proof that

162

the book must have been written *after* Cyrus appeared in history. The argument for two authors, based on subtle differences in vocabulary and literary style, is also weak. It can easily be explained by the simple fact that Isaiah has two different themes to develop in the two sections: first, a theme of darkness and judgment; second, a theme of hope and restoration. This, plus changes we might expect in anyone's style over a forty-year period, are as acceptable explanations for literary differences in the text of Isaiah as any two-author theory. It is important to note that the two-author theory fails to explain the substantial literary *unity* of the book. This unity is far more pronounced than any differences.

One of the themes that unifies this powerful book is that of Messianic prophecy. Because of Isaiah's focus on the coming deliverer and his powerful portrait in chapter 53 of the Messiah as a suffering Savior, Isaiah has rightly been characterized as the evangelist of the Old Testament. His writings are considered by some as gospel—the good news of what God intends to do for his people in and through the coming Christ.

Isaiah as Prophecy

Are there special rules for or difficulties in interpreting prophecy? What makes some sections of prophetic books so difficult to understand?

Isaiah is classified as a prophetic book, as are all the Old Testament books that follow Isaiah in the Bible. The prophets were special individuals chosen to speak God's word to their own generations. Some of them recorded the divine message in written form for the benefit of future generations as well as their contemporaries.

In general Christians think of the prophetic books as books whose content is primarily information about the future. While many predictions about events close at hand and events distant to the prophets' times are found in these books, we need to remember that the prophets' ministries were *primarily* to the people of their own times. The prophets thus spoke out against corruption in worship (as Isa. 1:11–15), and reminded God's people that he yearned for their love.

The prophets ruthlessly exposed personal sins and social injustice (Isa. 1:16, 17), and warned of divine judgment to come if sin were not abandoned (Isa. 22:6–16). Yet the prophets also reassured God's people that he would restore them when they returned to him (Isa. 54:7).

Frequently these themes are interwoven in prophetic visions of future events: invasion and judgment at the hands of a foreign country, the appearance of the Messiah, etc. The prophets constantly reflect the conviction that the future as well as the present is in God's hands, and that history is moving in a direction set by God. Since God controls the future, his prophets can describe future events with great certainty, and his people can look forward confidently to the fulfillment of the prophets' words.

But there are difficulties in understanding much of the future that the prophets describe. Prophecy tends to describe a coming event without putting that event in context. That is, the prophets do not say *when* a future event will take place and do not give details about *how* a particular event described fits in with other future events. It is as if someone in England in the year 1600 predicted a great civil war on a distant continent without saying it would take place 250 years later, without noting that before it happened the American continent would be settled, the American revolution would take place, and slavery would divide the emergent states. The prophecy would be accurate enough; but without a time frame and without some sense of historical context, an interpreter would have been hard pressed to explain just what it all meant.

Given this basic difficulty, it is still possible to develop guidelines that will help us understand prophecy. There are the generally accepted guidelines: (1) Determine whether the passage is about the prophet's own time or is predictive and concerns the future. (2) Determine whether a prediction is conditional or unconditional. Some prophecies are of the *if-then* type: "If you do such and such, then God will do such and such." Others are simple announcements of what God intends to do no matter what his people do. (3) Determine whether or not the prophecy has been fulfilled. For instance, the predictions concerning Jesus' death contained in Isaiah 53 have been fulfilled. What was future to Isaiah is past to us. (4) Determine whether the prediction has multiple fulfillment. This is a complicating factor in understanding prophecy. A prediction of a future event may, in fact, relate to *more than one* future event. For instance, warning of a foreign invasion may refer to an invasion that took place twenty years after the prophet spoke and yet also refer to a massive foreign invasion to take place at history's end that is *foreshadowed* by the first invasion. Or a judgment announced on the king of Tyre in Ezekiel 28 may suddenly shift and focus on the nature and fate of Satan.

Keep in mind that it is not easy to understand prophecy. The detailed charts concerning the future that some commentators and preachers sometimes try to fit prophetic teachings should be viewed with a certain amount of skepticism. Yes, every prophecy of Scripture that has been fulfilled has been fulfilled literally. Those events future to the prophet actually happened in space and time. And yes, we can expect the yet unfulfilled predictions of Scripture, such as the promise of a literal, physical return of Jesus, to certainly take place. But what we cannot know is the time, and what we cannot be certain about is just how the various events that still lie in the future will fit together as history unfolds.

And so we should read prophecy as the prophets intended. It is a message to us from God about future events that will help us put our present life in perspective. It is not intended to drive us to chalkboards to draw detailed charts. As Peter wrote after reminding us that this present world is destined to be destroyed by fire, "Since everything will be destroyed in this way, what kind of people ought you to be? You ought to live holy and godly lives as you look forward to the day of God and speed its coming" (2 Peter 3:11, 12). The Bible's words about tomorrow are written to remind us that our today is but a moment in time and to remind us to shape the values we live by in our present in view of eternity's endless extent.

Isaiah 2:10–21

What is that day mentioned in these verses? Is it the same as the day of the Lord mentioned elsewhere?

Yes. These theologically significant phrases are found frequently in the books of the prophets. They most often identify the events described as taking place at history's end (Isa. 7:18–25). However, "they always identify a period of time during which God personally intervenes in history, directly or indirectly, to accomplish some specific aspect of his plan" (*Expository Dictionary of Bible Words*, p. 211).

If we read all references to the "day of the Lord" or "that day" in the Old Testament, the dominant picture is of a period of terrible divine judgment poured out on unbelieving Israel (Isa. 22; Jer. 30; Joel 1, 2) and the unbelieving nations of the world (Ezek. 38, 39; Zech. 9). But while judgment is predominant, it is clear that the darkness of that day gives way at evening time to blessing, as a converted remnant of God's people is rescued and restored to the Promised Land (Jer. 30:19–31:40; Micah 4; Zech. 13).

Isaiah 4:2

Who is "the Branch of the LORD" spoken of in this passage?

Six Old Testament passages speak of the Messiah as the Branch (Isa. 11:1; Jer. 23:5; 33:15; Zech. 3:8; 6:12). The imagery is that of a sprout or descendant from David's line who comes to deliver God's people and to fulfill God's purposes in the world.

Isaiah 7:14

Did Isaiah really predict a virgin birth, or does the Hebrew word simply mean "an unmarried woman"?

The Hebrew word *'almah* is used in Genesis 24:43 and Proverbs 30:19 of an unmarried woman. However, Matthew 1:23, quoting Isaiah, uses the Greek word *parthenos*, which has the distinct meaning of *virgin*. This fact, along with the name given the child (*Immanuel* means "with us is God"), makes it clear that either Isaiah is referring directly to Mary in his mention of the virgin or that the woman he *does* refer to foreshadows Mary and the virgin birth of Jesus.

Isaiah 7:13–16

Who are all the people referred to in this famous prophecy? It doesn't seem to make any sense at all.

These verses are complicated, but they can be understood. At the time Isaiah wrote this, King Ahaz was under pressure from Syria and Israel to join a coalition formed to resist Assyria. Ahaz refused and was threatened with invasion by the two nearby kings. Isaiah was sent to tell Ahaz not to fear and to ask for a sign that God was speaking through his prophet. When Ahaz refused to ask for the sign, Isaiah announced God would give an authenticating sign *anyway*. Referring either to his son Shear-Jashub, then an infant in arms (7:3), or, as some believe, to a child who would be born to Isaiah's second wife-to-be (7:14), the prophet announced that the neighbors Ahaz feared would be crushed by Assyria "before the boy knows enough to reject the wrong and choose the right" (7:16).

This refers to a child's coming of age and becoming personally responsible to keep the law, the *bar mitzvah* age of twelve or thirteen. Thus, within a decade or so the neighbors Ahaz feared would be gone; but when the child reached twelve or thirteen he would "eat curds and honey" (7:22). There would be no agricultural products to eat, for the Assyrians would devastate Judah and destroy her crops.

All this came to pass. The fulfillment of this prediction served to authenticate the long-range prophecy embedded in the text: At some time in the future a virgin *would* have a child who would actually be

God with us in human form. Seven hundred years after Isaiah wrote this, an angel appeared to Mary and told her the time had come. Mary the virgin became pregnant, and the child she bore was Jesus the Messiah, God the Son, truly one with us in an incarnation foreshadowed and foretold by the prophet of old.

Isaiah 9:6
What are the meanings of the various names given to the person spoken of here?

While Hebrew poetry uses synonymous repetition, a significant distinction is drawn in this verse. The Messiah is a *child born* (referring to his human nature) but also a *son given* (referring to his deity). The titles that follow in verse 6 emphasize his deity. Everlasting Father is perhaps best understood as "Father (source) of Eternity." This title like the title Mighty God could never be ascribed to a mere human being. Verse 7 describes his destiny as the promised Messiah, Israel's future king. It is clear from this as well as other passages that the Old Testament does teach the amazing fact that God would enter the world he created as a human being. This incarnation is accomplished not only to keep God's ancient promises to Israel but also to enable him to suffer and die so that all who believe in him can be saved.

Isaiah 10:5–7
How could God permit a pagan army to devastate his people? And if he did, it certainly isn't fair to then punish the Assyrians for doing what he intended!.

The Old Testament portrays God as using war and natural disasters as instruments of judgment on sin. Isaiah makes it clear that the Lord *is* using this foreign army as the "rod of my [God's] anger" (10:5) to discipline his people. This is, in fact, a message of hope. It reminds the people of Judah that God remains in control of history, and there he continues to function as moral ruler of the universe.

The text itself explains Isaiah's announcement that God will judge the Assyrians. God's intention was to punish his people. The Assyrians' intention was to destroy them. God's use of the Assyrians was judicial and justified. The Assyrians' invasion of Judah was motivated by greed and a passion for glory and was not justified.

Isaiah 10:20

What is the remnant (often translated survivors in the NIV) that Isaiah and the other prophets speak of so frequently?

This significant term is typically used in a technical way in the Old Testament. The word itself, *sa'ar*, and its cognates, means to remain or survive and implies some catastrophic judgment that eliminates most of a group. In prophetic passages it is typically used of those who remain after a divine judgment. It also implies their conversion and restoration to fellowship with the Lord. The concept makes an important theological point, for it reminds us that mere physical descent from Abraham, Isaac, and Jacob did not save Israel, nor did mere ritual observance of the law. Only those in Israel who exercised personal faith in the Lord were members of the true Israel of God (Rom. 9:6; 11:1–6).

Time and time again terrible judgments purged ancient Israel of unbelief. And time and time again God gave his people a fresh start, building for the future on the remnant that was left after he had been forced to devastate the land.

Isaiah 14:12

Is the son of the dawn in this verse Satan, or is he the king of Babylon?

Son of the dawn in the NIV replaces *Lucifer* in older English versions. This verse as it is translated in the Septuagint (the Greek version of the Old Testament produced a century or so before Christ) is paraphrased by Jesus (Luke 10:18) in a way that obviously refers to Satan. This has led many commentators to see Satan as the subject of the original text. It is most likely, however, that the law of double reference, so important in understanding prophetic passages, applies here. Isaiah is describing the fall of Babylon personified in its kings. And yet the description also refers to Satan, whose attitudes and motives are mirrored in his autocratic human counterparts.

Isaiah 28:13

What does it mean for the Word of God to become "do and do"?

Various explanations have been suggested. In Hebrew the text of verses 10 and 13 read *tsaw tsaw, tsaw tsaw, qaw qaw, qaw qaw.* Thus, some people conclude the phrases are intended to represent drunken muttering and to imply that the Word of God has become nonsense to his people, the reason they will "fall backward, be injured and snared and captured" (v. 13). Others emphasize the words *so that* of verse 13 and assume that Israel has *substituted* words that are no better than drunken muttering for God's Word and thus is doomed. A third possibility is that the repeated "Do and do, do and do, rule on rule, rule on rule" (vv. 10, 13) represent a basic *misunderstanding* of God's Word. Treating Scripture as no more than a set of rules, God's people miss the message of grace, love, mercy, and faithfulness that is the essential context of God's law and of a personal relationship with the Lord.

Isaiah 41:8

How can Christians say that the servant in this verse is Christ, when it clearly says, "Israel, my servant"?

There are a number of "servant" passages in Isaiah. At times they do refer to the people of Israel (41:8–10; 42:18–19; 43:9–10; 44:1–3; 45:4; 48:20). But these references to Israel emphasize the fact that, although chosen by the Lord and strengthened by him, Israel has failed to fulfill God's purposes for her. Therefore, Isaiah introduces another servant. This servant, as the Messiah, *will* accomplish God's will. The four passages in Isaiah that speak of the Messiah as the servant of the Lord are 42:1–9; 49:1–7; 50:4–10; and 52:13–53:12. Together they describe Christ's serving attitude, his commitment to justice and to the mission set for him by God, and—most stunning—his suffering and death for the sins of God's people.

Isaiah 44:28; 45:1

The specific identification of Cyrus as the ruler who returns the Jews to their homeland proves that this part of the book must have been written after 539 B.C. It could not have been written by Isaiah, who died around 680 B.C.

This question assumes that God could not have revealed the future to Isaiah. Yet the Old Testament itself makes clear claim to God's practice of doing just this: revealing the future to and through his prophets (41:23; 45:21; 46:9–10; 48:3, 5). The difficulty is not with the Bible but with the critics who assume either that God does not know the future or cannot reveal it.

What evidence is there that predictive prophecy in Scripture accurately foretells the future? The following is a partial list of fulfilled Old Testament prophecy concerning Jesus Christ. Every one of these predictions was made hundreds of years before Jesus' birth, yet each was fulfilled literally and in specific detail.

Prophecy	Prediction	Fulfillment
To be the Son of God	Psalm 2:7	Matthew 3:17
To be a descendant of David	Jeremiah 23:5	Luke 3:23, 31
To be born in Bethlehem	Micah 5:2	Matthew 2:1
To be "from ancient times"	Micah 5:2	Colossians 1:17
To be called Lord	Psalm 110:1	Luke 2:11
To be "God with us"	Isaiah 7:14	Matthew 1:23
To perform healing miracles	Isaiah 35:5–6	Matthew 9:35
To be betrayed by a friend	Psalm 41:9	Matthew 10:4
To be sold for thirty coins	Zechariah 11:12	Matthew 26:15
The betrayal money to be thrown in God's house, then used for a potter's field	Zechariah 11:13	Matthew 27:5, 7
To be crucified	Isaiah 53	Matthew 27
To have hands and feet pierced	Psalm 22:16	Luke 23:33
To be crucified with thieves	Isaiah 53:12	Matthew 27:38
To have his clothes divided by lot	Psalm 22:18	John 19:23–24
To be forsaken by God	Psalm 22:1	Matthew 27:46
To be preserved from broken bones	Psalm 34:20	John 19:33
To be pierced	Zechariah 12:10	John 19:34
To be buried in a rich man's tomb	Isaiah 53:9	Matthew 27:57–60

These are just a few of the estimated three hundred prophecies about Jesus as Messiah that are found in the Old Testament. When compared with the fulfillment of these prophecies recorded in the New Testament, it becomes absolutely clear that the Bible does contain accurate predictive prophecy. And the argument that references to Cyrus *must* have been penned long after Isaiah died is shown to be an empty, meaningless complaint.

Isaiah 45:7

The purported statement by God that "I bring prosperity" may be in harmony with the notion that God is good. But surely the claim "I create disaster" cannot be harmonized with the idea of a good God.

This verse is often referred to so as to imply that God is the author of evil. The reason is that in the original, *ra'* is used both of evil and the consequences of evil, of a wrong act and of its repercussions.

Passages that assert that God "does no wrong" (Deut. 32:4) and that his eyes "are too pure to look on evil" (Hab. 1:13) make it clear that God does not do evil in the sense of doing wrong. At the same time it is clear that God *does* see to it that wicked acts receive the consequences they merit. Thus, God *does* create disaster in the same sense that a judge who sentences convicted criminals creates personal disasters for the guilty.

Isaiah 49:6

How can a God who loves all peoples adopt just one race as his chosen people? Does the Old Testament's claim that only the Jews are God's people make God out to be mean and narrow?

Not at all. Isaiah 49:6 makes it clear that God has always intended to make salvation available to everyone. This verse says of the Messiah, "I will also make you a light for the Gentiles, that you may bring my salvation to the ends of the earth."

It is important to put this question in the broadest possible context. Genesis chapters 1–11 relates God's dealing with the whole human race through general revelation and tradition. Because of the failure of humankind to know or submit to him, God chose one man, Abraham, and his descendants, the Jews, to be channels not only of his special revelation but also to be the womb within which a Savior for all humanity might be formed. God originally said to Abraham, "All peoples on earth will be blessed through you" (Gen. 12:3).

The Old Testament contains many instances where God's care extends to Gentiles as well as Jews. Among blessed Gentiles of the Old Testament are Rahab the harlot (Josh. 2), Ruth, Naaman (2 Kings 5), and the entire population of Nineveh (Jonah 4).

Isaiah 58:3–6

Is there any spiritual value in fasting?

Only one fast was commanded in the Old Testament. It was to take place on the Day of Atonement (Lev. 16:29). However, the Bible mentions a number of fasts associated with the threat of war (Judg. 20:26; 2 Chron. 20:3), with sickness (Ps. 35:13), and with mourning (1 Sam. 31:13; 1 Chron. 10:12). The New Testament often links fasting and prayer (Luke 2:37; Acts 10:30; 13:2 KJV). Even so, there are no instructions *to* fast other than the command "You must deny yourselves" on the Day of Atonement (Lev. 16:31).

While there is no reason *not* to fast if a person wishes or feels led to do so, Zechariah 7:9–10 reminds us that God is most concerned with justice, mercy, and compassion.

Jeremiah

Jeremiah

Who wrote this book, and what themes and issues does it deal with?

The book contains a number of prophetic sermons given by Jeremiah and later dictated to his secretary, Baruch (Jer. 45). Jeremiah lived during the last decades of the kingdom of Judah, through the reigns of Josiah, Jehoiakim, and Zedekiah. His messages are not reported in chronological order but are frequently dated by the name of the king in whose reign they were given.

Jeremiah's mission was to warn Judah of its impending doom and urge his countrymen to surrender to the Babylonians rather than to be destroyed in futile resistance. Jeremiah's words were deeply resented by Judah's rulers and her people, and the prophet was charged with various crimes, from undermining morale to treason.

Despite the dark tone of Jeremiah's ministry, the book also contains one of the Old Testament's brightest promises. Nested among the warnings of destruction is the good news that God intended to make a New Covenant with the people of Israel. It will replace the Mosaic covenant, whose laws were written in stone, with a law written on the heart. Both forgiveness and empowerment will flow, and God's cleansed people will at last live righteous lives and enjoy the full blessing of the Lord.

Jeremiah 1:2; 2:5

How did the word of the Lord come to Jeremiah and the other Old Testament prophets? Did they hear voices?

173

Such phrases as "the word of the Lord" and "God says" make it very clear that the Old Testament prophets were conscious of the fact that they were delivering God's word and not simply expressing personal opinions. The book of Hebrews notes that God spoke "at many times and in various ways" (Heb. 1:1). These ways may well have included an audible voice. They also involved such means as dreams, visions, and angelic visitors.

The avenue through which revelation came to the prophets and other writers of the Scripture is not the issue. The Bible says that these human authors were not the *origin* of their messages but that they "spoke from God as they were carried along by the Holy Spirit" (2 Peter 1:21). It is the written words of the Scripture that are inspired, that is, guaranteed to convey the message God intended. We can trust the Bible not because we are able to identify how God spoke *to* the prophets but because we know God spoke *through* the prophets (see Isaiah 44:28, page 169).

Jeremiah 2:13

What is "living water"? And what is so terrible about digging cisterns?

The expression *living water* means "*flowing* waters." Here the source of the flowing water is identified as a spring, a perpetual flow, bubbling up from within the earth. Such a spring not only provided man and beast with water but also was used to irrigate fields and grow crops. In contrast, those living in hilly, arid areas of Palestine survived only by digging household cisterns, usually in a series of three, to collect water for the family during fall and spring rains. If the sides of the cisterns cracked, the water disappeared into the earth, and the family had to desert its lands or die. The metaphor is therefore powerful: God is a spring, a source of ever-flowing waters. Idolatry is a series of cracked cisterns. The symbolism of living waters is carried over into the New Testament where Jesus, speaking of the Holy Spirit, promises all who believe in him a constant source of living water flowing from within (John 7:38).

Jeremiah 7:22–23

Does this statement that God never said anything about sacrifice in the Mosaic era prove that Leviticus was written after the seventh century B.C., when Jeremiah lived?

Not at all. The text says, "For *when I brought your forefathers out of Egypt and spoke to them*, I did not just give them commands about burnt offerings and sacrifices, but I gave them this command: Obey me." Jeremiah is referring to a specific incident recorded in Exodus, when God thundered from Mount Sinai. At that time God charged Israel to obey him (Exod. 19:5), and the people agreed to do so (19:8). The laws concerning sacrifice came later and were given to Israel by Moses after he met with God on the mountain for forty days. So Jeremiah's point is clear: The first issue in one's relationship with God is commitment to love and obey the Lord. Everything flows from that; without it nothing else counts. The worship of Judah in Jeremiah's time is meaningless, because it is ritual without relationship, duty without devotion, sacrifice without sincerity.

Jeremiah 7:31

What is Topheth and why does its existence near Jerusalem call for judgment?

A Topheth was a park or area where pagans practiced child sacrifice. Excavations near ancient Carthage have uncovered thousands of tiny burned bodies, most of children between birth and four years of age. The fact that such a district could exist in Judah reveals how terribly corrupt the people had become.

The horror of Topheth is underlined by a striking contrast. At times ancient peoples sacrificed their children in times of desperate danger (2 Kings 3:26, 27). But the children burned alive at a Topheth were sacrificed in the parents' hopes of obtaining some favor from a god or goddess—more wealth, recovery from an illness, etc. A child's life was traded away for some desired personal advantage. Today's Topheths are not parks, but clinics, and the bodies of the innocents are not buried, but ground up and washed away. In the abortion clinics of America lives are traded just as callously as in the ancient Topheths. There is little difference between the motives of the people Jeremiah condemns and those of moderns who don't want careers or vacations interrupted, who hope to avoid the consequences of their choices, or who simply find a child inconvenient. Our modern Topheths cry out as loudly for judgment as any grassy park near ancient Jerusalem. Nor can clean, comfortable offices disguise the reality of abortion any more than meadows could mask the horror of burning infants alive.

Jeremiah 12:1–6

*Do Jeremiah's frequent depressions and bouts with despair show
him to be an unspiritual man? Are real believers supposed to be
delivered from all that?*

It is a mistake to suppose that faith in God releases us from
painful emotions any more than faith in God frees us from physical pain
when we break a bone. We are always vulnerable to hurts as long as we
live in this world. And sometimes the hurts will seem too great for us to
bear.

Times of despair or depression are not necessarily symptoms of a lack
of faith. Instead they are opportunities for us to *demonstrate* our faith.
Jeremiah demonstrated his faith in a wonderful way. The prophet's frequent bouts with despair were caused by the anguish of seeing the doom
he had predicted come on the nation that rejected his message. They
were also caused by the growing antagonism of his own people. Still,
Jeremiah preached faithfully for some forty years. What Jeremiah's
expressions of personal grief teach us is that despite our pain, God will
give us the strength to continue and to triumph.

Jeremiah 22:24, 30

*How could God reject the family of Jehoiachin and say that
"none will sit on the throne of David," when he had promised
David that one of his descendants would always have right to the
throne?*

1 Chronicles 3:16–17 names seven descendants of Jehoiachin.
Strikingly, a tablet found in Babylon's Ishtar Gate reports that all seven
were made eunuchs (castrated) and so made unable to have children.
How then was the promise to David kept? Solomon had a brother named
Nathan, and seven sons of Neri, David's descendant through Nathan,
were adopted by Jehoiachin. Comparing 1 Chronicles 3:19 with Luke
3:27 we learn that Zerubbabel, who governed Judah in the time of Haggai and Zechariah, was of the Davidic line, a son of Pedaiah, brother of
Shealtiel, who was a descendant of Neri. While Jehoiachin's line did end,
Jesus was a descendant of David through a different branch of David's
family.

Jeremiah 23:31

What were false prophets, and what was their message? How could the people of Judah tell when a prophet was a false prophet?

False prophets appear in both the Old Testament and the New Testament. They were people who claimed to have God's message for others, but they had not been sent by God. The Old Testament gives a clear set of tests for recognizing false prophets in Deuteronomy chapters 13 and 18. The true prophet is a Jew, not a pagan, who speaks in the name of Yahweh, and who is authenticated as God's spokesman by the sure fulfillment of his predictions. The New Testament also gives a test by which to distinguish false prophets and teachers. The false prophet will deny Jesus as truly human and at the same time fully God (1 John 4:1–3).

There are additional signs of a false prophet reflected both in the Old Testament and the New Testament. Some of these signs are the following.

Doctrinal signs	*Jeremiah*	*2 Peter*	*Jude*
Introduce destructive heresies, denying the Lord who bought them	23:13	2:11	

Personality Signs			
Bold, arrogant	23:10	2:10	16
Despise authority		2:10	4
Follow corrupt desires of sinful nature	23:14	2:10	4, 19
Love profit		2:15	12

Ministry Characteristics			
Appeal to sinful desires	23:14	2:17	16
Promise freedom to the depraved	23:16–17	2:19	

While the false prophet may counterfeit godliness for a time, his doctrine, personality, or ministry will soon betray him, and true believers will be warned away.

Jeremiah 25:11

What seventy-year period is intended here? And what seventy-year span marked the Babylonian captivity? How does this period compare with the seventy years specified in Zechariah 1:12?

Jeremiah's seventy years seems to be a rounded-off period running from about 605 B.C., when King Jehoiakim was taken to Babylon, to 538 B.C., when Cyrus permitted the Jews to return home. This period represents *political* captivity. In contrast, Zechariah looks at the *religious* captivity. His seventy-year period probably runs from 586 B.C., when Solomon's Temple was destroyed, to 516 B.C., when the returned exiles finally completed rebuilding a new temple on the site of Solomon's temple.

Jeremiah 31

What is the new covenant of Jeremiah, and how does it relate to Israel and to the church?

The central provisions of the new covenant God promised through Jeremiah are found in Jeremiah 31:31–34. Key elements are: (1) The new covenant *replaces* the Mosaic covenant. The Mosaic, or law covenant, governed how believers related to God as the generations passed until history's end, when God would keep his ancient promises to Abraham. (2) The new covenant is made with the house of Israel and with the house of Judah. (3) The new covenant provides complete forgiveness of sins. (4) The new covenant provides for an inner transformation of the human personality by which God's laws are written within the heart. The imagery is one of a conversion that enables believers to gladly and willingly do all that the old law, written in tablets of stone, demanded that they do to live in fellowship with God.

To understand the implications of the new covenant, we need to understand that Jeremiah simply *predicted that it would be made* in the future. Jeremiah's words are prophecy. The New Testament tells us that the new covenant was *actually instituted* by the death of Christ. But we must remember that all of God's covenant promises are *eschatological*. That is, they look ahead to a future time at history's end when the promises will be kept in full. For this reason Paul writes in Romans 11:26–27 of the coming fulfillment of the new covenant's promises to Israel, "And so all Israel will be saved, as it is written: 'The deliverer will come from Zion; he will turn godlessness away from Jacob. And this is my covenant with them when I take away their sins.'"

How then can Paul speak of himself as a current minister of a new covenant (2 Cor. 3:6), and the writer of Hebrews explain the meaning of Christ's death for Christians in terms of fulfillment of the new covenant (Heb. 8–10)? The answer is found in a fascinating characteristic of biblical prophecy. Predictions and promises that have their *ultimate* fulfillment in the distant future *also have an impact on the believer's present!* For instance, the Abrahamic covenant promised to bless Abraham's offspring and give them the land of Canaan as their possession. The prophets teach that this promise is to be kept at history's end. But *if a given generation of Jews kept the law of Moses,* God promised that they would experience the *benefits promised in the Abrahamic covenant* (his blessing, and possession of the land) in their own time.

It is the same with the new covenant. The full benefits of Christ's death will be experienced by humankind only when Jesus returns. Then the new covenant promises will be *ultimately* fulfilled. But God promises us in the Bible that if a person believes in Jesus as personal Savior, the critical benefits of the new covenant—forgiveness and a conversion that works a personal inner transformation—will be his or hers *now.*

Thus the new covenant instituted by Christ has both present and future implications. We claim the benefits of the new covenant now by faith in Jesus. And we look forward to a time at history's end when God will pour out every blessing won for us by Christ—on us and on a converted Israel as well.

Jeremiah 31:29

This verse says, "The fathers have eaten sour grapes, and the children's teeth are set on edge." What does this proverb mean?

The proverb is a denial of personal responsibility. The persons who say it mean, "What is happening to us is our fathers' fault, and there is nothing we can do about it." Ezekiel 18 explores this issue and makes it clear that while a previous generations' actions may have an impact on today, each individual is responsible to God for his or her own choices and will certainly be rewarded or punished on the basis of his or her own acts.

Jeremiah 36:30

Jeremiah predicted that Jehoiakim would not have any son sit on David's throne. But 2 Kings 24:6 says Jehoiachin reigned after him. The Bible's rules say that if a prophet's words do not come true, he is a false prophet. This surely is a discrepancy.

Not at all. Gleason Archer points out that the verb *yasab* (sit enthroned) in Jeremiah's prophecy implies being firmly established as king over a period of time. Jehoiachin reigned only three months, and this during a frantic period when Jerusalem was under siege. The chances are he was never officially king, and he certainly was *not* established as king. At best his reign was unofficial and thus does not violate the prophecy of Jeremiah concerning Jehoiachin's line.

Jeremiah 43:7–13; 44:30

Jeremiah predicted a Babylonian invasion of Egypt. But there is no record that this happened. So how can one argue that Jeremiah was not a false prophet?

There is no record of such an invasion in the Bible. And critics have long pointed out that there was no mention in Egyptian or Persian sources of any Babylonian invasion of Egypt. However, a cuneiform tablet has now been found and translated which describes an invasion of Egypt that took place in Nebuchadnezzar's thirty-seventh year, 569 or 568 B.C. In addition, funerary texts now in the Louvre in Paris describe an invasion of the Nile Valley by an army of northerners. These records from both Babylon and Egypt make it clear that the predictions of an invasion made by both Jeremiah and Ezekiel (29) were fulfilled.

Lamentations

Lamentations

Who wrote this book, and what themes and issues does it deal with?

Tradition ascribes this book to Jeremiah, although the text remains anonymous. Its laments clearly date from the destruction of Jerusalem, and its setting is Babylon. If the aged prophet did write this book, it was after the last remaining Jews fled to Egypt against God's command and after a long journey to the land of their captivity.

Lamentations is a collection of five dirge poems. These are anguished funerary laments over the destruction of Jerusalem and the sufferings of its inhabitants. The first two and last two poems have twenty-two verses, each beginning with a different letter of the Hebrew alphabet. The middle poem has sixty-six verses, each triad beginning with a different letter.

181

Ezekiel

Ezekiel
Who wrote this book, and what themes and issues does it deal with?

The book was written by Ezekiel, a young man from a priestly family who was resettled in Babylon with a group of other aristocratic captives in 587 B.C. Ezekiel served as Jeremiah's counterpart, warning the Jewish community in exile that Jerusalem would surely be destroyed (chapters 4–32). After the fall of Jerusalem and the razing of the temple, the theme of this book shifts to one of hope, predicting the restoration of the Jews to the Promised Land and the building of a magnificent new temple (chapters 33–46).

Ezekiel emphasizes the holiness of God, particularly in his powerful description of the glory of God departing from the Jerusalem temple, which had been corrupted by the worship of pagan deities (chapters 8–11).

Ezekiel 1:28
What is the meaning of the glory of the Lord?

Ezekiel's vision featured four living creatures identified as cherubim (10:15) around God's throne, from which emanated a brilliant light, concealing and yet revealing a figure "like that of a man" (1:26). The identification of this man with the glory of the Lord is significant on three counts. First, the glory of the Lord is associated in the Old Testament with God's real presence and self-revelation. Second, Ezekiel at this stage of history sees much *more* of God than was revealed earlier.

At Sinai all that was seen was thunder and lightning. All Moses saw was the scintillating brightness associated with God's back (Exod. 33:12–23). After history and the prophets revealed more of God's character and purpose, Ezekiel saw God more clearly yet was still blinded by the light that shone from him. Ultimately God revealed himself fully in Jesus, and the true glory of the Lord was unveiled in him. Third, the glory of the Lord had previously been associated with the Jerusalem temple (2 Chron. 7:1–3). Now the glory appears to Ezekiel in Babylon. A vastly significant shift is about to take place in the flow of history and the experience of God's ancient people.

Ezekiel 3:16
What did Ezekiel's commission as a watchman imply?

Watchmen were posted on the tops of hills and city walls to guard against the approach of an enemy. They were responsible to warn their city of any impending danger. If their warning was ignored, they were not responsible for subsequent disasters. But if they failed to warn the city, they were held responsible for its fall. Ezekiel is appointed a spiritual watchman for his people. He must speak out in warning, but he is not responsible for how the Jews of the exile or the homeland respond to his words. This is often applied to the modern Christian, who has a word of hope and warning to share with the world. We are responsible to give warning but cannot be held responsible for how those we witness to respond.

Ezekiel 6:1
Why should Ezekiel prophesy "against the mountains of Israel"? Why not against the people?

The prophecy here and in chapter 36 is addressed to the mountains, which have witnessed the corruption of God's people by their worship of pagan deities at high places. Later the mountains are promised that they will see the restoration of the Jews to a land purified of idolatry (36:8–12).

Ezekiel 8–11
What was the meaning of Ezekiel's vision of the glory of the Lord departing the Jerusalem Temple?

The people of Judah foolishly thought that the mere presence of the temple of the Lord in Jerusalem would protect them (Jer. 7:4). Ezekiel's vision, which graphically describes idolatry taking place in the environs of the temple itself, makes it clear that God is *not* committed to defend a place corrupted by sin. It is his presence with a people, not the presence of a structure built of stones, that offers hope. The departure of the glory of the Lord, that visible expression of God's presence, symbolically underlined the truth preached by both Jeremiah and Ezekiel that Jerusalem was doomed.

Ezekiel 11:19

Doesn't flesh in the Bible symbolize man's sinfulness? How then can God call the new spirit he promises to put into his people "a heart of flesh"?

Flesh does not *always* symbolize sinfulness. Here it is in contrast with a heart of stone, which is a metaphor for a stubborn, obstinate resistance to God. A heart of flesh is warm, living, and responsive. The meaning of any biblical symbol or metaphor depends on the context in which it is used.

Ezekiel 16

What is an allegory, and how frequently are allegories used in the Bible?

An allegory is a story in which people, events, or things describe something other than themselves. While parables compare one thing with another, in allegories the qualities or relationships of the described people, events, or things are transferred to the people, events, or things actually being talked about. Thus Paul in Galatians 4:21–31 indicates that the story of Ishmael's expulsion from Abraham's home is an allegory indicating that there can be no mixing of law and grace.

The heading over Ezekiel 16 in the New International Version calls the story of Judah as an infant, exposed at birth to die but rescued by God and brought up carefully to be the Lord's bride, an allegory. Strictly speaking, it probably is not an allegory but rather an extended metaphor. The only image that the Bible itself identifies as an allegory is the one in Galatians.

Early Christian and many Jewish commentators tended to take an allegorical rather than literal approach to interpret the Old Testament.

Thus rather than look at historic events as having meaning in their own times and a message for their own people, many interpreters tended to seek hidden meanings in every story. For instance, to the allegorist Abraham's sending his servant for a bride for Isaac *really* is about God's sending the Holy Spirit into the world to woo humanity to belief, that they might become the bride of Christ.

Aside from the fact that the prophets and the New Testament do not rely on allegory to interpret earlier events, the great danger of allegorizing Scripture is that there is no way to identify correct or incorrect interpretations. When we focus on the literal meaning of the text, taking account of symbol and metaphor and parable but resisting the temptation to allegorize, the Scripture itself provides a check against misinterpretations.

Ezekiel 17:1–10

If allegories are dangerous, why does this chapter tell a story that the NIV identifies as an allegory, a parable (17:2)?

The problem here is that the New International Version translates *hida* as "allegory," while the companion term *masal* is translated "allegory" in other versions. It is best to treat *hida* as "a riddle"—a hard or puzzling question—and to take *masal* as "a parable," even though parables tend to rest on natural events rather than the clearly metaphorical events described here.

Even if this story were an allegory, note that it is immediately interpreted in 17:11–21. There is no room here for misinterpretation, for the text itself explains the symbolism clearly. Thus, even if this should be viewed as an allegory, it strengthens our objection to treating other stories as allegories. God does not intend to *obscure* truth but to reveal it. When an allegory or parable is unclear, the biblical text tends to explain it in context.

Ezekiel 18

This passage talks about the death of souls, yet it clearly bases life or death on an individual's behavior. How then can Christians argue that salvation is by faith rather than by works?

In the Old Testament *soul* does *not* indicate the immaterial part of man that persists after death as it commonly does to those who speak English. The Hebrew word *nepesh* occurs 750 times in the Old

Testament and is translated "soul" 119 times in the New International Version. Other occurrences of *nepesh* are rendered as "life," "being," "self," etc. Thus the warning in Ezekiel 18 that "the soul who sins is the one who will die" (v. 4) simply states that the person who sins will himself or herself suffer the penalty for sin.

But what penalty is in view here in Ezekiel 18? It is *not* eternal death but biological death. The city of Jerusalem and the province of Judah were about to be invaded by the Babylonians. The people had shrugged off any personal responsibility, arguing that they were being punished for the idolatry and sins practiced by their forefathers. They used this as an excuse to persist in their own sins. In essence they were saying, "It makes no difference what we do."

Ezekiel confronts this attitude with a simple truth. It *does* make a difference what men do. Yes, Jerusalem is doomed, and doomed by the sins of the preceding generations. But even in times of national disaster God makes a distinction between the wicked and the good. If a person persists in doing evil, he could count on dying in the coming Babylonian invasion. Thus, "the soul who sins is the one who will die." On the other hand, repentance and a commitment to do good will win survival.

Ezekiel 21:4

How can God say he will "cut off the righteous and the wicked" when Ezekiel has promised in chapter 18 that the righteous will live while the wicked die?

Ezekiel 21 is talking about the fact that the Babylonian invasion will *affect* all persons in Judah and Jerusalem. While "cut off" is frequently a euphemism for kill, here the prediction to Jerusalem warns that all its inhabitants will be removed from the city. In Ezekiel 18 the prophet addresses the inhabitants of Jerusalem and warns that the wicked will die while the good are saved but go into captivity. There is no conflict at all between the words addressed to Jerusalem and the words addressed to the city's people.

Ezekiel 24

What is intended by the imagery of the cooking pot in this chapter?

This is an image of the intensity of judgment. The pot is Jerusalem, the besieging army is the fire; the meat within is the inhabitants of the city. The fire chars the inhabitants who are then scattered. But the city is so polluted by the impurities (v. 11) that it, too, must be destroyed, melted down. Only in this way can the impurity caused by the pagan practices of its inhabitants be purged away.

Ezekiel 26:2–14

Ezekiel predicts that Nebuchadnezzar will take Tyre, but he never did. Does this failure make Ezekiel a false prophet?

The prophecy found here is against Tyre. But like many other Old Testament prophecies, the temporal elements are not distinguished. The description in verses 3 and 4 of the forces from many nations who break down the city towers and walls fits the Babylonian forces, and verses 7–11 describe the plunder of the shorebound city effected by Nebuchadnezzar. Verses 12–14, however, look *beyond* the Babylonian invasion and describe what happened when Alexander the Great swept along the coast and successfully attacked Tyre by throwing the stones of the ruined city into the sea to build a causeway to the offshore island where the city then stood.

It is not that the prophecy was unfulfilled. Rather, in this prediction, as in other Old Testament prophecies, the time element is undefined. The fulfillment of the prophecy took place in two stages separated by some 250 years.

Ezekiel 28:11–19

Why do some say that this passage describes the fall of Satan?

This reasoning is based on characteristics of Old Testament prophetic material in which certain persons, civilizations, or events are seen as symbols for other persons, civilizations, or events. For instance, the prophet Joel begins his prophecy with the description of a locust plague sent by God as a judgment on his people. In the middle of this prophecy Joel suddenly begins to speak about a great northern army destined to sweep over the land at history's end.

Here Ezekiel begins speaking against the prince of Tyre who exalts himself as a god (28:1). Suddenly the prophet shifts to speak of Satan, the hidden king of Tyre (28:11) who is the evil power behind the self-centered, materialistic culture of that ancient kingdom. The description of the king as being "anointed as a guardian cherub [angel]" (v. 14) who walked in Eden, the garden of God (v. 13), and was driven in disgrace from God's presence (v. 16), seems to be a much better fit with what Scripture suggests was Satan's original position and fall than with the posturing of some petty human tyrant.

Ezekiel 34:23–24

This verse says that God's servant David will rule over a restored Israel in the future. How can this be? Does God intend to raise David from the dead to fulfill this prophecy?

No, the reference is to the Messiah. He is identified as David because he is the descendant of David and will achieve even more fully all that the historical David achieved for his people. We see the same literary convention used in Ezekiel 37:24.

Ezekiel 37

Does the vision of a valley of dry bones describe the reestablishment of the state of Israel in 1948?

Possibly. The prophecy, interpreted in context, looks ahead to a time when the Jewish people are scattered throughout the nations with no homeland and no hope. The prophet sees them as dry bones, strewn across a desert valley. Then Ezekiel prophesies at God's command and the dry bones come together. Flesh and sinews are added, but as yet there is no life. Then Ezekiel is told to prophesy to the breath, and the great company comes to life (vv. 1–10).

The interpretation identifies each element of the vision. The bones are Israel. There is a return to Israel's own land, and there is a national conversion when God's Spirit gives his people life (vv. 11–14).

Those who believe that Old Testament promises to Israel should be understood literally rather than taken as metaphors of what God intends to do for and in the church think that the formation of the state of Israel in the ancient Promised Land might well be fulfillment of the first part of this prophecy. They see it as the coming together of the dry bones and their covering with flesh, and look forward to a future national conversion of Israel to its Messiah when Jesus returns.

Ezekiel 38 and 39

Who are Gog and Magog? Has their invasion of Israel taken place?

Much effort has been made to identify not only Gog and Magog but also Rosh, Meshech, Tubal, and other names given in these chapters.

Gog is the personal name of an enemy who has never been successfully identified with any historic person. Magog, in Genesis 10:2, is one of the descendants of Japheth, and thus identifies a people. But the prefix *ma* can mean "place of" in Hebrew, so the New International Version says, "Gog, of the land of Magog" (38:2). Meshech and Tubal (38:2, 3; Gen. 10:2; 1 Chron. 1:5) were peoples located in eastern Asia Minor.

The best answer we can give is to note that historically Israel and Judah were invaded from the north. The identifiable lands and peoples named in this prophecy lie to the north of the Promised Land, in the great Mesopotamian valley currently occupied by Iran, Iraq, and some of the former Soviet republics (38:6, 15).

Most students of prophecy see in these chapters a portrait of a great invasion of the Holy Land that will take place in the future, prior to the return of Christ. They particularly note that no historical invasion seems to fit Ezekiel's description of a supernatural intervention that destroys the invading army and requires seven months to collect weapons and bury the enemy dead.

Ezekiel Chapters 40–48

The temple described so carefully by Ezekiel has never been built. If this is a future temple, why would blood sacrifices be offered there, since Jesus' one sacrifice put an end to that Old Testament practice (43:18–27; compare with Heb. 9, 10)? If this is not a future temple, it was never built, so the prophet is wrong, and by the Old Testament's own criteria he is a false prophet.

The care with which the specifications of the temple, its courts, and its rooms are given makes it most unreasonable to argue that Ezekiel's temple is symbolic. It is also a fact that no Jewish temple meeting these specifications has ever been constructed on the temple mount. Thus, those who take Old Testament prophecy seriously believe that Ezekiel's temple will be constructed in the future and associate it with Christ's reign as Israel's promised Messiah.

But if the construction of Ezekiel's temple does lie in the future, why would its priesthood offer sacrificial animals there? Particularly, why would they officiate at the burnt offerings, sin offerings, and peace offerings required by Mosaic law as 43:18–27 describes? Since the one sacrifice of Jesus is sufficient to win complete forgiveness for all who believe, why a return to the Old Testament sacrificial system?

To answer this question, most theologians point out that the Old Testament sacrifices never did remove sins but were a reminder of man's constant need for forgiveness (Heb. 10:3, 4). They symbolized the future sacrifice of Christ. The offering of these sacrifices served as an expression of the faith of the worshiper. It follows that sacrifices made in any future temple may have nothing to do with removal of sins but will serve as reminders of the forgiveness God has won for us in Christ. It is significant that the Christian communion service is a memorial believers are to practice "until he comes" (1 Cor. 11:26). It is not impossible that sacrifices offered in Ezekiel's temple during Israel's millennial age would serve the same function as our communion and "proclaim the Lord's death" to remind humankind of the terrible cost of our redemption.

Daniel

Daniel

Who wrote this book, and what themes and topics does it deal with?

This book purports to have been written by Daniel, a Jewish nobleman who was taken to Babylon as an adolescent and advanced to high positions in the civil service of both the Babylonian and Persian empires. The first six chapters of Daniel are biographical and relate incidents that demonstrate God's sovereignty despite his people's subjection to pagan powers. The second six chapters are filled with visions and prophecies about the future. These are intended to communicate to Israel that God in his sovereignty knows and controls the future and will establish the Jews to their homeland at history's end. To demonstrate this theme of God's sovereign control, Daniel utters some of the most specific of the Old Testament's predictions about the course of history. These predictions were fulfilled so unmistakably that many critics have argued that the book *must* have been written in the second century B.C. rather than the fifth century B.C. setting of Daniel's story.

Daniel's Dates

Modern critics insist that there is proof that Daniel was written in the second century B.C. instead of the fifth century B.C. If that's true, the book must be a fraud and can hardly be viewed as Scripture, which if correct shows the whole notion that the Bible is inspired by God to be wrong.

191

There is no doubt that many believe the Book of Daniel is one of many religious writings dating from the second century, whose anonymous authors used the names of ancient heroes in their titles. This view is reflected in an article in *Bible Review* (August, 1989, p. 13), in which Marc Brettler writes: "Clear linguistic and historical evidence suggests that Daniel was written in the second century B.C.E. [Before the Common Era], yet the text itself implies it was written three centuries earlier. The author of Daniel made this false claim so his book would become an instant, ancient classic—and he succeeded."

The fact is, however, that "clear linguistic and historical evidence" does *not* suggest Daniel was written in the second century, and the notion that a newly created book could be foisted off on the Jews as an ancient work by Daniel is absurd. The Jews had a fanatically high regard for Scripture. Copyists followed strict rules to reduce the chance of even slight errors in transmission. Scholars debated the meaning of every phrase, and various interpretations were passed down from generation to generation. The idea that anyone in the second century B.C. could successfully claim his work as a book of Scripture composed by Daniel three centuries earlier and have it accepted by the community of Jewish scholars borders on the bizarre and at best must be considered irrational.

But what about the historic and linguistic evidence cited by the critics? One line of reasoning involves the description in Daniel 2, 7, 8, and 11 of the empires that succeeded Babylon—the Persian, Greek, and Roman Empires. How could Daniel have so accurately traced the division of Alexander's empire under his four generals, if the book were not written after all this happened? The believer's answer, of course, is that all predictive prophecy depends on the supernatural. It is not at all surprising that God, who controls the future, knew the future course of empires and would reveal it ahead of time through his prophet.

Other so-called historical evidence comes in the form of alleged inaccuracies that a real Daniel would supposedly have corrected. For instance, Daniel 1:1 says Nebuchadnezzar invaded Judah in the third year of Jehoiakim, while Jeremiah 46:2 places it in the fourth year of Jehoiakim. But recent understanding of Near Eastern dating systems has shown that the dating system used in Judah was different from one used in Babylon, and that this supposed inaccuracy is, in fact, a most compelling argument for fifth-century authorship. No Jew writing the Book of Daniel in the second century B.C. would have gone against Jeremiah 46:2 and dated the invasion using a Babylonian dating system three centuries out of date. There are a host of similar objections and responses. For instance, Belshazzar was long assumed to be apocryphal, because the Greek historian Herodotus, writing in 450 B.C., named

Nabonidus as the last king of the Babylonian empire. See, the critics shouted, Daniel is *wrong*. Then came the discovery of cuneiform tablets which revealed that Belshazzar was the son of Nabonidus and had been made co-ruler with his father. Suddenly it seemed that Daniel, in writing about the Babylon of 540 B.C., knew more about the situation there than Herodotus who wrote ninety years later. And, if the historian was in error about *recent* history, how could an unknown Jewish writer three hundred years later know about this lost fact of Belshazzar's co-regency?

As archeology has provided more and more information about the Babylonian-Persian period, detail after detail in Daniel's portrayal of the times, its customs, and even of individual personalities has been authenticated. There are still historical problems. But a clear pattern has been established: When new information becomes available, it is Daniel, not the critics, who proves to be correct.

How about the linguistic arguments? These hinge primarily on the notion that words borrowed from the Greek language are found in Daniel and that therefore the book could not have been written before the Hellenistic period initiated by Alexander about 330 B.C. Here, too, research has provided interesting information. Today only three words in the book are undoubtedly borrowed from Greek. All are names of musical instruments, listed in Daniel 3:5, 10, 15. Could these words appear in an authentic fifth century B.C. Babylonian or Persian document? Absolutely. Eighth-century B.C. Assyrian inscriptions mention Greek captives taken to Mesopotamia. The Assyrians and Babylonians were always interested in music. Why shouldn't they have learned from these Greeks? Furthermore, the Greek Alcaeus of Lebos in the *seventh* century B.C. mentions his brother serving in the Babylonian army. Neo-Babylonian tablets from the same century list supplies provided to Ionian (Greek) shipbuilders and musicians. The argument that three music words from the Greek indicate a second-century date of the writing of Daniel is slightly incredible. In fact, Daniel's writings contain at least fifteen Persian words that have to do with government and administration. Daniel applies these words as they were used by the Persians themselves. This supports the fifth-century date. Daniel's correct use of these words simply cannot be explained if the author were an unknown second-century writer unfamiliar with the details of Persian government three hundred years before his time.

It is amazing that, despite the host of evidence cited by conservative scholars, many people persist in holding the view that the Book of Daniel is a fraud perpetrated on the Jewish and Christian communities. Daniel is, in fact, inspired Scripture, an authentic account of the man whose adventures and visions it records. As Scripture, the prophecies of Daniel, many of which have been proven accurate by the passage of time, must be given serious attention by anyone interested in the Bible's picture of the future of the earth.

Daniel 2:2

The wise men of Babylon apparently were involved in many occult practices that the Old Testament forbids. How could Daniel be faithful to God and still be one of this class of people?

The text simply says that Daniel and his friends were trained in the language and literature of the Babylonians (1:4). It is important to note that, when Nebuchadnezzar wanted his dream interpreted, he "summoned the magicians, enchanters, sorcerers and astrologers" (2:2), and Daniel did not come with them. Only later was Daniel informed that the king had condemned all the wise men of Babylon (2:13). The conclusion we draw is that, while practitioners of the occult were *among* the wise men of that era, not all wise men were involved in occult practices. Actually, this is not at all surprising. Lists of college professors today include experts in engineering or psychology or education or whatever. Modern wise men usually concentrate their attention on one field. Apparently Babylon's wise men did also.

Daniel 3:28; 4:36–37

Was Nebuchadnezzar really converted to faith in the Lord?

This question cannot be answered. However, it is significant that unlike Pharaoh, Nebuchadnezzar did respond positively to God at each point of revelation (2:47; 3:28; 4:36–37). In the Old Testament, as well as in the New Testament, such a response to God is typically associated with faith rather than with unbelief.

Daniel 4:28–37

There is no historical corroboration of any seven-year illness of King Nebuchadnezzar. And it is most unlikely that a maddened king could have survived to recover his throne.

There is no doubt it is unusual for any oriental monarch to have survived a period when his personal control of events was weakened. But unusual does not mean impossible, particularly when the temporary madness was cast as discipline from God intended to humble a proud monarch without removing him. It is also not certain that seven years were involved. The Aramaic word used here means *"time* or *season."* A season was typically three months. So if the word was used in the sense of season, a little less than two years rather than seven years was actually involved.

Daniel 5:1

Why does this verse speak of a King Belshazzar when there was no such ruler?

See the question on the date of Daniel, pages 191–194.

Daniel 5:31

Who was Darius the Mede? Was he the same person as Darius the Persian?

There is, admittedly, great confusion over the identity of Darius the Mede who, Daniel says, "took over the kingdom, at the age of sixty-two" (5:31). The critics have argued that this is evidence of invention: Either the second-century writer did not know it was Cyrus the Persian who conquered Babylon, or he simply grabbed at a famous name to make his history sound more authentic. In view of discovery after discovery that has proven Daniel to be accurate and the critics wrong, it would be foolish to argue *from the absence of evidence* that there is no explanation for Daniel's statement. Arguments from a lack of evidence are always much weaker than arguments based on the existence of evidence.

It is quite evident from established dates and ages that Darius the Mede (Dan. 5:31) and Darius I could *not* be the same person. Who then could he have been? The text's careful use of terms indicates that Darius *received* the kingship, that he was *"made* king" (*homlak*) rather than *"became* king" (*malak*, the usual word indicating conquest or inheritance of a kingdom), which means that like Belshazzar this Darius was a subordinate ruler appointed by Cyrus to govern Babylon. There is no conflict here either with the practice of the Persian rulers to work through similarly empowered subject kings, or with Darius' decree addressed to various nations and men within the land he governed.

While various identities for Darius the Mede have been suggested, more light on the actual identity of this individual and the reason for his title, Darius the Mede, must await fresh archaeological discoveries.

Daniel 9:24

Daniel's prophecy of the seventy "sevens" seems to be one of the most specific found in the Old Testament. But if the prophecy really predicts the coming of the Messiah to set up his kingdom within 490 years of the decree to rebuild Jerusalem, this did not happen. If the prophecy does not specify this period of time, how is it to be understood?

First, it is necessary to understand the *content* of the prophecy. Daniel's phrases, and their most likely meaning, are the following:

1. To finish transgressions

   To put an end to man's rebellion, and thus to establish a new order on earth

2. To put an end to sin

   To establish a new and just society in which righteousness will triumph

3. To atone for wickedness

   To accomplish through the Messiah's self-sacrifice the atonement that makes forgiveness possible

4. To bring in everlasting righteousness

   To permanently establish a society in which justice, righteousness, and holiness mark every relationship

5. To seal up vision and prophecy

   To see the fulfillment of all the visions and predictions of the Old Testament prophets

6. To anoint the most holy

   To consecrate the Messiah or the temple of God and so officially inaugurate the rule of God on earth

It is clear from looking at this list that, despite the death of Christ, which has won our salvation, the other aspects of Daniel's prophecy have not yet been accomplished during the passage of nearly 2500 years.

Yet, the prophecy *does* speak of a period of 490 years, which is the idiomatic meaning of the Hebrew expression *seventy "sevens,"* or as older versions have it, *seventy weeks*. What is more, we *know when the 490-year period was to have begun*. Daniel 9:25 says the period begins with "the issuing of the decree to restore and rebuild Jerusalem." That decree was issued in the seventh year of Artaxerxes I, in 457 B.C.

It would seem then that history's flow, according the Old Testament prophets, should have ended 490 years later, about A.D. 34.

But it did not.

However, if we look closely at the 490-year period, we see it is divided into several groupings. The first is two sets of years, one set of seven sevens (forty-nine years, 9:25) and another set of sixty-two sevens (434 years, 9:25). According to Daniel 9:25, forty-nine years after the decree was issued, the city "will be rebuilt with streets and a trench." By 408 B.C., stimulated by Ezra and Nehemiah, that work was complete. If we subtract the set of sixty-two sevens, or 434 years, from the years that had already passed, we come up with a date of A.D. 27, the date most scholars believe that Jesus began his public ministry. Thus Daniel's prediction that after sixty-nine of his seventy sevens "the Anointed One, the ruler, comes" (9:25) would be completely accurate.

But what about the rest of the prophecy? And what happened to the seventieth "seven," the last seven years in Daniel's prophecy? Verse 26 says that after the sixty-ninth seven the Anointed One (the word is *Messiah* in Hebrew, *Christ* in Greek) "will be cut off, and have nothing." This is a clear Old Testament indication of the death of the Messiah. The prophecy of this verse goes on to predict the subsequent destruction of the city and the temple, after which "the end will come like a flood."

The point here is that we know from history that the seventieth seven-year period *did not follow directly upon the sixty-ninth*. After the Messiah appeared at the end of the sixty-ninth seven, a period of time passed before his death about A.D. 30. And another period of some forty more years passed before the Romans destroyed Jerusalem and its temple in A.D. 70. Clearly then, since verse 27 picks up the sequence of the final seven-year period, *an undetermined period of time is interposed between the end of the four hundred eighty-third year of Daniel's prophecy and the final seven years.*

If this understanding is correct, history's culminating events spoken of by the Old Testament prophets, and by Jesus in Matthew 24 and Mark 13, will take place in our future, when the final seven-year period of Daniel's prophecy begins.

Daniel 11–12

What events are described in the complex images and difficult language of these chapters?

Intense study of chapter 11 and comparison with the history of the area make it clear that much of this description has to do with rulers who lived between the time of Daniel and the New Testament era. Many, however, see 11:40 as a transition verse, shifting the focus of description from history past to the distant future and specifically to the last of Daniel's seventy sevens. The interpretation of the passage is complicated by differing views of prophetic passages held by Christians and also by the fact that prophecy frequently has dual reference. That is, a prediction might be of actions taken by the Seleucid Antiochus IV around 160 B.C. and at the same time foreshadow actions to be taken by a more distant, more powerful and evil ruler at history's end. While the complications of the passage are best left for commentaries to unravel, it is enough to note that every prediction made by Daniel that involves history past has been fulfilled literally. Thus we can assume that any predictions still unfulfilled will be fulfilled in just as literal a fashion.

Daniel 11:31

What is the "abomination that causes desolation" spoken of here?

In 168 B.C. Antiochus Epiphanes, intent on stamping out Judaism, erected an altar to Zeus in the Temple at Jerusalem and sacrificed a pig, an unclean animal, on it. While this event is taken by many to fulfill the prophecy, Jesus clearly spoke of Daniel's prophecy as something destined to be fulfilled in the future (Matt. 24:15). What is more, the abomination of desolation is to mark the initiation of great distress (literally, tribulation) spoken of by the Old Testament prophets (Matt. 24:21; Ezek. 5:9; Dan. 12:1; Joel 2:2), and to precede the return of Christ (Matt. 24:29–30).

Returning to the law of dual reference, it is not uncommon for focus to shift midway in the prophecy from one event or person to another that the first one foreshadows. And it is not at all uncommon for predicted events or persons to serve as symbols of even greater, similar events or persons destined to follow. Thus there is no reason why the abomination that causes desolation should not speak both of Antiochus's pollution of the temple and of a future desecration performed by an even greater enemy of God's people as history draws to a close.

Daniel 12:1

Who is Michael, the great prince?

According to Daniel 10:13 Michael is a chief prince or powerful angel. Daniel 12:1 indicates that he "protects your [Jewish] people."

Michael is mentioned by name here, in Jude 9, and in Revelation 12:7. The other angel whose name is given in Scripture is Gabriel, who is mentioned by name in Daniel 8:16; 9:21; Luke 1:19, 26.

Daniel 12:1–3

This is the first Old Testament passage to speak of a resurrection from the dead to everlasting life for some, and to "shame and everlasting contempt" for others. What does the Bible teach about resurrection?

The clearest teaching concerning resurrection is found in the New Testament, even though a number of Old Testament passages do hint at a deliverance that extends beyond this present life (Job 14:14; Ps. 17:15; 49:7–20; 73:23–26). Even more explicit predictions speak of God swallowing death (Isa. 25:8) and promise that "your dead will live; their bodies will rise" (Isa. 26:19). Daniel 12:1–3 contains the clearest of the Old Testament's teachings.

The clearest expression of resurrection is seen in Jesus. When raised, we will be like him (1 John 3:2), no longer flesh and blood but endowed with a transformed, imperishable and glorious body (1 Cor. 15:42–44).

What is most debated is the indication in Scripture that there is more than one resurrection. 1 Thessalonians 4:16 speaks of the "dead *in Christ*" (italics mine) rising up in the air to meet the Lord at his return. Revelation 20:5–6 speaks of dead saints coming to life at Christ's return to "reign with him for a thousand years," and says, "The rest of the dead did not come to life until the thousand years were ended." Later in the chapter John describes a judgment at which all the dead appear before God and are condemned to an eternity in the lake of fire (vv. 11–15).

The Bible clearly indicates a resurrection of the saved that precedes final judgment. Some speculate that there are *two* resurrections of the saved. One is a resurrection of Christians, those who are "dead in Christ" (1 Thess. 4:16). The other is a resurrection of Old Testament believers or of those who died during the final time of great tribulation (Rev. 20:5–6). Whatever the number and sequence of resurrections may be, the fact that bodily resurrection is taught in both Old Testament and New Testament is unmistakable. We can leave the details in God's hands and rest on the certainty that we will rise again to enjoy life everlasting in the presence of our Lord.

Hosea

Hosea

Who wrote this book, and what themes and issues does it deal with?

The prophet Hosea lived and preached in the northern kingdom, Israel, in the middle of the eighth century B.C. This book records his preaching to his countrymen, warning them of an Assyrian invasion. He identifies this invasion as God's judgment on his straying people. Hosea's personal experience served as a parable underlining his preaching. His wife abandoned him and turned to prostitution, just as Israel abandoned God and turned to idolatry. Yet Hosea continued to love her and years later took her back. The prophet's deed foreshadows God's similar action and serves as a promise that one day God, too, will restore his sinning people.

Hosea 1:2

How could God, committed to moral purity, tell Hosea to "take to yourself an adulterous wife"?

While some take this introductory verse to mean that Gomer was promiscuous when Hosea married her, others hold that Gomer was chaste when Hosea married her and only later turned to immorality. This argument seems irrelevant, for what is important is that God called the prophet to play his own role in a relationship that paralleled God's relationship with his people. Hosea himself was not immoral for marrying Gomer, any more than God was immoral for loving and remaining faithful to a woman (people) who was unfaithful to him. Legally

Hosea had a right to call for the execution of Gomer for her adulteries, even as God had a right to totally exterminate Israel for its centuries of unfaithfulness to him. The fact that Hosea and God both chose love over law reminds us that the highest morality of all is to seek to redeem the sinner.

It is also important to note, however, that the sins of both Gomer and Israel had painful consequences. Gomer was finally abandoned by her lovers and forced into slavery. Israel was invaded by the Assyrians and her people killed or dragged off into foreign lands. Often it is only when we experience the consequences of our sins that we will be open to the healing love extended to us by others and by the Lord.

Hosea 8:13

How can the prophet say here that Ephraim (Israel) "will return to Egypt" and then promise in 11:5, "He shall not return into the land of Egypt" (KJV)?

The New International Version removes this apparent contradiction by rendering 11:5 as a question "Will they not return to Egypt?" But the fact remains that the people of the northern Hebrew kingdom did not return to Egypt. They were taken north, not south, into Assyrian territory. How is this to be explained? Simply by pointing out that places are often used metaphorically in Scripture. Babylon is spoken of in Revelation, long after the destruction of the ancient city, as a metaphor of materialistic human society. Sodom served Isaiah as a symbol of wickedness long after the original city's destruction (Isa. 1:9–10). And here Egypt, the land where the Israelites were enslaved for such a long period, serves as a symbol of the slavery into which the coming Assyrian invasion will plunge the surviving inhabitants of the north.

Joel

Joel

Who wrote this book, and what themes and issues does it deal with?

Neither Joel nor his time are identified in the Bible. His message, however, is clear. The prophet sees a great cloud of locusts that devastates the Holy Land as a warning of an even more devastating invasion by foreign enemies, associated with the coming day of the Lord. Joel warns that a devastating judgment must purge God's people before history's end, when the Lord will provide the blessings that had been promised centuries before to Abraham's descendants.

Joel 1:15

What is the "day of the Lord" that Joel mentions five times in his short book?

The *day of the Lord* and *that day* are technical theological phrases used to identify any period of time in which God acts, directly or indirectly, to accomplish a specific purpose in his dealings with his Old Testament people. They are most frequently used by the prophets to speak of events to take place at history's end. These events include devastating judgments, as described by Joel and Amos, and a subsequent restoration of blessing as the covenant promises given to Abraham are fulfilled.

Joel 2:28–32

What is the significance of God's promise that he will "afterward . . . pour out my Spirit"?

See the discussion of this passage at Acts chapter 2, page 317.

Amos

Amos

Who wrote this book, and what themes and issues does it deal with?

Amos was a sheep rancher from Judah who was sent on a preaching mission to Israel sometime between 780 and 760 B.C. His message was one of warning and a bold call for a return to social justice and morality. The book reminds us that true piety will reflect a concern for the poor. Religious, moral, and social corruption go hand in hand.

Amos 1:3

What does the phrase "for three sins . . . even for four" mean?

It simply means "for repeated sins." God can forgive sins that we commit when we repent and turn away from them. Amos announced God's judgment on sins that peoples of his time kept on repeating with no thought of repentance or reform.

Amos 4:4

What is the significance of the repeated references to Bethel and Dan?

The Old Testament required God's people to worship the Lord only at one place, where he chose to "put his Name" (Deut. 12). That place was Jerusalem, where Solomon's temple stood. But Jerusalem was the political capital of Judah, the southern kingdom. When Jeroboam, a rival to Solomon's son, led the northern tribes to break away from the south, he feared that going to Jerusalem to worship would ultimately lead to a political reunification of the kingdom. So he set up worship centers at Bethel and Dan and devised an entirely new religious system patterned on but a corruption of the worship required in Moses' law. When God speaks contemptuously of Bethel and Dan and the sins committed there, he refers to the corrupt form of Yahwehism practiced at these worship centers.

Amos 5:21

Why does God say, "I despise your religious feasts"?

On the one hand, the religion practiced in the north was in constant violation of Moses' law (see above). But even worse, the people who enjoyed religion were morally corrupt. They claimed to sacrifice to God, but they trampled the poor, took and gave bribes, sold themselves to materialism, and deprived the poor of justice in the courts. God will not accept the worship of people so materialistic and uncaring, neither in Amos's time nor our own.

Amos 9

What future does Amos see for God's people?

Each of the Old Testament prophets, however bleak the warnings found in his book, ends with a note of hope. Chapter 9 of Amos is typical. Israel will suffer a devastating judgment that comes as a consequence of sin (9:1–10). Yet after the judgment God will restore his people. A descendant of David will sit on the throne, ruling not only Israel but all the nations. At that time the exiles will be returned to the Holy Land, and perpetual prosperity will follow.

This theme, echoed so frequently by all the prophets, has led many to expect the return of Jesus to initiate a restoration of the Jewish people to their homeland.

Obadiah

Obadiah

Who wrote this book, and what themes and issues does it deal with?

This brief, undated book contains a prophecy concerning the doom of Edom, a land whose people delighted in the fall of Jerusalem to an invading force. Jerusalem was successfully attacked several times in history, so there is no way to fix the date of this prophecy with any certainty. However, the prophecy reminds us of one provision of God's ancient covenant with his people: The Lord will "bless those who bless you, and whoever curses you I will curse" (Gen. 12:3).

Jonah

Jonah

Who wrote this book, and what themes and issues does it deal with?

Jonah is identified in 2 Kings 14:25 as a prophet who lived in Israel during the reign of Jeroboam II (793–753 B.C.). He predicted the expansion of the kingdom under this strong but wicked ruler of the northern kingdom. But when Jonah was commanded to go to Nineveh to announce impending judgment, the prophet fled in the opposite direction. At the end of the familiar story, Jonah's flight is explained. The patriotic prophet feared that if he preached in Nineveh, the capital of Assyria, its people might repent. Jonah wanted Nineveh destroyed, for this expanding northern power not only threatened his country but had been identified by earlier prophets as its destroyer.

Jonah was disciplined and given a second chance. At last the reluctant prophet did go to Nineveh. And the people of that great city did repent, and the city was not destroyed. In this, Nineveh served as a powerful object lesson to Israel. If only a doomed people will repent and turn to God, impending judgment can be avoided. Tragically, the people of Israel were as slow as Jonah to sense the meaning of the prophet's mission. Within a very few years, in 722 B.C., the Assyrians did sweep into the northern kingdom and put an end to Israel's existence as a nation.

The reference to Jonah in 2 Kings, and the historical setting of the ministry described in this book, make it clear that Jonah is not intended to be taken as a parable but as a historic account of the prophet's ministry.

206

Jonah 1:17

Could Jonah have been swallowed by a whale? And if he was, how could he have lived?

In the first place, the Hebrew text never says that Jonah was swallowed by a whale. This verse, however, speaks of a great fish that God specially prepared to swallow the drowning prophet and thus save his life. Despite a host of suspicious stories from the nineteenth century of people supposedly swallowed by whales and later recovered alive, we should not look for natural parallels to support the biblical account. It is clear from the text that Jonah describes a miracle, and the great fish was specially prepared by the Lord for its mission.

Jonah 3:3

Nineveh was not large enough in the eighth century B.C. for Jonah to have taken three days to cross. The Bible clearly is wrong here.

Nineveh in Jonah's day was a very large city with a population of at least 120,000 (4:11), some four times larger than the 30,000 in Samaria, the capital city of Israel. It is also true that cities of the flat Mesopotamian plain spread outward, rather than concentrate their population in the cramped, hilltop sites common to the Holy Land. Even so, a distance of three days does seem extreme, as the inner walls of the city had a length of only eight miles. The best explanation is that Jonah refers to the wider administrative district. We might call this "greater Nineveh." This view is supported by Genesis 10:11–12, which refers to an area that includes the cities of Rehoboth Ir, Calah, and Resen within "the great city" of Nineveh.

Jonah 3:10

How can Jonah be accredited as a prophet when the destruction he foretold did not happen?

Jonah himself recognized that there is a conditional element built into every Old Testament prediction of judgment. When the city was not destroyed, Jonah was angry and begged God to take his life. He had fled to Tarshish because he knew God as "a gracious and compassionate God, slow to anger and abounding in love, a God who relents from sending calamity" (4:2). When the ruler and people of Nineveh repented, God was able to deal with them in grace rather than in judgment.

It is very important when reading prophecies of divine judgment to keep this "implicit condition" in mind. The principle still operates today. All people are lost and doomed by sin. But all who turn to Christ will avoid judgment and instead experience the grace of our compassionate God.

Micah

Micah

Who wrote this book, and what themes and issues does it deal with?

The prophet Micah was a contemporary of Isaiah and ministered in Judah between 750 and 686 B.C. The book alternates between predictions of judgment and words of hope. While God rejects idolatry, injustice, and ritualism, he gladly pardons the penitent. Another major theme of Micah is that David's kingdom would be restored and enlarged under the coming Messiah.

Micah 6:6–8

How are these verses to be understood? It sounds as if a person can be saved if he or she will "act justly . . . love mercy and . . . walk humbly with . . . God."

It is always important to interpret any verse or passage in its context. This verse is addressed to people who, through descent from Abraham, Isaac, and Jacob, are in a special covenant relationship with God. However, to fulfill their obligation under God's law, these covenant people were called to a life of justice, mercy, and responsiveness to God. This prophet, like Amos, Isaiah, and many others, is deeply disturbed because God's people assume that they can win God's favor with ritual and sacrifice while ignoring the moral and social dimensions of a walk with God.

These same words might well be addressed to Christians today. They lay a foundation for any believer who seeks to live in fellowship with the Lord. They are not addressed to unbelievers, nor does it lay out a way of salvation or imply that a person's behavior is the basis of eternal salvation.

Nahum

Nahum

Who wrote this book, and what themes and issues does it deal with?

Nothing is known of the author, whose name means "comfort of the Lord." Most believe Nahum wrote between the fall of Thebes in 663 B.C., mentioned in 3:8–10, and the fall of Nineveh in 612 B.C. His words, spoken against the Assyrian capital, were intended to comfort Judah, which had been threatened by its great northern neighbor for decades.

Nahum 1:2, 3

How can we reconcile Nahum's portrayal of God as "jealous and avenging" with the notion of a God of love? How can we explain the note of joy in this book over the bloody destruction of Nineveh?

This common moral argument is based on several faulty assumptions. First is the assumption that a God of love cannot at the same time be a God who metes out terrible judgments on sin. Both the Old and New Testaments make it clear that this is a false assumption. Second is the assumption that vengeance in itself is sinful. While it is true that human beings are not to take revenge, the Bible clearly reserves for God not only the right but the obligation to take vengeance on sinners. Thus Paul quotes the Old Testament by saying, "'It is mine to avenge; I will repay,' says the Lord" (Rom. 12:19). God's vengeance cannot be criticized as long as it is not confused with vindictive retaliation.

211

Finally, the note of joy sounded in this book is completely understandable. The prophet's people have been threatened for decades by one of the most cruel, destructive peoples known to the ancient world. Who would not rejoice to see the threat removed and the persecutor of many nations humbled at last?

Habakkuk

Habakkuk

Who wrote this book, and what themes and issues does it deal with?

Habakkuk, like Jeremiah, prophesied during the last decades of Judah's existence as a nation. His was a unique concern: How could a holy God permit the sin the prophet observed in Judah to go unpunished? When God showed Habakkuk the punishment he was preparing, Habakkuk wondered how a holy God could use an evil people as his agent. The Book of Habakkuk warns Judah that judgment is surely coming, and demonstrates the need for the believer to rest his or her faith in God when devastating judgments fall.

Habakkuk 2

How can God as a judge justify giving success to a cruel people bent on conquest?

We human beings consistently assume that success is good, and that conquering nations or wealthy individuals is in some sense blessed. When Habakkuk raised the question of how God could permit a wicked nation to crush Judah, sinful though the people of Judah were, God pointed out that he was in fact punishing the Babylonians even as they achieved their greatest military successes. The principles of present judgment of the successful wicked that are spelled out in Habakkuk 2 are that (1) however great the successes of the wicked, they remain dissatisfied (2:4, 5); (2) the actions of the wicked arouse hostility and enmity (2:6–8); (3) the wealth and power they gain, rather than provide

213

them with security, makes them vulnerable to others who want their place (2:9–11); (4) the material things they gain are even now in a process of decay (2:12–14); (5) ultimately they will be repaid in kind by those whom they have mistreated (2:15–17).

The point here is that God does not let the wicked get away with anything. Instead, he has structured a truly moral universe in which wickedness creates the conditions for its own punishment, a universe in which the wicked, however well off they may seem, can never experience satisfaction and peace.

Zephaniah

Zephaniah

Who wrote this book, and what themes and issues does it deal with?

Zephaniah, a descendant of King Hezekiah, prophesied during the reign of godly King Josiah. Despite the religious reforms initiated by Josiah, the nation did not wholeheartedly return to the Lord. Zephaniah's book focuses on the coming day of the Lord (see Joel 1:15, page 202) and the judgments that will fall on God's people before restoration and blessing arrive.

Haggai

Haggai

Who wrote this book, and what themes and issues does it deal with?

Haggai was a prophet who lived among the little group of Jews who resettled Judah and Jerusalem after the end of the Babylonian captivity. The prophet gave a series of carefully dated messages to the postexilic community, calling them to finish rebuilding the Jerusalem temple, whose foundations had been laid eighteen years earlier. While the chosen people characteristically had ignored the earlier prophets, they responded enthusiastically to Haggai's urging and did complete the temple.

Haggai 2:6, 7

What does "the desired of all nations will come" mean?

The Hebrew word translated "desire" is *hemdat*, used both of highly esteemed persons and of valuable possessions. This is why some have taken the verse to mean simply that Gentiles would bring precious gifts to dedicate to God at the new temple in Jerusalem. However, the earliest Jewish commentators and most Christian interpreters see this as a reference to the Messiah. It is not that the pagan nations look for Israel's Messiah, but rather that people of every nation yearn for peace and a ruler who can bring it to them.

In fact, it was this temple, rebuilt by the little Jewish community and later expanded by Herod the Great to become a magnificent edifice, that Jesus, the Messiah, entered and at which he worshiped.

216

Zechariah

Zechariah

Who wrote this book, and what themes and issues does it deal with?

Zechariah ministered to the small Jewish community in Judah after the return of some of the Jews from the Babylonian captivity. He lived at the same time as Haggai, and his preaching, too, was instrumental in encouraging the Jewish people to finish rebuilding the Jerusalem temple that Nebuchadnezzar had destroyed.

The first part of this book, chapters 1–8, contains messages given between 518 B.C. and 520 B.C. These focus on the long period of time during which God's people would be forced to live as subjects to various Gentile world powers. The final prophecy, found in chapters 9–12, was given at a much later date. Some estimate it as late as 480 B.C. In this prophecy Zechariah looks far ahead and describes final judgment and the kingdom to be established by the Messiah at history's end. A number of prophecies in this section clearly refer to the first coming of Jesus and his earthly ministry.

Taking these sections together, we find that Zechariah's message is one of waiting and hope. The future God intends for his people is not always reflected in our present experience. But when it does come, it will be glorious indeed.

Zechariah 1–6

What does each of these eight night visions of Zechariah mean?

The chart below describes and summarizes the message of each of these visions. Remember that each vision, addressed to the postexilic Jewish community, was intended to encourage the Jews as they waited not just decades but centuries for God's promise of a Messiah to be kept.

The Vision	Its Meaning
Horsemen report the world is at peace (ch. 1).	God is not yet shaking the nations. It is not the time for Messiah to appear.
Horns, hewn away by workmen, one after the other (ch. 1).	Horns represent power. The four world empires described by Daniel must come and go before Messiah appears.
God sends an angel to survey Jerusalem (ch. 2).	God will protect the city with walls of fire until Messiah appears.
The high priest is cleansed and restored (ch. 3).	The coming Messiah will be God's anointed priest and remove Israel's sin.
God shows Zechariah two gold lampstands and two olive trees (ch. 4).	God will provide the poverty-stricken community with the resources needed to finish the temple.
Zechariah sees a flying scroll (ch. 5).	God will judge those who violate his word. Gentiles may rule the Holy Land, but God is still in charge.
A woman is placed in a basket and removed from Judea (ch. 6).	The woman is a personification of wickedness, which God will remove from the land after Messiah comes.
The high priest is crowned (ch. 6).	The Messiah is destined to be both priest and king.

Zechariah 7:5

What did God mean when he asked through Zechariah, "When you fasted and mourned . . . was it really for me that you fasted?"

The fasts mentioned in this chapter commemorated the initiation of the siege of Jerusalem and the fall of that city to the Babylonians. For nearly seventy years the Jews had remembered that terrible time with days of fasting and weeping. Now that the city was populated again, some residents of Judea were asking whether it was necessary to observe these traditional fast days. God's response was a pointed question. Were these fast days an indication of genuine repentance, or simply expressions of self-pity? Did the people fast for God, or for themselves? As the passage goes on, we see an important principle laid down. If real repentance is involved, the best way for God's people to display it is not by holding fast days but by commitment to a truly moral lifestyle: "Administer true justice; show mercy and compassion to one another. Do not oppress the widow, or the fatherless, the alien or the poor. In your hearts do not think evil of each other" (7:8–10). This is *still* the kind of "fasting" that God requires.

Zechariah 9–13

Why are the final chapters of this book so disjointed? The images don't seem to fit together. Is this an indication that some later writer or editor just took snatches of various prophets' work and patched them together as Zechariah's?

While these chapters were long criticized as disjointed, it was recently shown that this section displays a very complex and sophisticated literary form called chiasmus. In this form the material is balanced in a unique and complex way, as shown in the chart below, with theme set against theme in distinctive progression. Far from lacking unity, these chapters of Zechariah demonstrate a design that demands they be viewed as the work of a talented and cultured writer.

Zechariah 11:12–13

This passage is quoted in the New Testament as the work of Jeremiah, not Zechariah. Not only that, here the shepherd is paid thirty pieces of silver; in the Gospels it is Judas who gets the money. Surely these are serious discrepancies.

The first problem is resolved by noting that, in many manuscripts of the Hebrew Bible, Jeremiah was first in the collection of prophets, and his name was frequently used of the whole collection. Thus the phrase "in the prophet Jeremiah" need not mean that Jeremiah wrote the prophecy but that it was found in the collected works of the prophets.

Themes of Zechariah 9–13

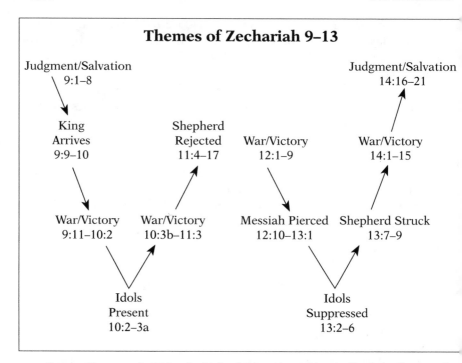

Source: Lawrence O. Richards, *Richards' Complete Bible Handbook* (Dallas: Word, 1987), 423.

The second problem is resolved by noting that both Old Testament and New Testament describe the same event accurately. The shepherd's ministry is viewed contemptuously by his people. All they offer him in payment for his services is thirty pieces of silver, the price Exodus 21:32 sets on a slave who is gored by an ox. This price is so demeaning that the expression "Throw it to the potter" is used, meaning "Throw it away." In Matthew the perspective changes, but the meaning is the same. Rather than that the Messiah asks for his just wages, Judas asks Israel to set a price on his master's head. The amount settled on is the same pittance Zechariah predicts: thirty pieces of silver. Israel considers her Messiah worthless. Later the betrayer fulfills the prophecy literally by throwing the money on the temple floor, where it is used by the priests to buy a potter's field to serve as a burial place for the indigent. If we note the change in perspective, from Messiah to Judas, the Gospel event fits the prophecy completely, even though the prophecy was penned some five hundred years before the events it describes.

Zechariah 13:6

Is this mention of wounds received in the house of a friend a reference to Jesus' sufferings at the hands of his own people?

No, although it has been taken this way by some commentators. This passage describes what will happen in Israel when the Messiah returns and cleanses his people from sin. Then false prophets will be ashamed and try to disguise themselves (13:4–5). The reference to wounds reminds us that false prophets at times abused themselves, hoping that the scent of blood would rouse the brutal deities they worshiped (compare 1 Kings 18:28). When confronted about their characteristic wounds, these false prophets will lie and answer, "Oh, I got these in a brawl at a friend's place the other day. We had a little too much to drink, you know."

This is not a Messianic prophecy.

Malachi

Malachi

Who wrote this book, and what themes and issues does it deal with?

Malachi is the last book of the Old Testament, written some four hundred years before Christ. The prophet wrote to confront the postexilic community with its slide back into the sins of indifference and materialism. While the book shows us the flaws in that ancient community and reflects tendencies in our own lives, it also reminds us that God keeps a record of individuals who are faithful to him in times of national decline. Malachi ends with a prediction that Elijah will appear to announce the coming of the long-promised Messiah who will save Israel at history's end.

Malachi 1:3

Does the phrase "Esau have I hated" really express God's attitude toward this person and his descendants? How can a God of love hate anyone?

The words love and hate in this passage are used in a legal sense. In ancient wills the phrase "I have hated" was used to reject decisively a person's claim to any part of the writer's estate that was to belong to another person. The prophet is reminding the Jews that they are the chosen people (the "loved" ones who have inherited the covenant first given to Abraham), while Abraham's grandson Esau was "hated" (did not inherit the covenant promise). The prophet cites historical as well as biblical evidence to underline his point. God restored the Jews to

Jerusalem, but the land of the descendants of Esau (the Edomites) lay barren when Malachi wrote this prophecy.

Malachi 2:11
Who or what is "the daughter of a foreign god"?

The phrase simply means a pagan woman. Marriages to pagans were forbidden by Old Testament law, because such relationships characteristically led to apostasy.

Malachi 2:15
Various English versions translate this verse differently. What is it saying?

The prophet speaks out against those who divorce their wives to marry younger, more sexually attractive women (2:14). While the Hebrew language here is difficult, the sense of verse 15 is, "No one who has done this has any share of God's Spirit. What is the [godly husband] concerned about? Godly offspring. So keep watch over your spirit and do not betray the wife of your youth." Verse 16 sums up: "'I hate divorce,' says the Lord God of Israel."

Thus Malachi calls the believer to set clear priorities in marriage. Be faithful to your wife. Be concerned not about sexual pleasure but about bringing up your children as godly men and women. Clearly this must be done in the context of a home where faithfulness, selflessness, and love rule.

Malachi 2:16
If God hates divorce, why did Old Testament law make divorce relatively easy to obtain? According to Deuteronomy 24, all a husband had to do was write a statement, "I divorce you," and the marriage was ended.

Both testaments realize that you can legislate action but that you cannot legislate attitude. Malachi makes it clear that the godly husband will have priorities in his marriage that guard him against passions that might cause him to divorce his wife to marry a younger woman. But what about the husband who is *not* godly? What about the abusive husband or the husband who lives promiscuously? What about the situation where a wife is abusive or unfaithful?

Commenting on such situations, Jesus explained that God permitted divorce "because your hearts were hard" (Matt. 19:8). Rather than force a couple to live in a relationship that had become destructive, God permitted divorce, even though this meant they fell short of his intent in creation.

As far as the written bill of divorce is concerned, this was provided for the wife's protection. The written bill of divorce was to prove that she was not legally bound to her ex-husband, and had the right to remarry. Without a written bill she had no such proof and so could not marry again. It should be noted that, in Old Testament society, while divorce was not unusually common, it was normal for divorced people to marry again.

Malachi 3:10

What is the storehouse to which tithes were brought? Does this verse imply that Christians must give their tithes to the local church rather than to missions?

The storehouses in this passage were those areas set aside in or near the temple for the storage of tithes paid in kind rather than in coin. While some preach from this verse and imply that it means Christians are to pay tithes to the local church, this application is not based on an accurate interpretation of the text. There is no real parallel between the Jewish temple at Jerusalem and a local Christian church; the only parallel is between a synagogue and a church. Moreover, tithing is an Old Testament concept, which has been supplanted by different principles of giving in the New Testament (see page 69).

Malachi 4:5

Has God's promise to send Elijah "before that great and dreadful day of the Lord" been fulfilled?

Jesus once remarked that the ministry of John the Baptist could be considered to fulfill this prediction of an Elijah-like prophet destined to appear before the judgment of the day of the Lord (Matt. 11:13–14; 17:12–13; Mark 9:1–13; Luke 1:17). The implication is that, because Jesus was rejected by the Jewish people, another person will fulfill this prophecy of Malachi before Christ's return. Some students of prophecy believe that the real Elijah will return to the earth as one of the two witnesses described in Revelation 11.

Matthew

Matthew

Who wrote this book, and what themes and issues does it deal with?

Matthew was one of Jesus' disciples. He wrote this book some time before the Romans destroyed the city of Jerusalem in A.D. 70. Matthew's Gospel is one of three that take a generally chronological approach to relate the story of Jesus' life. Telling the story of Jesus for a Jewish audience, Matthew frequently quotes or refers to Old Testament prophecies to demonstrate that Jesus is the Messiah whom the Jewish people expected. His Gospel explains why Jesus did not establish the earthly kingdom that the Jews expected. Matthew emphasizes teachings that explain how believers are to relate to the present spiritual kingdom of God; he also promises that Jesus will return to openly establish God's rule on earth.

Matthew is distinctive in his lengthy reports of Jesus' teachings. Among the longer passages are the Sermon on the Mount (5:1–7:27), instructions to his disciples (10:5–42), his teachings through parables (13:3–52), his comments on greatness in God's kingdom (18:1–20:28), and the preview of history's end (24:4–25:46).

Matthew 1:1–17

Were there really only forty-two generations from creation to Christ? How could that possibly be?

Jewish genealogies were not complete but typically selected and identified key ancestors. The three groups of fourteen are symbolic, most likely used because the numeric value of the name *David* in Hebrew is fourteen. The major purpose of this genealogy is to demonstrate that Jesus did descend from David's line, for the prophets declared that the Messiah would come from David's family.

No one today has genealogical data available to trace his or her ancestry back two thousand years. Yet the early Hebrew stress on racial purity, as reflected in the Bible's many genealogies, reminds us that many families in Israel were able to do just that. It is not at all surprising that the records of those in David's line would be carefully preserved. Interestingly, historians report that the emperor Domitian (A.D. 81–96) ordered all descendants of David to be slain. When two were identified from the genealogies and brought before the ruler, he saw their calloused hands and realized they were only poor farmers and let them go.

Matthew 1:6

Luke reports that Jesus descended from Nathan (3:31), but Matthew says his descent was through Solomon. Surely one of the two made an error.

The reason for the differences in the two genealogies has troubled scholars since the second century A.D. Several solutions have been offered that preserve the accuracy of both accounts. One familiar theory is that Matthew gives the line of Joseph, and Luke the line of Mary. From Joseph, Jesus inherited a clear right to the throne held by David's son Solomon; from Mary, his human descent from David was through another of David's sons, Nathan. Other theories suggest that both Matthew and Luke provide genealogies of Joseph but that one line is a throne-succession line, which finally jumped by default to Joseph's physical descent line. The other genealogy, the line of Solomon, died out. While we are unsure which of the various theories is correct, it is clear that each successfully handles the issue of an error in Scripture by showing how each genealogy not only can be correct but can support the Bible's teaching that Jesus is in David's royal line.

Matthew 2:1

Who were the "magi," and how did they know that a star would announce the Messiah's birth?

The popular ideas that the wise men were kings and that there were three of them are inventions not derived from the biblical text. In

Old Testament times magi were a scholarly class who advised Babylonian and Persian rulers. While we cannot identify the magi of the Bible, we do know that this scholarly class persisted in Persia into New Testament times and was at times influential in the Parthian kingdom east of Palestine.

We have no information on how these wise men recognized the star that announced Jesus' birth. Some suggest they relied on the prediction in Numbers 24:17: "A star will come out of Jacob; a scepter will rise out of Israel." A knowledge of this prophecy in the lands east of Israel is not at all unrealistic. A large and vital Jewish community thrived in the east from the time of the Babylonian conquest, and the fruit of their intense study of the Old Testament is available today in the Babylonian Talmud, one of the two major sources of religious tradition in Judaism.

Matthew 2:2

What was the star of Bethlehem?

Many attempts have been made to link the star that appeared at Jesus' birth with a natural astronomical phenomenon. Some have suggested a conjunction of planets, others a comet, still others a supernova. However, Matthew 2:9, which says that the star "went ahead of them until it stopped over the place where the child was," makes it clear that the star was a supernatural rather than natural phenomenon. This will trouble those who doubt the possibility of miracles, but it will hardly bother the Christian believer.

Matthew 2:6

Why does Matthew not quote Micah 5:2 accurately? If we changed the meaning of a verse of Scripture we would be roundly criticized.

Matthew does not change the meaning but rather paraphrases to bring out the intent of the text. Micah notes that Bethlehem is a relatively insignificant (small) city and yet is destined to be the birthplace of the Messiah. Matthew appropriately interprets this to imply that Bethlehem is not insignificant, because from it the ruler "who will be the shepherd of my people Israel" has actually come. This last phrase is not found in Micah but is taken from 2 Samuel 5:2.

Such a blending of different Old Testament texts in a single quotation (a conflate quotation) is not unusual (see also Matt. 27:9–10; Mark 1:2–3).

What we have in this quotation is not a misquote or an error but an authoritative, Holy Spirit-guided *interpretative paraphrase* of the Old Testament text intended to emphasize its original intent.

Matthew 2:6

Did the disciples of Jesus simply go back to the Old Testament after Christ's death and find parts of written prophecies that they twisted so they would appear to show Jesus was the Messiah?

The problem with this theory is that long before Jesus was born, the Jewish rabbis had identified and studied the key Old Testament Messianic texts. In his *Life and Times of Jesus the Messiah*, Edersheim lists 456 Old Testament passages applied to the Messiah or Messianic times by the "most ancient Jewish writings." A study of Edersheim's material shows that the disciples of Christ did *not* invent their applications of Old Testament passages to Jesus, but that most of these passages were recognized as Messianic long before Jesus was born.

Matthew 2:17

How many boys did Herod's soldiers actually kill? And what does the prophecy in Jeremiah have to do with the "slaughter of the innocents"?

Archaeological surveys of the Bethlehem area suggest that its population was between three hundred and one thousand in the first century A.D.. Given the larger number, one would expect no more than twenty and more likely a dozen or so male children two years old and younger. We are shocked by the brutality of the act, but the massacre is in fullest harmony with what is known of Herod's character and fierce defense of his throne.

The Jeremiah passage quoted is linked to this event. Jeremiah 31:15 portrays Rachel, the symbolic mother of the Jews, weeping as her descendants are torn from the Promised Land. Yet that prophecy is found in a context of the hope that despite the tears God promises the exiles will return. Now, despite the tears shed for the innocent victims of Herod's slaughter, their deaths underline the escape of the child Jesus, whose survival ultimately means restoration of humankind to a personal relationship with God. As tears intermingled with joy in Jeremiah's time, so tears and joy intermingle in Bethlehem. Each passage thus foreshadows salvation.

Matthew 3:2

Why did John preach, "Repent, for the kingdom of heaven is near"? What was the kingdom of heaven?

The *Expository Dictionary of Bible Words* (Zondervan) points out that "in the OT [Old Testament], 'kingdom' is best expressed by the idea of reign or sovereignty. One's kingdom is the people or things over which he or she has authority or control." The Bible portrays God's kingdom (heaven's rule) in several ways. On one hand, God is sovereign ruler of all creation, and the universe is his creation (Ps. 145:11–12; Dan. 4:3). At the same time the prophets foresee a time when God's disguised sovereignty is expressed in visible form here on earth. Daniel 2:44 says, "The God of heaven will set up a kingdom that will never be destroyed." In the New Testament another form of God's hidden kingdom is emphasized: God rules in the hearts and lives of Jesus' followers, and he works out his will for them through circumstance and, at times, miracle. Thus Christians are rescued from the domain of darkness governed by Satan and brought "into the kingdom of the Son he loves" (Col. 1:13).

In what sense then did John mean his announcement, "The kingdom of heaven is near"? It is certain that John's listeners thought at once of the earthly, political kingdom the prophets foretold. But John's proclamation was intended to draw attention not to a particular form of the kingdom but to the presence of the King. The kingdom was near because King Jesus was about to begin his public ministry. The kingdom was near (available) for anyone who truly believed in Jesus as Messiah and Son of God. By giving allegiance to the King, they could personally enter that realm where heaven rules. In that sense the kingdom of heaven is near to human beings today as well. All one needs to do is to bend his or her knee to the King. By that simple act of faith, he or she will be transformed and become a citizen of the kingdom of our God.

Matthew 3:11

How many kinds of baptisms are mentioned in the New Testament? And how was John's baptism different from Christian baptism?

This verse mentions three baptisms: of water, of the Holy Spirit, and of fire. So at least three baptisms are mentioned in the New Testament, and if we add Christian water baptism we have four.

John's water baptism was a symbol of repentance and commitment. The Jew who accepted baptism from John confessed his sins and expressed his determination to live a righteous life.

The water baptism practiced by the early Christian church was also a symbolic act. But rather than symbolize repentance, Christian baptism symbolizes the union of the believer with Jesus in his death, burial, and resurrection (see Rom. 6:1–4).

The baptism of the Holy Spirit is defined in 1 Corinthians 12:13 as that act by which the Spirit unites the believer to Jesus as a member of his body. This spiritual union is the reality symbolized by Christian water baptism.

The baptism of fire referred to in Matthew 3:11 has been understood in two different ways. Some take it as a reference to the fire that destroys the unrepentant (wheat and chaff, Matt. 3:12). Others emphasize the many symbolic references to fire in the Old Testament as a purifying agent (Zech. 13:9; Mal. 3:2–3). In this view the Holy Spirit and fire are closely linked, reminding us that when the Holy Spirit enters our lives he not only joins us to Jesus but also begins a purifying and cleansing process.

Matthew 4:5–10

Matthew and Luke differ in the order of the three temptations experienced by Jesus. They both cannot be right; one is obviously wrong—a biblical error.

The answer to this objection, and to others where a sequence of events differs in two Gospel accounts, is found in the fact that there is more than one way to appropriately order events in any historical record. Some histories are written chronologically. Others are written thematically; that is, events are reported in a sequence that develops the writer's theme rather than in a strict temporal order. We understand this as a methodological matter, and we surely do not accuse a thematic author of error simply because he treats events out of chronological sequence. We would charge Matthew or Luke with error only if there were evidence that *each claimed* to be reporting the three temptations chronologically.

So the question is, Do Matthew and Luke claim to report the temptations in temporal sequence? A look at the original Greek manuscript makes it clear that Matthew was writing chronologically. He says, "then" (4:5, *tote*) and, "again" (5:8, *palin*). These terms specifically indicate sequence. So Matthew does claim to provide a chronological report of the temptations. But Luke simply links the events by the Greek words *kai* and *de*, translated "and" (Luke 4:2,6). These conjunctions have no specific chronological implications and link the temptations very loosely.

Rather than that the two accounts prove an error in the Bible, the original language makes it very clear there is *no* conflict and that Luke purposely and consciously abandoned chronological order to develop a thematic point (see comments on Luke 3:1, page 283).

Matthew 5:1-12

What does "blessed" mean, and how are these classes of people we would consider to be disadvantaged actually blessed?

The Greek *makarios* is sometimes rendered "happy" in modern versions. But this misses the point of the underlying Hebrew concept. We might express it better in the interjection: "Oh, the blessedness of . . . ." The basic idea is that the person who is blessed has been favored by God in some important way.

The Beatitudes do not claim that those who are poor in spirit, who mourn, or who hunger and thirst for righteousness are happy. Rather they claim that such persons are *better off* than those characterized by opposite qualities. Many books have been written exploring the exact meaning of such phrases as "poor in spirit" (Matt. 5:3). The chart below summarizes likely interpretations of each Beatitude and the reason that a person characterized by this trait is blessed by God and better off than one who lacks it.

The Beatitudes

poor in spirit (v. 3)	utterly dependent on God	inherit God's kingdom
those who mourn (v. 4)	sensitive to and contrite for sins	will be comforted (see also Isa. 61:1–3)
the meek (v. 5)	gentle, without malice to others	will inherit the [new] earth
those who hunger and thirst for righteousness (v. 6)	eagerly desire personal righteousness and social justice	will be satisfied when Messiah comes and establishes both
the merciful (v. 7)	show forgiveness and compassion	receive mercy from God
the pure in heart (v. 8)	moral purity vs. external piety	will see God (experience his presence)
the peacemakers (v. 9)	encourage reconciliation, with God and others	model themselves on God and thus earn the description, 'sons'
the persecuted for righteousness (v. 10)	committed to what is right	enjoy now what it means to live in God's kingdom

Matthew 5:13

How can salt lose its saltiness? What does this saying mean?

In the first century A.D., salt was used not only to flavor food but also as a preservative. Most salt was rock salt, obtained from salt marshes, and not the purified substance we know or that the ancient world derived from evaporated seawater. This salt was mixed with soil, deteriorated under high heat, and was leached away by water. Thus it lost its saltiness and became useless as a preservative. Jesus here warns his disciples that they can serve as a preservative in society only if they retain their virtue and refuse to adopt the world's low, changing moral standards.

Matthew 5:17

How did Jesus fulfill the law and the prophets?

Typical interpretations suggest Jesus intended to claim he would fulfill the predictions of the prophets concerning the future, or that he was the one the prophets spoke of. However, Jesus here expresses another idea entirely. It was the goal of every rabbi in Judaism to "fulfill" the law in the sense of explaining its true meaning. Jesus simply said that his teaching rather than abolish the Old Testament law and prophets in fact explained the real meaning of the earlier revelation.

Note that in Matthew 5 he goes on to do exactly this. Whereas earlier interpreters of the law focused on acts (do not murder, do not commit adultery, etc.), Jesus shows that the law's commands actually point to man's inner attitudes. The righteousness that the law points to requires that man be rid of the anger that leads to murder and the lust that leads to adultery. In saying that his hearers would never even be able to glimpse God's true kingdom "unless your righteousness surpasses that of the Pharisees and teachers of the law," Jesus makes it clear that a relationship with God requires an inner transformation that will make an individual truly good.

Matthew 5:29

How can plucking out an eye or cutting off a hand prevent sinning? Did Jesus really mean a person should do this?

Most people take these words as hyperbole intended to emphasize the fact that sin is so serious it must be dealt with in a radical way. The specification of "right eye" (5:29) and "right hand" (5:30) are references to one's best eye and hand and are added pointers to Jesus' intent. Whatever may feed the imagination and lead to sin must be expunged. Rather, the Bible's prescription for godliness calls on us to think about things that are true, noble, right, pure, lovely, and admirable —the excellent and praiseworthy and not the depraved and degenerate (Phil. 4:8).

Matthew 5:38–47

Does Jesus' rejection of the Old Testament teaching of an eye for an eye show that this was a primitive teaching unworthy of being ascribed to God?

The Old Testament principle was intended to limit the punishment that could be imposed for a hostile or accidental act. Far from being primitive, it was morally advanced for the time (see comments on Exod. 21:23–25, page 61). Jesus did exactly what he had done in the other teachings recorded in Matthew 5: look behind the law to expose the principle it expressed. In the case of this law, which in essence outlawed vengeance, the underlying principle is forgiveness and grace. Rather than strike back we are to adopt God's approach and love even those who have become our enemies.

Matthew 6:22–23

What does "if your eyes are bad" mean, and why is this serious?

The point of this analogy is that, as a lamp provides illumination that enables a person to find his or her way, so the eye lets in light that enables a person to make moral choices. A bad (*poneros*, connotes "evil") eye distorts light, and thus one's moral choices are made without a clear focus on what is right or wrong. Scholars disagree whether this metaphor goes with verses 19–21 or with verse 24. If the former, Jesus reminds us that the selfish person is spiritually and morally blind. If the latter, Jesus says that a person who divides his attention between God and material possessions will develop moral and spiritual blindness.

Matthew 7:6

What is the meaning of Jesus' warning not to give dogs what is sacred or to throw pearls to swine?

The context focuses on judging actions and thus implies the establishment of well-defined moral standards. In 7:3–5 Jesus warns his listeners to evaluate themselves by their standards, not to evaluate others. In 7:6 he warns them not to seek to impose high moral standards on unbelievers. The point of the analogy is that "dogs" are incapable of recognizing the sacred, and that "pigs" care nothing for pearls. Why then should we expect those without any relationship with God to accept the moral standards of believers? Rather than respond to efforts at moral uplift, the corrupt are more likely to turn "and tear you to pieces" (Matt. 7:6).

The way to affect society is to focus on the Gospel and its promise of personal relationship with God. Morality follows conversion, rather than precedes it. The believer who attempts to use biblical standards to reform society is putting the cart before the horse and will not prevail.

Matthew 7:28–29

How was the teaching of Jesus different from that of the Jewish teachers of the law?

Several books were written in the 1970s and 1980s to show that Jesus was simply another Jewish rabbi whose teachings were squarely within one or more of the rabbinical traditions of his time. Most of these books ignore or discount the central, radical teaching of our Lord that he is the Christ (the Messiah) and the Son of God, coequal with God the Father. They also discount observations such as the one found in this verse that sets Jesus apart from contemporary teachers.

What made Jesus' teaching seem different in the eyes of his contemporaries? Even in the first century, teachers of the law relied on interpretations and insights of many generations of rabbis who had lived before them. This approach, the citing of earlier authorities for one's own teachings, has remained characteristic of rabbinic Judaism. But Jesus did not cite earlier authorities, but spoke as if he himself had complete authority to interpret Scripture and explain God's will. Christians argue that he did have this authority, because Jesus was God incarnate, the giver of the Scripture.

Matthew 8:2

Why did the leper ask to be made clean rather than to be healed?

He did ask to be healed. In Judaism a person with an infectious skin disease was ritually unclean and could not participate in the community's religious life. He or she was also forced to live in isolation from others. When cured, the leper visited a priest, who certified his or her recovery, and pronounced him clean. Thus in asking Jesus to make him clean, the leper expressed his faith that Jesus could cure him of the disease and restore him to fellowship within the faith community.

Matthew 8:17

Does this quotation of Isaiah 53:4 imply that believers are guaranteed physical healing by Christ's death?

Matthew's quotation of Isaiah 53 points us to the entire context of the chapter, not just this one verse. That chapter points out that the Messiah will suffer for sinners and in taking their sin upon himself will heal them spiritually, giving them new life. But throughout Scripture spiritual and physical healing are linked, even as are sin and sickness. Thus Matthew's quotation points to the fact that Jesus, in bearing the sicknesses of the ill of his day, demonstrated his messiahship; it also points to the ultimate fulfillment of the promise of total healing embedded in Isaiah's description of the suffering servant.

It is true that the atonement guarantees physical healing, just as it guarantees spiritual healing. But that guarantee is for history's end, not for today. Even the apostle Paul did not claim healing when he was ill. He begged for it; but when told healing was not God's will, Paul rejoiced in the fact that God would provide the strength the apostle needed to accomplish the Lord's goal, in spite of his sickness (2 Cor. 12:7–10).

Matthew 8:20

What did Jesus mean when he spoke of himself as "the Son of Man"?

Matthew ascribes this title to Jesus thirty-two times. It shows up fourteen times in Mark, twenty-six times in Luke, and twelve times in John. The phrase *son of* here emphasizes Jesus' identity with the human race. He became a true human being. The most important implication of this truth is rooted in the Old Testament concept of the *go'el*, or "kinsman redeemer." In Old Testament law a near relative had both the right and obligation to come to the aid of a helpless and enslaved relation, as well as the right to avenge such a person's murder. In becoming human, Jesus became our kinsman, and thus won the right to become our redeemer. While in some contexts Jesus used the title *Son of Man* simply as a way of naming himself, in others the title emphasizes not only his humanity but also his commission to save a helpless humanity trapped in bondage to sin.

Matthew 8:22

How could Jesus be so unfeeling as to tell a bereaved young man to leave his father unburied and to immediately follow him?

First, the young man was not bereaved, because his father was not dead. Jewish burial customs involved the disposal of the corpse immediately upon death. If the father had died, the young man already would have been on the way to the tomb with the corpse. In fact, the young man said that he wanted to follow Jesus but not until his father died. He placed his filial obligation to his father above his commitment to the Son of God. Thus Jesus' response was not unfeeling but a clear call to put God first in everything—even above what we feel we owe our parents.

Matthew 8:28

Are demons mythical beings? If not, where did they come from? Can Christians be demon possessed today?

The New Testament treats demons as real beings. Most scholars identify them with angels that chose to rebel against God and follow Satan. Volume 2 of *A Contemporary Wesleyan Theology* sums up the New Testament teaching on demons this way:

As spiritual beings, demons are unclean, they are vicious, intelligent, and able to attack human persons with moral and spiritual pollution as well as with physical harm and abuse. Throughout the Gospels (Matt. 8:16; 17:18; Mark 9:25; Luke 10:17, 20) demons are shown to be spiritual beings. In some cases such as the Gadarene demoniac (Mark 5:2–16; Luke 8:27–38) and Mary Magdalene, out of whom Jesus cast seven demons (Mark 16:9; Luke 8:2)—numerous demons may possess one person. The apostles Paul and John likewise lend support to the spiritual nature of demons in such passages as Ephesians 2:2; 6:12; and Revelation 16:14, among others.

Both Old Testament and New Testament forbid God's people to have anything to do with any form of the occult and thus to withdraw from anything that might possibly involve evil supernatural forces (see also 1 Cor. 10:20–21). While various Gospel references indicate that demons can oppress and possibly even possess the unwilling, the New Testament also reminds us of truths that put the demoniac in perspective. Jesus remains the ultimate power in the universe, and demons can be cast out in his name (Acts 19:15–16; Acts 16:18). What is more, Christians are indwelt by the Holy Spirit, so they can take comfort in the words of 1 John 4:4: "The one who is in you is greater than the one [Satan] who is in the world."

Matthew 8:28–34

Matthew tells of two maniacs in Gadara. Mark 5:1–20 and Luke 8:26–39 speak of only one maniac, and Luke places him in Gerasa. Surely at least one is in error.

The most likely location of the event reported in all three Gospels is Gadara. Most believe Gerasa reflects a scribal error involving the substitution of *r* for *d*, letters which look very similar in Aramaic.

Were there one or two maniacs? Is this a contradiction? Not necessarily. After all, Matthew does not suggest there was *only* one maniac. He simply remembers and concentrates attention on one.

Suppose you told a friend, "Jim was at the party but came late," while a another person told the same friend, "Jim and Carl came late to the party." Should you be charged with an error because you failed to mention Carl when telling about Jim? Of course not. Why then should the New Testament be charged with an error because Matthew only mentioned one of the two maniacs, while Mark and Luke mentioned both?

Each writer agrees on the central elements of the story. Jesus demonstrated his power over demons by casting them out of their human victims and permitting them to go into a herd of pigs, which dashed into the water and were drowned. To insist that Matthew made an error simply because he did not mention both maniacs hardly seems reasonable under the circumstances.

Matthew 9:1–8

What point was Jesus making when he asked, "Which is easier to say, 'Your sins are forgiven,' or to say 'Get up and walk'"?

It is clearly easier for a person to *say*, "Your sins are forgiven." Why? Because there is no way to prove that a person's sins are or are not forgiven. On the other hand, it is no light matter to say, "Get up and walk," for everyone will know whether the speaker has that kind of authority. If a cripple does get up and walk, the power of the speaker is proven. If not, he is exposed as a fraud. Thus when the cripple did get up and walk, Jesus' claim to the right to forgive sins was authenticated by the miracle of healing.

Matthew 9:16–17

What did Jesus mean by his reference to putting a new patch on old clothes and new wine in an old wineskin?

Jesus had been criticized for associating with sinners rather than separating from them, as the Pharisees did (9:9–13). Even the followers of John the Baptist could not understand why Jesus did not follow accepted religious practices and fast twice a week. Jesus' reference to new cloth and new wine was a way of saying that the truths he taught could not simply be patched on to Judaism or poured into the old religious framework. Jesus' teaching was so dynamic and new that it called for a totally new way of thinking about holiness and living a godly life.

Matthew 9:23

What were flute players and a noisy crowd doing outside the house of a dying girl?

Our culture takes a solemn approach to death, and those attending a funeral are generally quiet and very reserved. In first-century A.D. Judaism a death was greeted with loud wails and great crowds of mourners gathered to noisily express their grief for the family, often accompanied by shrill music. What Matthew describes was the typical reaction of the neighborhood to a death in one of its families.

Matthew 10:1

What were "evil spirits"?

Evil spirit is another name for the angels who followed Satan and rebelled against God. They are the same as the demons of the Gospels. (See explanation of Matthew 8:28, pages 236–237).

Matthew 11:12

What is the meaning of Jesus' words, "The kingdom of heaven has been forcefully advancing, and forceful men lay hold of it"?

The context shows that Jesus identified the appearance of John the Baptist as one of history's turning points. Jesus' own ministry, marked by miracles, a great flurry of demonic activity, and intensifying opposition from the Pharisees, demonstrates that the kingdom of heaven is advancing in spite of fierce resistance. Satan and humanity may fight against God, but the advance of God's kingdom is irresistible.

Matthew 11:14

How could John be Elijah? What did Jesus mean when he made this identification?

The last book of the Old Testament, Malachi, announces that God will send Elijah to his people before the "great and dreadful day of the LORD comes" (Mal. 4:5). Some take this prediction to refer to the actual Elijah, who was taken up into heaven without experiencing biological death (2 Kings 2:11). Others see Elijah as a type of the last great prophet, and understand the prediction to mean that an Elijah-like prophet will appear just before history's end. Here Jesus tells his listeners that if they had responded to John's message with faith—and thus had accepted the one John announced as their Messiah—John could have been considered to have fulfilled Malachi's prediction. Jesus implies that, since the Jewish people did not turn to Christ as their Messiah, another person will appear in the future to fulfill Malachi's prediction before God's kingdom is established on earth.

Matthew 11:16–17

What did Jesus mean by comparing his generation to children playing in the marketplace?

"We played the flute for you and you did not dance" refers to children playing wedding. "We sang a dirge, and you did not mourn" refers to children playing funeral. The pouting children in Jesus' story complain, because whatever they try to play, their companions won't join in. In the same way the adults of Jesus' time would not respond to God, whether the Lord spoke to them through the ascetic John or through the warm and caring Jesus.

Matthew 11:29

What is Jesus' "yoke," and how does a person "take it up"?

It was common in the first century A.D. to speak of "the yoke of the law" (see Acts 15:10). The intent was to present the law as a responsibility, a task to perform, which every adult Jew took up when he or she reached the age of moral responsibility. Yet, in practice, wearing the yoke of the law proved to be a wearying burden. Then Jesus appeared with a new and exciting revelation of the Father (Matt. 11:27), offering those who came to him a very different yoke to carry. In contrast to the law, which Israel had reinterpreted as a rigid set of rules one had to follow to win favor with God, Jesus offered grace, love, and forgiveness. Truly his yoke *is* easy, and the burden that comes with faith in him is light.

How do we take his yoke upon us? Jesus said, "Come to me, . . . Take my yoke upon you and learn from me" (11:28–29). We are to turn to Jesus by faith, accept his gracious offer of salvation, and then learn to live the new life he gave us by responding daily to his Word.

Matthew 12:8

What does "The Son of Man is Lord of the Sabbath" mean?

Jesus had just rejected one of the Pharisees' rulings on how a person was to keep the Sabbath day. Old Testament law simply said that a person was not to work on the seventh day and should keep it holy. The rabbis, debating what "work" involved, had developed a host of special Sabbath rules. For instance, spitting on soft ground was work, for the earth might be turned by the spittle. In Matthew 12 the disciples' act of plucking heads of grain that grew near a path fell under the rabbis' definition of work.

Jesus rejected this interpretation as missing the intent of Sabbath law. He pointed out that God had permitted a more serious violation of ritual law on one occasion when David and his men had been famished (12:3–4; 1 Sam. 21). In that case, the priests who served in the Lord's house had worked on the Sabbath (Matt. 12:5). But the saying in question means simply that Jesus did not rest his case on such arguments. Instead, Jesus spoke authoritatively. As the one who instituted the Sabbath, Jesus was "Lord of the Sabbath," with every right to say what God did and did not intend by the command to keep the Sabbath holy.

The next incident illustrates and demonstrates this point. Jesus heals on the Sabbath, proving his authority, and announces that it is "lawful to do good on the Sabbath" (12:12).

Matthew 12:24

Who or what was Beelzebub?

The name originally ridiculed a pagan deity, Baal-Zebul (exalted Baal) by distorting his name to Baal-Zebub (lord of flies). By New Testament times the name was given to Satan, the "prince (ruler, or chief) of demons."

Matthew 12:30

In this verse Jesus says, "He who is not with me is against me."
But in Mark 9:40 Jesus says, "Whoever is not against us is for us."
This is a contradiction that cannot be explained.

There is no need to explain away supposed contradictions that do not exist in the first place. In Matthew Jesus deals with the conflict between God's kingdom and the forces of evil. Here no one can be neutral. If one is not *for* Jesus, one is necessarily *against* him.

In Mark the disciples saw someone cast out demons in Jesus' name and forbade it "because he was not one of us." Clearly if a person publicly identifies his actions with Jesus, he cannot be against Jesus. What bothered John was not the man's relationship with Jesus but the man's relationship with the disciples: "He was not one of us" (Mark 9:38).

How foolish we would be if the Methodists tried to rule the Baptists out of the kingdom of God, not because of their attitude toward Jesus but because they were not one of the Methodists! And it is foolish to imagine that there is any contradiction between these two sayings of Jesus, which deal with totally different situations.

Matthew 12:31

What is "blasphemy against the Spirit" and why is this an unforgivable sin?

Look at the context. The Pharisees have just credited Satan with the miracles that Jesus performed through the power of the Holy Spirit. It is this sin—observing a miracle performed by the Spirit and ascribing it to Satan—that Jesus says will not be forgiven.

This reference to an unforgivable sin has troubled many unnecessarily. Those who are concerned that they have done something for which Jesus will not forgive them show a very different attitude from the Pharisees, who refused to accept even the most compelling evidence that Jesus was the Son of God. The person who rejects the Spirit's message about Jesus will not be forgiven. Anyone who seeks Jesus' forgiveness certainly has not committed the unforgivable sin.

Matthew 12:36

What does Jesus mean by giving account for "every careless word"?

One young woman I knew felt that this verse condemned casual conversation. She thought she was supposed to talk only about God and Jesus. But that is not Jesus' point. He simply means that it is the careless words, the words we speak when we are not consciously thinking about being spiritual, that reveal our hearts. A prime illustration is in this chapter. When Jesus entered a synagogue and found a man with a shriveled hand, the Pharisees challenged Jesus about whether it was lawful to heal on the Sabbath. They didn't care about the man's suffering, even though any one of them would have lifted a sheep out of a pit where it had fallen on the Sabbath. The Pharisees simply did not stop to think that their focus was on what was lawful, while they overlooked human suffering, or how different their values were from those of Jesus.

It is the same with us. Careless words, words we utter without thinking about what they imply, reveal our hearts. God is not so concerned about our Sunday pieties as our hearts on Monday.

Matthew 12:40

Jesus predicts he will be in the tomb three days and three nights. But the Bible seems to indicate he was crucified on Friday and raised Sunday morning. This is not seventy-two hours.

The text does not say seventy-two hours, but "three days and three nights." According to Hebrew reckoning, a day began at six P.M. and lasted until six P.M. the following day. This period was called a night and a day—a twenty-four-hour period involving both the hours of darkness and the hours of light. In the idiom of the first century, "three days and three nights" simply indicated that three separate twenty-four-hour periods would be involved and did *not* mean that the entirety of all three periods were included. Three days and three nights would be accurate in identifying only part of the first day and part of the third day. Thus Christ's prediction of "three days and nights in the heart of the earth" would be fulfilled if he died Friday afternoon about three and was raised early Sunday morning.

Matthew 12:43–45

What did Jesus mean by his story of a cast-out demon who returns to an unoccupied house and brings other evil spirits with it?

Jesus clearly intended this parable to apply to "this wicked generation" (v. 45). His point seems to be that the Messiah has come and is cleansing the house of Israel of evil spirits and illnesses. But that house remains empty, because the people refuse to believe in Jesus and invite him in as their Messiah. As a result, they are totally vulnerable. The evil spirit Jesus casts out will return with reinforcements, and the final state of the nation will be worse than it was before the Messiah came.

Matthew 12:46

Does the word brothers *here mean other children of Mary and Joseph, or does it mean other close relatives?*

The Catholic church holds that Mary remained a "perpetual virgin" after Jesus' birth, and that the Greek word *adelphos* here indicates Jesus' cousins rather than half-brothers born to Mary and Joseph. This is a most unlikely and strained interpretation of the text, especially in view of Matthew 13:55–56, where the people of Jesus' hometown name his brothers as James, Joseph, Simon, and Judas, and also mention his sisters.

Matthew 13:3

What are parables?

The word *parable* means "to set alongside." Parables are sayings, stories, or metaphors that teach truths by comparison. Most of Jesus' parables are vivid illustrations drawn from ordinary life, intended to help his listeners understand spiritual truths. But the parables in Matthew 13 are intentionally obscure. The parables about the kingdom of heaven were intended to unveil secrets about God's plan to the disciples while keeping them from the unbelieving crowd (13:10). These parables contrast the visible earthly kingdom that the Jewish people expected the Messiah to institute with the hidden form of God's kingdom that exists during our present age. The parables of Matthew 13, and their surprising teachings, are summarized below.

Parables of the Kingdom

The Parable	Expected Form	Unexpected Characteristic
1. Sower 13:3–9, 18–23	Messiah turns *Israel* and all *nations* to Himself.	*Individuals* respond differently to the Word's invitation.
2. Wheat/tares 13:24–30, 37–43	The kingdom's righteous citizens *rule over* the world with the King.	The kingdom's citizens are *among* the men of the world, growing together till God's harvesttime.
3. Mustard seed 13:31–32	Kingdom *begins* in *majestic glory.*	Kingdom *begins in insignificance;* its greatness comes as a surprise.
4. Leaven 13:33	Only righteousness enters the kingdom; other "raw material" is excluded.	The kingdom is implanted in a different "raw material" and grows to fill the whole personality with righteousness.
5. Hidden treasure 13:44	Kingdom is *public* and for all.	Kingdom is *hidden* and for individual "purchase."
6. Priceless pearl 13:45–46	Kingdom *brings all valued things* to men.	Kingdom demands *abandonment* of all other values (cf. 6:33).
7. Dragnet 13:47–50	Kingdom begins with initial separation of righteous and unrighteous.	Kingdom ends with final separation of the unrighteous from the righteous.

Matthew 13:31–32

Jesus was certainly wrong about the mustard seed being the smallest of all seeds. This is an example of the fact that the Bible errs in scientific matters.

Here Jesus referred to the black mustard, which had the smallest seed of any plant cultivated in Palestine. It would be ridiculous to suppose that Jesus was making a botanical pronouncement about every seed on earth. In popular Jewish idiom the mustard seed was the smallest measurable seed, and the weight of it was viewed as the least that could be weighed using a balance scale. Jesus made a point by referring to a tiny, familiar seed viewed as totally insignificant by his contemporaries, yet which generated a large plant that might grow to a height of ten feet. So the kingdom Jesus introduced might seem insignificant to his generation, yet it would grow to become a great movement.

Matthew 14:3

Did Herod die shortly after Jesus was born? Who is this Herod, and who are the other Herods of the New Testament?

The chart on the following page identifies the various members of the Herod family, the areas they ruled, and references to them in the New Testament.

Matthew 15:3–8

How could dedicating a gift to God release an adult child from any obligation to care for his aged parents?

Jesus refers not to any Old Testament legal principle but to a rabbinical ruling. He points out that the command to honor one's parents implies an obligation to be responsible for them when they are old and infirm. But the rabbis had interpreted the Old Testament law on vows in such a way that a person might declare any assets *Corban* (set aside for donation to the Temple treasury). A person making such a declaration did not actually give his assets to the treasury but used the goods or money he had dedicated for his own benefit instead. In essence, the rabbis' interpretation of the law on vows—a mere human tradition—set aside a direct command of God.

Matthew 15:21–28

How could Jesus be so callous as to refuse to help the Canaanite woman and refer to her people as dogs?

There is significant theological interplay in the dialogue between Jesus and this woman. She referred to Jesus as "Son of David"

THE HERODIAN FAMILY

GENERATION I

HEROD THE GREAT
King of Judea
37–4 B.C.
Matthew 2:1–19
Luke 1:5

GENERATION II

Son of **Doris**
Antipater

Sons of **Mariamne**
Aristobulus
Alexander

Son of **Mariamne** of Simon
Herod Philip
4 B.C.–A.D. 34
(First husband of Herodias
—Matt. 14:3, Mark 6:17)

Sons of **Malthace**
•**HEROD ANTIPAS**
Tetrarch of Galilee
4 B.C.–A.D. 39
Luke 3:1, 19–20, Mark 6:14–29
Matt. 14:1–11
Luke 13:31–33, 23:7–12

•**ARCHELAUS**
Ethnarch of Judea
4 B.C.–A.D. 6
Matt. 2:22

Son of **Cleopatra**
•**HEROD PHILIP**
Tetrarch of Iturea and Trachonitis
4 B.C.–A.D. 34
Luke 3:1

GENERATION III

Herod of Chalcis
A.D. 41–48

•**HEROD AGRIPPA I**
King of Judea
A.D. 37–44
Acts 12:1–24

Herodias
Consort of Herod Antipas
Mark 6:17
Matt. 14:3

GENERATION IV

Bernice
became consort of her
brother
Acts 25:13

•**HEROD AGRIPPA II**
Tetrarch of Chalcis and
of northern territory
A.D. 50–70
Acts 25:13–26:32

Drusilla
married "FELIX
procurator of Judea
A.D. 52(?)–59(?)
Acts 24:24

Salome
Matt. 14:1–11
Mark 6:14–29

Reigning rules of New Testament note are in capitals,
wives and relatives by marriage are in bold face.
Other members of the house designated by • .

(v. 22), a title identifying the Jewish Messiah. Jesus responded by saying that he was "sent only to the lost sheep of Israel" (v. 24). That meant that he truly was the Jewish Messiah. As a Gentile, the woman had no right to him or the benefits he brought to his own. His "bread" was for the children of Israel, not the "Gentile dogs," a common Jewish euphemism for Gentiles. The woman did not argue but agreed. She had no right to the benefits Jesus brought, and admitted that the children were to be fed first. But in saying that even the dogs eat the leftover crumbs, the woman expressed great faith. Jesus responded to her not because she had any claim on him but because the grace of God he brought was enough to meet the needs of the Jewish people, with enough left over to satisfy the Gentiles. Seeing her faith, Jesus granted her request.

The lesson here is important. No one today can claim to have a right to God's grace. But faith brings us to Jesus anyway and gives us the benefits he died for.

Matthew 16:18

Is Peter the "rock" on which the church is built? The Catholic church sees this pronouncement as Jesus' appointment of Peter as the first pope. Protestants disagree. Who is right?

Even the Catholic interpretation of this verse does not universally support the official interpretation. The church fathers reflect three theories: (1) Peter is the rock on which the church is built; (2) Peter's confession of Christ is the rock on which the church is built; (3) the truth Peter confessed—that Jesus is the Christ, the Son of God—is the rock on which the church is built. Most Protestants agree with those church fathers who took the third view (see also 1 Cor. 3:11).

Matthew 16:18

What are the "gates of Hades"?

The word *gates* is often used to refer to fortifications or powers. Thus the gates of Hades would be the powers of hell. Similar expressions are found in Job 17:16; Psalm 9:13; 107:18; and Isaiah 38:10 and in both pre-Christian Jewish and pagan literature. In these references "gates of Hades" seems to refer to death and dying. Jesus was announcing that death itself had no power against the church he was about to establish.

Matthew 16:19

*What are the "keys of the kingdom of heaven"? How are people
"bound" or "loosed" on earth so as to affect their status in
heaven?*

In biblical times keys represented authority stewards possessed to deny or provide access to a ruler (Isa. 22:15, 22). Binding and loosing is illustrated in Luke 11:52, where Jesus remarks that the teachers of the law had "taken away the key to knowledge" and thus had "hindered those who were entering [the kingdom of heaven]." The best way to understand the passage in Matthew is to see the keys as the knowledge of the gospel, and binding and loosing as the effect of the response to the gospel. That is, those who respond to the gospel proclamation are loosed, able to enter the kingdom, while those who refuse the gospel invitation are bound, unable to enter. It should be obvious that a person is not loosed or bound because of what another individual does here on earth. And it's equally obvious that when Jesus made this pronouncement concerning binding or loosing, he did so as an expression of heaven's decree.

Were the keys Jesus mentions given to Peter alone, to all the disciples, or to the whole church? It is interesting and perhaps significant that Peter was privileged to preach the first gospel message to the Jews (Acts 2) and to the Gentiles (Acts 10), thus turning the key and opening the door of the knowledge of salvation to both divisions of humanity. At the same time, anyone who shares the good news of Jesus with another exercises the power of the keys and, on the basis of God's Word, we can pronounce the individual who believes as loosed from his sins and the individual who rejects Jesus as bound to them.

Matthew 16:24

*How does a person deny himself, take up his cross, and follow
Jesus? What is the believer's "cross"?*

It is important to note that Jesus did not say disciples were to take up his cross but their cross. In the New Testament the cross is often used as a symbol of Christ's death and the entire meaning of that death. At the same time it is a symbol of God's will for Jesus Christ, who went to the cross in obedience to the Father's will.

It is this second meaning that Jesus uses here. A disciple's cross is whatever God's will for him or her may be. To deny oneself, then, is to consciously reject one's own will in favor of doing God's will. This does not mean we are never to do anything we like to do or even want to do.

God's will for the Christian is described in Romans 12:2 as "good, pleasing and perfect." The true disciple decides that when what he wants and what God wants conflict, he will deny himself and follow Jesus' example to do the will of God.

Matthew 16:26

How can a person "forfeit his soul" if he or she fails to take up Jesus' cross and follow him? The Bible says that salvation is by faith.

The solution to this supposed doctrinal contradiction is grammatical. The Greek word *psyche* is translated as 'his life' in 16:25 and 'his soul' in 16:26. In both cases its meaning is "the man himself" and follows the Aramaic pattern of using *nephesh* (the Hebrew equivalent of the Greek *psyche*) as a reflexive pronoun. Jesus is saying that the disciple who fails to deny himself, take up his cross daily, and follow Jesus, will lose the new person he might become in Christ, while the disciple who surrenders his old self will gain not his soul or his life but the new self God's Spirit seeks to help him become.

Matthew 16:28

Jesus said that some living then would not die until they "see the Son of Man coming in his kingdom." Two thousand years have passed, all of Jesus' first-century followers have died, and Jesus has not yet returned. Was he wrong in this case?m

There are two different views of what Jesus intended by this prediction. Literally translated, this phrase says that some would not die until they saw Jesus *coming with his reign.* Either view resolves the apparent contradiction, and each depends on our understanding of "coming with his reign." The first reflects 2 Peter 1:16: "We were eyewitnesses of his majesty." Many interpreters regard the transfiguration, which follows immediately after Matthew's account (17:1–8), as a vision of Jesus as he will be revealed in his return. Thus some (actually three) of the disciples "standing here" did see Jesus transfigured, coming in his kingdom majesty, "with his reign."

The second interpretation focuses on the day of Pentecost, when the Holy Spirit came upon the disciples and united them to Jesus and one another as Christ's church (Acts 2). This interpretation construes "with his reign" as the present form of God's kingdom, where Jesus rules in the hearts and lives of believers.

Matthew 17:17

Whom did Jesus mean when he spoke of an "unbelieving and perverse generation"?

The two words together indicate an unbelief that has its roots in moral failure, a willful neglect, or twisting of evidence to avoid an obvious conclusion. In applying these terms to this "generation," he certainly extended his condemnation beyond the disciples to the whole nation to which he had come. As for the nation, individuals would appeal to Jesus for healing, and people would acknowledge the fact that his miracles were evidence of his deity, and such would turn to him as the Son of God. As for the disciples, their failure to trust fully in the name of Jesus was demonstrated in their inability to cast out the demon that bound the man's son.

Jesus' response is best understood as an anguished cry. In view of all he had done and all he had said, how could this people to whom he had come with God's word still fail to believe? How could his disciples fail to grasp the extent of the power available to them through his name? They had performed a rite of exorcism and expected that the mere form would prevail. They had failed to realize that the power of Jesus was tapped by relationship—a relationship of complete dependence expressed by prayer.

Matthew 17:24–27

What was the temple tax, and what did Jesus mean by telling Peter that "the sons are exempt"?

Each Jewish male between age twenty-five and fifty was to pay an annual tax to support the temple services. Originally this tax was to be paid at the time of each census (see also Exod. 30:11–16). When asked if Jesus paid this tax, Peter blurted out, "Yes, he does" (Matt. 17:25). Later Jesus rebuked Peter, pointing out that human rulers hardly taxed their own children. Surely then the Son of God was not liable to pay a tax to God (17:25–26).

There is a further implication here. The early census tax on which this first-century tax was based was imposed by God on his covenant people. Since God does not tax his own children, the census and temple tax underline the fact that mere physical descent from Abraham, Isaac, and Jacob did not automatically make anyone a child of God. Only a personal faith like that of Abraham could do that.

Matthew 18:4

What made the child in this verse an example of greatness in God's kingdom?

It was his responsiveness to Jesus' call. Christ had come to his own people, but the nation either hesitated or rejected Christ's call to accept him as their Messiah. Yet when Jesus called a little child, the child unhesitatingly came to stand among them (18:2). Responsiveness to Jesus' word is still the key to greatness in God's kingdom.

Matthew 18:8–9

How will cutting off a hand or plucking out an eye keep a person from sinning? Didn't Jesus teach that sins come from the heart?

Yes, he did (Matt. 16:15–20). For an explanation of the strong warning contained in Jesus' imagery here, see the explanation of Matthew 5:29, page 232.

Matthew 18:17

What does it mean to treat a person like a pagan who will not listen when confronted about a sin committed against a fellow believer?

Jesus' teaching emphasizes the necessity of confession and reconciliation within the community of faith. Christ lays down a pattern of intensifying confrontation to be followed when a believer refuses to deal with any act that has hurt another follower of the Lord. Two interpretations are possible: (1) The unrepentant believer is to be ostracized (disciplined) by the church; or, (2) when a believer refuses to accept the church's efforts to help settle the dispute, the believer who was harmed is free to take the offender to secular courts.

Matthew 18:35

If God will not forgive a person who fails to forgive others, then salvation is not by faith, and Jesus' sacrifice did not win forgiveness for us. There is a real doctrinal conflict.

Jesus' story is not intended to teach God's way of salvation, but it is told in response to Peter's question in 18:21: "Lord, how many times shall I forgive my brother when he sins against me?" Christ's point is simply that it is unthinkable that we, who have been forgiven a great and unpayable debt of sin by God, should be unwilling to forgive the paltry debts others may owe us.

But Jesus goes on to point out that there are serious consequences to an unforgiving attitude. A person who is unwilling to forgive has not really understood grace or appropriated God's forgiveness. An unforgiving spirit blocks us from a personal experience of God's forgiveness and the joy of fully experiencing the peace with God that Christ's sacrifice won for us.

Matthew 19:6–9

Jesus said, "What God has joined together, let man not separate," and that a person who remarries "except for marital unfaithfulness" (19:9) commits adultery. Why then do some churches permit divorce and remarriage?

It is always dangerous to interpret any verse out of its context in the flow of a passage. These verses have to be understood by looking at the whole of what is happening here. When we trace the argument, we see that neither of these verses means what some people assume they say.

Jesus was asked about divorce by the Pharisees, whose claim to spiritual superiority rested on their zealous efforts to keep God's law. Was divorce law to be interpreted loosely, as by the contemporary school of Hillel, so that a person might divorce and remarry for any and every reason? Or was divorce law to be interpreted strictly, as by the school of Shammai, and permitted only for some type of marital unfaithfulness? Rather than answer this question about Mosaic law, Jesus pointed out that the creation story showed that God's intent was a lifelong union of one man and one woman.

Unsatisfied, the Pharisees returned to the issue of law. "'Why then,' they asked, 'did Moses command . . .'" (19:7)? Jesus responded that Old Testament law permitted divorce "because your hearts were hard" (19:8). That is, God knew that sin would so distort some relationships that divorce would be necessary for the well-being of the people involved. In saying this, Jesus utterly rejected the basic assumption the Pharisees made concerning relationship with God. They assumed that the law was the highest standard of all, and that by keeping it faithfully one could win God's favor. Jesus showed that God's intent was the highest standard, and that the law was a lowered standard, evidence of God's willingness to deal with sinful humanity's failings in grace.

What did Jesus mean when he said, "What God has joined together, let man not separate" (19:6)? The Old Testament's one pronouncement on divorce (Deut. 24:1–3) commanded the husband to give the wife a written bill of divorce when the marriage was dissolved. There was no prescription here to bring the issue to Moses, to the priests, or to others trained in the law to decide whether the couple could or could not divorce. Yet the Pharisees were constituting themselves an ecclesiastical court, as if they had the right to say to some, "You can divorce," and to others, "You cannot." It was this, the assumption that some ecclesiastical court can grant a divorce, that Jesus rejected when he said, "Let man not separate."

In context then, "Let man not separate" does not prohibit divorce but does reaffirm the principle that the decision concerning when a marriage has become destructive and must end can be made only by the persons involved. While the exception clause ("except for marital unfaithfulness") suggests that in some cases the act which institutes a second marriage may not involve adultery, Jesus' statement that adultery is involved calls on us to treat marriage as sacred and divorce as something never to be undertaken lightly.

Jesus' statement that one who divorces and remarries commits adultery underlines a critical reality. Every time we fall short of God's intent, we sin. The Pharisees had trivialized divorce and remarriage by arguing about when it was lawful, rather than by humbly confessing that each broken marriage was evidence of man's sinful condition and called for tears and admission of sin. Remarriage, implied by the divorce law of the Old Testament, was permitted by God. But, technically, initiating the new union did involve the sin of adultery. How good to know that this sin, too, can be forgiven, and that God does graciously give to those who fail another chance to build a marriage that seeks to approach God's ideal.

Matthew 19:16–22

Does Jesus' response to the man who asked what to do to inherit eternal life imply that one can earn salvation by good works?

Not at all. Instead Jesus called on the young man to look into the mirror of the law and discover that he was a lost sinner. To do this, Jesus recited the responsibilities toward other people that were engraved on the second stone tablet given Moses at Mount Sinai. The young man claimed to have kept those rules. Then Jesus commanded the young man to sell all he had and to "come, follow me" (v. 21). This the young man refused to do and so violated the first and great commandment of the law: "You shall have no other gods before me" (Exod. 20:3). This wealthy man's response showed that he valued his wealth more than the command of Jesus, who was God in the flesh.

A person may be blameless in keeping one or more of the Ten Commandments. But he or she can never keep all the commandments, and so has sinned. The Ten Commandments are a mirror. If we look into that mirror honestly, it reveals our flaws and drives us to Jesus to be saved.

Matthew 20:1–16

Were the workers right to feel the owner of the vineyard treated them unfairly? What did Jesus mean by telling this story?

Jesus' story was intended for those who assume that spiritual achievement is a matter of working harder than others. We can understand why those who worked all day in the vineyard were upset when those who worked only a couple of hours were paid a full day's wages (one denarius). But Jesus' point was that the owner chose to be gracious rather than to deal with his workers on a legal, "fairness" basis. If God were fair and paid us what our actions merit, none of us would be saved. How wonderful that God has chosen instead to relate to us in grace!

Matthew 20:29–34

Did Jesus heal two blind men, or just the one man who is mentioned in Mark 10:46 and Luke 18:35–38?

It's not at all uncommon for three people reporting on the same event to mention different details. There is no conflict at all in the three reports, for the details supplement rather than conflict with each other. The three accounts fit together to tell the following story.

Bartimaeus heard of Jesus when he entered Jericho but was unable to attract his attention at that time. After Jesus finished teaching in the city, Bartimaeus, joined by another blind man, shouted out for help as Jesus was leaving the city. This time Christ heard the cries and stopped to heal both blind men.

Matthew 21:2

This verse mentions two donkeys: a mother and its foal. But Mark 11:2 and Luke 19:30 only mention one. Who is right?

Again, this is not an either-or issue. The accounts agree that Jesus entered the city riding the young donkey. The fact that Mark and

Luke did not mention the mother donkey does not in any way imply she was not there.

Certainly no one would accuse reporters of error when they merely emphasized different but nonconflicting details of the same news story. For the same reason, it makes no sense at all to accuse the Gospel writers of discrepancies when their stories differ in certain extraneous details.

Matthew 21:7

Why did Jesus enter Jerusalem riding a donkey?

It was in part to fulfill a prophecy found in Zechariah 9:9. But this triumphal entry had additional significance. In biblical times, when a ruler rode a horse, it signified warlike intentions. In contrast, riding a donkey was symbolic of peaceful intent. Jesus' entry into Jerusalem on a donkey was a symbolic statement of his intent not to establish an earthly kingdom at that time.

Matthew 21:12–13

In what sense was the temple a "den of robbers"?

Visitors to Jerusalem had to obtain the wood, animals, and other items involved in offering sacrifices at the temple. In addition, other currencies had to be exchanged for authorized temple funds. Some early Jewish documents indicate that not only was this commerce permitted in the temple environs but that the family of the high priest received a part of each business' profits and that fraud was widespread. For instance, someone might bring a lamb to the temple. A corrupt priest might find some blemish on the lamb that disqualified it as a sacrificial animal, forcing the worshiper to sell it at a loss and buy a qualified lamb at an inflated price. Later the first lamb would be resold and used as a sacrifice.

Matthew 22:32

How does the Old Testament statement "I am the God of Abraham, the God of Isaac, and the God of Jacob" prove the doctrine of resurrection?

Jesus' argument hinges on the tense of the Hebrew verb. He points out that the Old Testament does not quote God as saying "I *was* the God" of these patriarchs. Instead the Lord said, "I *am*." This clearly implies that Abraham, Isaac, and Jacob still live, even though they died long before God spoke these words to Moses.

Thus the Sadducees' theological position that a person who died will not be resurrected was disproved, and the Pharisees' position that there will be a resurrection of the dead was given biblical support.

It is important to note that Jesus treated the Scriptures with such respect that he drew support for a central doctrine from the mere tense of a verb. If Scripture is so reliable that a vital doctrine can be supported by such a small detail, it follows that Scripture is God's Word in its entirety.

Matthew 22:41–46

What was the point of Jesus' challenge to the Pharisees to explain how David could call the Messiah "Lord"?

Jewish tradition placed great weight on ancestry and viewed an ancestor as superior to his descendants. Thus the Messiah, as a descendant of David, should by rights have shown respect for David by calling him Lord. This was a common expression of respect. Christ challenged the Pharisees to explain how David could refer to the Messiah as Lord in a well-known messianic Psalm. The implication, which the Pharisees refused to acknowledge, was that the Messiah was also the Son of God—exactly what Jesus claimed for himself.

Matthew 23:13–29

What is a woe?

Jesus used this word as an exclamation, both of grief and denouncement. Here Jesus rendered a judicial verdict on many practices of the Pharisees, but did so with a heavy heart.

Matthew 23:13–15

What is a hypocrite?

The original word described an actor in a Greek play who held a mask in front of his face to represent himself as the character he was playing. The word eventually meant anyone who behaved insincerely or attempted to be something he was not. Jesus' harshest denunciation of the Pharisees was for playacting at piety when their inner motivation was selfish and self-serving.

Matthew 23

What did Jesus mean when he told his disciples, "Do not call any-one on earth 'father,' . . . Nor are you to be called 'teacher'"?

In New Testament times there was a clearly defined process by which a person was recognized as a teacher of the law. That process involved a long period of discipleship during which the candidate was trained by a recognized sage (rabbi). Those who had been through this process were held in great awe in Judaism and viewed as religious authorities. They were addressed with great respect as "teacher" or "father," and their interpretations of divine law were considered to be as binding as the law itself.

In the context of this chapter condemning contemporary "teachers of the law and Pharisees" (v. 13), Jesus was warning his disciples against the development of a hierarchical approach to Christian faith. Rather than set up some men as authoritative interpreters of God's will, the Christian is to regard all believers as brothers and sisters, and all are to appeal together to Christ, whose teachings alone are authoritative.

This theme is developed later in the New Testament epistles, and particularly in Romans 14, where believers are commanded to be personally responsible to Christ as Lord and not to another's interpretations of God's will.

Matthew 23:16–22

What does it mean to "swear by" something? And what does Jesus' teaching imply?

It was common in first-century Judaism to bind a promise or commitment by swearing by something precious. The same thing is common in our day: "I'll never do it again. I swear it, by my mother's good name." However, this practice led to a debate between the rabbis over what oaths were binding and must be kept, and which might be disregarded. Thus if one made a commitment and swore by the temple, the rabbis held that the oathmaker might fail to keep his promise without any penalty. But if he swore by the gold in the temple, he had to keep his word.

While Jesus derided the rabbis' foolish rulings, the real problem resided in their notion that a person could give his word and then violate it without doing wrong. In Matthew 5:37 Christ taught, "Simply let your 'Yes' be 'Yes,' and your 'No' be 'No'; anything beyond this comes from the evil one."

Matthew 23:34–36

How could Zechariah son of Berechiah be the last of the martyrs? And wasn't Zechariah the son of Jehoiada?

Twenty-seven different individuals named Zechariah are mentioned in the Old Testament. The Zechariah who was the son of Jehoiada was martyred three centuries before the death of the prophet Zechariah, who was the son of Berechiah. The critics complain of an error because other Jews were martyred after the son of Jehoiada. This assumes that Jesus made a mistake or there was a copying error that confused the names. The simplest explanation is that both Zechariahs were martyred and that Jesus knew exactly what he was saying when he identified Zechariah the son of Berechiah as the second of the two martyrs.

Matthew 24:3

What did Jesus' disciples mean when they asked about "the end of the age"?

The Old Testament prophets described in some detail how history would end: a devastating period of judgment followed by the initiation of a glorious era instituting Jewish domination of the world under the promised Messiah. When the disciples asked about "the end of the age" they were thinking of the end of Gentile domination of the Holy Land and the initiation of the promised era of prosperity and peace.

Matthew 24:15

What is "'the abomination that causes desolation' spoken of through the prophet Daniel," which Jesus said would indicate that the end was at hand?

See the discussion of this phrase under Daniel 11:31, page 198.

Matthew 24:21

What does the phrase "great distress" mean, and how does it relate to Old Testament prophecy?

The Greek word is *thlipsis* and is used in the Septuagint to translate words describing a period of intense tribulation and suffering associated with the judgments to take place before the Messiah comes. In using this phrase and describing this period as a time of "unequaled" anguish, Jesus not only refers to Old Testament prophecy but confirms the predictions of the prophets concerning the future of the world and the future of the Jews as God's chosen people.

Matthew 24:34

How could Jesus say, "This generation will certainly not pass away until all these things have happened"? In fact, that generation is long dead, and Jesus' predictions have not yet been fulfilled.

The answer to this supposed error in Scripture hinges on our understanding of the word translated "generation" (*genea*). One possible meaning is that *genea* is used here in the sense of "race" or "people." In this case Jesus would be saying that God would preserve the Jewish race until his return. While there are other interpretations, this one seems to best fit the context and certainly resolves the supposed error in a way that does no violation to the language or grammar of the text.

Matthew 26:39

What was the cup that Jesus begged God to take from him, and how was this prayer answered?

Many assume that the cup was Jesus' coming crucifixion. However, Hebrews 5:7, describes Jesus' Gethsemane experience and says that "he offered up prayers and petitions with loud cries and tears to the one who could save him from death, *and he was heard because of his reverent submission*" (italics mine). This may indicate that the cup was not Christ's death on the cross but rather death itself. Jesus died according to God's will, and in answer to his prayer was raised from the dead.

Matthew 27:9

Does this verse wrongly attribute to Jeremiah a prophecy actually made by Zechariah? This clearly is an error.

When the Hebrew Old Testament scrolls were organized, Jeremiah came first among the prophets. It was common to refer to Jeremiah and simply mean, "One of the prophets." So this is not an error at all but reflects a convention with which Matthew was completely familiar.

Matthew 27:26

Why was Jesus flogged if he was going to be crucified?

The soldiers used a *flagellum*, a leather whip into which metal, bone, or other sharp-edged weights were plaited. This kind of whipping often killed victims by itself. Those about to be crucified were often whipped first, with the intent of weakening the condemned so that they would take less time to die.

Matthew 27:51

What was the significance of the tearing of the temple veil from top to bottom?

A thick, woven veil separated the innermost room of the temple from an outer room. Priests entered the outer room daily to worship and to maintain a fresh supply of the bread and oil there. The innermost room was entered only once a year by the high priest, who entered on the Day of Atonement carrying sacrificial blood which he sprinkled on the Ark of the Covenant. The veil was significant, for it symbolized a basic spiritual reality. Despite God's love for Israel, his Old Testament people were not permitted to come freely into his presence. The splitting of the veil when Jesus died symbolized the gospel truth that through Christ believers can now "approach the throne of grace with confidence" (Heb. 4:16). Nothing can separate the believer in Christ from God the Father.

Matthew 28:14–15

Does the story told by the soldiers of the disciples stealing Jesus' body make more sense than the Christian position that Jesus rose from the dead?

Not really. In New Testament times, guards who fell asleep on duty were executed. No first-century guard would willingly tell his superiors that he had fallen asleep. The only reasonable explanation for this story is the one given by Matthew: The guards were bribed to say that Jesus' disciples stole the body while they slept.

There is, of course, another problem. If the guards really were asleep, how could they know that the disciples had come and taken the body? They could have known this only if they were awake and saw the disciples. But if they had seen the disciples, these armed men would surely have prevented the theft.

In fact, the only reasonable explanation is that given by Matthew. God sent angels to open the tomb of Jesus, and it was a living Jesus who left the grave where his body had been laid.

Mark

Mark

Who wrote this book, and what themes and issues does it deal with?

Mark's Gospel is the shortest of the four biblical accounts of Jesus' life and ministry. Tradition identifies John Mark, the young man who deserted Paul's team on his first missionary journey (Acts 12:25; 13:5), as the writer of this book. Mark was given another chance by Barnabas, Paul's original missionary partner (Acts 15:36–41), and later was reconciled to Paul (Col. 4:10; 2 Tim. 4:11). Later still, Mark became a companion of Peter (1 Peter 5:13), and this Gospel reflects Peter's eyewitness account of Jesus' life.

The Gospel of Mark is a fast-moving, intense narrative of Jesus' life and works. Mark's Gospel lacks the extended accounts of Jesus' teaching found in the other Gospels. Instead it focuses on Jesus' actions. Christ is portrayed as a vigorous man, using his unquestionable authority to deal with opposition, sickness, and even evil spirits. Mark engages in no theological polemics, but confronts the reader with a vivid picture of one who acted as, and claimed to be, the Son of God.

Mark 1:4

What is "a baptism of repentance," and what does it have to do with winning forgiveness of sins?

The Greek construction in the phrase *baptism of repentance* uses a genitive of quality. This means that the baptism was intended to indicate that repentance had already taken place, or that the baptism was a sign that the individual was repenting then. The word for repent, *metanoia*, means "a change of mind." In Scripture *repentance* indicates a much deeper, more radical, total change. This is no mere "I'm sorry," but a revolutionary reorientation of heart and life in which a person turns from sins to God. Such repentance, which is in itself an act of faith, leads to the forgiveness of sins. This, too, is implicit in the Greek, where *eis* here indicates an "end result."

Mark 1:8
What does it mean to be baptized with the Holy Spirit?

The problem in understanding this phrase is rooted in the fact that it is used one way in Scripture and another in one of our contemporary theological traditions. In the Bible, baptism with the Spirit refers to that work of the Holy Spirit by which the believer is united to Christ and to other believers. This definition is derived from 1 Corinthians 12:13: "For we were all baptized by one Spirit into one body—whether Jews or Greeks, slave or free—and we were all given the one Spirit to drink" (see also Rom. 6:3–8). This first took place on the day of Pentecost, commonly identified as the "birthday of the church" (Acts 2:1–4; see also Acts 10:45–47; 11:15–17).

In one contemporary theological tradition, however, the phrase *baptism of the Spirit* identifies the doctrine that God the Holy Spirit fills and empowers believers. This baptism of the Spirit is a "second work of grace," believed to happen subsequent to salvation. Many in this tradition see speaking in tongues as the sign of an authentic baptism of the believer by the Spirit.

When a person uses this phrase, it is important to know whether he or she uses it biblically or theologically. And it is important not to read into any New Testament passage its theological rather than biblical meaning.

Mark 1:23
What is an "evil spirit" and where do evil spirits come from?

See the discussion of Matthew 10:1, page 238.

Mark 1:41
Why did Jesus touch the man with leprosy when he healed him?

Most of the miraculous healings Jesus performed were accomplished simply by his speaking a word of command. In this case, however, he spoke and touched the leper as well. The reason for this lies in the nature of the disease, which made a person ritually unclean and led to his isolation from others. The leper was not allowed to join the community in worship and could not even be touched by any person who was ritually pure. When Jesus, moved by compassion, touched the leper, he was responding not only to the man's need for healing but also to his terrible sense of isolation from others.

Mark 2:4
How can a person dig through a roof?

The flat roofs of ordinary homes in New Testament Palestine were constructed of poles covered with layers of branches and dried mud. The men who carried their paralyzed friend to Jesus did, literally, dig through these layers to let their companion down through the hole.

Mark 2:15
Why was Jesus criticized for eating with "tax collectors and 'sinners'"?

Old Testament religion called for strict separation of "clean" and "unclean." For instance, certain ritually unclean animals could not be eaten. A menstruating woman was temporarily unclean, and her husband could not have sex with her during this time. Dead bodies were unclean, and those who touched them were to wash their clothing and were themselves unclean until evening. The notion of separation of the clean and unclean had been extended in first-century Judaism to define interpersonal relationships. Those who were most zealous to keep God's Old Testament laws looked down on their more lax coreligionists and were quick to label other sinners as unclean. The religious people felt that any association with sinners would contaminate them, just as would touching a ritually unclean object.

Jesus' actions then were totally incomprehensible to the Pharisees and other religious leaders. How could Jesus have anything to do with such people? That surely must contaminate him. They did not realize that Jesus had come to earth for the express purpose of reaching sinners with the good news that God—unlike the religious persons—loved them and would accept all who came to him in faith. Rather than draw back in fear that he might be contaminated, Jesus sought out society's outcasts to save and transform them.

Mark 2:17

What did Jesus mean when he said, "I have not come to call the righteous, but sinners"?

Jesus was first of all stating his mission on earth: to reach out to sinners with the good news of God's love and forgiveness. But Jesus was also making an acute psychological observation. The person who considers himself or herself righteous will not listen to an invitation to repent and be saved. That person relies on good works to merit favor with God. The person who knows he or she is a lost sinner will be ready to hear the gospel and eager to respond to its invitation.

Mark 2:21

What did Jesus mean by likening his message to new wine and new cloth?

See the discussion of Matthew 9:16–17, page 238.

Mark 2:26

Mark says Jesus identified Abiathar as high priest when David's men ate sacred bread at the tabernacle. But the Old Testament says Ahimelech was high priest. So the Bible does contain mistakes.

But Jesus' words do not imply that Abiathar was already high priest. The literal Greek text says, "in the time of [*epi* with the genitive] Abiathar the high priest," that is, during the lifetime of the Abiathar who became high priest. If we take what Jesus said in the way his words must have been understood in the first century A.D., there is no conflict here at all.

Mark 2:27

What did Jesus mean when he said, "The Sabbath is made for man, not man for the Sabbath"?

Jesus meant that the Sabbath was intended as a grace gift, given to human beings by God. It was not intended to be a straitjacket. It follows, therefore, that it is lawful to do good to one another on the Sabbath, without the kind of restriction on response to human need shown by the Pharisees' attitude toward the paralytic whom Jesus healed.

It is fascinating to read the hundreds of pages of detailed discussion by early rabbis of what a good Jew could or could not do on the Sabbath. It all hung on this simple commandment: "Remember the Sabbath day by keeping it holy" (Exod. 20:8) and the proscription on doing any work on that day. This led the rabbis to classify thirty-nine kinds of "work" a person could not do on the Sabbath, including tying and untying. A later expression of this ruling says, "It is forbidden to tear or twine even threads or hairs. . . . A knot . . . is likewise forbidden to be untied. In case of pain it may be loosened through a Gentile."

Jesus' remark puts the Sabbath in a very different perspective: The Sabbath is God's gift to humanity, so human needs have priority. To make keeping the Sabbath a burden by giving human traditions that define "work" priority over human need is to misunderstand the meaning of the Sabbath entirely.

Mark 2:27
What did Jesus mean when he called himself "Lord even of the Sabbath"?

See the discussion at Matthew 12:8, page 240.

Mark 3:6
Who were the Herodians?

The name suggests they were influential Jews who were supporters of Herod's policy of accommodation with Rome. When the Pharisees began to plot against Jesus because his Sabbath healings demonstrated a significant challenge to their religious views and popularity with the people, the Herodians seem to have joined them out of fear that Christ's growing following might upset the tense political situation in Palestine.

Mark 3:29
What is the unforgivable sin?

See the discussion of Matthew 12:31, page 241.

Mark 3:31

Did Jesus have brothers and sisters?

See the discussion of Matthew 12:46, page 243.

Mark 4:24–25

What did Jesus mean, "With the measure you use, it will be measured to you"?

When grain was bought or sold it was poured into a measure, a basket, or a square wooden box. Often a dishonest man would use two measures, a smaller one for selling and a larger one for buying. Jesus' words then are a warning. If a hearer responds to what Jesus said, God will respond to him. If anyone fails to respond, God will not respond to him. As a result, one who responds will be "given more"; one who does not, "even what he has will be taken from him."

Mark 4:31

Jesus was wrong in saying that the mustard seed is the smallest of seeds. So the Bible does contain an error.

See the discussion of Matthew 13:32, page 244.

Mark 5:1–16

There is a discrepancy among the Gospels as to how many demon-possessed men there were. Surely this shows there are errors in Scripture.

See the discussion of Matthew 8:28–34, page 237.

Mark 5:34

Does this verse show that if a person has enough faith he or she can always expect to be healed of an illness or disease?

Numerous instances of healings by Jesus are reported in the Gospels, many associated with the sick person's faith (Matt. 8:1–3; 9:20–22; Acts 5:16; 14:9). Other healing miracles are reported with no mention of faith at all (Matt. 9:23–26; Mark 6:5; Acts 3:1–10; 8:7; 28:8). Certainly it was faith that brought the sick to Jesus, as in the case of this woman who firmly believed that if she could only touch the Lord she would be healed.

While faith leads us to Jesus, confident that he can heal, even the firmest faith will not guarantee healing. This is illustrated by the apostle Paul, who appealed to the Lord three times for healing of what may have been a serious and disfiguring illness. Instead of healing Paul, the Lord announced that he would provide enough grace to allow the apostle to live victoriously with his problem (2 Cor. 12:7–10). Later Paul, rather than tell Timothy to pray for healing, advised him to "use a little wine" to deal with his chronic stomach problems (1 Tim. 5:23; see also Phil. 2:27). Surely no one would charge these leaders of the early church with a lack of faith.

James does tell the sick to have the elders pray over them. But the notion that Christians can claim physical healing as a right, or that having faith guarantees healing in every case, is simply not supported by either the Bible's explicit teachings or its reports of illnesses and healings.

Mark 5:39

Each of the Gospels reports that Jesus said Jairus's daughter was "not dead but asleep." But each evangelist also describes the ridicule of the crowd, who knew she was dead.

There is no way to know for certain what Jesus meant. It is possible the girl had slipped into a coma, and that Jesus aroused her. It is also possible that Jesus used the expression in view of the fact that he intended to "awaken" the young girl shortly. It is significant that Jesus used a similar expression in speaking of Lazarus, who had been dead for several days (John 11). The Bible frequently uses *sleep* as a euphemism for death. This is a beautiful testimony to the fact that biological death is not the end for any human being.

Mark 7:3

What was the "tradition of the elders"?

The Babylonian captivity launched a great movement toward the study of the Old Testament Scriptures (Ezra 7:10). Convinced that disaster had struck the nation because their ancestors had ignored God's Word, the Jewish people searched the Scriptures diligently to learn how to live to please God and to avoid future disasters.

Over the centuries this movement generated a large body of material containing the interpretations of generations of men who had given their lives to the study of and explanation of Old Testament law. By the time of Jesus anyone who was considered an expert in the law was expected not only to know the Old Testament text but also to interpret it in light of the exposition of sages who had gone before. In fact, the Old Testament was interpreted through the body of traditional interpretations, so that in a sense tradition was given more weight than Scripture.

Jesus was rigorous in his criticism of those whose grasp of the Old Testament was distorted by mere human tradition. In this passage Jesus goes on to attack the Pharisees and teachers of the law who criticized him for not keeping tradition. Their religion all too often was nothing more than letting go "of the commands of God and . . . holding onto the traditions of men" (Mark 7:8).

Christ's words are a warning to us today. While we want to honor and study the insights of great students of God's Word, we must never forget that Scripture is the authority and not any human being's interpretation of it.

Mark 7:11

What was "Corban" and how did it enable persons to avoid obligations to elderly parents?

See the discussion of Matthew 15:3–8, page 245.

Mark 7:24–30

How could Jesus reject the plea of the Syrophoenician woman and even imply that she was a dog?

See the discussion of Matthew 15:21–28, page 245.

Mark 7:36

Why would Jesus tell onlookers not to tell others he healed the deaf and dumb man, when, according to Mark 5:18–20, he had commanded a man healed of demon possession to tell others?

The old saw "Circumstances alter cases" surely applies here. There is one obvious difference between the circumstances of these two incidents: The miracle of 5:18 was performed in a pagan land; that of 7:36 was in Jewish territory. There are other differences, too. The demoniac was eager to follow Jesus; the Jewish crowds were excited and curious but not committed to him. Also, the demoniac was to give personal testimony about what the Lord had done for him, but the crowds could only talk about what they had seen Jesus do for others. Commentators have drawn various conclusions from these differences. Perhaps the most telling observation is that Jesus called for silence here, as in Mark 1:44, so that his teaching might be emphasized and because excitement about his miracles might have touched off a messianic insurrection based on misunderstanding of his real purposes.

Mark 8:11

Why did the Pharisees demand a "sign from heaven"? Jesus had already performed many notable miracles authenticating his claim to being God's messenger.

The text says the Pharisees intended to "test" Jesus (the same word in Greek is also translated "tempt"). They were unwilling to accept the miracles Jesus had performed and wanted some higher kind of sign from heaven that was unmistakably from God. The reaction of the Pharisees to Jesus' miracles, even when they discounted them as demonic in origin, reminds us of an important truth. No proof is enough to create faith in a person who resolutely refuses to believe. Christ's later miracle of raising Lazarus and even his own subsequent resurrection failed to convince the religious zealots. We can never present enough evidence to compel anyone to believe. Faith is a choice. When we choose to believe, we realize how much evidence there is, so that faith is more reasonable than unbelief.

Mark 8:15

What was the "yeast of the Pharisees and that of Herod"?

According to Matthew 16:12, Jesus was referring to the teachings of the Pharisees and Sadducees. Many of the Herodians were Sadducees.

Mark 8:34–37

What is meant by the following words of Jesus: "He must deny himself and take up his cross and follow me. . . . What good is it for a man to gain the whole world, yet forfeit his soul?"

See the discussion of Matthew 16:24, page 248.

Mark 9:1

How could people living in Jesus' day see his kingdom "come with power"? It is now two thousand years later, and Christ has not come with power yet.

See the discussion of Matthew 16:28, page 249.

Mark 9:11

How can Jesus say here that Elijah has come first, but is quoted by Matthew as saying that John could have fulfilled the Old Testament prophecy of Elijah if the Jews had accepted Jesus as their Messiah (Matt. 17:12–13)?

The disciples raised the question in view of Jesus' announcement that he had to suffer and die (Mark 9:9–10). Jesus said that Elijah would appear and "restore all things" (Matt. 17:11).

Where is room then for Jesus' death, if John fulfills the Elijah prophecy? Both Gospel accounts agree that John's ministry fulfills the requirements of the Elijah prophecy. Mark is simply more emphatic, in view of the question raised by the disciples. Elijah *has* come, but Jesus, the Messiah, must still die.

Mark 9:25

Why does Matthew's Gospel describe this boy's affliction as epilepsy, while Mark reports that Jesus diagnosed his problem as a "deaf and mute spirit"?

Matthew describes the symptoms exhibited by the boy: not merely deafness but also seizures suggestive of epilepsy. Mark's report is the most extensive found in any Gospel and includes Jesus' revelation of the cause of the epileptic symptoms: demonic possession.

Mark 9:40

Is Jesus inconsistent when he says here that anyone "not against us is for us," and says just the opposite in another situation?

See the discussion of Matthew 12:30, page 241.

Mark 9:42–49

Was Jesus' real intention to cut off a hand or blind an eye that might involve a person in sin?

See the discussion of Matthew 18:8–9, page 251.

Mark 9:50

How can salt lose its saltiness?

See the discussion of Matthew 5:13, page 232.

Mark 10:9

What is Jesus' teaching on divorce?

See the discussion of Matthew 19:6–9, page 252.

Mark 10:17–21

Does Jesus' instruction to the rich young ruler imply that a person can be saved by good works?

See the discussion of Matthew 19:16–22, page 253.

Mark 10:25

Why were the disciples so amazed when Jesus remarked that it is hard for a rich man to enter the kingdom of God?

It was commonly believed in first-century Judaism that wealth was evidence of God's favor. Moreover, wealth permitted a person to do those generous good deeds that were thought to earn God's favor.

The theological basis for this view is rooted in Deuteronomy, which promises Israel prosperity if they love and obey God (Deut. 30:1–10). This promise was applied inappropriately in the first century A.D. to individuals. So Jesus stunned the disciples not only by rejecting popular opinion but by indicating that wealth actually made it hard for a person to enter the kingdom of God. Jesus' point was that a person with great material possessions is unlikely to give priority to spiritual things.

This thread of teaching on material possessions also has roots in the Old Testament. In Psalm 73 Asaph realizes that the wicked wealthy are not blessed by God but actually have been placed "on slippery ground" (Ps. 73:18). Wealth tends to distort an individual's perspective on life and drain any sense of need for God.

Mark 10:38

What were the cup and the baptism Jesus challenged James and John to share?

James and John had asked for exalted positions in the kingdom they thought Jesus was about to establish on earth. Jesus challenged them by pointing to his own cup and baptism, here images of suffering (Ps. 75:8; Isa. 51:17) and of trouble (Ps. 18:16; 69:1–2; Matt. 3:10). Christ's point was that as he had to pass through intense suffering, be raised from the dead, and be exalted as Lord, so his followers would only attain future exaltation by suffering and serving others.

Mark 10:46–52

Mark speaks only of one blind man, Matthew and Luke mention two. Is this an example of errors and conflicts among the Gospels?

See the discussion of Matthew 20:29–34, page 254.

Mark 11:12–14

Why did Jesus curse the fig tree? And why do the accounts of the cursing differ?

This has been called one of the most difficult stories in Scripture. It helps to recognize that the Old Testament often pictures Israel as a vine or tree, intended by God to produce fruit (Isa. 5:1–5; Hos. 9:10; Nah. 3:12).

The leaves and the fruit of the fig tree develop at the same time. Even though it was not the season for figs, the fully leafed tree Jesus and the disciples saw should have had fruit. Most commentators agree that the fig tree and Jesus' curse were symbolic, linked with Jesus' angry purging of the temple. The tree represented God's people, apparently very religious (the fully leafed tree) but without godliness (the fruit). Thus the cursing of the fig tree was an acted-out parable, symbolizing the judgment of God on a hypocritical and faithless generation.

While the accounts in Matthew and Mark differ slightly, each ties the cursing of the fig tree to the cleansing of the temple, which gives the story its significance. Matthew 21:19 notes, "Immediately the tree withered," while Mark 11:20 says, "In the morning . . . they saw the fig tree withered from the roots." But this is no conflict, if we understand that the leaves immediately dropped as the tree began to wither, while the next day the process was complete and the tree was "withered from the roots." Certainly the event was striking enough to make the disciples comment on both days.

Mark 11:23–24

Did Jesus really mean for his disciples to move mountains by prayer? What about all the people who have prayed and believe that they have received what they pray for but still don't really receive it?

These particular words of Jesus are not found in the earliest and best Greek manuscripts, and many believe they were not in Mark's original work. However, the saying itself is authentic, and is also found in Matthew 17:10.

The best way to understand the first part of the saying is to observe that mountains serve in the Old Testament as a symbol of a great difficulty (Zech. 4:7). So Jesus' statement can be taken metaphorically to indicate that the believer can appeal to God in prayer for that which human resource cannot accomplish.

Unfortunately, some have taken Jesus' promise about believing out of the context of Scripture's total teaching on prayer. Answers to prayer do not depend on how firmly we believe or how fervently we pray. They depend on God, who graciously responds to the needs of his people and acts in our behalf. Jesus does not say that belief is a condition we must meet to have our prayers answered; rather, he is speaking descriptively. When we pray, and God's Spirit speaks to our hearts in such a way that we know we have been heard, thereby giving us faith's inner confidence, then we know that God will answer our prayers. Belief is an inner sign that God intends to respond, not a precondition we must meet before God will listen to us.

Mark 11:27–28

Why was the issue of authority so important to the chief priests and teachers of the law?

In first-century Judaism the Sanhedrin, a sort of supreme religious and secular authority, was considered to be the final judge of Scripture's meaning and practical application. The authority anyone exercised in Judaism was ultimately drawn from this body. Jesus had never been given the stamp of approval of these religious leaders, yet he not only taught and performed miracles but took it on himself to throw out of the temple the merchants who were licensed by the chief priests. Christ revealed the emptiness of their claim of authority by challenging them to render an official verdict on John the Baptist's ministry. When they refused, knowing that whatever answer they gave would be used against them, they in essence abdicated the authority they falsely claimed to have and surrendered any right to challenge Jesus.

Mark 12:13–17

Why was the issue of taxes so sensitive in first-century Palestine? And what was the trap the Pharisees set in asking Jesus about them?

The burden of taxes was extremely heavy. Jews owed a tithe of income to the temple. The Herods, who ruled as petty monarchs under the Romans, also demanded taxes. In fact Herod Archelaus, who governed Judea, imposed such heavy taxes that the Romans deposed him to head off a revolt. In addition, oppressive taxes were imposed by the Roman government. This last tax not only strained the economy but also aroused religious opposition. There was continual theological debate over whether it was treason to pay taxes to foreign rulers, since God alone was king of Israel. The heavier the taxes became, the more popular this teaching was with ordinary people. So when the Pharisees posed their question to Jesus, they expected that either he would say taxes should be paid to Rome, thus taking a most unpopular stand they could use against him, or that he would say taxes should not be paid to Rome. If Jesus said the latter, the Roman governor might move against him to head off a tax revolt. Such a revolt, based on this very teaching, had taken place in Palestine around A.D. 6.

Jesus thwarted them completely by borrowing a coin, pointing to Caesar's image on it, and telling them to let Caesar have what was his and to be sure to give God his due.

Mark 12:26

How did Jesus' quotation of God's words "I am the God of Abraham" thwart the Sadducees? And what does it tell us about Scripture?

See the discussion of Matthew 22:32, page 255.

Mark 13:14

What is the "abomination that causes desolation"?

See the discussion of Matthew 24:15, see page 258.

Mark 13:22

Deuteronomy 18 indicates that performing miracles is a sign that a person is God's spokesman. How then could Satan empower Antichrist to perform miracles?

It is true that performing miracles was generally considered a sign that a prophet was a "man of God" (2 Kings 1:10). However, this alone was not enough to prove God had sent an individual as his spokesman. Deuteronomy 13:1–4 says that even if a person "announces to you a miraculous sign or wonder" and it actually comes to pass, that prophet is not to be listened to if he calls on Israel to "follow other gods." Deuteronomy 18:17–23 adds that a true prophet "from among their brothers" will speak in Yahweh's name and will demonstrate his calling by predicting future events in the name of the Lord, which events invariably come true.

So miracles alone are not enough to demonstrate that a person has been empowered by God. The Bible describes Satan as a real being, a fallen angel with great powers. Modernists may see Satan as a myth and miracles as a way primitive peoples explained natural phenomena. But the Bible takes Satan and miracles seriously and describes a spiritual warfare between the forces of evil and those of God.

Mark 13:30

Jesus was wrong, because the generation that lived then did pass away before the things Jesus described happened.

See the discussion of Matthew 24:34, page 259.

Mark 14:22–24

Does Jesus' statement, "This is my body. . . . This is my blood," mean that the communion elements are actually changed into Christ's body and blood?

The Roman Catholic Church takes these words literally and promotes the doctrine of transubstantiation. This theory holds that, when consecrated by a priest and taken into the body, communion bread and wine are said literally to become the body and blood of Jesus. Lutherans hold a doctrine of consubstantiation. This means that the body and blood of Christ are said to be present *along with* the bread and wine the worshiper partakes of in communion. Most other Protestants believe that Christ was speaking metaphorically, and that the bread and wine are symbols of Jesus' body broken on Calvary and the blood he shed there.

Interestingly, early in the Reformation the Protestants, Luther of Germany and Zwingli of Switzerland, attempted to unite their movements. They failed, falling out over Luther's angry insistence that when Jesus said, "This is [Greek *estin*] my body," he meant that the bread is actually Christ's body. Zwingli just as vigorously argued for a symbolic interpretation of Jesus' words. He pointed out that Christ also said, "I am the gate for the sheep" (John 10:7). The Greek word translated "am" in this verse is just as emphatic. But Luther surely didn't believe that Jesus was present in the splinters of a gate.

While the theological differences will undoubtedly continue, there is no reason why "This is my body" cannot be understood as a metaphorical statement. It does not require us to believe that bread and wine actually become Jesus' body and blood when taken at the Lord's Supper.

Mark 14:36

What was the cup Jesus wanted to pass from him? Was this prayer answered, or not?

See the discussion of Matthew 26:39, page 259.

Mark 14:61–65

Did Jesus really claim to be God? Many people who read the Bible say he did not and that this belief is a notion fostered later by the disciples, especially the apostle Paul.

Whatever some may assert from a vantage point thousands of years later, it is clear that Christ's enemies understood him to claim deity as "the Son of the Blessed One" (v. 61). This claim was also made at other times and in other ways (John 6:31–38; 8:52–59; 14:8–12).

Anyone who is willing to take the Gospel accounts of Jesus' life as they stand, without rejecting passages they happen not to like, will be driven to the conclusion that Jesus firmly believed himself to be, and presented himself as, the Son of God, coequal with the Father. (See also the discussion of Philippians 2, page 355.

Mark 15:25

At what hour was Jesus actually nailed to the cross? This verse says at "the third hour," while John 19:14 indicates the trial was still taking place at "about the sixth hour." How can this discrepancy be explained?

Matthew and Luke agree with Mark that Jesus was hanging on the cross when a great darkness, lasting till Jesus' death at the ninth hour, shrouded the scene. Since these three evangelists counted the hours from sunrise, the crucifixion would have taken place about 9 A.M., the darkness would have fallen about noon and lasted until 3 P.M.

The best explanation is that John was using the official system, based on the Roman civil day, rather than on Jewish custom. In the Roman system, numbering the hours began at midnight rather than at dawn. Thus the Roman sixth hour would have been the Hebrew first hour, and no conflict at all exists.

But why would John use the Roman system? All agree that John's Gospel was the last written and that John probably lived in Ephesus, the capital of a Roman province. John also wrote to a predominantly Gentile church, who themselves were accustomed to the Roman way of numbering the hours. In essence, then, the readers of John's account would have understood Christ was crucified about 9 A.M. and died about 3 P.M. These are the same times indicated in the Gospels that used the Palestinian custom of reckoning time.

Mark 15:26

The different Gospel accounts report different charges attached to Jesus' cross. Is this an example of an error in the Bible?

Roman custom decreed that a person on the way to execution would wear, or have carried before him, a whitened wooden board on which the charges against him were written in ink or burned into the wood. At the execution, this summary of charges was attached to the cross above the victim. No Gospel account records the entire inscription. But rather than consider the differences to be errors, the different accounts enable us to reconstruct the whole list of charges: This is Jesus of Nazareth the king of the Jews.

Mark 15:44
Why was Pilate surprised that Jesus "was already dead"?

Crucifixion was an extremely painful and typically long, drawn-out form of execution. The individual was placed on the cross in such a way that to breathe he had to force his body erect, pushing against the nails in his feet and at the same time pulling against those in his hands. The pain and effort often extended several days, until the victim could no longer lift his body.

Pilate was surprised because Jesus had died in some six hours, a very quick death for one who was crucified. Remember that the soldiers broke the legs of the two thieves crucified with Jesus so they could not lift themselves up to breathe and so that they would die before nightfall and the beginning of the Jewish holy days (John 19:32).

Mark 16:1
Do the accounts of those who visited the tomb and saw Jesus on that resurrection morning differ? Does this imply error in the Bible?

No. None of the Gospel writers claims to list in order every resurrection morning occurrence. Students of the Bible have harmonized the Gospel accounts and determined that the most likely sequence of events is as follows:

Three women start for the tomb	Luke 23:55–24:1
They find the stone rolled away	Luke 24:2–9
Mary Magdalene leaves to tell the disciples	John 20:1–2
Mary the mother of James sees the angels	Matthew 28:1–2
Peter and John arrive and look in the tomb	John 20:3–10
Mary Magdalene returns, sees angels, and then sees Jesus	John 20:11–18
Mary, the mother of James, returns with other women	Luke 24:1–4
These women, too, see the angels	Luke 24:5; Mark 16:5
The angel tells them Jesus is risen	Matthew 28:6–8
They are met on departing by Jesus	Matthew 28:9–10

Mark 16:9–20

Do these verses belong in the Bible? If not, how did they get there?

The earliest Greek manuscripts, along with patristic evidence, suggest that Mark's Gospel ends at verse 8. Church historian Eusebius, in the A.D. 300s, noted that "accurate" copies of Mark ended at verse 8. This view was taken by most of the early church fathers. Also, modern scholars have argued that these additional lines cannot have been written by Mark because of differences in the language used in these verses from that used in the rest of the book.

While not every scholar agrees that the evidence is strong enough to completely reject these verses, most feel the weight of evidence indicates verses 9–20 are not authentic Scripture but were added later in an attempt to round off the seemingly abrupt ending of Mark at verse 8.

Luke

Luke

Who wrote this book, and what themes and issues does it deal with?

Luke was a medical doctor, a convert who accompanied Paul on his later missionary journeys (see also Col. 4:14; 2 Tim. 4:11; Philem. 24). Luke is the only Gospel writer who was not an eyewitness to events he describes. Instead Luke took the role of a careful historian and drew his account from a number of sources. Many believe that Luke researched this Gospel and interviewed many individuals during the two years that Paul was under arrest in Caesarea (Acts 23–26). Surprisingly, this Gospel is the longest book in the New Testament. In his "orderly account" of Jesus' life (Luke 1:3), Luke includes six miracles and no less than nineteen parables not mentioned by the other Gospels.

Luke writes in beautiful, polished Greek, the mark of a highly educated person. Most assume that he shaped his account to appeal to the Hellenistic mind, displaying Christ as the fulfillment of the Greek ideal of excellence. Luke portrays Christ relating comfortably to all sorts of people and concerned about everyone. Vivid character sketches help us sense the power and emotion of the human drama enacted wherever Jesus went. Yet more than any other Gospel writer, Luke emphasizes the Holy Spirit: filling Jesus, leading him, and at work through Christ's miracles.

It is also notable that Luke is very sensitive to women, mentions many, and shows Christ's affection for the often disregarded sex.

While this Gospel, as do the others, concludes with the life, death, and resurrection of Jesus, Luke continued his history in another book, Acts, which traces the development and spread of the Christian church.

282

Luke 1:6

Does the statement that Zechariah and Elizabeth observed all
God's commandments "blamelessly" imply that they were sinless?

No. The Hebrew word translated "blameless" in the Old Testament, which underlies this statement in the Gospels, indicates that
the person so described "accepted God's way and sought to live by it.
When he or she fell short, God's way prescribed confession and provided
sacrifices for restoration" (*The Expository Dictionary of Bible Words*, p.
128). We know that David sinned, yet he correctly pled his own blamelessness in prayer (Ps. 18:23; 26:1).

The New Testament speaks frequently of blamelessness not to imply
sinless perfection but to exhort us to commit ourselves to live a moral
life guided by the Word of God.

Luke 2:1–2

Is there any secular record of the census Luke reports?

It is known that the Roman governor Quirinius took a cen-
sus in A.D. 6 when he was governor of Syria. Since this would be after
Herod's death and after Jesus' birth, some assume that Luke made a mis-
take and mixed up his dates. However, records of the time suggest
Quirinius may have served two terms in Syria, one before and one after
Jesus' birth.

Another possibility is that the word *prote*, translated "first" here, may
be used in the sense of "earlier" or "prior." In this case Luke would be
referring to a census earlier than that taken by Quirinius. Undoubtedly
people living in first-century Palestine would have remembered the census Luke alludes to, and it is not surprising that no written record of
that census should have survived two thousand years.

We do have copies of a census decree issued by a Roman governor in
Egypt, which shows that it was customary for individuals to return to
their original family homes to be counted. We also know that census
taking was not unusual. The Romans listed their citizens and their property every five years and implemented this policy throughout the empire
in 5 B.C.

Luke 2:14

What did the angels really say, and what did it mean?

The King James rendering, "Good will to men," does not translate the Greek correctly. Here the New International Version's rendering, "On earth peace to men on whom his favor rests," is correct. This means that Christ, the Prince of Peace, had arrived to give inner peace to humankind.

Luke 2:22–24
What law required Mary to bring Jesus to the temple and make an offering?

Old Testament law decreed that a woman was ceremonially unclean after childbirth and required her to make a sacrifice after thirty-three days for her ritual purification (Lev. 12:1–5). This brought Mary to the temple, where she offered two young birds. At the same time Jesus, as Mary's firstborn son, was presented to the Lord and "bought back" with another sacrifice. It is interesting to note that Mary's offering of two young birds rather than a lamb indicated the family was very poor.

Luke 3:1
What year did John begin his ministry? And why did Luke take such care to identify it?

Luke was a careful historian who verified his facts. In providing this kind of detail Luke makes sure we realize he relates real history, not a so-called religious history that contains a large dose of fantasy and fiction. As for the year John began to minister, this depends on whether Luke used the Roman or the Syrian system of reckoning. By the Roman system, John would have begun to minister sometime between August A.D. 28 and August A.D. 29. By the Syrian system, John's ministry would have begun between the fall of A.D. 27 and the fall of A.D. 28.

Luke 3:3
What is repentance?

See the discussion of Matthew 3:2, page 229.

Luke 3:8
What did the Jewish leaders mean when they said, "We have Abraham as our father"?

Abraham was the original recipient of God's covenant promise. The Jews relied on their physical descent from Abraham for a guarantee of their right to a privileged relationship with God. John the Baptist ridiculed this position, saying that God could turn stones into children of Abraham. This hyperbole was intended to drive home an important truth that was developed later by Jesus and by the apostle Paul. The characteristic of Abraham which won him God's blessing, and which wins us blessing as well, is faith. Thus those who have faith are the true, spiritual descendants of Abraham (John 8:31–41; Rom. 4:12–17; Gal. 3:6–9).

Luke 3:23–37

Why does Luke's genealogy of Jesus differ so significantly from the genealogical record provided by Matthew?

See the discussion of Matthew 1:6, page 226.

Luke 3:38

How could Adam be "the son of God"? Christians claim that Jesus alone was God's Son. Does this verse imply that Adam was God?

The phrase *son of* is used in different ways in the Bible. A son of the prophets may be a member of that class of persons; the son of a ruler is often a successor, even though not of the same family; *sons of God* is used in the Old Testament to identify angels. It is important to know in what sense *son of* is used in any context. In this genealogy, *son of* is used in the sense of "springs from." All those named in the list spring from their earlier ancestor, Adam by direct creation, the others by natural biological generation. Christians are called the sons of God as well, a term intended to emphasize our membership in God's family through spiritual rebirth. The New Testament makes it very clear that Jesus was the Son of God in an entirely different sense, for Jesus alone is presented as God's "One and Only" Son (John 1:1–14), coexistent with the Father from eternity.

Luke 4:1–13

The order of the three temptations of Jesus differs in Luke from the order given in Matthew. The two accounts cannot both be accurate, so the Bible must be in error.

See the discussion of Matthew 4:5–10, page 230.

Luke 4:22–28

What are "gracious words"? And why did Jesus' neighbors turn on him so viciously so soon after commending him?

It is best to understand "gracious words" in the sense of "words about God's grace." The New International Version may be wrong in translating the phrase *emartyroun autō* as "spoke well of him" rather than "bore him witness." Jesus' neighbors agreed that Jesus said amazing things about God's grace but did not necessarily have a positive attitude toward him. However, when Jesus clearly said that God's grace would be extended to the Gentiles when his own people rejected him, his neighbors became violently hostile. Before we criticize them too severely, we must remember that the Jews had suffered intensely under Roman rule, and that earlier revolts had been put down bloodily. The people were desperate for the appearance of a Messiah, whom they fully expected to crush the Gentiles and exalt Israel. They did not want a prophet who said that God's grace extended to their oppressors.

Yet the reaction in Jesus' hometown foreshadows the reaction of the nation, just as the story of Elijah and the widow of Zerephath foreshadows the grace God will pour out through Jesus on all people.

Luke 4:33

What are demons, and where do they come from? Are demons active in our world today?

See the discussion of Matthew 8:28, page 236.

Luke 5:21

Who were the Pharisees and teachers of the law who so quickly aligned themselves against Jesus?

The Gospels mention several groups when reporting opposition to Jesus. Those mentioned most often are the Pharisees, the Sadducees, the chief priests, and the teachers of the law. The first two groups were religious parties that held distinctively different theological positions in Judaism. The chief priests included the high priest and other high officers in the temple hierarchy, who were usually Sadducees in their theological orientation. The teachers of the law were rabbis, or sages, who were recognized authorities on the teachings of the Old Testament law. They frequently served as judges in deciding civil and criminal cases on the basis of Old Testament law. A teacher of the law might be oriented either to the theological position represented by the Pharisees or to the position taken by the Sadducees. Most often when Jesus spoke of Pharisees and teachers of the law he meant rabbis who approached the law as theological Pharisees.

To further complicate the situation, most Pharisees were actually middle-class lay persons who chose to live by the strictest interpretation of God's law. While the number of actual Pharisees was small, with estimates of their membership ranging up to six thousand in Palestine, their zeal was greatly admired by the general population, and their influence was immense. In contrast, the Sadducees were typically upper-class individuals, whose wealth and social position led them to support accommodation with the political status quo.

Although the Pharisees and Sadducees were constantly at odds on religious and political issues, they joined forces in several attempts to discredit Jesus and finally in the plot to get rid of the troublesome teacher entirely.

The *NIV Study Bible* summarizes the characteristics of the Pharisees' and Sadducees' beliefs in the following chart:

Pharisees

1. Along with the Torah, they accepted as equally inspired and authoritative all material contained within the oral tradition.

2. On free will and determination, they held to a mediating view that made it impossible for either free will or the sovereignty of God to cancel out the other.

3. They accepted a rather developed hierarchy of angels and demons.

4. They taught that there was a future for the dead.

5. They believed in the immortality of the soul and in reward and retribution after death.

6. They were champions of human equality.

7. The emphasis of their teaching was ethical rather than theological.

Sadducees

1. They denied that the oral law was authoritative and binding.

2. They interpreted Mosaic law more literally than did the Pharisees.

3. They were exacting in Levitical purity.

4. They attributed everything to free will.

5. They argued there is neither resurrection of the dead nor a future life.

6. They rejected a belief in angels and demons.

7. They rejected the idea of a spiritual world.

8. Only the books of Moses were canonical Scriptures.

Luke 5:36–39

What is the meaning of new patches on old clothes and new wine in old wineskins?

See the discussion of Matthew 9:16–17, page 238.

Luke 6:20

Matthew reports that Jesus said the "poor in spirit" were blessed. Luke leaves out "in spirit," making the meaning very different. This is certainly a discrepancy in the Gospel accounts.

In the first place, as anyone who travels and speaks in various places knows very well, the same sermons and messages are given many times and often are slightly adapted to fit new audiences. It would be foolish to assume that Jesus gave his Sermon on the Mount only one time, or that he failed to use his comments on its various themes over and over again. The Beatitudes must have been spoken dozens of times as Jesus traveled in Galilee and in Judea. One should not assume that a difference in reports of Jesus' comments on a familiar theme must describe the same incident. The differences in the accounts are not discrepancies in the Scriptures.

Note that Luke says specifically that Jesus looked around at his disciples, defined in verse 17 as "a large crowd" of followers, and shaping his words to their condition said, "Blessed are you who are poor." In this context *poor* and *poor in spirit* are equivalents and convey the same thought: A grinding poverty drove most of the ordinary folk of first-century Palestine close to despair and focused their hopes not on this world but on the appearance of the Messiah or on the next world. The destitute seem more likely to sense spiritual needs than the prosperous. The poor are blessed for they, far more than the well-to-do, yearn for the kingdom of God.

Luke 7:8

What did the centurion mean when he said both he and Jesus were men "under authority"?

The centurion meant that as an officer in the Roman army he could trace his authority back to the emperor himself. Thus when he spoke an order, he spoke as a representative of the greatest power on earth and would be obeyed. In saying this, the centurion confessed his faith that Jesus could trace his authority back to God and that when Jesus spoke he spoke with the full authority of God himself, and his word carried the full power of God here on earth. Thus if Jesus simply spoke the word, the centurion's servant would be healed, because distance was no obstacle to God.

Luke 7:11–17

How many people did Jesus bring back to life after they had died?

The New Testament records three such incidents. There is the raising of the widow's son reported here; the raising of the ruler's daughter, reported in Matthew 9:18–25; and the raising of Lazarus, reported in John 11. Since the Jews buried persons who died as quickly after their death as possible, the raising of Lazarus was the most impressive. The ruler's daughter had just died, for she was still in her house. The widow's son had died very recently, for the crowd was carrying his bier to the place of burial. But Lazarus had been dead and buried for three days, proof positive of Christ's authority over humanity's greatest enemy, death.

Yet there was a basic difference between these resuscitations and Jesus' own resurrection. Each of the three Jesus raised returned to normal biological death. They were destined to die again. When Jesus returned to life, a great transformation had taken place—he had a resurrected body not subject to the limitations imposed on normal human beings. Thus while the raising of these three people uniquely demonstrated the extent of Jesus' authority, he was "declared with power to be the Son of God by his resurrection from the dead" (Rom. 1:4).

Luke 7:28

How can a person who is "least in the kingdom of God" be greater than John the Baptist, whom Jesus called the greatest of "those born of women"?

John was the greatest in that he had the privilege of announcing the imminent appearance of the Messiah whom the prophets had foretold. But the people who actually enter the kingdom are greater than John in the sense of having an even higher privilege. We need to remember that John was in prison at this time. He was executed before the death and resurrection of Christ, which led to the initiation of the church age and its expression of the kingdom of God on earth.

Luke 7:47

Does this story make love for God, rather than faith, the condition of salvation? Is this a theological discrepancy?

Jesus makes it clear to this woman that "your faith has saved you" (Luke 7:50). Her love, expressed in a generous gift that represented a person's life savings, showed that the woman realized she had been forgiven. Love is uniformly presented in the New Testament as response to God's grace, never as an act or attitude that God subsequently rewards.

Luke 8:26–39

The Gospel writers disagree on how many demon-possessed people Jesus cured in this case. The details make it clear that all the writers are recounting the same incident, but differences in the accounts make it clear that one of them is wrong.

See the discussion of Matthew 8:28–34, page 237.

Luke 9:23–26

What does Jesus' warning about self-denial and losing one's soul mean?

See the discussion of Matthew 16:24, page 248 and 16:26, page 249.

Luke 9:53

Why did the Samaritans refuse to offer Jesus hospitality simply because he was heading toward Jerusalem?

The Samaritans and Jews were much like the modern Israelis and Palestinians; centuries of mutual antagonism had resulted in intense hostility between them. This hostility went back to the initial rebuilding of the Jerusalem temple by Jewish exiles returning from Babylon in the 400s B.C. At that time a Samaritan offer to help was rejected, and the Samaritans were told they had no part of Israel's God. The theological rift deepened over the centuries. Many pious Jews traveling to Jerusalem to celebrate religious holidays chose to cross the Jordan River and take the long route rather than the shorter, easier route through Samaritan territory. Despite the hostility, the tradition of hospitality was so embedded in each culture that even a traveling Jew could normally expect some

Samaritan to give him shelter at night. However, Jesus' group was traveling to Jerusalem to take part in the religious celebration from which Samaritans were excluded. This was apparently too much for the villagers to handle, and they refused to shelter Christ's company.

Luke 9:59-60

Was it heartless of Jesus to demand that the young man who wanted to follow him leave his dead father and come along immediately?

See the discussion of Matthew 8:22, page 236.

Luke 9:62

What did Jesus mean when he said no one can look back after putting his hand to the plow?

When farmers plowed they set the course of their furrows by picking out two objects (one farther away than the other), lining them up, and keeping the one directly behind the other. This enabled the farmer to make a straight furrow, which would set the pattern for plowing the entire field.

If the farmer looked back and took his eye off his guide, the furrow became crooked and the pattern of the entire field was thrown off. Similarly, if a person intends to follow Jesus, he must not look back at old priorities (guidelines). If he does, the whole pattern of the life Jesus intends him to lead can be thrown off.

The decision to follow Jesus means making him the one guiding priority in our lives.

Luke 10:18

When did Jesus "see Satan fall like lightning from heaven"?

The New English Bible renders this verse: "I watched how Satan fell, like lightning, out of the sky." This version reflects one of two main interpretations of the text, that the effect of Jesus' ministry on earth was to destroy the power of Satan. This view is supported by frequent Gospel references to Jesus' defeat of demons and of Satan himself. The other interpretation takes Jesus' words as a reference to that long-ago time when Satan sinned and was expelled from his high position by God (see also Isa. 14:12). In either case, Jesus' words underline his own claim of a power far greater than that which Satan himself exercises, a power so great that he can even give his disciples authority to "overcome all the power of the enemy" (Luke 10:19).

Luke 10:29

According to Jesus' story of the good Samaritan, what does it mean to be a neighbor?

The teachers of Jewish law generally understood the Old Testament command to "love your neighbor as yourself" (Lev. 19:18) as a decree to do good to one's fellow Jew. While the law protected aliens and called on the Jews to treat a foreigner well, it clearly made a distinction between the obligation owed to a foreigner and to a fellow Israelite.

Jesus' story defines the concept of neighbor to include foreigners and implies that any person in need is our neighbor. We are to show the stranger the same compassion and love we would display to our family.

Luke 10:42

What did Jesus mean when he told Martha that "only one thing is needed"?

Mary's priority was listening to Jesus. This had precedent over Martha's priority, putting on a good meal. Some manuscripts say "only a few things" are necessary, perhaps indicating that Martha only needed to prepare a few dishes and not the more impressive meal she was slaving to make ready. Even a one-dish meal, common in Palestine, would be sufficient. While there are various interpretations, all focus on this central fact: Mary's priority of listening to Jesus had precedent over Martha's priority of putting on a good meal.

Luke 11:2–4

Why is this version of the Lord's Prayer different from that of Matthew?

Jesus undoubtedly taught this model prayer more than once. He was under no obligation to repeat himself word for word.

Luke 11:13

Luke says God will give the Holy Spirit to those who ask him. Matthew 7:11 says God will "give good gifts to those who ask him." How can this discrepancy be explained?

Jesus undoubtedly repeated the teachings he gave his disciples, just as he did with his public sermons. Luke's material on prayer in chapter 11 is unique. It is not repeated in the other Gospels. Yet the teaching is essentially the same. God is our heavenly Father, who will certainly do no less for us than an earthly father would do for his children. In fact, God will do far more for us than sinful human beings will, even to give us the promised Holy Spirit when we depend fully on (ask) him.

Luke 11:24

What does the parable of the evil spirit leaving and then returning to a house mean?

See the discussion of Matthew 12:43–45, page 243.

Luke 11:34

What did Jesus mean when he said, "Your eye is the lamp of your body"?

See the discussion of Matthew 6:22–23, page 233.

Luke 11:42–44

What are woes?

See the discussion of Matthew 23:13–29, page 256.

Luke 13:16

Is Satan the cause of our diseases? The Bible says he kept the crippled woman "bound for eighteen long years."

Satan is certainly portrayed as the enemy of human beings and is directly charged with bringing on the disasters, including sickness, that struck Job. In addition, the Gospels ascribe to demonic beings many of the illnesses that Jesus cured. So clearly Satan can be the cause of human illnesses. But to say that Satan can be the cause of some illness does not imply that he is the cause of all illness. The Bible far more often links sickness with sin (Deut. 28:20–25; Ps. 103:3; Isa. 1:5–6; Hos. 5:13–14). This does not mean simply that sickness is punishment for sin but also that sickness is a consequence of sin. Modern medical science is becoming increasingly aware of the genetic link to many of our most serious diseases. Although created perfect, Adam's fall introduced into the human race a deadly deterioration that is physical as well as spiritual. While Satan may be involved in certain cases of illness, and divine punishment in others, most illness is a result of our human condition, of being members of a fallen race.

Luke 13:19–20

What do the parables of the mustard seed and the yeast teach in these verses?

It is important to remember that the stories and parables Jesus used were told often and in different contexts. At times the same story in a different situation makes a different point. In Matthew 13, the mustard seed and yeast emphasize the growth of the hidden form of God's kingdom that Jesus is about to introduce. In Luke the focus shifts slightly. The same parables emphasize the power that exists in the tiny mustard seed and in the yeast. Although a mustard seed and yeast exist only as specks, each possesses a power to grow and to transform its surroundings.

Luke 13:23

Jesus uses the word compel *in his parable of guests called to a ruler's banquet. Does this imply that God not only chooses those who will be saved but also that they have no choice in the matter?*

It is true that the word used here, *anankazo*, does mean to "force" or "compel." It is used only nine times in the New Testament. Each time the context determines the kind of compulsion that is involved. This is important, for this word is used of both external, physical force and of inner pressures or responses to moral suasion. Here the compulsion has rightly been described as "an insistent hospitality." What is truly significant about the story is not the word *compel* but the king's command to search the street (*plateia*, a highway) and the alley (*rhyme*, the narrow lanes where the poor and ignored lived). The gospel invitation is for all, and the servants of heaven's King are to be sure each person receives his or her invitation.

Luke 14:26

How could Jesus suggest that a disciple should hate his or her parents? The Old Testament says we are to honor our parents. This surely is a moral discrepancy in the Bible.

Hate is used here in a special sense (see Rom. 9:13). Jesus uses a familiar formula that his hearers would have understood. When the claims of God and family conflict, the disciple must give God priority.

Luke 14:34

How can salt lose saltiness? This must be a scientific error in the Bible.

See the discussion of Matthew 5:13, page 232.

Luke 16:8

How could Jesus approve of a clearly dishonest steward? Is this a moral discrepancy? The Bible should consistently call for honesty and speaking the truth.

Jesus did not commend the steward for his dishonesty. He pointed out that the dishonest steward was wise, for he realized that money was to be used to prepare for his future. The Pharisees, against whom this story was directed, loved money and wealth for itself. They failed to realize that money is of no value in itself, but that material resources can be wisely used to advance kingdom causes.

Luke 16:19

Is Jesus' story of the rich man and Lazarus to be taken as a parable or as a report of something that really happened?

Many argue that Lazarus and the rich man were real, specific individuals, because Jesus does not use names in other stories of illustration. Whether they were fictional or real, the story describes death as a transition for both lost and saved individuals. The rich man is portrayed after death as fully conscious and self-aware, but "in torment."

Lazarus is also fully conscious and self-aware, at "Abraham's side," a phrase used in the first century to describe Paradise.

Luke 17:1–10

What is the point of this confusing response of Jesus to the disciples' request to "increase our faith"?

Jesus had just told his disciples to forgive again and again. The disciples were aware of how difficult this was. They asked Jesus to increase their faith. Jesus dismissed their request, saying, "If you have faith as small as a mustard seed, you can say to this mulberry tree, 'Be uprooted and be planted in the sea,' and it will obey you" (v. 6). He then told a story about a servant who did the day's tasks his master set for him and served his master dinner. When the day was done, he expected no praise because he had only done his duty.

The disciples, in asking for more faith, had missed the point. Faith might be fine for planting mulberry trees in the sea. But Jesus, their Master, had commanded them to forgive. The issue here is not one of faith but of obedience.

This passage illustrates a principle we must use to solve many Bible difficulties. Jesus' familiar words and images were repeated over and over during his three years of ministry. They frequently were applied to make different points. To understand the image, we must look carefully at the context in which it is used.

Luke 17:37

What does Jesus mean, "Where there is a dead body, there the vultures will gather"?

In context, Jesus' point seems to be that where the spiritually dead are found, judgment will follow.

Luke 18:1–9

Jesus seems to suggest that God is like an unjust judge. Is this in conflict with the New Testament's image of God as a loving father?

This is an example of teaching by contrast. Jesus' point is that if a poor widow can get justice from an unjust judge, surely one of God's dearly loved children can be assured that God will act in his or her behalf.

It is exactly because God is *not* like the unjust judge that we can have such confidence in prayer.

Luke 18:19

Here Jesus clearly denies that he is God, for he says, "No one is good—except God alone."

No, Jesus is pointing up a discrepancy in the rich ruler's greeting. It was the rich ruler who said, "Good teacher" (master). Either the ruler must regard Jesus as a flawed human being and thus not good in any absolute sense, or he must regard Jesus as God and thus not merely as another teacher of God's law. In fact, Jesus' response to the rich ruler demonstrates, rather than denies, the fact that he is God and must be approached as such.

Luke 19:8–9

Was Zacchaeus saved because he gave ill-gotten wealth back to those he defrauded?

Just the opposite. Zacchaeus's actions demonstrated the reality of his change of heart. Salvation is the cause of this kind of transformation. It is never a reward merited by right actions.

Luke 19:30

The Gospel writers disagree over whether there was one animal or two involved in Jesus' triumphal entry into Jerusalem. This surely shows there are errors in the Bible.

See the discussion of Matthew 21:2, page 254.

Luke 20:44

What is the implication of David calling the Messiah "Lord"?

See the discussion of Matthew 22:41–46, page 256.

Luke 21:32

How can Jesus' statement that "this generation will certainly not pass away until all these things have happened" be explained?

See the discussion of Matthew 24:34, page 259.

Luke 22:19–23

How can bread and wine be the body and blood of Jesus? Yet people tell us to take the Bible literally.

See the discussion of Mark 14:22–24, page 276.

Luke 22:36

How could Luke report that Jesus told his disciples to buy swords? In Luke 22:49–51, Jesus told Peter, who drew a sword, "No more of this." Is this inconsistent?

It is best to take Jesus' words as sad irony. Earlier Jesus told his disciples to take no bag (supplies) or purse (money) on their preaching ministry but to rely on the hospitality of those they ministered to. Now he reverses these instructions, knowing full well that, rather than a welcome, his followers will soon find only hostility and rejection in their homeland. It is interesting that the disciples were able to produce "two swords" (Luke 22:38). Apparently they were intensely aware of the growing hostility to Jesus and were fearful. Significantly, when they tried to use these weapons later, Jesus rebuked them (vv. 49–51). For this reason some take Christ's words about buying swords as an oblique reference to the time of crisis the disciples were about to face.

John

John

Who wrote this book, and what themes and issues does it deal with?

This Gospel was written by the apostle John, one of Christ's original twelve disciples. It is the last Gospel written, probably dating from the A.D. 90s. It is also the only Gospel that does not rely on chronology for its organization. Instead John develops themes found in Christ's teachings, woven into seven major discourses, or lengthy teachings.

The other Gospels are generally understood to have been directed toward various first-century ethnic-cultural groups: Matthew toward the Jews, Mark toward the Romans, Luke toward the Greeks. In contrast, John's Gospel has been called the universal Gospel; it deals with those issues of life and death, faith and unbelief, light and darkness that are vital to all people of every time and place.

John's Gospel has also been called a theological Gospel. His book emphasizes key themes reflected in central theological terms that are repeated again and again. Often his main concepts are pairs: life versus death, light versus darkness, belief versus unbelief, truth versus falsehood, love versus hate. Certainly the key word in this Gospel is *belief,* or *faith,* found ninety-eight times in the Greek text. According to John, "These are written that you may believe that Jesus is the Christ, the Son of God, and that by believing you may have life in his name" (John 20:31).

In view of this purpose, it should not surprise us that John, more than the other Gospels, makes absolutely explicit the full deity of Jesus. Christ was in the beginning with God (1:1–4), is equal with God (5:18), claims deity (9:35–37; 10:36), announces himself to be the I AM (*Yahweh*) of the Old Testament (8:58), and affirms that he existed with God "before the world began" (17:5). The people of Jesus' time understood and rejected this claim. Now John, from the perspective provided by the resurrection, reaffirms Christ's claims and calls everyone to faith in Jesus Christ as Lord.

John

Key words in John and their meanings:

Know This is a relational term, used both of initiating a relationship with God at the time of salvation and of living in daily fellowship with God through loving obedience (see 8:19, 31–47; 10:4; 14–15; 1 John 4:15–16).

Word A name ascribed to Jesus that presents him as the one who reveals the Father and as the creative power who by merely speaking brought the universe into existence.

World A theological term (*kosmos*) that portrays human society apart from God, warped and driven by sinful passions.

Life A reference to biological life at times, but more importantly to spiritual life: a vitalizing power provided by God, who plants his own ever-living nature within us.

Death Biological death at times, but most frequently a description of the spiritual state of lost human beings, isolated from God and morally corrupt. Only the gift of spiritual life, found in Jesus Christ, can counteract the forces of death or break its grip on the human personality.

Light The term often implies holiness, but in John the emphasis is on illumination. As the light of the world, Jesus shows us the way to God and the way to live to please God.

Darkness Morally this word describes sinful acts and sinful lifestyles. Theologically, *darkness* depicts the dominant evil power that holds sinners in its grip, blinding them to the gospel's offer of salvation.

Belief John does mention a superficial belief in Jesus found in those who were awed by his miracles but were unwilling to commit themselves to him. But John also uses this key term as a faith-response to God, by which a person commits himself or herself to the Lord and receives life from God's Son. In the Gospel of John, as in the other New Testament documents, a true or saving faith will exhibit itself in a life of love for God and obedience to him.

Unbelief This is not doubt or uncertainty but represents a decision not to trust oneself to Christ or believe God's Word about him. Unbelief is a moral and spiritual issue, not an intellectual one.

Truth John uses this word more than all the rest of the New Testament writers combined. John's focus is the link between truth and reality as reflected in both the Hebrew and Greek terms. Something is true because it is in harmony with reality. We can know the truth (that is, experience reality) by trusting God and keeping (doing) Jesus' words. As we obey Jesus, we find that life really is what is described for us in God's Word.

Falsehood This is not so much a matter of lying to God as it is a matter of deceit or illusion. Human notions of what life is all about are tragic distortions of what is real. Only God's Word unveils truth, and only by adopting for ourselves a perspective on life shaped by God's Word can we escape the world of illusion and discover truth.

Love This is one of the most critical concepts in the Bible. It is emphasized not only in John but in each of the New Testament books. Love can only be understood by reference to God and his love for us demonstrated in Jesus. We then respond to God's love, both by obedience to his commands and by loving others as he has loved us. John makes it clear that love is not something natural in human beings, but that real love must be created in us by God. As we respond to Jesus, his love will fill us and flow through us to others.

Hate As a theological term in John, *hate* speaks of the deep antagonism that the unsaved world feels toward Jesus and toward his followers.

John 1:1

The Greek leaves out the definite article in the phrase "and the Word was God." Without the definite article the verse seems to teach the Word was "a" god.

The Jehovah's Witnesses use the lack of the article to argue that Jesus, while special, was not actually God. But in Greek usage the subject of a phrase is distinguished from the predicate by use of the definite article. By leaving the article out John, in fact, makes it clear that the Word *is identical with* God. The New International Version here is absolutely accurate.

John 1:17

Does the saying "The law was given through Moses; grace and truth came through Jesus Christ" imply a conflict between the Old Testament and the New Testament?

Not at all. The law that unveiled God's standard of righteousness *was* given through Moses. Jesus was the primary source of God's revelation of his grace. John speaks here in a historical sense. Moses and Jesus were focal points of revelation, the first emphasizing righteousness, the second emphasizing grace. There is no conflict, because the believer who lives in the age of grace is called on to live a righteous life, but the Old Testament saint who lives in the age of the law was no less a recipient of God's grace.

John 1:26

How many baptisms are there, and what does each involve?

See the discussion of Matthew 3:11, page 229.

John 1:51

What did Jesus mean when he spoke about the "angels of God ascending and descending on the Son of Man"?

Jesus referrs to the vision of Jacob reported in Genesis 28:10–17, when the patriarch saw a stairway upon which angels passed from earth to heaven and heaven to earth. The imagery speaks of communication, of a point of access between heaven and earth. In this saying Jesus takes the place of the stairway, in essence affirming that he himself is the portal between heaven and earth, the one through whom access is gained.

John 2:9

Did Jesus turn the water into an alcoholic beverage, or does wine here refer to grape juice?

Many Christians who are rightly concerned about the misuse of alcoholic drinks in our society have argued that Jesus could not have turned water into wine. They feel that it must have been grape juice. This is not supported by the text, by the culture, or by the rest of Scripture's references to wine.

On the one hand, wine in Scripture is a symbol of joy and blessing, as in Psalms 4:7 and 104:15. Wine was drunk at feasts, given as a gift (1 Sam. 25:18), and praised by the psalmists. Wine was also used in offerings made to God (Exod. 29:40). Paul recommended that Timothy use

wine medicinally (1 Tim. 5:23). And certainly the wine at Cana was fer-
mented, not fresh, grape juice. But this should not be taken as a blanket endorsement of the use of alcohol.

Both testaments decry drunkenness and disapprove of love for alcoholic beverages (Prov. 20:1; 21:17; 23:20). Drunkenness characterizes
pagans, not Christians (1 Peter 4:3), and there is no excuse for excessive
drinking (Eph. 5:18). It should be noted that wine was usually mixed
with three or four parts water and not as it is normally drunk today.

John 2:14

*The other Gospels picture Jesus as driving the moneychangers out
of the temple the week before his death. John places this incident here at the beginning of his ministry. Who is right, and who
is wrong?*

Some assume that only one cleansing of the temple took place,
and noting that John's Gospel is not ordered by chronology, believe this
is the same incident that took place at the end of his ministry. But John
mentions at least three Passovers (2:13, 23; 6:4; and 11:55; 12:1; 13:1).
Adult male Jews were to come to Jerusalem to worship at each, so there
is no reason why Jesus would not have visited the temple several times.
There is also no reason to suppose Jesus did not become incensed at the
misuse of God's temple more than once and did not cleanse the Temple
at least twice.

John 3:5

*What did Jesus mean when he said a person must be "born
[again] of water and the Spirit"?*

What Jesus intended by these symbols is still debated. Some
see this as a *hendiadys,* both words meaning the same thing. Others suggest that water refers to John's baptism and the Spirit refers to his ministry. Possibly Jesus was saying that repentance, signified by baptism,
is essential but not enough. Only an inner transforming work of the
Spirit of God can bring a person into the kingdom of heaven.

John 3:10

*Why should Nicodemus be expected to "understand these
things"?*

Nicodemus was a very important person. As "Israel's teacher," he was a recognized authority on the Old Testament. Jesus implied that the Old Testament teaches a new birth, and so his own reference to being born again should not have shocked his visitor. Does the Old Testament teach this? Yes. Through Ezekiel God promised to take away his people's heart of stone and give his people a new heart (Ezek. 11:19), and through Jeremiah God promised to write his law on the heart rather than on tablets of stone (31:33).

John 3:18

If people are condemned for not believing in Jesus, how can God judge pagans who have never had a chance to hear? Is this fair?

The verse does not teach that pagans are condemned for not believing in Jesus. All who are lost are condemned for their own sins. This verse simply means that anyone who does not believe in Jesus stands condemned, for only faith in Jesus can reverse the sentence God has been forced to impose on lost humanity. This has motivated the missionary effort to reach every tribe and tongue and people with the gospel.

For the question of whether the pagans have a fair chance, see the discussion of Romans 2:12–16, p. 329.

John 5:16

Isn't John's Gospel anti-Semitic? He constantly portrays the Jews as persecuting Jesus.

Some may view this verse as anti-Semitic, and those who are anti-Semitic may wrongly use John's language to support their views. However, in John's Gospel, *the Jews* is invariably a reference to those religious leaders who were hostile to Jesus. It is not a reference to the Jewish people in general, nor does it display hostility. It is instead simple descriptive language.

Rather than being anti-Semitic, the New Testament is actually pro-Semitic. The earliest Christian community was entirely Jewish. Paul expressed a deep sense of obligation to his own Jewish people. He not only sought to bring the gospel to them first (Rom. 1:16) but would gladly have surrendered his own salvation if this would have meant the salvation of his fellow countrymen (Rom. 9:3–5). True Christians can hardly be antagonistic to a people so dear to God's heart, whose own Messiah suffered and died to be our Savior.

John 5:17

Why did the Jewish leaders try to kill Jesus just for saying that like God he was simply working?

Jesus justified his own works of healing on the Sabbath by arguing that God did not stop working on the seventh day. That is, natural law still operated; a broken bone continued to mend, a cut continued to heal. But in identifying his acts with the creative works of his Father, Jesus was rightly understood as claiming to be God. The religious leaders "tried all the harder to kill him" (v. 18) because they considered this blasphemy.

John 5:28–29

Jesus said those "who have done good" will awaken to eternal life, while those "who have done evil will rise to be condemned." This certainly contradicts other Bible passages that suggest works cannot save and that a person must be saved by faith.

In interpreting any statement of Scripture, it is necessary to read it in its context. Verse 24 sets that context, saying that "whoever hears my word and believes him who sent me has eternal life." Thus the particular good work in this passage is to hear the word and believe.

It is true that doing good works is a product of faith (James 2:17–18). So one might argue that only those with faith do the "good" Jesus refers to here. However, the fact is that in context Jesus is speaking of the specific good work of hearing and believing.

John 6:53

What does it mean to "eat the flesh of the Son of Man and drink his blood"?

Jesus here uses a very powerful metaphor. This simply means to participate fully. For the question of whether the communion elements actually become the body and blood of Christ, see the discussion of Mark 14:22–24, page 276.

John 6:66

This verse says that many disciples of Jesus stopped following him after they heard his sermon on the bread of life. Does this mean that some who were saved were lost again?

This would only be true if *disciple* and *convert* were synonyms. In fact, they are not. The word *disciple* is used not only of committed followers of Jesus but in several other ways as well. The word also refers to the twelve whom Jesus trained personally and then commissioned to be apostles, to followers of various other theological or political schools (Matt. 22:16; Mark 2:18), and of loose adherents of a movement, including the movement associated with Jesus during his lifetime (John 8:31; 13:35; 15:8). These were people who were attracted to Jesus and followed along for a time. But by calling such people Jesus' disciples, the Scripture does not imply that they had either faith in him as the Son of God or commitment to his kingdom.

John 8:1–11

Should this story be included in the Gospel of John?

There are a few, a very few, words or verses that nearly all scholars agree may not have been found in the original copy of a Gospel or an epistle. In each case doubts arise not from a passage's teaching but because the passage in question is not found in various ancient manuscripts.

In the first century all books were copied by hand. In the case of the New Testament, manuscripts were taken throughout the Roman world and copied again and again. It is not surprising that most manuscript copies made in Alexandria, for instance, might have slight differences in words or letters from manuscripts copied in a different place. This has interested a group of scholars called lower critics, who study different families of New Testament manuscripts. They attempt to explain any differences and try to determine how the original most probably read.

As I noted, there are amazingly few words or verses still in question. One of the best-known New Testament scholars suggests that all the words in question would fill only one half of one page in a Greek New Testament, and not one questionable word affects a major New Testament doctrine or substantial fact.

All this explains why some people question whether John 7:53–8:11 is actually part of the original text of John's Gospel. These verses are not found in the oldest manuscripts we have, and this passage is not discussed in the earliest commentaries on John's Gospel. For these reasons, most scholars doubt that John included this story in his Gospel. At the same time, most scholars also are impressed by the story and its spirit and point out that it may well be an authentic report of something Jesus actually did that was woven into John's Gospel at some later time.

John 8:11

Does Jesus' refusal to condemn the woman caught in adultery show he rejected the harsher penalties imposed by Old Testament law? Certainly we can conclude that Jesus did not support capital punishment.

It is always questionable to try to argue general principles from just one situation. This is especially true when several principles are involved. The death sentence for adultery, although found in Old Testament law, was seldom imposed for adultery. In this case Jesus' adversaries clearly tried to entrap him. If he confirmed the death sentence, Jesus would seem to be acting contrary to the word of mercy and grace he emphasized in both his acts and his teaching. If Jesus rejected the death penalty, he could be accused by the religious leaders of trying to overthrow the Law of Moses.

Rather than fall into the trap Jesus avoided it. In saying, "If any one of you is without sin, let him be the first to throw a stone" (v. 8), Jesus confirmed the death penalty in principle. In saying, "Neither do I condemn you," Jesus affirmed the forgiving grace of God, which he consistently taught and exhibited. But Jesus did more. In calling on the woman to "go now and leave your life of sin," Jesus showed us that forgiveness is a dynamic alternative, which serves righteousness as surely as punishment does. The forgiven sinner experiences an inner transformation and will now choose not to sin. Thus both law and grace uphold righteousness, and the person who loves God can offer the condemned of humanity a way out of the dilemma caused by sin.

John 8:44

What did Jesus mean when he said that his opponents belonged to their "father, the devil"?

It is common for us to expect children to bear a resemblance to their parents. After all, anyone who springs from a person with a large nose or a square jaw is likely to have that feature also. All Jesus means here is that the same thing is true in the spiritual realm; a person is likely to resemble the spiritual head of his or her family.

Since Satan is a liar and a murderer, those who told lies about Jesus, who rejected the truth he taught, and who tried to kill him for sharing God's good news showed a family resemblance to Satan rather than to God. If they had been members of God's family they, like God, would have loved rather than hated Jesus.

John 8:58

Why did people try to stone Jesus when he claimed that "before Abraham was born, I am"?

The name *Yahweh*, the Old Testament covenant name of God, is built on the Hebrew verb translated "to be." God told Moses to tell the Israelites in Egypt that "I AM has sent me to you" (Exod. 3:14). Thus the Jews rightly understood Jesus to claim to actually be Yahweh of the Old Testament. Since they did not believe him, they intended to stone him to death for blasphemy. Stoning was the traditional form of execution in Israel.

John 9:2

Why did the disciples ask who had sinned when they observed a man who was born blind?

Popular theology held that severe illness was punishment for sin. The man the disciples asked about was born blind, so the physical disability preceded any moral choices he might have made. This made the disciples wonder if perhaps his blindness was a punishment for a sin of his parents rather than one of his own.

Jesus' answer, "Neither this man nor his parents sinned, but this happened so that the work of God might be displayed in his life" (v. 3), was decisive. Jesus did not reject the idea that sickness might be punishment at times (Acts 12:19–23). It did put to rest the superstition that sin is always the cause of sickness. In fact, Jesus' reply reminds us that God can have a positive purpose in permitting illness and can use it to display his work in our lives. At times, that display can be through a healing, as the blind man experienced. But it can also be by providing grace along with the disability, so that God's power might be revealed in our weakness (2 Cor. 12:9).

John 10:34

What did Jesus mean by calling Old Testament saints gods? Does this lessen his own claim to be the Son of God, which his enemies here reject?

Jesus quoted Psalm 82:6. The Psalm addresses those who serve in some position as judges, and they are addressed as *elohim* and "sons of God," because they share in a function which is, in the last analysis, God's function as judge.

Jesus' enemies had just rejected the evidence of Christ's miracles and condemned him for claiming to be God (John 10:33). Christ's argument was that if Scripture calls mere mortals who receive the divine Word by the courtesy title "gods," he himself, "whom the Father set apart as his very own and sent into the world," had a far greater right to claim deity. Jesus is God, and his miracles corroborate his claim.

John 11:49–52

How could a man of corrupt character like Caiaphas prophesy? Can God speak through people who are not believers?

John points out that Caiaphas "did not say this on his own." It was an unwitting prophecy. John also makes it clear that he spoke "as high priest," crediting the office rather than the character of the man.

On the one hand, we need to remember that God is not limited. At one time he spoke even through a donkey (Num. 22:21–35). On the other hand, we are clearly taught in 2 Timothy, 2 Peter, and Jude that a corrupt or immoral character is a sign of a false prophet.

John 12:24

It is not correct to say that a grain of wheat dies. What it does is germinate. Here is another example of scientific error in the Bible.

Jesus was not making a pronouncement for a botany text but was drawing an analogy rooted in every farmer's experience. The seed a person keeps remains a single seed, and if one plants the seed, it is gone. However, that seed's "death" results not in loss but in multiplication; the planted seed "produces many seeds." Jesus applies his metaphor to our lives by pointing out that a believer can either hold tightly to his own life or surrender it to God. By hating (decisively rejecting) the world's claims and choosing to follow Jesus (v. 25), a person actually gains rather than loses, even though the choice to follow Christ involves surrender of many things.

It is foolish to charge Jesus or the Bible with scientific error when Jesus simply describes what every farmer experiences and applies it as a metaphor to encourage commitment.

John 13:8–10

Why did Jesus insist on washing his disciples' feet, and what did he mean by "a person who has had a bath only needs to wash his feet"?

The streets in Palestine, even in cities like Jerusalem, were dusty. When a visitor entered a house it was courteous for the host to call a slave to wash a visitor's feet. Peter objected to Christ washing his feet because he thought it was demeaning for Jesus to do a servant's job.

Jesus insisted for two reasons. First, he provided an example of the attitude his followers should adopt toward one another (13:13–17). Second, this symbolized the cleansing of Peter's personality to make him fit for God's kingdom. To understand the implications, we need to remember that baths were not taken in the home but in outside facilities. Even a freshly bathed individual would return home with dusty feet. Many sermons have been preached on this text, suggesting that the bath Jesus referred to is salvation, and that as we live in the world we are dirtied by sins of commission and omission. Thus we need to confess our sins daily, that Jesus might cleanse us just as he cleansed Peter's feet so long ago.

John 13:34–35

How is this a new commandment? The Old Testament certainly tells believers to love their neighbors (Lev. 19:18).

Love itself is not new. It pervades the Old Testament as well as the New Testament. As Paul says, the law itself can be summed up in the practice of love (Rom. 13:8–10). But several things *are* new in John 13. (1) There is a new relationship. We are to "love one another." Participation in the body of Christ creates relationships that are far more intimate than that of neighbor to neighbor. In Christ we are brothers and sisters. (2) There is a new standard. The Old Testament says, "Love your neighbor as yourself" (Lev. 19:18). Jesus says love one another "as I have loved you." Jesus loved us more than he loved himself and gave himself for us. (3) There is a new outcome. "By this all men will know that you are my disciples." The reality of Jesus among his people is communicated by the visible expressions of love in the Christian community.

John 14:2

What did Jesus mean when he said there are many rooms in his Father's house?

In biblical times larger homes were built with many rooms constructed around an open inner court. Frequently each member of the extended family—parents, married and single children, grandchildren, and grandparents—had rooms of his or her own in the family home. What Jesus implied in promising that "in my Father's house are many rooms" was that God would welcome Christ's followers into his own eternal household, that there would be a place for them in God's own home when Jesus returned.

John 14:6

How can Christianity claim to be an exclusive faith? Why should Christians deny others the right to approach God in their own way?

No one can deny others the right to attempt to approach God in their own way. But Jesus insisted that the only way to reach God was through faith in him. Christians simply agree with God by saying that today's Jews, Muslims, Hindus, Buddhists, or cult members cannot be saved apart from personal faith in Jesus as God's Son and their Savior. No Christian has the right to revise Scripture or rewrite the teachings of Jesus. The notion that all religions worship the same God is flatly contradicted by the Bible, as is the popular view that all religions lead to God.

John 14:12

How can believers "do even greater things" than Jesus did?

It is not a miracle for a Pete Sampras or Andre Agassi to win a tennis tournament. But if I won a pro tournament, it would be a greater thing than what they do, for I am a sixty-year-old duffer. Jesus' miracles amazed his observers, but then, Jesus is God. Jesus can be expected to do what God can do.

This helps us understand Jesus' enigmatic saying that those with faith in him will do greater things than he has done. As Jesus lived by God the Father's will, so will those with faith also live. And it is far greater for us to do this, because we are sinners. The sinless Jesus lived in unbroken fellowship with his Father. As Christ constantly performed compassionate and good works, so the person with faith will reach out to others in love. And this is a far greater thing for us to do, because we are essentially selfish, which Christ was not but was perfect love. The things we do are greater only in this sense of being more miraculous, considering who we are.

It is important to note that verses 12 and 13 are linked with verse 14. How can we do these greater things? Only by relying fully on the power of God, by asking him, and by letting him act through us.

John 14:28

If Jesus is truly God, how could he say, "The Father is greater than I"?

Christians agree with the statement, expressed in the Westminster and many other catechisms, that the three persons of the Godhead "are one God, the same in substance, equal in power and glory." This statement focuses on the essence of who God—and thus who the Father, Son, and Holy Spirit—is. But Jesus was speaking as the Son incarnate. Philippians 2:7 reminds us that in taking on humanity Jesus "made himself nothing, taking the very nature of a servant." So the Father was greater than Jesus in his incarnate state, although not in his essential nature as God the Son.

John 15:6

Does Jesus' warning that unfruitful branches will be burned indicate that a believer can be sent to hell if he or she "does not remain in" the Lord?

Jesus' metaphor of the vine and the branches is specifically about bearing fruit. Jesus is not talking about being saved or lost, and his imagery should not be applied to that issue. He is speaking of maintaining a daily relationship with him (remaining in him) through obedience, especially to his command to love. This is essential for fruitfulness. The reference to burning is not a threat but drives home a point that was well understood by first-century farmers. The trunks and branches of most trees can be used even when they are dead. But the wood of a grapevine is gnarled and twisted and utterly useless. Thus farmers can do nothing but burn vines that do not produce. Jesus here reminds us that God has saved us so that we might bear fruit.

That is all we can do. If we fail to remain in Jesus and so cut ourselves off from the source of fruitfulness, our lives become meaningless. We find our purpose in life by remaining close to Jesus and letting God produce fruit in us.

John 15:18

What is the "world" that hates the followers of Jesus?

The *Expository Dictionary of Bible Words* notes that John uses *kosmos* (translated here as "world" in a distinctive theological sense:

[To] portray human society as a system warped by sin, tormented by beliefs and desires and emotions that surge blindingly and uncontrollably. The world system is a dark system (Eph. 6:12), operating on basic principles that are not of God (Col. 2:20; 1 John 2:16). The entire system lies under the power of Satan (1 John 5:19) and constitutes the kingdom from which believers are delivered by Christ (Col. 1:13–14). Its basic hostility to God is often displayed (page 639).

John 16:5–16

What biblical evidence is there that the Holy Spirit is a person rather than an influence, an "it"?

The *Zondervan Dictionary of Christian Literacy* (1987) sums up the evidence:

When Jesus spoke of the Holy Spirit, our Lord chose the personal pronoun "he," even though "spirit" in Greek is a neuter word (John 14:17, 26; 16:13–15). Christ promised to send his disciples "another Comforter" when he returned to heaven, and he identified the Spirit as the promised one. The word in Scripture for "another" is *allos*, a Greek term meaning "another of the same kind" in distinction to *heteros*, meaning "another of a different kind." Christ, the second person of the Godhead, was to send the Spirit, equally God, to live within those who believe.

There are many other indications that the Spirit is a person and not a force or influence. The Holy Spirit knows and understands (Rom. 8:27; 1 Cor. 2:11), can be insulted (Heb. 10:29), can be lied to (Acts 5:3), can be resisted (Acts 7:51), and can be grieved (Eph. 4:30). The Holy Spirit teaches (John 14:26), intercedes (Rom. 8:26), convicts (John 16:7–8), bears witness (John 15:26), and guides (John 16:13). Each of these activities testifies to the fact that the Spirit is a person, not an impersonal influence.

The Holy Spirit is also a divine person. The Bible clearly identifies the Spirit as God by the titles it gives him. He is the eternal Spirit (Heb. 9:14), the Spirit of Christ (1 Peter 1:11), the Spirit of the Lord (Isa. 11:2), the Spirit of the Sovereign Lord (Isa. 61:1), the Spirit of the

Father (Matt. 10:20), and the Spirit of the Son (Gal. 4:6). No other being apart from God bears such divine titles.

The deity of the Spirit is shown in other ways. He is omnipresent, as only God can be (Ps. 139:7; 1 Cor. 12:13). He is all-powerful (Luke 1:35; Rom. 8:11). He was an agent in Creation (Gen. 1:2; Ps. 104:30), and has power to work miracles (Matt. 12:28; 1 Cor. 12:9–11). The Spirit is the one who brings us new birth (John 3:6; Tit. 3:5). It was the Spirit who raised Jesus from the dead and who brings God's resurrection life to you and me (Rom. 8:11). The Holy Spirit can be blasphemed (Matt. 12:31–32; Mark 3:28–29), and lying to the Holy Spirit is said to be lying to God (Acts 5:3–4). The biblical testimony is clear. The Holy Spirit is a person. And the Holy Spirit is God.

John 16:23

What does it mean to pray in Jesus' name?

The phrase "in my name" occurs often in this lengthy discourse (14:13–14,26; 16:23–24, 26). People in biblical times considered that a name communicated something of the essence or character of the person named. To pray in Jesus' name means to approach God through Jesus and to identify the content and motivation of one's prayers with all that Jesus is.

John 17:23

Why has God not answered Jesus' prayer that his followers be "brought to complete unity" in him?

The assumption that this prayer has not been answered rests on misinterpretation. This verse has often been taken as an appeal for organizational unity; an appeal that all Christians unite to form a single denomination or worldwide church.

In fact Jesus defined his meaning when he asked that "all of them may be one, Father, *just as you are in me and I am in you*" (italics mine) (v. 21). Jesus frequently claimed to live in perfect union with God and expressed that relationship by doing God's will (John 5:19–20; 6:38; 8:28–29; 12:44–45; 14:9–11). Christ did not pray that all Christians become members of a world-church organization but that like Jesus himself we live our human lives in intimate union with God, doing his will, and thus remaining in him, letting him live out Christ's life in us.

John 19:11

Whom did Jesus refer to when he told Pilate that the one who handed him over to Pilate was "guilty of a greater sin"?

Most commentators agree that Jesus referred to Caiaphas, the high priest, who represented the nation in delivering Jesus to Pilate for judgment and demanding the death sentence.

John 19:14

Was Jesus crucified on a Friday?

See the discussion of Matthew 12:40, page 242.

John 20

Do the Gospel accounts of what happened Easter morning conflict? If so, how can anyone say the Bible is without error?

See the discussion of Mark 16:1 page 279.

John 20:22

This verse says Jesus gave the disciples the Holy Spirit. But later Jesus told his disciples they would have to wait to receive the Spirit in the future and to wait until he "comes on you" (Acts 1:8). Surely one of these verses is in error.

Calvin saw in this verse the description of a partial gift of the Spirit, who was to be given fully on Pentecost, and suggested that the Spirit was given "in such a way that they were only sprinkled with his grace and not saturated with full power." Another explanation is that John, whose Gospel makes no pretense of chronological organization, takes this opportunity to sum up the meaning of Christ's death and resurrection in which believers are empowered by the gift of the Spirit to fulfill their commission as his witnesses. A third possibility is that the Spirit was given to the disciples at this time, but that his baptizing work (1 Cor. 12:13), by which they were united to Christ and one another as the church, took place at Pentecost. Any of these three possible explanations successfully defends the passage against the charge of error.

Acts

Acts

Who wrote this book, and what themes and issues does it deal with?

The Book of Acts was written by Luke, who also produced the Gospel that bears his name. Acts continues the story of Jesus, showing what he accomplished after his resurrection through his followers. Acts is the only New Testament book to give a narrative history of the early church, describing the explosive spread of Christianity throughout the Roman Empire within just three decades. On another level, Acts is the story of Peter and of Paul, the greatest of the apostles, who took the lead in spreading the gospel to first-century A.D. Jewish and Gentile communities.

Acts 1:5

What is the "baptism of the Spirit"?

See the discussion of Mark 1:8, page 263.

Acts 1:18

The accounts of Judas's death (see also Matt. 27:5) are clearly in conflict. So here is another error in the Bible.

These accounts are not clearly in conflict. Judas hung himself, and later the rope broke. His decomposed body broke open when he was cut down, or fell. Or, as some have suggested, *hung* here means he was impaled after he flung himself off a cliff. Either of these scenarios removes any supposed conflict in the accounts.

Acts 1:26

If the apostles drew lots to find God's will, would that be a good way for Christians to make choices today?

In Old Testament times the high priest consulted the Urim and Thummim to seek direction from God. Most believe these were colored stones, or lots, placed in a pocket sewn into the vestlike ephod he wore. God indicated his will by directing the high priest's hand to the correct lot. This is the tradition the apostles followed when they were unable to tell which of two qualified candidates God intended to fill the place left empty by Judas.

However, many have noted that this took place before the coming of the Holy Spirit at Pentecost. No other reference is made in the New Testament to seeking God's will by resorting to lots or any other form of chance. With the coming of the Spirit, believers were guided by him as he spoke to them directly or to them through others.

Acts 2:6

Is speaking in tongues always a sign of the coming of the Holy Spirit in a person's life?

While this view is held by some, no such teaching is found in the New Testament epistles. There is another explanation for the incidents of Christians speaking in tongues reported in Acts. Acts 2 reports a coming of the Spirit on the believers in Jerusalem that was marked by the sound of "the blowing of a violent wind" (v. 2), by visible flames, and by speaking in tongues. The three signs are never mentioned together again. Speaking in tongues is found again in Acts 10:46 and 19:6. In the first case, tongues were the decisive sign to the Jewish believers that God had, in fact, chosen to grant salvation to Gentiles who believed in Jesus (Acts 11:15–18). Acts 19:6 describes a dozen men who believed John the Baptist's message about the imminent coming of the Messiah. They spoke in tongues and prophesied after their conversion to Christ. There seems to be no compelling reason for the granting of this sign, as there was in Acts chapters 10 and 11. Even so, these two incidents hardly seem sufficient basis for such a significant doctrine. This is especially true since 1 Corinthians 12:10 indicates that some but not all Christians will be given the ability to speak "in different kinds of tongues."

Acts 2:16–21

Why did Peter quote this extended prophecy from Joel? Certainly all that Joel predicted did not happen on Pentecost and has not happened yet.

Peter quoted this passage (Joel 2:28–32) to show that what the people were witnessing—their sons and daughters filled with the Spirit and prophesying—was predicted in the Old Testament as a sign that will initiate the last days. Peter went on, without implying that the judgment aspect of the end times would happen at that time, to say, "And everyone who calls on the name of the Lord will be saved." This passage thus sums up God's program for the gospel age: The Spirit has come, giving all who call on the Lord salvation before judgment falls.

Acts 2:38

Peter tells his listeners to repent and be baptized "for the forgiveness of your sins." What does repentance have to do with forgiveness?

Repent means to change one's mind or direction in life. In this sermon Peter called on the crowd to change their mind about Jesus, who had been rejected by Israel and crucified. In this case to repent would mean to acknowledge the resurrected Jesus as "both Lord and Christ" (3:36), and thus receive God's forgiveness.

Acts 2:44–45

Do these verses teach a kind of Christian communism?

What they teach is Christian love expressed by a sharing of material resources with those in need. Acts 5:4 expresses one difference between the early church and communism. The early church recognized the right of its members to their own property, for Peter said to Ananias, who had pretended to give all the proceeds from the sale of some property to the church, "Didn't it belong to you before it was sold? And after it was sold, wasn't the money at your disposal?" (Acts 5:4). Communism rejects the right of personal property and says that all belongs to the community (the state).

Acts 4:6

How can this verse call Annas the high priest, when we know that the Romans deposed Annas from office in A.D. 15?

Some assume the Annas identified here as high priest was Jonathan, son of Annas, who became high priest in A.D. 36. However, we know that Annas controlled the priesthood through his sons and son-in-law Caiaphas. Despite the Roman intervention, Annas was considered by the Jews to be the rightful high priest even after he was deposed.

Acts 4:13

What did the leaders mean by identifying Peter and John as "unschooled, ordinary men"?

First-century A.D. Judaism made an important distinction between those who were trained in Old Testament law and those who were unschooled. The trained were held responsible for their first violaton of the law. But the unschooled were not held responsible for a first offense. Instead they were instructed and warned not to commit the offense again. It has been suggested that the phrase "They were unschooled, ordinary men" represented a legal determination, meaning all that the Sanhedrin could do was warn the disciples "not to speak or teach at all in the name of Jesus" (Acts 4:18). Because the Sanhedrin was the official interpreter of divine law, their command would be binding in Judaism, and the disciples could be punished for any future offense.

Acts 5:1–11

Nothing in the Old Testament or New Testament suggests that lying to God merits the death penalty. Certainly there is a moral discrepancy here between what happened to Ananias and Sapphira and Jesus' call for love and forgiveness.

It is a mistake to dismiss the conspiracy of Ananias and Sapphira lightly. Peter pinpoints Satan's personal involvement in the incident and notes that those two not only attempted to deceive the Christian community but also assumed they could lie to God. The immediate and decisive judgment of Ananias and his wife caused "great fear [awe]" to seize "the whole church and all who heard about these events" (v. 11). Thus the judgment was punishment of wrongdoing, a reminder to the church to take God seriously, and a witness to the whole city that God truly was among this group that followed Jesus as Messiah.

Acts 5:32

How can obedience be the condition for receiving the Holy Spirit? Doesn't the Bible teach that all Christians have the Spirit?

1 Corinthians 12:13 says that "we were all baptized by one Spirit into one body," and Romans 8:9 says that "if anyone does not have the Spirit of Christ, he does not belong to Christ." The apparent conflict is removed, however, when we realize that frequently in the New Testament obedience to Christ or to the gospel is a euphemism for and has the same meaning of faith in Christ or of a faith-response to the gospel (see also Rom. 15:18; 16:26; 2 Thess. 1:8).

Acts 5:36

Josephus assigns the revolt of Theudas to 44 A.D., at least ten and perhaps as many as fifteen years after Luke puts these words in the mouth of Gamaliel. So Luke is in error.

It is a little naive to charge Luke with an error at this point. The history of Palestine under the Romans is filled with reports of rebellions and incidents involving many more than four hundred men. There is no reason not to suppose that Gamaliel and Josephus refer to different events entirely. This is not surprising, as Theudas, like Judas, was a common name, a short form of Theodoros, the Greek form of the Hebrew name Nathaniel.

Acts 7:6

Is Stephen's four-hundred-year figure correct? If so, Exodus 12:40–41 must be in error.

Any literary document has to be interpreted by the literary conventions of its times. Rounded numbers are frequently used not only in the Bible but in our own day.

Everyone would understand exactly what we meant if we said our nation was founded two hundred years ago, even though the actual bicentennial took place in 1976.

Acts 7:14

Here is a clear discrepancy. Exodus 1:5 says the descendants of Jacob were seventy in all, while Stephen says there were seventy-five.

Gleason Archer, in his *Bible Difficulties* (Zondervan, 1982), argues that both texts are right. He notes that the Hebrew text of Exodus 1:5 bases its calculations on the sixty-six direct descendants identified in Genesis 46:26–27, plus the two sons of Joseph, plus Joseph and his wife.

However, the Septuagint, which is the Greek translation of the Old Testament completed over a century before Christ, says in Exodus 1:5 that "all who came with Jacob into Egypt, who issued from his loins, apart from the wives of the sons of Jacob, were sixty-six persons. And the sons of Joseph who were born to him in Egypt were nine persons. All the souls of the house of Jacob who entered Egypt were seventy-five." Thus the Septuagint includes nine offspring of Joseph rather than two, which assumes that Joseph's sons Ephraim and Manasseh later had seven sons who were considered to be among the seventy-five original Jewish immigrants. Thus both the Hebrew version of Exodus 1:5 and the Septuagint version are correct, and Stephen was right in identifying seventy-five offspring, even though Exodus 1:5 says there were seventy. Both figures are accurate, because the two traditions used different methods of calculation.

Acts 8:13, 20

If Simon the Sorcerer believed and was baptized, how could Peter later threaten him with hell?

Scripture, as well as experience, demonstrates that there is counterfeit as well as genuine belief in Jesus. Christ described the initial response of "the man who hears the word and at once receives it with joy. But since he has no root, he lasts only a short time. When trouble or persecution comes because of the word, he quickly falls away" (Matt. 13:20–21). We have no way of knowing whether Simon's response and repentance were genuine or whether they were entirely superficial. Peter's analysis that Simon's heart was "not right before God" (Acts 8:21) implies he was never converted.

Acts 9:2

How could the high priest in Jerusalem give Saul authority to seize Jews in Damascus, which was not Jewish territory?

In the Roman Empire people of a given nationality were considered to be subject to the laws of their own lands. Thus disputes involving Jews would be settled by Jewish courts. Of course, a dispute between a Jew and a Roman would be settled in a Roman court, with the Roman undoubtedly favored. This concept of law meant that a Jew anywhere in the Roman Empire was considered to live under authority of Jewish law. Since the Sanhedrin was the supreme court of Judaism and the high priest its highest officer, the high priest could grant Saul the legal right to seize Jews *anywhere* and bring them back to Jerusalem for judgment.

Acts 9:1–9

Why are there such differences in the two accounts of Paul's conversion? Surely there is some discrepancy here.

It's true that some hold there is a contradiction between Paul's first account (Acts 9:7) of his conversion, and his second account (Acts 22:9). In older versions Acts 9:7 describes Paul's companions as speechless, hearing "the sound" (*tes phones*) but seeing no one. Acts 22:9 seemed to report that they heard "the voice" (*ten phonen*) of the one talking. The New International Version resolves the supposed conflict by correctly rendering a distinction made in the original through the cases used with each verb. Thus the two accounts report: "They heard the sound but did not see anyone" (9:7); and, "They did not understand the voice of him who was speaking to me" (22:9).

The charge of contradiction is resolved, and we see that the real problem is the failure of older versions to correctly translate the original manuscript.

Acts 11:19, 27

What were the prophets of the early church? Do we have them in the church today?

The New Testament speaks of a spiritual gift of prophecy, and we first meet New Testament prophets here in Acts. In New Testament references, prophets preach and explain God's Word, exhort believers, and in some cases foretell the future (Acts 13:1; 15:32; 19:6; 21:9–10; Rom. 12:6; 1 Cor. 12:10; 13:2, 8; 14:3, 29–39). Some Christians believe that the foretelling aspect of New Testament prophecy ended with the completion of the New Testament itself (1 Cor. 13:8). Others insist the gift of prophecy is still exercised in the modern church but that a prophet's words are always to be tested by the conformity of his message to Scripture.

Acts 12:15

What did the people in Mary's house mean when they said, "It must be his angel"?

The reference is to Peter's guardian angel (Heb. 1:14). First-century A.D. Jews commonly believed guardian angels strongly resembled the people they were serving. While Luke accurately reports the remark, his report should not be taken as evidence that this belief, reflected nowhere else in Scripture, was correct.

Acts 15:29

What was meant by each of the four requests the Jerusalem council made of Gentile believers?

The Jerusalem council rejected the view of the Judaizers (Jewish Christians who argued that Gentile believers must subject themselves to the entire law of Moses). The council affirmed the principle of salvation by faith, and observed that biblical standards of righteousness were well known through the teaching of Moses' law in synagogues throughout the empire (15:21). However, the letter did pinpoint four areas in which Jewish believers were deeply offended by common elements of the prevailing Gentile culture and asked Gentile Christians to be sensitive to their Jewish brothers' convictions. Since sins in the Old Testament are also sins in the New Testament, we need to interpret these four issues as practices that are not clearly identified as sins. For instance, idolatry is sin. But some Gentile Christians shopped at temple markets for meat (1 Cor. 8). This was most likely the "food polluted by idols," mentioned by James (Acts 15:20). To abstain from "the meat of strangled animals and from blood" relates to Jewish food laws, which forbade the consumption of blood and thus of animals which had been strangled rather than bled when slaughtered. The word translated "sexual immorality" is *porneia* (v. 20), a very broad and general term that is hard to translate. Since all Christians are called on to abstain from sexual immorality, it is likely this term relates to the loose way in which sexual matters were discussed and joked about in the first century, rather than actual sex sins.

Acts 15:39

*Was Paul a hypocrite? He urged others to reconcile their differ-
ences but became so angry with Barnabas that he broke up with
his friend.*

Paul was not a hypocrite. But he was a fallible human being.
None of us are without weakness; all of us are susceptible to sin. Note-
worthy is the fact that Barnabas's investment in young Mark paid off.
Later Mark not only wrote the Gospel that bears his name but also
became reconciled to Paul, who wrote to Timothy to, "get Mark and
bring him with you, because he is helpful to me in my ministry" (2 Tim.
4:11). This tacit admission that he was wrong clears Paul of the charge
of hypocrisy but not of acting foolishly in breaking up with Barnabas
over giving Mark a second chance.

Acts 17:16–34

*Paul quoted a pagan poet in his address to the Athenians as if it
were Scripture. Does this mean that other writings beside the
Bible contain divine revelation?*

There is a difference between quoting a poet in the introduction of a sermon to establish a point of contact with one's audience and
using a biblical text as an authoritative expression of truth. Paul did not
quote the Old Testament in his sermon in Acts because the Athenians
did not acknowledge it as an authority. However, the central truths
expressed in his sermon—that God has established a day of judgment,
that he calls everyone to repent, that he has appointed Jesus and proved
this by raising him from the dead—are all biblical concepts that were
totally foreign to the philosophies of the Athenians. Whatever use Paul
made of pagan poets, his religious beliefs were clearly rooted in the Jewish Scriptures and God's further revelation in Jesus Christ.

Acts 19:1–7

*If the Holy Spirit is given to all believers (Rom. 8:9), how did it
happen that these believers did not receive the Spirit until Paul
laid hands on them?*

Paul asked these disciples if they had received the Spirit when
they believed. He clearly assumed that if they were believers they would
already have the Spirit. A few questions revealed that these men had not

324 New Testament

yet heard of Jesus but had responded to the call of John the Baptist to repent in preparation for the appearance of the Messiah. As soon as they heard of Jesus they were baptized, and "when Paul placed his hands on them" (during the baptism) the Spirit came upon them. There is no conflict with Romans 8:9 here, for the Spirit did come on these disciples of John when they believed in Jesus.

Acts 21:11

Why did Paul disobey the Holy Spirit and insist on going to Jerusalem after being warned that he would be imprisoned there?

Some have assumed that Paul went to Jerusalem in direct disobedience to the Holy Spirit. However, the text simply indicates that the Spirit led prophets to predict what would happen to Paul in Jerusalem. It was the prophets themselves who, out of concern, urged Paul "not to go up to Jerusalem" (21:12). No verse states Paul was directed not to go to Jerusalem. So it is best to assume that the messages were intended to prepare Paul for what lay ahead, not to warn him off.

Acts 21:20–26

Was Paul being hypocritical to undergo a Jewish rite, when he was the one who argued so strongly that Christians are not bound by Jewish law?

There is a difference between imposing Jewish ceremonial law on Gentiles and refusing to let Jews express their faith within the framework of their ancient heritage. Many first-century Jewish Christians expressed their faith in traditional ways by keeping the Old Testament's religious holidays and following ancient customs. Just as early Christianity did not require Gentiles to adopt a Jewish lifestyle, it did not require Jewish believers to adopt a Gentile lifestyle.

Paul as a Jew had a perfect right to adopt a Jewish lifestyle when among Jews and a Gentile way of life when among Gentiles. But, note that when a direct conflict arose between adapting to the culture and following basic Christian truths, Paul refused to compromise (Gal. 2:3).

Acts 23:6

Paul resorted to a trick to divide the Sanhedrin. Was this a morally flawed course?

Some certainly have charged Paul with insincere maneuvering here. Since the Bible does not present any human being other than Jesus as perfect, this charge, even if true, would hardly discredit Scripture. However, it is not at all necessary to take Paul's statement in this way. What Paul may well have been saying is, "The real issue here is resurrection from the dead." This is, of course, the issue in Christianity itself. The Book of Romans points out that the resurrection declared (proved) Jesus to be the Son of God (Rom. 1:4). Paul's statement in the Sanhedrin led to acrimonious argument between the Pharisees, who believed in resurrection, and the Sadducees, who did not. The flaring up of this long-standing dispute led to violence, and the soldiers had to rescue Paul yet again. It is unlikely that Paul could have foreseen this result.

Acts 28

What happened to the apostle Paul following the narrative of the Book of Acts?

The Book of Acts closes with Paul in prison awaiting trial. Hints from Paul's New Testament letters and references in early Christian documents suggest the following reconstruction of his life.

Paul was released from this first imprisonment, during which he wrote the first letter to Timothy. Paul traveled to Spain to open yet another mission field. Some time later Paul was arrested again and taken back to Rome. During this imprisonment Paul wrote his second letter to Timothy. This time Paul was condemned and was executed in Rome sometime before A.D. 70 as was the apostle Peter.

Romans

Romans

Who wrote this book, and what themes and issues does it deal with?

This first epistle in the New Testament is a letter written to Christians in Rome by the apostle Paul. It is perhaps the most theological of the New Testament letters, and its teaching, with that of Galatians, was central to the Protestant Reformation of the sixteenth century.

The theme of Romans is righteousness. Paul shows that no human being possesses righteousness (chapters 1–3), but that God provides righteousness as a free gift to those who believe (chapters 4–5). God's righteousness is not simply legal but an inner dynamic that makes it possible for believers to live a righteous life here and now (chapters 6–8). Paul then demonstrates that God's righteousness has operated throughout sacred history (chapters 9–11). The last chapters of Romans show how the new community formed by Christ is to live out his righteousness daily (chapters 12–16).

Romans 1:7

What is a saint?

Paul uses the word *saint* as a synonym for *Christian*. The biblical usage differs from the Roman Catholic understanding, which is that a saint is a person with an exceptionally holy life, whose unique relationship with God is confirmed by authenticated miracles performed on behalf of those who appeal directly to that person.

Romans 1:18–20

*How much can be known about God apart from the special reve-
lation God has given us as recorded in Scripture?*

Theologians divide revelation into two major categories: natural revelation, which includes all that can be deduced about God from
his creation, and special revelation, which includes all that God has
revealed to human beings as recorded in Scripture.

In this passage Paul affirms that God's "eternal power and divine
nature have been clearly seen" in the creation. Specifically, the creation
demonstrates the fact that God exists and that God is all-powerful.

This passage, however, does more than affirm that such evidence
exists. Paul says that "God has made it [his existence and power] plain
to them," and that these truths are "understood from what has been
made." If we liken creation to a radio transmitter constantly sending
out a message, we would say that human beings have built-in radio
receivers pretuned to God's station. Human beings are, therefore, "without excuse," because a refusal to acknowledge God can only reflect a
wickedness that suppresses what is already known.

Romans 1:18–32

*Are pagans who have never heard the gospel really lost? If so,
this is not fair at all.*

Paul has just shown that all human beings have a basic knowledge of God communicated through creation. Paul has also argued that
human beings willfully suppress this knowledge of God. In the rest of
the chapter he goes on to trace the spiritual and moral decline exhibited in human cultures where this knowledge of God is rejected.

Paul's argument establishes two points. God does speak to all people.
Faith is a response to God's self-revelation, and whatever the content of
that revelation (Gen. 15:4–6), all have an opportunity to respond in faith
to natural revelation. While we might argue that belief in Christ is necessary for salvation, another might say that if a person did respond to
God's natural revelation, the Lord would see that in some way that person heard the gospel. However, all such argument is hypothetical, for
Paul's point is that human beings do not respond to natural revelation.
In fact, their suppression of the known truth about God proves that
human beings truly are lost. For if humanity were responsive to God,
his revelation would draw them to him as a young person is attracted
to a girlfriend or boyfriend. The fact that knowledge of God repels human

beings shows how sin has twisted humanity, and how great our need of salvation really is.

Romans 1:27

Why is the Bible so repressive when it comes to alternate ways of expressing love? If a real love exists, what is wrong with homosexuality?

The Bible consistently views homosexuality as a sin, a shameful perversion of the sexual capacity God granted human beings at creation. Homosexuality is identified as a detestable perversion that defiles the individuals involved (Lev. 18:22–23). Romans adds that it involves shameful lusts and unnatural and indecent acts.

While some modernists reject the Bible's moral codes, and some churches claim that Scripture's antagonism to homosexuality is culture bound, no one who accepts the Bible as God's Word and submits to the Bible's authority can acquiesce to the notion that homosexuality reflects a morally acceptable alternate lifestyle.

Romans 2:6–7

How does this passage's teaching that a person can earn immortality by "persistence in doing good" match up with Paul's doctrine of justification of the wicked person who does not work for salvation (Rom. 4:5)?

Paul does not assume that anyone will in fact win salvation by working for it. This is a foolish belief he contradicts constantly in Romans and his other letters (see also Rom. 3:20). So it follows that, whatever Paul means here, he cannot be suggesting that a person can earn salvation by his good works.

What then is Paul doing? Most commentators note that Paul develops the principle expressed in verse 6: God judges each person "according to what he has done." In essence, a person's approach to life as expressed in his or her acts demonstrates the orientation of his or her life. Those who focus on future glory demonstrate a "persistence in doing good" that leads to eternal life. A focus on future glory suggests a believer whose hope is in God, and who as a consequence persists in good works not to earn salvation but to express relationship with the Lord.

Romans 2:12–16

How can people who have never heard of God's law be held responsible for breaking it? God surely is not being fair when he condemns human beings for committing sins they did not even know were sins.

Paul agrees completely with this point of view. In fact, he makes it clear that God will not judge pagans on the basis of a biblical law they never knew. That is the point of these verses. They remind us that in every society human beings adopt certain standards of right and wrong. And when a person does wrong—by the standards of his own society—that person is accused by his or her conscience of wrongdoing.

How then will God judge those "apart from the law"? He will use "the requirements of the law that are written on their hearts." The pagans will be judged by their own standards, and everyone will be convicted, for every human being has sinned and done that which he or she knows to be wrong.

It is important to note here that while conscience is universal and defines areas in which standards exist, the contents of conscience, in the sense of what specifically are judged to be right and wrong, differ across cultures. Thus every society, for example, has some kind of standards in the area of sexuality, although not every society holds that premarital sex is wrong. In no society, however, is any and every kind of sexual activity considered morally right.

Romans 3:25–26

How could Old Testament saints have believed in Jesus? He had not yet come and suffered for them. And if they could not believe him, how could the "sins committed beforehand" have been forgiven by God?

It is important to make a distinction between the basis of salvation and the content of faith. The basis of salvation, whether of an Old Testament saint or a New Testament believer, is and has always been the death of Christ as an atoning sacrifice. God is free to forgive because Christ has died for our sins. In this day and age, after the cross, Christ is the content of our faith as well as the basis of our salvation. Our faith response to the gospel of Jesus Christ saves us.

However, in earlier times the content of faith was not the same as the basis of salvation. Genesis 15:6 says Abraham "believed the LORD and he credited it to him as righteousness." What was it that Abraham believed? It was God's promise that Sarah would have a son. Abraham did not know about Jesus' future death on the cross, and God did not reveal it to him. Abraham simply believed what God did reveal, and God credited that faith to him as righteousness, on the basis of Jesus' future sacrifice of himself in payment for Abraham's as well as our sins.

The content of faith in different biblical eras is not as different as it may seem. God spoke to Abraham, and Abraham believed God. God speaks to us in the gospel, and when we respond by trusting ourselves to Jesus, we, too, believe God. It is faith in God as he reveals himself to us in his Word that is and always has been saving faith. It is the death of Christ in full payment for our sins that has made it possible for God to be just and at the same time to justify (pronounce "innocent") those who believe.

Romans 5:12

How is it that "death came to all men" through Adam's sin? Certainly this is not fair. Why should innocent descendants suffer because of what some distant ancestor did?

Paul's point is that sin is something like a genetic defect. This defect expresses itself in acts of sin for which each person is personally responsible. As far as judgment is concerned, individuals are judged not for Adam's sin but for their own personal sins (Rev. 20:11–15). So no one who is innocent will suffer unfairly.

However, the Bible clearly says that spiritual and biological death are realities. Human beings age and die. Too often our sinful nature controls our actions, and we are insensitive to God apart from a spiritual awakening. This condition is a consequence of Adam's original disobedience to God. Rather than cry "Unfair," human beings need to recognize the fact that Romans 5 describes the reality of their desperate situation. Because this is the way things are it is urgent that every person turn to Christ.

We need also to recognize an even greater unfairness: It was unfair for God's Son to suffer for the guilty. Yet he did suffer and in his suffering became the agent through whom God in grace repaired the damage caused by Adam's fall.

Romans 6:1–4

What baptism is Paul speaking of in this passage?

As noted in the discussion of Matthew 3:11 (p. 229), the Bible uses the word *baptism* in several different ways. Here the baptism is spiritual. It is defined in 1 Corinthians 12:13 as that by which the Holy Spirit unites the believer with Jesus as a member of his body. The theme of spiritual baptism is union with Christ. This is exactly the theme developed in this passage. We have been united to (baptized into) Jesus Christ, so his death is counted as our death. Even more exciting than this is the fact that because we have been united to Christ we also share in his resurrection. Through Christ God's resurrection power flows into us and we are enabled to live holy, righteous lives.

There is a modern, though imperfect, analogy to this. When a husband and wife are united in marriage, many states consider each person a full partner in all that the other possesses. A destitute woman might marry a man who has accumulated millions. Suddenly the law treats her as if she herself had accumulated these riches; the wealth is hers as well as his. Similarly, faith brings us into such an intimate union with Jesus that God views his death for sin as our death, and all that was won in Christ's resurrection also becomes ours. This great baptizing work of the Spirit of God is the basis for the Christian's power to live a holy life. This theme is developed in the rest of this powerful chapter.

What then is water baptism? The baptism performed by John the Baptist was rooted in the Jewish practice of taking ritual cleansing baths. With John it was transformed into an act signifying repentance and thus an inner, spiritual cleansing. In contrast Christian water baptism is perhaps best understood as an act symbolizing our identification with Jesus in his death and resurrection.

Throughout the history of the church, three forms of water baptism have been practiced. Water has been sprinkled on new believers, poured over new believers, or the new believers have been immersed in water. Each mode of baptism has a long and well-authenticated tradition. Those who practice immersion, however, suggest that their mode of baptism best symbolizes the spiritual reality portrayed in Romans 6.

Romans 7:6

If a person is "released from the law" he or she is free to sin. May Christians do anything they want to do?

In Romans Paul talks about righteousness. The rest of the book makes clear that God does expect believers to live righteous lives. A problem arises when we assume that it is necessary to be "under the law" (see Rom. 6:14) to be righteous.

God's Old Testament law, especially the Ten Commandments, is first of all a standard that provides a critical definition of right and wrong actions. Second, that law also provides insight into the character of the God who gave it and thus reveals him as a person. Third, the law served as a way through which the Old Testament saints related to God. Those who sought to please him obeyed the law and were rewarded; those who were indifferent to God and disobeyed were punished.

The problem with the third function of the law was, as Paul says, that it was "weakened by the sinful nature" (Rom. 8:3). The law defines good, but human beings are sinful and the law is unable to make anyone good. Furthermore, God's law stimulated the sinful nature to the extent that Paul says the command "Do not covet," in fact, "produced in me every kind of covetous desire" (Rom. 7:7–8). Somehow, as for the child who is told not to eat the cookies her mom has set aside, prohibition seems only to strengthen desire.

When Paul says the Christian is released from the law, he speaks of the third function of law by saying that we no longer have to relate to God through the commandments. Instead we relate to God directly through his Spirit. We seek to please him yet rely on him to enable us to do what is right and good. This basic attitude toward God stimulates our new, God-given nature and not our "sinful passions [which were] aroused by the law" (7:5). As a result we "bear fruit to God" (7:4). Or, in the words of Romans 8:4, we find that "the righteous requirements of the law [are] fully met in us, who do not live according to the sinful nature but according to the Spirit."

Paul's point in Romans chapters 6–8 is that God does expect Christians to be righteous and to fully meet all the requirements of his moral law—and even more. But we cannot reach that goal by telling ourselves, "It's the law, we must do it." We reach that goal by loving Jesus, by desiring to please him, and by relying on the Holy Spirit to guide and enable us. When we live close to Jesus, we will not choose to sin, and the evidence that we are living a life pleasing to him is that none of our choices will violate the standards of righteousness provided in God's Word.

No, a person who is free from the law is not free to sin. He or she is free to be righteous.

Romans 7:14, 19

If a believer is a "slave to sin," why keep on trying to do right?

Theologians disagree as to whether Paul here describes his experience as a Christian or his experience before his conversion. The first view is the better one. In it Paul continues the theme he introduced in chapter 6 of freedom from God's law.

The Christian truly does have the desire to do what is good. But the problem is that Christians (as well as non-Christians) have what the Bible calls a sinful nature. This is identified theologically by Paul as "the flesh." In himself Paul had no ability to live the truly good and holy life he yearned to live. Paul sought to relate to God through the law and tried to do what was good. But as long as he did this, he failed.

This point should not be misunderstood. Earlier Paul spoke of coveting, of wanting something that belongs to another (7:7). For many people, the inner desire of coveting leads to stealing, which is coveting in action. Many of the good people in this world would never steal, so they might count themselves as righteous. But Paul, who likewise would never steal, looked inside and saw that his desire itself was sin. You and I can control our actions, but which of us can control our desires? Paul did not say that an external, behavioral goodness is impossible but that we discover our enslavement by sin when we look within and judge not only our acts but also our desires. And try as he might, Paul could not control this inner self. It was not subject to his conscious self. In fact, his conscious self seemed to be controlled by the inner desire.

Later, in chapter 8, Paul cried out in glad relief. What the law could not do, God has done by giving us his Spirit. When we rely fully on the Spirit and are led by him, the Spirit of Christ enables us to meet fully all the requirements of the law, including the command, "Thou shalt not covet." Through Jesus we are changed within. By the Spirit's enabling power our changed selves, not our "flesh" or sin, can be in control.

Romans 8:28

How can Christians say that everything that happens is good? When we see all the tragedy and suffering in the world, this appears to be the grossest hypocrisy.

This verse does not say that everything that happens is good. It says, "In all things God works for the good of those who love him, who have been called according to his purpose." This is a very different proposition. Many things that happen to believers are bad in every sense of that word. Yet Paul assures us that God is great enough to bring something that is good for us out of the most terrible tragedy.

It is also important to understand the word *good*. The Greek word here is *agathos*, which means good in the sense of useful or beneficial. What happens to the Christian may not be pleasant, but God is at work in our most painful situations so that what happens becomes beneficial rather than harmful to us.

Romans 8:29

The Bible talks about predestination and foreknowledge here and in other passages. Does this mean that God chose those who will be saved and chose others to be lost?

Christians differ on the meaning and implications of what the Bible says about predestination. The Greek word *proorizo* means to "mark out ahead of time" or "to predetermine." It is found only six times in the New Testament (Acts 4:28; Rom. 8:29–30; 1 Cor. 2:7; Eph. 1:5, 11). One Protestant tradition argues that God simply knew those who would respond to the gospel and predetermined that those persons would be "conformed to the likeness of his Son" (Rom. 8:29). Another Protestant tradition holds that humanity is so ruined by sin that apart from an irresistible application of God's grace no one would be able to respond to the gospel. Thus predestination applies to salvation itself. No Protestant tradition currently argues for double predestination—the idea that God actively chose who would be lost even as he actively chose some to be saved.

The whole debate recognizes a tension that exists in Christianity as a revealed religion. The Bible portrays God as an all-powerful, completely sovereign individual. Yet the Bible also portrays human beings as morally responsible beings with freedom of choice. These two teachings, that God is sovereign, and that human beings have free will, seem to us to be in such clear conflict that for one to be true the other must be false. And so we intuitively feel that when we emphasize one, it must be at the expense of the other.

In fact, it is exactly at this point that we are forced to affirm what seems to us a paradox. The Bible makes a valid offer of salvation to whoever chooses to believe. We are called on to share this gospel with all humankind. The Bible also reveals a God who is sovereign in the fullest sense. He is the Lord of the past, the present, and the future. All of this is under his complete control. We are called on to acknowledge this God, to worship and adore him. We are not called on to decide how both strands of biblical teaching can be in full and total harmony with reality.

This is to some a very unsatisfactory answer. But when we come to what seem to be theological discrepancies in the Bible, we are forced to make a very basic decision. Is God truly God, and are we merely creatures? If so, we must recognize that our understanding, our logic, is nothing compared with his vast understanding. Simply because we cannot understand is no reason to doubt what God has revealed. At such times we confess our positions as creatures, bow before him in wonder, and remain absolutely confident that in eternity the seeming conflict will be resolved.

Romans 9:1–16

What is the point of Paul's constant references to the children of the patriarchs?

In this chapter Paul argues a very specific point. God acts freely without being bound by what human beings do. The Jews believed God was bound by his covenant promises to favor Abraham's descendants. Paul argues that physical descent is not relevant, because faith is the key to a relationship with the Lord. To prove this he points out that Isaac and Ishmael were both children of Abraham, but only Isaac was given the covenant promises. The Jews' argument was that Ishmael's mother was a slave. So Paul goes on to point out that Jacob and Esau were twins, and God preannounced his choice of Jacob before either of the boys could have done anything to affect God's choice. When God said, "I will have mercy on whom I will have mercy" (v. 15), he was not asserting favoritism but rather attesting that he acts freely without being bound by man's actions in any way.

How wonderful this is! If God were bound by our actions, he would be bound to punish us, because we have all sinned. But he is not bound, so he can do as he chooses. And what he has chosen is to have mercy and compassion.

Romans 9:13–15

God announces he is free to act and then says he hated Esau. Is that compassion? It sounds totally unfair.

See the discussion of Malachi 1:3, page 222.

Romans 9:17, 22

How can anyone justify the morality of God causing someone to sin, so he can show how righteous he is by punishing them?

The verse does not say or suggest that God made Pharaoh sin. It simply asserts that Pharaoh, by the providence of God, occupied the position of Egypt's ruler and so played the role assigned to him. Pharaoh chose to resist God's will. As a result of his free choice Pharaoh and Egypt were punished. Note, however, that God "bore with great patience the objects of his wrath" (v. 22). Pharaoh was given chance after chance to repent, as succeeding plagues, each one more severe than the one before, witnessed to God's power and Pharaoh's sin.

For more about this incident, see the discussion of Pharaoh's hard heart, Exodus 4:21, page 51.

Romans 10:4

What does "Christ is the end of the law" mean?

The Greek word for "end," (*telos*) should be taken here in the sense of "goal" or "fulfillment." *Law* is a reference to the whole body of Old Testament revelation. This verse refers to Christ's fulfillment of Old Testament prophecies and types, with the result that "there may be righteousness for everyone who believes."

Romans 11

What happened to all the promises given to Israel by the Old Testament prophets? Did God take them back when the Jews refused to acknowledge Jesus as Messiah?

Christians have treated Old Testament prophecies in two ways. One tradition suggests that predictions about the future of Israel are now being fulfilled in the church. That is, predictions that the Messiah would rule over an Israel regathered to the Promised Land are to be understood symbolically and are fulfilled in Jesus' present rule in the hearts of believers, who possess spiritual rather than material blessings. The other Christian tradition believes that the predictions concerning the future of Israel are not symbolic and are not fulfilled in the church but will be fulfilled here on earth when Jesus returns.

Paul indicates in this chapter that Israel has been set aside temporarily to benefit the Gentiles but that in the future all Israel will be saved. Certainly God has a future for his Old Testament people, even though Christians may not agree as to just what that future holds.

Romans 12:20

What does it mean to "heap burning coals" on a person's head by doing good to those who harm you?

There are a variety of explanations, none of which is certain. Some associate the burning coals with purification (see also Isa. 6:6–7) and suggest that the Christian's radical response to injustice will lead to the conversion of the wicked. Others see an association of the burning coals with the fiery judgment of the wicked. In this case the Christian, by doing good in return for evil, makes sure the wicked will receive even more severe judgment.

In any case, Paul clearly calls on us to leave judgment in God's hands and accept the privilege of doing good.

Romans 13

Are Christians supposed to submit to laws that are unjust? What about the involvement of Christians in civil disobedience, such as in the civil rights movement and pro-life demonstrations?

Paul's point is simply that the Christian is to be a good citizen and obey civil laws not only because of the threat of punishment but because this is generally the right thing to do. No one has seriously suggested that in cases where man's law directly conflicts with God's law the Christian is to obey man rather than God (see also Acts 4:19–20).

It is important to realize that Christians can uphold human law in either of two ways. One way is to obey a law. The other is to accept the punishment the law decrees. A person who flees to avoid punishment does not uphold the law; but one who accepts whatever penalty the law decrees does uphold it.

In cases of civil disobedience, in which a believer is compelled by conscience to disobey a law of the state, the believer can show respect for the law by accepting the punishment.

Romans 14:1

What are the "disputable matters" this passage mentions?

Some acts, such as robbery or adultery, are clearly identified in Scripture as sins. There can be no dispute about whether a person who practices these is doing right or wrong. Other things are not clearly identified. Is it right to eat meat? Can a Christian smoke? Is social drinking acceptable?

Paul's point in this passage is that in areas such as these where Christians can and do dispute what is right and what is wrong, they are not to let their personal convictions affect their relationships with other believers who hold different convictions. They are to remember that Jesus is Lord, and each Christian is responsible to him to do that which he or she believes is pleasing and acceptable to Christ. Christians are not lords to fellow Christians and must extend to them the freedom to chose and to do what they are convinced in their hearts is right.

1 Corinthians

1 Corinthians

Who wrote this book, and what themes and issues does it deal with?

This letter was written to the church of Corinth by the apostle Paul, the founder of that church. The letter is a response to a number of questions and problems that had arisen in the church. The book, frequently called the New Testament's problem epistle, is usually outlined by the different problems that Paul dealt with.

1 Corinthians 2:16

What does Paul mean when he says "We have the mind of Christ"?

Paul is referring to Isaiah 40:13. This great passage comforts Israel by praising the greatness of her God. Among its many affirmations of God's greatness, Isaiah asks, "Who has understood the mind of the Lord?" God's thoughts are simply beyond our comprehension.

In 1 Corinthians 2, Paul points out that God not only has revealed his truth in words taught by the Spirit but also has given his Spirit to those who believe in Christ to interpret and apply those words. Thus the believer is able to make judgments about all things because "we have the mind of Christ." Jesus actively leads and guides his own, and the believer's insight into God's will for him or her is not subject to assessment by others.

1 Corinthians 5

What right does the church have to discipline members? Doesn't Romans 14 say to accept rather than judge others?

Christians have no right to judge others' convictions, their motives, or what a fellow believer is convinced is God's will for him or her. Church discipline has nothing to do with any of these things. Instead church discipline has to do only with the habitual practice by Christians of those things the Bible clearly identifies as sin. In this case the church does not judge the sinning believer but agrees with God's pronouncement that a particular behavior is sin. God determines what is sin; the church simply agrees with God when it acts to discipline a fellow believer.

It should be noted that church discipline involves a process of confrontation as described in Matthew 18:15–17. This is intended to bring about the repentance and restoration of the one who sins. If that person fails to respond, the final step is to expel him or her from the church. Even this is not intended as punishment. Rather, the church, by acting out on earth the reality of sin's spiritual impact of separating the believer from fellowship with God, seeks to help the sinner to grasp the consequences of his sin and repent.

1 Corinthians 5:5

What does it mean to "hand this man over to Satan"?

Some take this to mean that in expelling the sinner the church puts him out and into the devil's territory. The phrase "so that the sinful nature may be destroyed" is taken as a reference to the anguish such a person will feel and so be moved to repent. Or Paul may be implying that an expelled person becomes vulnerable to Satan, who is now allowed to afflict him with physical suffering. A third possibility is that Paul expects the expelled person to die, in which case Satan's share is nothing more than his body, while his spirit will be saved.

1 Corinthians 6

Is it ever right for a Christian to take another believer to court? What can a believer do if he is defrauded by a brother, and the brother will not let the church mediate the dispute?

Paul urges Christians to take their differences to the church for mediation by brothers rather than to the secular courts. Many see in this passage an absolute prohibition against suing a fellow Christian, whatever the merits of the case.

The problem with this interpretation is that it fails to take into account the emphasis in the Old Testament on the responsibility for self-purification in the faith community. A person in Israel who had knowledge of a violation of the law was responsible to bring that violation to the attention of local judges. In the New Testament a person who is offended by a sinful action is responsible to go to the offending person (Matt. 18:15–17), and if that person does not listen, to enlist others and ultimately the church to confront the offender. There is nothing spiritual about letting oneself be victimized, whether by a Christian or a pagan.

Many try to resolve the conflict by pointing out that Matthew 18:17 concludes the process by saying if the person will not respond to church discipline, the church is to "treat him as you would a pagan or a tax collector." Under this theory a person who rejects arbitration by the church puts himself outside the community of faith and can be sued as could any pagan.

1 Corinthians 7:10–11

How can some Christians say divorce and remarriage are permissible, when these verses convey God's command not to separate from spouses, or to remain unmarried?

First, note that there was no concept of legal separation in first-century A.D. law, so that both *separate* and *divorce* in this passage refer to divorce.

Some background is important. The Corinthians had heard Paul speak favorably of the unmarried state (7:1). Some had misinterpreted this to mean that marriage was not spiritual. They had either begun to refrain from sex or to actually divorce their spouses in a mistaken effort to follow Paul's advice. Paul makes it clear that sex in marriage is important and is not to be given up (7:3–5). He also makes it clear that the Christian is not to initiate a divorce, even if his or her spouse is a pagan (7:10–14).

Paul then goes on to discuss the case of a believer whose pagan spouse is unwilling to live with him or her. In this case, Paul says, the believer is "not bound," a phrase which is best understood to imply both a valid divorce and a right to remarry.

What is important in seeking to understand this passage is to first note that Paul deals with specific situations that have arisen in Corinth. It may not be wise to apply what Paul says about this specific situation to every possible situation in which divorce is considered. Second, we must compare what is taught here with the rest of the Bible's teaching on divorce and remarriage. (See the discussion of Matthew 19:6, page 252.)

1 Corinthians 7:12, 40

If Paul's letters really are Holy Scripture and authoritative, how could Paul make a distinction between his personal advice and a command of the Lord? Are we forced to conclude that Paul's letters are not really the Word of God?

In 7:12 Paul indicates that while on one point he is quoting Jesus, on the other he is not. Verse 40 expresses Paul's informed opinion, formed under the guidance of the Holy Spirit.

It can be debated whether or not Paul knew when he wrote his letters that they would be recognized by the church to be as surely words from God as were the Old Testament Scriptures. But clearly they were so recognized, even by the apostle Peter, in Paul's own time (2 Peter 3:15–16). If Paul was aware of the inspired nature of his writings is completely irrelevant to the issue of whether or not they were inspired.

1 Corinthians 8–10

Why all this fuss about food sacrificed to idols and idol feasts? What is the problem here?

Two different issues are involved in these chapters. The first is rooted in the fact that most meat in first-century A.D. cities was purchased at temple markets. The animals had been brought as sacrifices, and the priests sold the unburned parts to support their activities. Some felt it was shocking for Christians to buy meat there and that food sacrificed to idols had a pagan taint. Those who enjoyed their steaks and roasts responded that, as Christians, they realized idols had no real existence. So buying meat offered to them was irrelevant.

A second problem arose when a believer was invited to a banquet by a pagan friend. It was customary in those days to dedicate a banquet to a particular deity, and Christians were divided as to whether a believer should participate.

Paul deals with these issues in three ways. (1) He points out that there is some truth to each side of the argument. Idols do *not* represent real deities. On the other hand, demonic beings are behind paganism. (2) The fact that each side appeals to truth is a problem that exists in every dispute. We know only in part. Because our knowledge is incomplete, we can never dogmatically insist that we are right and our brothers are wrong. Thus, when Christians come to a dispute like this one, they must approach it on the basis of love rather than knowledge (8:1–3). (3) Finally, Paul points out that historically, close association with idolatry has led to immorality (10:1–10).

Throughout these chapters Paul intersperses his teaching with practical applications. Since Christians approach differences in love, they stand ready even to abandon their rights if insisting on them might harm a brother or weaken them. Because eating at a dinner dedicated to a pagan deity signifies participation in the cult, Christians will reject such invitations. However, if invited to a pagan's home for dinner, there is no harm in eating the main dish, unless the host makes a point of saying the animal was sacrificed to an idol. Even then one is to refrain not because this is wrong but because it might give the host a wrong impression.

Paul sums up his advice simply: "Whether you eat or drink or whatever you do, do it all for the glory of God. Do not cause anyone to stumble, whether Jews, Greeks, or the church of God" (10:31–32).

1 Corinthians 9–10

What rights do Christians have, and what is our attitude to be toward them?

Paul refers to the Christian's freedom to take any course of action not clearly identified in Scripture as sin. In Romans 14 Paul argues that Christians should not judge one another in these areas but are to give each other the freedom to do whatever each considers will please the Lord. In these chapters Paul reminds us that other people should be more important to us than insistence on our own so-called rights. We should be most concerned about doing what benefits others.

1 Corinthians 11

Why does Paul make such an issue of having women cover their heads? Does the whole passage take a demeaning view of women and prove Paul was a male chauvinist?

It is true that this passage has been quoted as evidence of Paul's chauvinism. But to draw such conclusions is possible only by seriously misinterpreting what Paul says. In fact, Paul strongly maintains the significance of women and their right to participate fully as members of Christ's church. A clear explanation is provided in the Zonder-van *Expository Dictionary of Bible Words*, p. 328.

The passage (11:2–6) explores what is proper in worship. Paul argues that the women in Corinth should wear a veil, as the women in other churches did (v. 16). There is a mix of the cultural and theological reasons for this. Within the culture, and especially to those of Jewish background, appropriate feminine dress on such a public occasion called for a veil. The women of Corinth were apparently so excited about the Christian message of freedom and equality that they reacted by rejecting feminine dress and asserting their equality by traditionally masculine behavior.

In the above passage, Paul protects this freedom of women. But he clearly does not approve of their symbolizing their liberation by praying and prophesying with their heads uncovered (v. 5). It is in effect a denial of their femininity. He refers to creation and shows that there is a creation order that includes both men and women (vv. 3, 7–10). Men and women are interdependent in God's design for the universe (vv. 11–12). It is the glory of each being within creation to proudly take the place God has assigned.

Paul writes that "the head of every man is Christ, and the head of the woman is man, and the head of Christ is God" (v. 3). This defines the flow of the creation order: Christ flowed from God the Father, man came into being by Christ's activity as Creator, and woman was taken from the side of man. In this verse, then, the order of creation is established. There is no suggestion here of inferiority, for Jesus is and always was the complete equal of the Father.

Thus Paul's appeal is not that women take a subordinate place in the church. His appeal is that they recognize the fact of an order in creation that is unchanged by the wonderful message that in Christ all are equal (Gal. 3:26–28).

What is a woman to do? Simply this: She must live within the culture as a woman rather than deny her womanhood by dressing as would a man. A woman in the Corinthian church was to pray and prophesy with her head veiled, and a man in Corinth was to function with his head unveiled. Neither need deny his or her identity within the creation order to affirm significance in the body of Christ. A man can be proud of his place as a man. And a woman can be equally proud of her place as a woman.

1 Corinthians 11:17–34

What was wrong with the way the Corinthians celebrated the Lord's Supper?

In first-century A.D. culture, wealthy individuals had poorer "clients" whom they helped and who owed them a variety of duties. Some see in this description a corruption of the Lord's Supper by the wealthy who linked it with a common cultural practice in which clients were invited to the home and either served an inferior meal or waited while more important guests ate.

Paul reminds the Corinthians that the Lord's Supper is a celebration of their shared faith, whose meaning is corrupted by the humiliation some well-off Corinthians heaped on their brothers and sisters by treating them so meanly.

1 Corinthians 12–14

What is Paul talking about in these chapters? Why is there so much emphasis on speaking in tongues?

While 12:1 in our Bible versions begins, "Now about spiritual gifts," the word *gifts* is lacking in the original. Paul's subject is spirituality not simply spiritual gifts.

This discussion was vital because the Corinthians had carried into their Christian experience pagan notions about spirituality. In that culture, ecstatic experiences were taken as evidence of intimate contact with the gods. Thus epilepsy was called the divine disease. Falling down in an epileptic fit was often described by the phrase "and the god took him." Oracles like that at Delphi might breathe volcanic fumes; the resultant muttering was interpreted by priests as messages from the gods. Thus the apparently similar gift of speaking in tongues deeply impressed the Corinthians and was taken as evidence of the spirituality of the speaker.

Paul explains in 1 Corinthians 12 that *all* the gifts are expressions of the Spirit's presence in the believer's life, and that all believers are essential, even as every member of a living body is necessary for it to function. In 1 Corinthians 13 Paul teaches that love is the real indication of one's closeness to God and thus of his or her spirituality. In 1 Corinthians 14, Paul returns to the question of speaking in tongues and calls for this gift to be exercised in an orderly way in church meetings. Throughout these chapters Paul takes the position that, while a valid spiritual gift, tongues speaking is not a premier gift. He says, "I would rather have you prophesy. He who prophesies is greater than one who speaks in tongues" (14:5).

The chapter concludes with further instructions on how to conduct an orderly and proper worship service.

1 Corinthians 14:34

How can Paul say that women should remain silent in the church,
when he has just said in 11:5 that they should pray and prophesy
with heads covered?

Several interpretations of this passage have been suggested.
(1) Paul is laying down a principle of submission that is binding on all
churches of every time and culture. In this view there would undoubtedly be a conflict with 1 Corinthians 11:5. (2) Paul is calling for church
services to take forms that are appropriate to their society. If it is cul-
turally disgraceful for women to speak up in a particular kind of meeting, and if a church service is perceived as that kind of meeting, then
women should keep silent in the church. With this in view, in 11:5 Paul
simply refers to a different kind of meeting, perhaps a home study group
in contrast to a larger congregational meeting. (3) Paul is dealing with
a specific situation in which the women are being disruptive. Paul's command to remain silent is intended to correct this problem, not as a universal prohibition.

There is no completely compelling explanation of these verses, despite
the fact that the disruption of worship is undoubtedly the subject Paul
deals with in this passage. At the same time, either the second or third
explanation above satisfactorily resolves the charge of error or discrepancy in the Bible.

1 Corinthians 15:29

What is meant by baptism for the dead? Does Paul suggest that
we follow such a rite?

Some in Corinth held the view that there is no resurrection
of the dead. Paul directly confronts and corrects this notion by showing that the resurrection of Jesus is a keystone of faith and the guarantee of our own resurrection. He then mentions a particular practice of
the Corinthians. Some of them, concerned about departed relatives, had
undergone baptism as surrogates for them so the deceased would not
miss out on its benefits. Without at all condoning the practice, Paul simply points out that the Corinthians were being inconsistent. If death is
the end, and there is no resurrection of the dead, why in the world would
they undergo baptism in their behalf?

2 Corinthians

2 Corinthians
Who wrote this book, and what themes and issues does it deal with?

This second letter in the New Testament that is directed to the Corinthian church was also written by Paul. His earlier epistle led to the resolution of some of the problems he dealt with. But there were still those in Corinth unwilling to submit to the apostle's authority and who actively tried to undercut it.

In this very personal letter Paul responds to some of the charges. Paul shares not only his motives but also the principles of ministry on which he operates. He urges the Corinthians to be as responsive to him as he always has been to their needs and concerns.

2 Corinthians 1:1
What was an apostle? How many apostles were there in the early church?

The Greek word *apostolos* means "one who is sent." An apostle was a personal representative of the one sending him. In the church the term applied in a unique sense to the twelve disciples of Jesus and to the apostle Paul. However, the word is also used in the more general sense of early Christians who traveled widely to share the gospel with others (see also Acts 14:14; 1 Cor. 12:28; 2 Cor. 11:13). It is probable that we would call those who were designated apostles in this general sense missionaries.

48   New Testament

2 Corinthians 4:4

Who is the "god of this age"? Doesn't the Bible teach there is only one God? If there are more, the Bible must be in error.

The reference here is to Satan, who exercises a certain amount of authority in this present age. The use of this title in no way suggests that Satan is anything but a created being, whatever his pretensions.

2 Corinthians 5:10

Romans 8:1 says, "There is now no condemnation for those who are in Christ Jesus." But this verse says Christians must "all appear before the judgment seat of Christ." Is this contradictory?

The "judgment seat" is the *bema*, a platform from which public announcements were made. This included announcements of both rebukes and honors. The large *bema* in Corinth has been uncovered by archaeologists, and it was undoubtedly the same stage that Paul had in mind when he wrote these words about the Christians' appearance before Christ. That appearance is not for judgment as to our salvation but for the evaluation of our works. On the basis of how we have lived for our Lord we will receive his praise or his rebuke.

2 Corinthians 6:14

What does it mean to be "yoked together with unbelievers"?

Paul makes an obvious but oblique reference to an Old Testament law which forbids the teaming of two kinds of animals, such as a donkey and an ox (Deut. 22:10). Paul is simply saying that Christians are not to form partnerships with unbelievers, an injunction which has been applied to relationships ranging from business partnerships to marriage.

2 Corinthians 7:4

Is Paul being hypocritical in telling the Corinthians, "I have great confidence in you"? After all, this is the one church Paul flatly says is unspiritual (1 Cor. 3:1–4). This looks like an insincere attempt to manipulate the folks at Corinth and certainly violates Paul's own rules of Christian conduct.

Paul is aware of the weakness of the Corinthians yet is absolutely sincere in his expression of confidence. The explanation for this is found in 2 Corinthians 4 and 5. There Paul teaches that "what is seen is temporary, but what is unseen is eternal" (4:18). He goes on to point out that love is the motivating power that leads to the transformation of the believer (5:14). In the same verse Paul explains that Christ died for all, so that believers might "no longer live for themselves but for him who died for them and was raised again." Since the purpose of Christ's death was to create a people who would live for him, Paul cannot imagine that Christ's death would be in vain. Paul—despite the disappointing evidence of the Corinthians' present behavior—is totally confident of their transformation. Thus he is both totally realistic about his beloved Corinthians and at the same time absolutely confident in them.

2 Corinthians 12:2

Does this phrase indicate that Paul thought of creation in pagan cosmological terms?

Paul is using a common expression to indicate a place that lies beyond earth's atmosphere (the first heaven) and space (the second heaven). There is no implication here that Paul accepts a primitive or any other cosmology. Third heaven simply means God's presence.

2 Corinthians 13:10

Paul spoke much in the last three chapters of this book about his authority. But in Matthew 20 Jesus implies that spiritual leaders must be among their Christian brothers rather than over them. Isn't Paul out of step with Jesus in this matter?

The basic meaning of authority is freedom of action. Paul as an apostle was granted a certain area in which he had freedom to act, and that area included authoritative interpretation of God's will to the church. Paul was granted this authority for building up the church, not for personal power. It is significant that when Paul warns the Corinthians to respond to this authority, he says they must do so because Christ "is not weak in dealing with you, but is powerful among you" (13:3). Even if the Corinthians refused to respond to his authority, Paul would do nothing to punish them but would rely on Christ to discipline them and thus prove "that Christ is speaking through me" (13:3).

Galatians

Galatians

Who wrote this book, and what themes and issues does it deal with?

The apostle Paul wrote the letter to the Galatians. The book was a response to Jewish teachers who infiltrated the churches in Galatia and insisted that to be saved and to grow in the Christian life a person had to be subject to Old Testament law. Many in Galatia were influenced by this teaching, which Paul directly confronted in this brief book.

Galatians 1:4

What does Paul mean by "the present evil age"?

The phrase, which occurs several times in the New Testament, simply contrasts that period of human history with the age to come when Christ returns.

Galatians 3:26–4:7

Why does Paul say that we become sons, or children, of God? How can we be adopted by God if we were already created by him?

Paul is speaking of the Christian's adoption into the family of God. According to the Roman adoption formula, a person undergoing it became a son of the father. This was a very significant transaction. A person who was adopted was no longer considered a member of his pre-

350

vious family and owed no obligation to his old father. Instead, his obligation was to his adoptive father. The resources of the adoptive son were considered to belong to the new father. In a similar way the adoptive son came into possession of all the father possessed, for each became obligated to the other.

In undergoing adoption as sons, Christians are released from any obligation to sin and Satan and become responsible only to God. At the same time all the believer possesses belongs to God, yet all of God's infinite resources are placed at the believer's disposal.

Galatians 5:2–3

How can Paul say that "Christ will be of no value" to Christians if they accept circumcision?

In the Old Testament, circumcision is a symbol of identification with the Jewish people and participation in the covenants given to them. Paul says that as long as a person seeks to attain righteousness through the Mosaic law, Christ will be of no value to him. Why of no value? Because the power of Jesus is released by faith, not by works. As we rely on him and reject every attempt to rely on our own effort, Christ will make a difference in our present life.

Galatians 6:2, 5

How can Paul say, "Carry each other's burdens," and in the next breath say, "Each one should carry his own load"?

The answer is clear in the Greek text, although not in our English versions. In 6:2 the word is *baros* "an unusually heavy load," while 6:5 uses the word *phortion* "the normal load carried by a soldier on duty." There is no conflict at all.

Ephesians

Ephesians

Who wrote this book, and what themes and issues does it deal with?

Ephesians, another of Paul's letters, is frequently called a Christological epistle, because Christ is its central theme. In this letter Jesus is presented as the head of the church, which is both his body here on earth and the family of God. Paul's concern is that we Christians learn to live with one another as members of that body and as children in that family.

Ephesians 1:7

Why all these references to the blood of Christ? Do they mark Christianity as a primitive religion?

The phrase "the blood of Christ" is frequently used in the New Testament to indicate the death of Jesus and to sum up its meaning for humankind. The doctrine of Jesus' substitutionary death is hardly primitive. In ancient religions, sacrifices were viewed as bribes offered to the gods to win their favor. Only the Judeo-Christian tradition sees animal sacrifices as types, or instruments of instruction.

In the Old Testament, animal sacrifices drove home the truth that sin deserves death but that God will accept a substitute in place of the sinner. Each sacrificial animal foreshadowed the work of Christ on the cross where our sins were paid for by God himself. Thus the blood of Christ constitutes not a demeaning bribe intended to influence a hostile deity but the full revelation of the grace of a God who loves mankind so much that he was willing to suffer the penalty for sin that his justice decreed.

Ephesians 1:11

How can God be fair and yet predestine some but not all persons, for salvation?

See the discussion of Romans 8:29, page 334.

Ephesians 4:8

Paul misquotes Psalm 68:18 here. How can he use a misquote to make a point?

In fact, Paul illuminates the meaning of the Hebrew text. His point is that Christ has triumphed, and in his triumph he has taken spoils not to keep but to distribute as gifts to men. Paul does not misquote the Psalm; he interprets it.

Ephesians 5:22

What does "Wives submit to your husbands" mean? Is Paul promoting male superiority and the subordination of women?

The Greek word used here, *hypotasso*, implies subordination of oneself to someone or something, whether a slave to a master or a citizen to the government. But the way the word is used throughout the New Testament reveals that submission is a most complex concept. It may be forced (Luke 10:17) or voluntary (James 4:7), to social structures (Rom. 13:1), to individuals (1 Peter 2:18). Most importantly, Christians voluntarily submit to each other in various Christian relationships. Here submission speaks equally of concern for others and respect for their roles and gifts (Rom. 12:10; Eph. 5:21; Phil. 2:3–4; 1 Peter 5:5). It is particularly important in understanding the implications of submission to remember that Christ called on spiritual leaders to live as slaves (*doulous*) to other believers (Matt. 20:27).

In the context of Christian interpersonal relationships it is clear that a wife's submission to her husband does not mean either inferiority, surrender of one's identity, or abject subservience. Instead, the command suggests that the wife minister to the husband by taking the lead in responding to him, even as he takes the lead in treating her with love.

Ephesians 5:23

What does it mean that "the husband is the head of the wife"? What does it not mean?

What it does not mean is that the husband has the right to make every decision in a marriage and that the wife's sole role is to obey. *Head* is not a synonym for *boss*.

In fact, Paul goes on to define exactly what he means by *head* in the context of the marriage relationship. The husband's headship over the wife is modeled on that of Christ over the church. Christ exhibited his headship by loving the church and giving himself for her, "to present her to himself as a radiant church, without stain or wrinkle or any other blemish." The husband who fulfills his role as head of his wife will love her selflessly and will be willing to give up his own aspirations to help his wife achieve her full potential as a person.

Ephesians 6:8–10

How can Paul compromise what is morally right by condoning slavery! Why didn't he and other New Testament writers come out against such a criminal institution?

In the Roman Empire as many as one-fifth of the people were slaves. This pervasive institution could not have been overthrown without an armed revolt that would have torn the empire apart, cost millions of lives, and driven the Western world into premature dark ages where brigands and pirates would have raged unchecked. Thus the early Christians were concerned with living godly lives in the world as it was, not as idealists might say it should be. The apostles wisely refrained from confusing the gospel of Christ with a demand for social reform that in the first century A.D.would undoubtedly have been considered rebellion against the Roman state.

What we must understand is that it was the Christian message that ultimately eradicated slavery. We see this reflected in Paul's letter to Philemon. Paul urges Philemon to welcome back his runaway slave Onesimus not merely as a slave but as a brother. An individual who is perceived as a brother in the Lord will hardly be treated as a mere slave.

Philippians

Philippians

Who wrote this book, and what themes and issues does it deal with?

Paul wrote this brief letter to the Philippian Christians while he was in prison in Rome. He wrote to thank them for a gift and to respond to their concern for his safety. The theme of the book seems to be joy. The words *joy* and *rejoice* are found some sixteen times in its four short chapters.

Philippians chapter two contains one of the New Testament's most significant Christological statements. Here Paul portrays Jesus as God when he surrendered the prerogatives of deity to enter the human race, die for our sins, and then become exalted once again to be Lord of all.

Philippians 2:7

Does "being made in human likeness" imply that Jesus only seemed to be human and was not really God in the flesh?

The word for "likeness" falls in the Greek word group *homoioo*, words frequently used in statements that make comparisons. This word suggests a similarity, a resemblance. The Greek term is used in several New Testament passages (Heb. 9:17; Rom. 8:3; Phil. 2:7). The word does not in any way suggest that Jesus only seemed to be a human being. The *Expository Dictionary of Bible Words* observes, however, that Jesus is never said to be in the likeness of God. It adds, "Jesus in his person perfectly represented God as he truly is. Jesus could not perfectly represent man as he is, however, since humanity is tainted by sin.

Jesus' human nature was untainted by sin. Thus, Jesus is the image of humanity as it will be renewed when the drama of redemption is complete" (p. 352).

Philippians 3:6

How can Paul be "as for legalistic righteousness, faultless," when the Bible says that all have sinned and come short of God's glory?

Paul says that he did not violate the law as it was interpreted by the rabbis of his society. This does not mean that he did not sin (see discussion of Rom. 7:6, page 331).

Philippians 3:10–11

What does Paul mean when he says he hopes "somehow, to attain the resurrection from the dead"? Was he really that unsure of his own salvation?

In Romans 8:11, Paul wrote of one of the amazing benefits of knowing Jesus: "If the Spirit of him who raised Jesus from the dead is living in you, he who raised Christ from the dead will also give life to your mortal bodies through his Spirit, who lives in you." That is, even though we live now in a mortal body, and sin is our ever-present companion, God's Holy Spirit is a present source of resurrection power that enables us to live a new kind of life now. This is what Paul is talking about in Philippians—not the future resurrection to take place when Jesus returns but a present experience of resurrection life as he seeks to follow Jesus now.

Colossians

Colossians

Who wrote this book, and what themes and issues does it deal with?

Paul wrote this powerful New Testament letter. Many believe he was trying to counteract certain heresies. Paul's teaching corrects the notion that the material world and everything in it are evil while the immaterial realm of God is good. In this belief system Jesus either did not become a true human being or he was not God; spirituality is essentially a matter of the mind and inner being; either one must punish and deprive the physical nature to strengthen the spiritual, or one may let the body do what it wants, based on the supposition that nothing done here can be good anyway or have any significant impact on the inner, spiritual, good man.

Paul responds strongly, saying that Jesus Christ is God. It was "by Christ's physical body through death" that our salvation was won. God not only entered the material world, but it was what he did in the world that accomplished salvation. Thus, what a person does in the body is related to spirituality. In the last chapters of this brief book, Paul describes the way Christians are to live out their spirituality in everyday life.

Colossians 1:20

Does Paul's teaching that on the cross Jesus reconciled "to himself all things, whether things on earth or things in heaven, by making peace through his blood," imply that everyone will be saved in the end?

Reconcile means "to bring into harmony with" and indicates a change in personal relationships between human beings, especially between human beings and God. The particular word used here, *apokatalasso*, is an intensive word which means "to restore harmony completely." The concept of reconciliation has two dimensions. The first, reflected here, is that God has effected reconciliation between God and humanity through Christ, so that our sins no longer count against us (see also Rom. 5:10–11). There is no longer any reason why human beings should view God as an enemy; he has demonstrated that he is our friend. The second aspect of reconciliation is experiential. We must accept Christ and thus be reconciled (see also 2 Cor. 5:18–20).

Always remember that two persons are involved in salvation's wondrous transaction: God, who has acted to save us; and the individual human being, who must respond with faith and must appropriate the benefit of what God has done. This passage makes it clear that God has done his part completely. Now it is up to us.

Colossians 2:14

How has the cross "canceled the written code" and "disarmed the powers and authorities"?

The passage is theologically significant. The word *regulations* suggests a posted edict, binding on all citizens, while *written code* suggests an IOU or acknowledged personal debt. Paul is thus speaking of the Mosaic law and the guilt that breaking the law brings. Both of these are canceled by the cross. The word translated "cancel" is *exaleipho*, "to wash out." In New Testament times this word was used in the sense of dismissing a legal charge and of annulling a law. Paul says that both the law's decrees and the guilt that the law generates no longer exist for Christians. In Christ we have been saved and transported into a realm in which we respond directly to God's Spirit who lives within to guide us.

The principalities and powers to whom Paul refers are Satan and his forces who kept mankind captive. The cross means victory to the believer and defeat for the forces of evil.

Colossians 2:23

What does Paul mean by "sensual indulgence"?

Paul is speaking against asceticism. The ascetic foolishly limits his notion of the flesh to the physical body, hoping to gain spiritually by fasting, by beating himself when he feels certain natural urges, by denying his body a blanket when it is cold, etc. Paul observes that such things "have an appearance of wisdom," that is, they look good on a resumé. But, in fact, they "lack any value in restraining fleshly indulgence." This is because the flesh is not just the body but the total human personality as warped by sin. So the ascetic's pride in his spiritual superiority, or the despair he experiences as he tries to convince himself he is pleasing God are just as much fleshly indulgence as is gluttony.

It is important to understand that true spirituality is living a human life in union with God, and to learn to live the kind of life that pleases him. This life is described in Colossians 3 and 4.

1 Thessalonians

1 Thessalonians

Who wrote this book, and what themes and issues does it deal with?

This letter was written by Paul to the church at Thessalonica and is one of the earliest of the New Testament epistles. It was written to encourage a church that was undergoing local persecution. It is most noted for a wonderful passage that describes the return of Christ for his church.

1 Thessalonians 4:13–18

Paul's picture of Jesus' return certainly differs from that given by Christ himself. Where is the great distress and the darkened sky of Matthew 24?

People sometimes assume that Christ's second coming is something that will happen in ten minutes. They forget that the first coming covered a thirty-year period. Why then try to squeeze everything the Bible links to Jesus' second coming into a single day?

Christians debate just how the event described here, commonly called the rapture, relates to other events associated with Jesus' second coming. But it is a characteristic of Bible prophecy to describe what will happen without providing a chart that shows timing and sequence. If we accept the basic notion that the second coming is not a single event but a series of events that will take place over a period of time that may extend to years, there is no conflict between this passage and any teaching of either Jesus or the Old Testament prophets.

2 Thessalonians

2 Thessalonians

Who wrote this book, and what themes and issues does it deal with?

Paul wrote 2 Thessalonians as a follow-up to his first letter. This letter was written to correct misunderstandings about Christ's second coming and what must happen at history's end. Some in Thessalonica thought Christ had already returned. Paul makes it clear in chapter 1 that when he does, a very public judgment will take place, and in chapter 2 that certain events must happen just before Christ arrives on earth.

2 Thessalonians 1:5–10

This is a terrible picture of a vengeance that goes beyond any punishment human courts decree. How can this be harmonized with the Bible's picture of a loving God? Why are people punished just for failing to heed the gospel?

Paul assures the members of this persecuted church that their tormentors will be judged. They will be punished for troubling God's people (including persecution, imprisonment, impoverishment, and murder) and for refusing to "obey the gospel." This phrase means the acceptance of God's message and faith in Jesus Christ.

This passage makes some very basic points. First, God does not ignore evil done to his own people. He will balance the books and see that justice is done. Second, to persecute God's people and reject God's love are not misdemeanors like jaywalking. These are capital crimes. And well

361

they should be. God gave his Son for us. Jesus suffered not mere physical death but the wrenching agony of the sinless one who became sin when he accepted the full weight of all mankind's wickedness. To hear of what God has done and then in effect to spit in the face of Christ's sacrifice by refusing to believe in him is the ultimate insult to God's majesty.

Finally, God is both loving and just. If a person will not respond to God's love, that person must accept what God's justice decrees. The fact that his justice is so terrible is itself evidence of the appalling nature of the sins he punished.

Rather than raise questions about the nature of God, a passage like this should raise questions about the nature of sin and the nature of a humanity so depraved that it not only rejects the sacrificial love of God but persecutes those who accept it.

2 Thessalonians 2:11

How can a God of love send "a powerful delusion" and cause the unsaved to believe Satan's lie?

This delusion is given to those who have already refused to respond to the gospel and shown themselves to be God's enemies. God does not keep the saved from believing in Jesus. He here announces that, since people will not believe in the gospel, he will cause them to believe in Satan's lie and so follow him to destruction. The powerful delusion is a judgment on those who have already committed sins. It should not be mistaken for a sin that God will later judge.

1 Timothy

1 Timothy

Who wrote this book, and what themes and issues does it deal with?

Paul wrote this book as a letter to Timothy, his young co-worker. It is a book of advice on how to minister successfully.

1 Timothy 1:8–11

Why does Paul say the law was made not for good men but for sinners and the ungodly? Doesn't the law show us how to do what is right?

Paul makes a simple but very important point. The law identifies wrong acts and says, "Don't do this." In fact, all our laws are like this. Take, for instance, a law that says, "Don't beat your wife." Why was this law put on the books? Because some men beat their spouses, and the legislature decided to pass a law against such behavior. If every man loved his wife and did not abuse her, would there be any need for such a law? Of course not. And if every man loved his wife and did not abuse her, would that law ever have to be applied? Again, of course not. It follows then that the law is not for the good husband but for the bad husband who does what the law says not to do. That law is totally irrelevant to the good husband who would never do such a thing.

It is the same with God's law. Will the person who walks with Jesus steal or commit adultery or murder? Of course not. So those laws are irrelevant to that person and do not apply. Those laws are there for the evil person to convict him of his wrongdoing, and have no impact at all on the person Jesus has made truly good.

1 Timothy 2:4

If God wants all people to be saved, why doesn't he just save them all?

One of the mysteries of our faith is that God has not chosen to do everything that he would like to do. This verse tells us that God yearns for everyone "to be saved and to come to a knowledge of the truth." At the same time we know from many Scriptures that not all human beings will choose to trust God and be saved. Apparently God found it necessary to protect the freedom of the individual to choose, even though this gift of personal responsibility meant that far too many would use their free will to choose not to be saved. So there is no real contradiction here, any more than there would be if you or I would say, "I wanted to eat those cookies, but I chose to stay on my diet."

1 Timothy 2:12

Paul always was a male chauvinist, and here is the proof: This verse does not "permit a woman to teach or have authority over a man." How can a book that is so antiwoman be held up as God's Word?

The Bible is not antiwoman. The New Testament makes it clear that women as well as men are full participants in Christ's church and like men are given a full range of spiritual gifts. In Romans 16 Paul mentions many women by name, calls them his fellow workers, and identifies Phoebe as a deaconess of a local church.

When you consider the total testimony of the Bible on the subject, you realize that women are both validated and appreciated.

At the same time, this passage does seem to restrict women from a position associated with teaching or having authority over men in the church. It seems best to take this as a reference to the role of elders in the church, who were responsible for the spiritual supervision of the congregation and for giving authoritative interpretations of the Scriptures when issues were in dispute. Just why women were not to take this role is not really understood. Paul gives an explanation which is rooted in theology rather than in any customs of the times (see 2:13–14).

The issue we face is whether there is conflict or discrepancy here. In this case we have to say that there is no real conflict. The importance of a person within the church, and his or her value as a person, does not hinge on being eligible for a particular leadership role. After all, most men will not be elders either, and many are ruled out by falling short of some qualification listed in 1 Timothy 3. Whatever restrictions this verse may place on women in church leadership (and the exact nature of this restriction is debated), the fact of a restriction in no way implies an essential subordination of women in ministry to the church.

1 Timothy 2:13–15

What does Paul mean when he says that "women will be saved through childbirth"? Is this just another demeaning view of women, meaning essentially that men should keep their women barefoot and pregnant?

There have been three major interpretations of this difficult verse. (1) The believing woman will be kept safe while bearing children. (2) The believing woman will be kept safe because of the birth of the child Jesus. (3) The godly woman will find fulfillment in her role as wife and mother.

There is a vast difference between the promise of fulfillment for women in the wife-mother role and the thought that this role is demeaning to women. In fact, this interpretation would give the role of wife-mother a new dignity, because women who find themselves as housewives are as significant as those who make a mark in a business or other career.

1 Timothy 3:12

Does "the husband of but one wife" mean that a man who has remarried after being widowed or divorced cannot serve as a church elder?

This requirement has been understood in different ways. Most often those who take it as restrictive apply it to divorce and remarriage but not to being widowed and remarried. Others take it to mean that the elder must be a "one-woman kind of man." Still others suggest it means an elder must be married rather than single. Whether divorce and remarriage disqualify from leadership depends on one's view of divorce (see the discussion of Matt. 19:6, page 252). It is best to understand this verse as a requirment of sexual purity, forbidding any violation of God's law on marriage whether in the form of polygamy or any marital unfaithfulness.

2 Timothy

2 Timothy

Who wrote this book, and what themes and issues does it deal with?

This is another letter written by Paul to his younger friend and apprentice, Timothy. This letter was written during Paul's second imprisonment in Rome, shortly before his death. It gives further instructions to Timothy on how to lead the church and continue Paul's missionary work after the great apostle is gone.

2 Timothy 3:16

Does Paul's saying that "all Scripture is God-breathed" imply that God dictated the Bible to its human authors?

The books of the Old Testament and New Testament clearly reflect the distinctive traits of the individuals who penned them. Whatever this verse may imply, it in no way suggests the writers were mere puppets who woodenly wrote down what God said to or in them.

The term *God-breathed* is a powerful image that calls to mind the ships that plied the Mediterranean with their sails filled with the wind. Similarly, the human authors were filled with the Spirit. They were carried along in their writing so that although they used their own words they recorded accurately and authoritatively the exact message God intended to communicate.

Titus

Titus

Who wrote this book, and what themes and issues does it deal with?

This letter of Paul was, like the two letters to Timothy, written to a younger leader in the church. It is filled with advice and guidance. Most of the topics touched on in the two Books of Timothy are also found in this short letter to Titus.

Titus 1:15

What does Paul mean when he says, "To the pure all things are pure"? This sounds like the Christian can do anything, and it will be all right.

Not at all. Most interpret the verse in this context to mean that Christians, who have been purified by Christ, are free to accept the good gifts that God gives them and to enjoy them without pangs of conscience. On the other hand, the ascetics and the Judaizers set up all sorts of restrictions and rules, but despite all their efforts nothing they did was pure or acceptable to God.

Another possible way of looking at this verse is fascinating. This is true particularly in view of the common argument raised by pornographers that there is nothing dirty about their work and that only dirty-minded people would see any harm in it. It is only those who have been purified by Christ who can truly see the beauty in what God has created. Pornography perverts the beauty of the human body into something prurient because of the corrupt minds and consciences of the viewer. It is not the Christian who objects to pornography who has the dirty mind. That mind belongs to the purveyor of filth who has taken something essentially pure and made something dirty of it.

Philemon

Philemon

Who wrote this book, and what themes and issues does it deal with?

This brief letter of Paul is written to a wealthy man about a runaway slave. The slave, Onesimus, has come to know Christ through Paul's ministry, and Paul urges his owner, Philemon, to welcome him back as a slave who is now also a brother. This reconciliation is important, first because Onesimus apparently stole something from his master when he left and is vulnerable to severe legal punishments, and second because first-century Christians had committed themselves to live within rather than outside the laws of the land. As a good Christian, Onesimus would be expected to show the reality of his conversion by doing what the culture defined as right, even though this was painful to him.

Hebrews

Hebrews

Who wrote this book, and what themes and issues does it deal with?

The author of the book of Hebrews is unknown, although many possible writers have been suggested. The Greek style, and particularly the typically rabbinical treatment of Old Testament texts, rules out the apostle Paul as author but does not help us identify anyone else. Suggestions as to possible authors have included both Apollos and Priscilla.

This book was directed to Hebrew Christians who apparently were being influenced by Judaizers to turn back to their old ways rather than go on in their Christian faith. Thus the author shows, point by point, how Jesus is superior. He is greater than angels, brings a better revelation than that of Moses, has a more effective priesthood than the Old Testament priests, administers a better covenant, offers up a better sacrifice, and in every way is superior to the old religion that Christianity had supplanted.

Hebrews 1:3

This verse says Jesus is a representation of God. But didn't Jesus say he was God, not just a representative of God?

The Greek word is used of the image impressed on a coin by the original stamp. It is the exact representation, with no deviation at all from the original mold. Far from implying that Jesus is an imperfect copy of God, this verse affirms his complete identity with God and his accurate representation to us of all that God is.

Hebrews 1:6

Here Jesus is called the firstborn. To be born clearly indicates that at one time a person did not exist. If Jesus is a created being he surely is not God. It looks like the Bible writers themselves disagree about who Jesus was.

The word *firstborn* is used in Scripture to indicate that someone holds a special position in the family. Here and in Romans 8:29, Colossians 1:15, 18, and Revelation 1:5 it is a technical theological term indicating that Jesus has the highest rank in the family of God and a unique relationship with the Father. It in no way suggests that Jesus is a created being.

Hebrews 4:15

How could Jesus be "tempted in every way" when he had no sin nature as we do? And could he have really given in to temptation? If not, how could Jesus' temptations be real?

The sin nature has nothing to do with perceiving or *feeling* temptations. It does, however, have a lot to do with *giving in* to temptations. Because Jesus was a real human being he could feel hunger, rejection, and anger. He could experience loneliness and yearn for love—in short, he could feel every pressure that we feel. He knows how much life can hurt and how strong the urge to do wrong can be. Because of this he can sympathize with our weaknesses.

In fact, Jesus knows the pull of temptation far better than we do. How can this be? Well, who would know how much it cost to refuse to tell a captor a military secret, the person who blurted it out in five minutes, or the person who refused to tell and subsequently took the punishment for five hours? It is obvious that the person who better understood the temptation to tell so as to avoid pain is the one who withstood the pain longest.

It's like this with temptations. We all too often give in to temptations and then complain about how strong they were. But Jesus *never* gave in. He experienced the strength of every pull on human nature to the fullest extent. Oh yes, Jesus knows how much it hurts to be a human being and knows it far better than you and I. And knowing, he cares and sympathizes with us sinners even when we fail.

Hebrews 5:8

If Jesus was God, how could he have "learned obedience" and been "made perfect"? God is already perfect and already knows everything. So it follows that Jesus is not God.

Our daughter Sarah was afraid of riding a two-wheeler for several years. She had a bike and told her friends, "I know how to ride." In fact, while she knew the theory, she had not had the experience. There is a big difference in knowing something intellectually and actually experiencing it. Even though God knew obedience intellectually far better than we ever will, it was only when Jesus became a human being and lived an obedient life that he knew obedience experientially.

Made perfect is used here in the sense of being made fully equipped for a task. Jesus' obedience equipped him for the task of saving us, for only a sinless person was qualified to serve as our Redeemer. Thus there is no conflict at all between this verse and the Christian doctrine of the deity of Jesus.

Hebrews 6:4–12

This passage is confusing. Whom is it about, believers who turn away from Jesus and are lost again, or people who never believed in Jesus? What does this passage really teach?

This passage has been and still is much debated by Christians. On the one hand, it describes people who have "once been enlightened, who have tasted the heavenly gift, who have shared in the Holy Spirit." This seems to decisively identify Christians. On the other hand, the indication that they might "fall away" and then never be "brought back to repentance" fits neither the Calvinist's conviction that a person once saved cannot be lost again, nor the Arminian's view that one who does fall away and loses his or her salvation can certainly be restored to a state of grace.

The best way to deal with the passage seems to be to take it as a hypothetical statement the author intended to use to shake the readers out of a foolish position. Rather than grow to maturity on the sure foundation laid by Christ these believers wavered between full commitment and a return to Judaism. They were challenged by the author's question. A paraphrase helps us see the author's point:

What would you want to do? View your failure as a falling away from God, so that access to him is now lost? How then would you ever be restored—you who have been enlightened, tasted the heavenly gift, shared in the Holy Spirit, and known the flow of resurrection power? Do you want to crucify Jesus all over again, and through a new sacrifice be brought back to repentance? How impossible! What a disgrace! This hints that Jesus' work for you was not enough.

The fact that this *is* hypothetical is made clear in verse 9, where the author says, "Even though we speak this, dear friends, we are confident of better things in your case—things that accompany salvation." The writer sees his readers not as lost but simply as wavering, foolishly failing to see that Jesus saves completely. They lack the confidence to go on in their newfound faith.

Hebrews 13:17

This verse tells Christians to obey their leaders. Is this in conflict with Romans 14, which teaches individual responsibility to Christ? If we obey others, that means they make our decisions for us. What about Jesus' teaching in Matthew 20 that leaders are to be servants, not bosses in the church?

The solution to this apparent conflict in teaching is found in the subtleties of the original language, which our English versions fail to reflect accurately. The original reads *peithesthe tois hegoumenois hymon kai hypeikete*. Each of these words is significant.

Peithesthe is from *peitho*, which literally means "let yourselves be persuaded, or convinced." A fair translation is, "be open to the persuasion of your leaders."

Tois hegoumenois hymon is translated "your leaders." The key term is used of rulers and princes, but the original meant to lead or guide. Here the spiritual leader is cast as one in the church who has traveled along the road toward godliness and, as a valid model, is able to point others to that way.

Hypeikete is the single word that our English versions render "submit to their authority." The word is rightly translated this way. But originally it was used, as in classical Greek, to describe soft and yielding substances. The root meaning is not "give in" but "be disposed to yielding."

If we put this together, we see that the verse has none of the tone of harsh command that seems to come through in the English. Rather, the writer says, "In your relationship with those who are your leaders and guides to godliness, be sure you maintain a yielding disposition and remain open to their persuasion." The passage goes on: "They keep watch over you as men who must give an account. [Be responsive] to them so that their work will be a joy, not a burden, for that would be of no advantage to you."

This is not in conflict at all with Romans 14 or other New Testament passages that affirm the freedom and responsibility of the Christian and the servant nature of spiritual leadership. Leaders are to remember to be servants. The rest of us are to remember to be responsive and not so hard headed that we are unwilling to listen to or be persuaded by those who are further along in the Christian life than we.

James

James

Who wrote this book, and what themes and issues does it deal with?

The author of this epistle is not James the apostle but James the brother of Jesus, who was converted after Jesus' resurrection and became a leader in the early church (Acts 1:14; 15:13). This very early book was probably written before the first missionary push beyond Judea that incorporated a large number of Gentiles. James is not concerned with the issues that the apostle Paul had to confront. Rather than attempt to define salvation by faith, James writes a very pastoral letter in which he urges Christians to lead a life that is appropriate for believers.

James 1:13

How can James say God does not tempt anyone? Weren't Adam and Eve tempted in the Garden of Eden? And didn't the Holy Spirit himself lead Jesus out into the wilderness to be tempted by the devil?

The same Greek word is translated both "tempt" and "test." This causes some confusion. The key to understanding this passage is to note that James specifies that God does not tempt anyone with *evil.* He then goes on to show that the pull toward evil comes from within us, not from outside actions by God or anyone else.

An important distinction is to be made here. God put the forbidden tree in the garden not to trap Adam but to permit him an opportunity to make a moral choice. Because of this, he became more than just a puppet who served God because he had no choice. The reason Adam made a wrong choice and disobeyed was because he failed to use his full capacity to choose, which God intended as a good gift to strengthen his moral character and fulfill his spiritual destiny. It is the same with those things we experience as temptations. They are opportunities for us to joyfully and willingly submit to the will of God and thus grow in grace and maturity. The person who gives in to temptation and does evil must not blame God, because the evil was not in the situation but in the man's response to it.

James 2:14–26

James says a person is justified by works. In Romans 4 Paul says a person cannot be justified by works, but by faith alone. Surely there is a doctrinal conflict here.

James makes it clear he contrasts a kind of faith that exists as mere intellectual belief with a kind of faith that involves a transforming commitment to God. The devils believe God exists, James says, and they tremble. What the devils do *not* do is commit themselves to God and so experience the kind of transformation available to the believer. We can catch the thrust of James's argument in a paraphrase, which reflects the fact that *justified* is not only a forensic term but also can mean to corroborate or confirm. Understood in this way, there is no conflict between James and Paul. Each affirms salvation by faith, and each asserts that those who believe must and will do good works (see also Eph. 2:9–10; Titus 3:5).

What good is it, my brothers, if a man claims to have faith but has no deeds? Can such faith save him? Suppose a brother or sister is without clothes and daily food. If one of you says to him, "Go, I wish you well; keep warm and well fed," but does nothing about his material needs, what good is it? In the same way, faith by itself, if it is not accompanied by action, is dead.

But someone will say, "You have faith, I have deeds."

Show me your faith without deeds, and I will show you my faith by what I do. You believe that there is one God. Good! Even the demons believe that—and shudder.

You foolish man, do you want evidence that faith without deeds is useless? Was not our ancestor Abraham considered righteous for what he did when he offered his son Isaac on the altar? You see that his faith and his actions were working together, and his faith was made complete by what he did. And the Scripture was fulfilled that says, "Abraham believed God, and it was credited to him for righteousness," and he was called God's friend. You see that a person is justified by what he does and not by faith alone.

In the same way, was not even Rahab the prostitute considered righteous for what she did when she gave lodging to the spies and sent them off in a different direction? As the body without the spirit is dead, so faith without deeds is dead.

A dead faith will not produce good works, and so the good works produced by a true faith in God show how God was totally justified in proclaiming Abraham righteous when all he had was faith.

1 Peter

1 Peter

Who wrote this book, and what themes and issues does it deal with?

This book was written by the apostle Peter. It is directed to Jewish believers scattered throughout the Roman empire. A major theme of the letter is suffering. It teaches how the Christian can live victoriously even while suffering unjustly.

1 Peter 3:19

How could Jesus preach the gospel to "the spirits in prison" after his death? Does this imply that people have a second chance to be saved after they die?

Not at all. Hebrews 9:27 says, "Man is destined to die once, and after that to face judgment." Peter is saying that Christ preached to the earth's inhabitants by the Holy Spirit, who gave them God's message through Noah. Their spirits are now in prison awaiting judgment. Jesus spoke to them *before* they died, not after.

1 Peter 3:21

Does baptism save us? And if so, of what kind of baptism does Peter speak?

This is another one of the Bible's more difficult passages. The thought is not hard to understand, but people tend to snatch the verse out of context and try to understand it without seeing it in context. We must remember that Peter draws a comparison between the days of Noah and the age of Christ. His analogy is intended to show the far-reaching effect of Jesus' work. To do this he goes back to the Genesis flood and compares the Christian experience to the experience of the eight people who were carried in the ark through the waters of raging judgment. Baptism is used here to indicate our union with Christ (see the discussion of Matthew 3:11, page 229, and Romans 6:1–4 page 330). Like Noah and his family, we Christians have been lifted beyond danger of judgment and deposited in a new world in which we are to live new lives. Freed by Jesus, we are to live these new lives not "for evil human desires, but rather for the will of God" (4:2).

Note the appropriateness of the analogy. Noah and his family were snatched from an old world that was destined for destruction and carried safely through the waters of judgment in the ark. When the waters receded Noah made landfall on a changed earth, empty of human habitations, rich with new, budding vegetable life. In the same way we have been lifted out of the spiritual kingdom ruled by Satan, which is destined to be judged by God, carried through the judgment in Christ, and brought into the kingdom of God's son. Now we live in that kingdom and everything about our lives is fresh and new.

2 Peter

2 Peter

Who wrote this book, and what themes and issues does it deal with?

The veracity of this second letter written by the apostle Peter has been challenged by many but has rightly found its place in our New Testament. The subject matter is very different from that of Peter's first letter. Here Peter, rather than write of the danger posed by those causes the church suffered from outside, writes about the false prophets and false teachers who constituted a danger from *within* the early church.

2 Peter 3:3–4

Both modern geology and modern biologists insist that the earth is of great age, and the features of our planet as well as the characteristics of all living things can be explained by processes that human beings can observe in nature.

The view that "everything goes on as it has since the beginning of creation" is a uniformitarian assumption. Such an assumption undoubtedly does undercut evolutionary theory. However, Peter's warning is addressed to those who dismiss the possibility of divine judgment by saying, "It hasn't happened yet." Peter's response? "Oh, yes, it has. God brought a flood on the earth that destroyed an earlier civilization."

There *is* a direct conflict between the theory of evolution and the biblical view of reality. See the discussion of Genesis 1, page 15.

1, 2, 3 John

1, 2, 3 John

Who wrote these books, and what themes and issues do they deal with?

These three brief letters were written by the apostle John late in the first century A.D. John's letters are pastoral in nature. They consistently emphasize fellowship and love as the church's best protection against antichrists who had already infiltrated the believing community.

1 John 1:9

What does it mean to confess sins?

The Greek word means "to agree with" or "say the same thing as." God calls believers to acknowledge that their wrong acts are sin. This verse promises that when we acknowledge our sins to God rather than deny or excuse them he will forgive our sins and keep on purifying us from all unrighteousness.

This teaching is vital, because people who deny or excuse their sins erect a wall that prevents the Lord from actively working in their lives. Being honest with God about our failings enables the Lord to keep working in our lives and continue the process of our inner transformation.

1 John 2:15–17

What are the world and worldliness?

The "world," or *kosmos* is used in a theological sense by John. He portrays human society as a system warped and twisted by sin. Worldliness is the driving force that motivates the lost and warps human society. It is the cravings of the sin nature, the passion to possess what can be seen, and the pride one feels in achieving things apart from God. The worldly Christian is not a person who drinks or smokes but a person whose drives, motivations, and responses are like those of the unsaved.

1 John 3:9

In 1:8 John says that "if we claim to be without sin, we deceive ourselves and truth is not in us." Here John says, "No one who is born of God will continue to sin." This is confusing.

The New International Version, unlike some older versions, emphasizes the meaning of the verb tense. John does not suggest that the Christian will be sinless but that the true Christian will not make sin a habit. There is no conflict between John 1:8 and this verse.

1 John 5:6–7

What does John mean by the water, blood, and spirit that give a uniform testimony to the deity of Jesus?

Many different interpretations of these verses have been offered by commentators throughout church history. Some link the water and blood to the liquid that flowed from Christ's side on the cross. Others have seen in it a symbol of the Old Testament sacrificial system, with its rites of purification by water and blood. Most today see a reference here to the water of Christ's baptism, which initiated his public ministry, and the blood that flowed at its end. In this view, the entire ministry of Jesus on earth is understood as giving witness to his deity. This witness was confirmed by the Spirit at his resurrection and is applied by the same Spirit to our hearts as we believe.

1 John 5:14

How can John tell us that we will receive what we pray for if we ask according to God's will? This is an empty promise, because no one on earth can be sure he or she really knows God's will.

John's point is that the Christian can be absolutely sure of access to God, and that if they live close to the Lord they will be sensitive to his will and ask accordingly with great confidence. As Peter Marshall remarked, "When we learn to want what God wants, we have the joy of receiving his answer to our petitions."

Jude

Jude

Who wrote this book, and what themes and issues does it deal with?

The book was written by Jude, a half-brother of Jesus who like James became a leader of the early church. Jude's theme is the danger to the church from false teachers.

Jude 9, 14

How can Jude refer to details of Moses' death that aren't found in the Old Testament and may even have come from nonscriptural religious literature? How can Jude quote as authority the book of Enoch, which was never considered one of the sacred writings? Does this show that the Bible is simply a religious book and not a unique revelation from God?

Jude's quoting the book of Enoch illustrates that there may well be authentic traditions that were expressed in folktales and religious writings current in the first-century A.D.. There is no reason why Jude, under inspiration, did not select just such authentic traditions from works that were in large part works of fiction. After all, we are familiar with historical novels whose fictional characters interact with real persons in situations that are accurately portrayed. The fact that Jude included these traditions demonstrates their authenticity.

Revelation

Revelation

Who wrote this book, and what themes and issues does it deal with?

The Book of Revelation was written by the apostle John. It was written in the last decade of the first century A.D. and portrays a vision John had while in exile on the Mediterranean island Patmos. The stunning images that flash across the pages of this book remind us of the most visionary of Old Testament prophets and are understood in different ways by Christians. All agree, however, that the book serves as a powerful confirmation of the fact that God is in complete charge of history. It is also agreed that, although God's sovereignty may be challenged, evil will be judged, and those who are saved will be rewarded at history's end.

Revelation

How has the book been interpreted by Christians?

Christians have taken some five different approaches to Revelation. Just how details within this book are interpreted depends on the way in which the book is viewed. *The Revell Bible Dictionary* sums up the five views as follows:

1. *Preterist*. Revelation describes conditions existing when John wrote the book. Christians were persecuted under the Emperor Domitian. John uses symbolism to disguise what is essentially a polemic against the Roman Empire and an effort to encourage Christians.

2. *Historicist*. Revelation previews the Christian era. The trumpets, seals, and bowls of judgment are different periods of history. The Reformers attempted to identify the events of chapters 4–16 with a chronology of the Western church from the first through the 18th centuries.

Modern historicists see Revelation as a nonchronological panorama of history. Seven separate parallel visions portray, from slightly different viewpoints, the age between Christ's first and second comings. Modern historicists are found among Christians of Reformed background, Mennonites, Southern Baptists, and others.

3. *Idealist*. Revelation has no relationship to history, but rather uses symbols familiar to first-century readers to portray the timeless conflict between good and evil.

4. *Futurist*. Revelation 4–16 is a portrait of future events that will take place at history's end. The events described are the same as those found in OT and Mt. 24 descriptions of a great tribulation to take place prior to the establishment of God's Kingdom.

5. *Apocalyptic*. Revelation was composed following the established tradition of Jewish apocalyptic writings, of which some 100 are known to exist, characterized by complex symbolism and cryptic language.

The Revell dictionary concludes: "Whatever approach is taken, Revelation remains a powerful affirmation of the ultimate triumph of God."

Revelation symbols

How is anyone ever to understand all the symbolic language found in this book? If it cannot be understood, what value is there in it?

This objection raises two kinds of issues; first, what do specific symbols mean and how can they be understood, and second, how are we to understand generally obscure language that may or may not be symbolic?

Many of the specific symbols can be identified quite accurately. Some are explained in the text. For instance, the seven candlesticks and seven stars of Revelation 1:20 are said to represent seven churches in Asia and their angels (messengers or leaders). Other symbols hark back to the Old Testament and can be explained by reference to previous revelation. thus the tree of life (2:7; 22:2) is symbolic of eternal life (see also Gen. 2:9), the rod of iron in 2:27 shows the role of Christ in judgment (Ps. 2:9), and the key of David in 3:7 is a symbol of Messianic authority (Isa. 22:22). Other symbols cannot be so easily understood. Their interpretation often depends on the reader's approach to interpreting the book as a whole. For example, the first beast of Revelation 13:1–10 is understood by the futurist to be an individual, the Antichrist, while the historicist sees the first beast as a symbol of anti-Christian world government. Both, however, agree that the symbol is rooted in the Book of Daniel, chapter 7. Even when the specific symbolism is not understood, the imagery is typically quite clear. The vision of the glorified Jesus described in Revelation 1 conveys a powerful impression of glory and majesty. This is true even for those who have not traced the symbolism back to images of God found in the Old Testament. We, like John, suddenly are confronted by a Jesus who is not the "meek and mild" Christ of his first coming, but the glorious and fearful judge humanity must face when he comes again.

Our failure to identify each symbol does not mean that we cannot understand the text. In fact, understood or not, the symbols that appear so frequently in Revelation convey perhaps even more clearly than mere description the meaning and impact of Christ's reappearance at history's end.

The same can be said of so-called obscure language. For instance, in writing chapter 9 John clearly struggled to find words to describe what he saw. But this is only to be expected. If a person living two hundred years ago were transported suddenly to Chicago to witness jets flying out of O'Hare and streams of vehicles rushing along expressways, he would find it almost impossible to explain what he saw. The world of two hundred years ago simply had no words for these modern phenomena. Our time traveler would be forced to use whatever words and concepts were available to him to describe something that must be witnessed to be really understood.

It is exactly this way with much of Revelation. John described what he saw. But he was forced to use the words and concepts available to him in his century. While we may not be able to accurately reconstruct what he saw from the descriptions he gave, we still can sense the essential meaning: The world trembles under God's judgment before humanity's final revolution and Satan's last snarls of hatred and antagonism.

Can we explain everything in Revelation? No. Can we understand the vision conveyed by this stunning book? Yes. And only too well.

Revelation 2–3

What were the seven churches? Were they real or symbolic?

The letters are addressed to seven cities in Asia Minor. A study of the details of each letter shows John had an intimate knowledge of the actual cities, their products, and their characteristics.

To some interpreters these are representative churches whose characteristics reflect strengths and weaknesses of local churches everywhere. In this view we are to compare our own churches with these seven model congregations and apply Christ's advice to correct our weaknesses.

To others these churches represent the history of Christianity itself. Each congregation reflects traits of Christendom, from the apostolic age to the period just before Jesus returns.

Whether or not a symbolic dimension exists, a study of the flaws of the seven churches and the words Jesus addresses to each can surely be applied to guide local congregations today.

Revelation 7:1–8

Who are the 144,000 described here?

The text identifies these as members of the twelve tribes of Israel. Historians see these numbers as symbolic, chosen to represent the full number of the saved. Futurists see them as literal members of Israel's twelve tribes, chosen to serve God as missionaries during the earth's final, tumultuous and terrible years. This idea is based on the common use of a seal to identify ownership and the setting apart of something for a specific purpose. John specifies the tribal groups from which the 144,000 are drawn. His specificity is not characteristic of symbolic language. Whoever the 144,000 are, they are not the so-called saved who earn their way into God's future kingdom by witnessing for him now, as the Jehovah's Witnesses cult teaches.

Revelation 11

Who are the two witnesses of this chapter?

The interpretation of this depends on one's approach to the book as a whole. The futurist sees in this a description of two persons specially empowered by God to announce in Jerusalem the coming judgment, despite the supernatural powers of Satan arrayed against them. The number of days is exactly half the seven-year tribulation period of Daniel chapters 9 and 11. Some even go so far as to identify one of the witnesses as Elijah. This fulfills the prediction of Malachi 4:5–6. Others take this whole description as symbolic, a picture of the church's witness despite the hostility of a godless society.

Revelation 12–13

Who are the woman, the dragon, and the two beasts?

How these are interpreted depends on one's approach to the book as a whole. In chapter 12 the dragon is clearly Satan, and most agree the woman is Israel, while the child she gave birth to is Jesus. Those who see this description as a vision of events at history's end see a final, great persecution of the Jewish people stimulated by Satan. Those who see Revelation as a series of images intended to describe the hostility between good and evil, God and Satan tend to see the woman as the church and the whole description as symbolic of a timeless struggle.

Similarly, the futurist sees the first beast as the Antichrist and the second as the false prophet. Together with Satan they form a counterfeit trinity that tries to establish dominance over humankind before being destroyed at Christ's personal intervention (see also Rev. 19:19–21). Historicists take the two beasts as symbolic of anti-Christian government and false religion.

Revelation 13:16

What is the mark mentioned in this verse?

The text tells us only that a mark on the hand or forehead will be required if a person is to buy or sell in the lands controlled by the beast. The beast is identified by interpreters either as the Antichrist, a person, or as anti-Christian government. Some have observed that the supermarket checkout process may indicate the nature of the mark. Just as a scanner reads the price code printed on each grocery item, so a scanner might read a number tattooed on a hand or forehead and automatically credit or debit a person's checking account. By making sure that only someone who has given allegiance to the beast is given a number, a government could exercise total control over its citizens.

Revelation 13:18

What is the meaning of the number 666?

There is no agreement on the meaning of "the number of the beast." Some note that while seven is the symbolic number of God, six "is man's number" because it falls short of perfection. Others note that in Hebrew and Greek, letters originally had numerical values. *Aleph/ alpha* was equivalent to one, *beth/beta* to two, and so on. So it is possible that the number 666 represents the numerical values of the true name of the beast or Antichrist. The problem is that this approach is open to abuse. In fact, it was used in the 1940s to justify the teaching that either Mussolini or Hitler, among others, was the Antichrist.

Ultimately, no one knows just what this numerical hint to the beast's identity means. Many prophetic utterances in Scripture are understood only after, and not before, their fulfillment.

Revelation 16:16

What is Armageddon?

This verse describes a great army gathered to resist God at history's end. Armageddon is a place name, meaning "the mountain of Megiddo." Many assume that this verse refers to a wide valley lying below Mount Megiddo in Israel.

In popular parlance the word Armageddon has come to mean a great, destructive battle that will mean the end of the world, such as might be expected from a nuclear holocaust.

Revelation 18

How can this chapter describe the fall of Babylon? Babylon fell hundreds of years before John wrote. Does he refer to Rome?

Quite frequently in Scripture a place serves as a symbol for something significant that happened there. Babylon provides one of the clearest examples of this phenomenon. Based on the theme of human pride and self-confidence introduced in the Genesis description of events at Babel (Gen. 11:4), and on Isaiah's portrayal of the Lucifer-like arrogance of this city (Isa. 14:22–15), "Babylon the Great" frequently in Scripture symbolizes human achievement in a society constructed without reference to God. In Revelation Babylon is a symbol of man's materialistic and spiritual efforts to construct a society apart from God. As this final book of the Bible shows, all such efforts are doomed not only to fail but also to earn God's judgment.

Revelation 20:2

What is the thousand years spoken of here? Is Satan bound now? At what time has he ever been bound? And what does "bound" mean?

Many in the early church understood this passage to refer to a future period when Jesus would reign over the earthly kingdom promised to the Jews by the Old Testament prophets. During that age Satan would be kept from influencing humankind, and God would fulfill his promise of an idyllic age, powerfully described in passages like Isaiah 65:20–25 and Amos 9:14, 15. The theological position of these church fathers, called *chilists,* and reflected in modern *millennialism* takes Old Testament prophecies literally and holds that God will restore the Jewish people to a favored position here on earth. At the same time the saints of the Christian era will serve with Christ as rulers of a world finally at peace. Although the Old Testament does not specify the length of the messianic era, early chilists and contemporary millennialists take the one thousand years of Revelation 20, associated with Christ's victory over the forces of evil, as an expansion of Old Testament revelation.

Nonmillennialists dismiss this view, convinced that the one thousand years is symbolic and that the binding of Satan refers to his inability to prevent the preaching of the gospel of Christ.

Revelation 19:20; 20:7–15

Is the fiery lake, and the lake of burning sulfur, mentioned in these verses what people mean when they speak of hell? If so, how could God condemn human beings to such a horrible fate?

This lake is a place of endless torment where the unsaved dead, self-conscious and fully aware, will spend eternity. This is not a pleasant prospect by any means, and no sensitive individual takes pleasure in contemplating this as the fate of even the most wicked of human beings.

However, we must understand those lines of biblical teaching that put hell in perspective. First, the doctrine of hell underlines something we commonly dismiss: the utterly appalling and loathsome nature of sin. If a loving God finds hell a necessity to purge wickedness from his universe, we can hardly treat any sin lightly.

Second, the doctrine of hell reminds us of how fully God shared his image and likeness with human beings. Each human being is far too significant to simply snuff out, as if the individual never had existed at all. When God created human beings he planted eternity within them. Endless existence is the destiny of every person.

Third, we need to remember a remark made by Jesus. God did not create hell for human beings but "for the devil and his angels" (Matt. 25:41). While human beings may share Satan's destiny, it was the devil's original sin that made hell a necessity. It was for Satan that hell was created in the first place.

Finally, we need to remember that God has done everything possible to make sure that human beings will *not* go to hell. God so loved our lost race that he gave his Son to rescue us from judgment. Only those who refuse to respond to God as he reveals himself first in creation and then compellingly in Jesus Christ will be lost. Human beings go to hell by their choice, not by God's. And they go there despite the fact that God made every effort to provide salvation to all.

Revelation 21:10–21

If the new Jerusalem is the heaven that Christians speak about, not many folks are going to make it. Even at 1500 miles square the city could house only a fraction of the people who have populated the earth.

Those who have raised this argument have not read the chapter carefully. The New Jerusalem is not heaven; it is the capital of an entirely new universe created by God as the home of a redeemed humanity.

John's vision of the new relationship that will exist between God and man is much more significant than his spectacular description of the New Jerusalem. He said, "Now the dwelling of God is with men, and he will live with them. They will be his people, and God himself will be with them and be their God. He will wipe every tear from their eyes. There will be no more death or mourning or crying or pain, for the old order of things has passed away" (21:3–4).

This picture of our future is far more important than foolish debates over the size of the new Jerusalem. When we understand what lies ahead, we cannot help but cry out with John, "Amen. Come, Lord Jesus" (22:20).